A Liberal-Labour Lady

"Men" Who Are Making B.C.
No. 4

BRITISH CANADIAN PRESS SERVICE

HON. MARY ELLEN SMITH, M.P.P.

MARY ELLEN is not a man, but she is the mother of several men, and one of the real makers of B. C. Born in Devonshire, England, famous for scenery, clotted cream and pretty faces, she came to Vancouver Island nearly thirty years ago as the bride of Ralph Smith, labor leader. Helped her husband become one of the foremost parliamentarians in Canada and minister of finance in B. C. Member of the Legislature since 1918 and first lady to become a cabinet minister in the British Empire. Is the mother of much valuable social legislation for women and children. Principal hobby, making speeches and jollying the "mere men".

A Liberal-Labour Lady

The Times and Life of Mary Ellen Spear Smith

VERONICA STRONG-BOAG

© UBC Press 2021

All rights reserved. No part of this publication may be reproduced, stored in a retrieval system, or transmitted, in any form or by any means, without prior written permission of the publisher, or, in Canada, in the case of photocopying or other reprographic copying, a licence from Access Copyright, www.accesscopyright.ca.

30 29 28 27 26 25 24 23 22 21   5 4 3 2 1

Printed in Canada on FSC-certified ancient-forest-free paper (100% post-consumer recycled) that is processed chlorine- and acid-free.

Library and Archives Canada Cataloguing in Publication

Title: A Liberal-Labour lady : the times and life of Mary Ellen Spear Smith / Veronica Strong-Boag.
Names: Strong-Boag, Veronica J., author.
Description: Includes bibliographical references and index.
Identifiers: Canadiana (print) 20210259906 | Canadiana (ebook) 20210259922 | ISBN 9780774867245 (hardcover) | ISBN 9780774867252 (softcover) | ISBN 9780774867269 (PDF) | ISBN 9780774867276 (EPUB)
Subjects: LCSH: Spear Smith, Mary Ellen, 1863-1933. | LCSH: Women legislators – British Columbia – Biography. | LCSH: Legislators – British Columbia – Biography. | LCSH: Women cabinet officers – British Columbia – Biography. | LCSH: Cabinet officers – British Columbia – Biography. | LCSH: Suffragists – Canada – Biography. | LCGFT: Biographies.
Classification: LCC FC3825.1.S64 S77 2021 | DDC 971.1/03092—dc23

Canada

UBC Press gratefully acknowledges the financial support for our publishing program of the Government of Canada (through the Canada Book Fund), the Canada Council for the Arts, and the British Columbia Arts Council.

This book has been published with the help of a grant from the Canadian Federation for the Humanities and Social Sciences, through the Awards to Scholarly Publications Program, using funds provided by the Social Sciences and Humanities Research Council of Canada.

Printed and bound in Canada by Friesens
Set in Garamond by Apex CoVantage, LLC
Copy editor: Deborah Kerr
Proofreader: Kristy Lynn Hankewitz
Indexer: Judy Dunlop
Cover designer: George Kirkpatrick
Cover images: Frank Leonard photo, 35220 Vancouver Public Library; Major James Skitt Matthews photos, AM54-S4-: Ports N30, N32, and P1400, City of Vancouver Archives.

UBC Press
The University of British Columbia
2029 West Mall
Vancouver, BC V6T 1Z2
www.ubcpress.ca

This volume is dedicated to Maleyk, Justice, Helios, and Laniākea Bighorn, and to William, Benjamin, Connor, and Camryn Ross. May their courage, intelligence, and good hearts construct the better world dreamed of by their great-grandmother Daphne Bridges, an English immigrant who chose Canada. Mary Ellen Smith never read George Bernard Shaw's *The Intelligent Woman's Guide to Socialism and Capitalism* (1937), but Daphne did.

Contents

List of Figures / ix

Acknowledgments / xi

List of Abbreviations / xiii

Introduction: Worker, Settler, Liberal, Feminist / 3

1 Setting the Stage in British Mining Villages, to 1892 / 10

2 Replenishing the Empire, 1892–1900 / 31

3 From Nanaimo to Ottawa and Back Again, 1900–11 / 55

4 Boom, Bust, War, and Death, 1912–17 / 78

5 Independent Liberal Lady? 1917–20 / 106

6 From Hope to Disillusion, 1920–28 / 139

7 On the Margins, 1928–33 / 172

Conclusion: British Columbia's Famous Pioneer Politician: Making History / 199

Notes / 203

Index / 257

Figures

From Northumberland to British Columbia, 1892 / 32
Nanaimo, 1905 / 42
Ralph Smith, 1902 / 61
"The Woman's Cause Is Man's," 1913 / 85
"Too Proud to Speak," 1913 / 87
"As It Should Be," 1917 / 90
Ralph Smith, 1916 / 93
"Why Not a Woman and an Independent?" 1918 / 115
"Electors, Attention!" 1918 / 118
Mary Ellen Smith, 1918 / 122
"Women in Public Life," 1918 / 124
Mary Ellen Smith at home in her modest apartment, mid-1920s / 130
"Striving for 'Mothers' Pensions,'" 1920 / 135
"The Largest Vote Cast for Any Candidate," 1920 / 146
A lonely figure on the left, c. 1920 / 148
"'Men' Who Are Making B.C.," 1921 / 149
A terrifying figure, 1928 / 158

Sending women home, 1922 / 175
"Vote Liberal," campaign poster, 1930 / 177
"Speaking of House-Cleaning," 1928 / 178
"Startling Exposure!" 1928 / 181
The veteran, officially dated 1918, but probably c. 1928 / 186

Acknowledgments

The 2019–21 COVID-19 pandemic and Boris Johnson, Donald Trump, and Canada's own perfidious politicians, notably Premiers Jason Kenney, Doug Ford, and Brian Pallister, provided special impetus for *A Liberal-Labour Lady*. Today is a far more "woke" age than that which produced Mary Ellen Spear Smith. Accolades, however, should be directed elsewhere. Most of all, this volume owes a debt to the scholarly and activist cultures of redress and fair dealing that emerged in Canada and globally in the half century after the 1960s. Like the earlier liberal-labourites and liberal-feminists highlighted here, that culture demanded a reckoning with history. These pages are one result. More particularly, they benefitted from the generosity of Linda Kealey, Christopher Bridges Ross, and Joan Sangster, who commented on a penultimate version of the manuscript. Also to be thanked are two thoughtful anonymous assessors for UBC Press; my editors Darcy Cullen, Karen Green, Deborah Kerr, Katrina Petrik, and Carmen Tiampo; Linda Hale, who shared her early findings on Mary Ellen; and the archivists and other scholars who are identified in the notes. Christopher Ross also provided invaluable research assistance with the British material. The Social Sciences and Humanities Federation of Canada, the fruit of much collective effort, supported decades of research that helped make everything possible. All that talent gives me hope.

Abbreviations

BCFL	British Columbia Federation of Labour
CCF	Co-operative Commonwealth Federation
CPR	Canadian Pacific Railway
ILO	International Labor Organization
IODE	Imperial Order Daughters of the Empire
LCW	Local Council of Women
MWMLPA	Mine Workers and Mine Laborers Protective Association
NCWC	National Council of Women of Canada
NMA	Northumberland Miners' Association
NVCMLC	New Vancouver Coal Mining and Land Company
PPEL	Pioneer Political Equality League
TLC	Trades and Labor Council
TLCC	Trades and Labor Congress of Canada
UBC	University of British Columbia
UWC	University Women's Club
WCC	Women's Canadian Club
WCTU	Woman's Christian Temperance Union
WLA	Women's Liberal Association

A Liberal-Labour Lady

Introduction:
Worker, Settler, Liberal, Feminist

A Liberal-Labour Lady tells the story of Mary Ellen Spear Smith (1863–1933), British Columbia's first female member of the Legislative Assembly and the British Empire and Commonwealth's first female cabinet minister. Talent, industry, opportunity, and oft-mentioned good looks catapulted her from obscurity in Victorian England's mining villages into the upper ranks of imperial Canada's respectable society. In the late nineteenth and early twentieth centuries, this miner's daughter and miner's wife refashioned herself as a lady with a mission. Mary Ellen, as she was familiarly known, channelled a politics of hope for White workers, settlers, reformers, and women, even as she ignored Indigenous Peoples and sought to exclude Asians from the body politic. She worked for the taming of capitalism and patriarchy, the prevention of class and gender wars, and the reinforcement of the era's "settler project." She is often remembered for her insistence on *both* equal wages for equal work and that no child be labelled illegitimate *and* on sterilization of the "unfit" and that no Asian person gain equal rights of citizenship. In both rejecting and reinforcing injustices, this flawed but extraordinary woman deserves far more than canonization or condemnation. This biography attempts that fair hearing.

Mary Ellen's tale advances here, as it did for many decades in life, alongside that of her husband, Ralph Smith (1858–1917). Married for almost thirty-five years, they were partners in family and political matters. Ralph initially loomed larger in Britain and Canada, but Mary Ellen gradually overtook him in the public spotlight. His premature death ensured that she would make her own mark in history. No study of either would be complete without the other, but equally so, this liberal-labour lady merits centre stage, as indeed Ralph himself was sometimes inclined to admit.[1] Daughters, wives, and mothers supply more than truncated reminders of dominant men.

Both Mary Ellen and Ralph became adults in Northumberland, England's northernmost county, in mining villages that were restive with Methodism, cooperation, unionism, and liberal-labourism. In demanding greater democracy and a share in capitalism's rewards, such Northumbrians were often radicals of their day. When the couple emigrated to the coal city of Nanaimo, British Columbia, in 1892, they carried their founding politics, but these evolved with their changed circumstances. The Smiths joined an imperial settlement movement that placed the British at the top of a racial meritocracy, viewed other Europeans as potentially compatible, and treated women and men of Indigenous, Asian, and African origins as largely unfit for inclusion in the nation. As capitalism widened the gulf between rich and poor in the new land, just as it had in the old, Mary Ellen and Ralph intended Britannicization, liberal-labourism, the "New Liberalism" of their age, and feminism to mobilize class and gender partnerships in the extension of democracy for preferred citizens. By the First World War, this agenda had taken them far. Ralph had captained the Trades and Labor Congress of Canada and served in the BC and Canadian legislatures, and Mary Ellen had moved to the fore of a broad-based feminist movement.

In 1917, Ralph's unexpected death, just after his appointment as the BC minister of finance, launched Mary Ellen's independent political career. Governor General Lord Grey (1851–1917) described her as "comely,"[2] and good looks were significant in fortifying her crusading gifts as a "free woman" – a politically charged moniker, when anti-slavery campaigns were still in living memory, and the New Woman and, soon enough, the Flapper were judged threats to the sexual status quo. In a 1918 provincial by-election in Vancouver, arguably the city with the dominion's most diverse suffrage movement, the recent widow won a tough campaign. As a pioneer female MLA, Smith sought to marshal a broad progressive coalition for women's minimum wage and mothers' pensions. Such New Liberal legislation was to underpin a modern state committed to a "fair deal," a core labourist value much invoked by suffragists,[3] for favoured peoples. In the 1920 provincial election, the veteran returned to the Grit fold and topped the polls. For some months in 1921, her reward was a place in cabinet. That appointment without portfolio again propelled Mary Ellen into the history books.

In fact, Canadian Liberals had little place for a feminist activist, especially one with a labourist history. As progressive gains stalled in a disappointing decade, Mary Ellen became better known for her anti-Asian prejudices. Barely winning the 1924 BC election, she languished. Four years later, she was shunted off to Esquimalt, Vancouver Island, where she would lose to a Conservative chieftain. Her defeat, and that of the provincial Liberal Party, left her a limited role as a defender of feminist causes whose time appeared to have come and gone. By her death in 1933, Mary Ellen's vision of a partnership between White women and workers in the humanization of capitalism and the assault on patriarchy lay in tatters, even as race remained a key marker of entitlement in BC and Canadian politics.

Like all biographies and histories, *A Liberal-Labour Lady* is partial. Surviving sources are often fragmentary, and few diaries or private letters offer intimate details. Mary Ellen's feelings about her life as a daughter, mother, wife, friend, and activist can be only dimly glimpsed. She and her family received at best brief mention in the institutional archives of Britain, British Columbia, and Canada. Documentation is especially slim for the early years in mining communities, and the limited legislative and state records for early-twentieth-century British Columbia further handicap recovery. Papers from the women or the organizations with whom Mary Ellen associated are likewise inadequate, and few private records of her male contemporaries remembered a female interloper. Indeed, we have no visual image of Mary Ellen before the First World War. Such recurring omissions and losses often mean that highflying women, indeed the "second sex" generally, readily slip from history. Until now, that has been the fate of this volume's liberal-labour lady.

Fortunately, the increasing digitization of many BC, Canadian, and British newspapers and magazines allows for unprecedented retrieval. Although influential feminist and labour publications such as Toronto's *Woman's Century*, Victoria's *The Champion*, and Vancouver's *Labor Statesman* await readily available electronic formatting, many of their issues survive in other forms to illuminate the landscape that moulded Smith and her contemporaries. The social media of its time, the print press was directed at both popular and particular audiences, from women to workers, businessmen, and activists. It offers a rich, diverse, and commonly highly partisan portrait that stands at the heart of the arguments in these pages. Read carefully, it reveals "many different voices" and sometimes "spaces where women spoke directly to other women" in critical "debates about gender roles and the relations between the sexes."[4] A dedicated contingent of feminist journalists, increasingly well documented by critical scholars, everywhere enriched discussion of the "New Day" promised by female enfranchisement.[5] Politics loomed large in much coverage of pioneers, a preoccupation that inevitably shaped this book. In Britain's Mother of Parliaments, trailblazing MPs such as Conservative Nancy Langhorne Astor (1879–1964) and Labour's Ellen Wilkinson (1891–1947) were both targets of and contributors to a print gaze that complicated and challenged democracy.[6] The same was true for Mary Ellen, as a feminist activist and later a politician. This overdue biography relies on the resulting treasure trove, with all its favouring of the public over the intimate and of men over women. The alternative is to omit a female torchbearer when we remember the past.

A Liberal-Labour Lady depends as well on expanding scholarship on workers, settlers, liberals, and women in both Britain and Canada. Overlapping worlds of debate and engagement in the issues of the day set the crucial context in which Mary Ellen emerged as a suffragist and MLA.[7] We have learned a great deal about the substantial and diverse resistance to the capitalist status quo offered by miners, workers in general, and labourist movements in the late nineteenth and early twentieth centuries. Their commonplace privileging of male breadwinners is now an acknowledged part of that story.[8] The world of British settlement and imperialism (or "Britannicization"), dispossession of Indigenous Peoples, and racism has similarly inspired important studies that inform this volume. Upper-class women or, more rarely, their less socially elevated sisters, such as Mary Ellen, are now identified as significant agents in transnational encounters that negotiated relations of class, race, and gender. They could be both heroic and imperious.[9] Liberalism, often said to be Canada's dominant ideology, has likewise provoked lively scholarly debate that shaped understanding here. Its recurring (but commonly unacknowledged) advancement of a White male elite once again undermined democracy even as its claims for a meritocracy sometimes left doors ajar for less privileged communities.[10] New scholarship on the suffragist generation in the English-speaking world has also significantly informed my interpretation. Female activists were a complicated lot, far more than merely democracy's readily forgotten shock troops or a White "God's police," as they have been dubbed in the Australian context.[11] It is no longer possible, as their enemies preferred, to ignore suffragists as key intervenors in crucial questions of their age. The courage, complexity, and limitations of the women (and the men) who were enrolled in the "Great Cause" of enfranchising women need a reckoning if we are to understand the evolution of Canada and the British world.

Newspapers, magazines, and state documents spotlight public life, but no one is entirely comprehensible without reference to their family. With Ralph Smith, a miner, Methodist, cooperator, unionist, and politician,[12] Mary Ellen was one part of a power couple for many years. His response to the class, gender, and racial conflicts of their age, as well as his endorsement of her talents, helped prepare her for community leadership as their children grew to maturity. One (step-)daughter and four sons were similarly essential to the private and public lives of their parents. Offspring and other kin surface here as regularly as the scanty records permit, tangible reminders of private interests behind public acts.

As an activist wife, a responsible parent, and a talented politician, Mary Ellen was never among the "gentle ladies of the Avenue," the self-satisfied and circumspect occasional do-gooders pilloried by sister suffragist Nellie L. Mooney McClung (1873–1951) in her memorable 1915 polemic, *In Times Like These*. As Mary Ellen moved from Britain to British Columbia, from miner's kin to settler newcomer to parliamentary lady over the course of seven decades, she was inspired by diverse gender protocols in developing a self-conscious performance of meritorious femininity. In Northumberland, as a young Methodist who was destined to become a collier's wife, she absorbed certain codes of behaviour. Priorities included religious faith, hard work, and wifely and maternal duty. Tough women strengthened mining communities. On the other hand, as an avid reader and motivated student of the world around her, Mary Ellen observed a pervasive "cult of true womanhood" associated most closely with the middle class. Centred on religiosity, gentleness, and purity, it promised public respectability and moral authority, important considerations for someone whose future involved significant social mobility and claims to superiority on the settlement frontier. Her early musical training, which prepared her to solo in Nanaimo operas and operettas and for intimacy with Zoe Lafontaine (1841–1921), the wife of Liberal prime minister Wilfrid Laurier (1841–1919), likewise influenced her presentation of gender and class. Further complicating Smith's staging of self was the rise of the so-called New Woman at the end of the nineteenth century. Distinguished by wage earning (often in professions), independence, and intelligence, this controversial figure had power, as demonstrated by Mary Ellen's recurring tributes to female nurses, teachers, lawyers, social workers, and other such pioneers. She also took heart from the courage of political trailblazers, including McClung, who became an MLA in Alberta in 1921, Agnes Campbell Macphail (1890–1954), who entered the House of Commons in the same year, and Britain's Margaret Bondfield (1873–1953), elected in 1923. In short, she channelled currents of her age that underscored women's potential. Even as blind spots crippled her vision, notably regarding race relations, Smith established herself as a campaigner with broad appeal for Canada's settler electorate.

Despite differences, versions of womanhood pervasive in the Victorian age and beyond were heavily oriented to heterosexuality and, to put it bluntly, to women's management of dominant males.[13] In some respects like Britain's second female MP, Viscountess Astor, Mary Ellen put that message to work as a gifted entertainer and speaker. Few commentators of either gender failed to mention her physical attractiveness, melodic voice, personality, quick wit, and charm. As revealed by her lengthy track record of sympathizers and loyalists, as well as executive offices in diverse clubs, women regularly succumbed to her magic. So too did men. In public, she deftly employed diverse styles of persuasion. As with most suffragists, maternal virtues stood centre front in her justifications for causes from child welfare, eugenics, and temperance to equal wages, Asian exclusion, and the vote. Both her sex's natural inclinations and her own history of child raising legitimized engagement in government and society. Mary Ellen was equally renowned for deploying womanly wiles to gain ground against the recalcitrant, including BC and Quebec premiers and Canadian prime ministers. Male listeners, whether veterans, unionists, businessmen, or legislators, could expect to be teased and cajoled into at least the semblance of gentlemanly conduct. Her third major approach to winning support relied on reason: she became a fount of irrefutable evidence of "women worthies" from the Bible to modern literature, science, and law. Natural justice demanded a fair deal for men's equals. Smith's diverse weapons of persuasion – from the maternal to the seductive and the reasoned – mounted a powerful arsenal in advancing a settler agenda, reforming capitalism, and challenging patriarchy. During her heyday, she had few peers in Canada; perhaps only McClung could outdo her in handling an audience.

Even with mastery of the tools of manipulation, public advocacy was always risky for women. Origins in working-class or otherwise suspect populations made champions especially vulnerable to denunciation and trivialization. Feminists in particular were closely monitored for inferiority and fallibility. Like Nellie McClung, who livened up suffrage speeches by mocking the disparagement of her foes, Mary Ellen had to withstand and deflect slurs on her femininity and reputation.[14] As suggested by her reflections on "snobocracy" and her membership in a literary club that rejected higher education as the premier sign of intellectual merit, she was sensitive to her precarious status as a working-class immigrant with relatively little formal schooling. Nor as a woman could Smith escape the insults that arose as she aged and lost the beauty that long held her in good stead with men in particular. Credibility on the public stage was hard and courageously won.

After her death in 1933, Mary Ellen Spear Smith barely survived in the public imagination, a seeming confirmation of democracy's inevitability and, equally so, of women's preordained limits in public life. This book charts a far more complicated truth. How could any single individual live up to the massive expectations, whether for success or failure, imposed on suffrage stalwarts in their own time and subsequently? Simultaneously intrepid and flawed, Mary Ellen stands as a key figure in the compromised struggle for greater justice in British Columbia and Canada during the late nineteenth and early twentieth centuries.

1
Setting the Stage in British Mining Villages, to 1892

Mary Ellen was born a miner's daughter and soon became a miner's wife. Almost three decades in England's colliery communities, first briefly in the southwest and then more influentially in the northeast, notably Northumberland, preceded her departure for Canada. At some level, she always remained a northern Briton, and her voice never lost the accent shared by many new Canadians from that region of the "Old Country," as it was commonly called. As she moved from daughter to wife and mother, often in the shadow of male relatives, notably her publicly minded husband, Ralph Smith, these years helped prepare her for life in British Columbia and the Dominion of Canada. Old lessons resonated even as she boldly moved to defy the odds for a working-class woman.

The Spears

Mary Ellen was born in 1863 to a mining family in Cornwall, circumstances that did not invoke music, romance, or high prospects. Her parents, Mary Ann Jackson (1837–95) and Richard Sleep Spear (1839–1913), had roots deep in England's southwestern counties, with their deposits of copper, tin, and arsenic. Life there was often hard. Joining the waves of migrant hewers who contributed industrial sinew to the British Empire's "replenishment of the earth" in the nineteenth century, the family would travel from Cornwall and Devon to Northumberland, and then to the United

States and Canada.[1] Like many migrants, Mary Ann and Richard pursued ambitions that exceeded their limited beginnings.

In Cornwall and Devon, the Spears depended on diggings, which produced a rich living for dynastic landlords such as the Russells, a prominent Whig family that held various titles in the English peerage, including Duke of Bedford. In contrast, most working people survived by the skin of their teeth. In the nineteenth century, their hardscrabble lives, invoked on the sidelines of the BBC *Poldark* drama (2015–19), suffered in the struggle with resource depletion, growing pollution, market competition, and persistent rock falls and flooding. The prevalence of the tributing system in Cornish mines, essentially a form of self-employment much like the zero-hours contracts of the twenty-first century, kept toilers vulnerable and handicapped the era's fledgling trade union movement.[2]

In mining, men dominated the waged labour force. Women, often dubbed "bal maidens" in a mix of Cornish and English, nevertheless regularly worked on-site and in processing ore, as did children. Exposés in Victorian newspapers and government inquiries increasingly roused public outrage at evident distress and possible sexual impropriety. One result was Britain's 1842 Mines and Collieries Act, which excluded all women and all children under age ten from underground labour. Yet, for all its evident brutality, mining was often preferable to unregulated servitude in agricultural and domestic labour. Well after Mary Ellen left for Canada in 1892, some Cornish and Devon women, like "Pitt Brow lasses," "Tip Girls," and "Pit Bank women" elsewhere in England, persisted in heavy work at light pay near the top of excavations. Ultimately, however, for all their proof of women's capacity, such jobs threatened evolving notions of gendered respectability that required decent wives to toil at home. Only male miners ultimately won kudos as working-class heroes, strong men enrolled in industrial capitalism's dangerous and essential toil.[3]

When Devon-born Mary Ann Jackson married her sweetheart, Richard Sleep Spear, in 1862 in the Cornish copper-mining parish of Calstock, they initiated an ambitious partnership of the type that underpinned much male employment. Setting up house in the nearby village of Gunnislake, the Spears produced their first child, Mary Ellen, on October 11, 1863. However, unlike the pattern in most miners' families, she was not followed in short order by numerous siblings. A brother, William John (1868–1919), would not arrive for five years. That gap helped keep Mary Ann healthy enough to join Richard in the vibrant regional community produced by temperance societies and Primitive Methodist chapels (a puritanical form of Christianity that stressed strict morality while offering the hope of salvation). Nor did the small household require the relentless domestic labour commonly demanded of daughters. Mary Ellen's talents, like her brother's, could be cultivated. Music, both singing and playing the piano and the organ, became a mainstay of family life and a sign of propriety and ambition.

Britain's Mining Communities

Almost immediately after Mary Ellen's birth, the family moved to Tavistock, Devon, birthplace of her parents, in search of pit jobs for Richard. That move produced no security. Soon enough, the Spears joined other economic refugees further fleeing bleak prospects. Whereas some tested the diggings in South Africa, South America, Australia, and North America, many desperate and hopeful travellers took advantage of new railways to reconnoiter northern England and Scotland, where booming coalfields buttressed the expanding British Empire with the promise of better jobs than traditional agricultural or newer factory employment. Substantial ore reserves, rising industrial demand, and proud miners produced relatively high wages in the counties of Northumberland and Durham, and married men often received a rent allowance or free housing plus financial help in case of injury.[4] Such pitmen have been reckoned "probably the highest paid proletarians anywhere in the world outside the USA."[5] Prospects for a breadwinner wage for adult males promised family security and respectability for those who survived toil in the depths of the earth.

Underground labour was never for the faint of heart. Even as new technologies and protective legislation gradually improved its safety, tragedy dogged the industry, with a British miner being "killed every six hours, seriously injured every two hours and injured badly enough to need a week off work every two or three minutes" between 1868 and 1919.[6] In Earsdon, Northumberland, the birthplace of Ralph Smith, some eighty miners died in 1860, followed by another two hundred in 1862,[7] a casualty rate that taught hard lessons. The toll of industrial diseases was less visible, but underground workers' lungs were commonly "loaded with black matter, solid or fluid, like printers' ink, or common ink, or lamp black, or charcoal powder, all insoluble and tasteless." Asthma and bad health haunted miners and their families, adding to domestic labours and fears.[8]

Though occasionally charged as feckless, thriftless, and failures in combating "the many risks of a dangerous occupation,"[9] nineteenth-century hewers nevertheless won a heady place in the pantheon of working-class heroes. Popular tabloid coverage of pit disasters fuelled the industry's association with a hypermasculinity of physical performance and courage. In tests of manliness, miners, such as Richard Spear and Ralph Smith, had no reason to kowtow to would-be social superiors. As they backstopped Britain's industrial machine, Northumberland and Durham communities seethed with restiveness, and northern coalfields developed a reputation for producing radical hard men and strong women who denounced any status quo that did not accord respect.[10] Only the ordinary British soldier, the so-called 'Tommy,'[11] would rival pitmen in the popular imagination. This reputation long empowered politicians with mining backgrounds and helps explain why the British Conservative prime minister, Margaret Thatcher (1925–2013), later set out to break miners in the great strike of 1984–85. Canadian hewers likewise shared in the pit legend, providing a powerful genealogy for would-be politicians such as Ralph Smith and, by extension, his helpmate.

Despite their dangers, restive northern mining villages drew diverse job-seekers. Northumberland's 1891 census reported birthplaces well beyond the British Isles, including "Sweden, the United States, Canada and even on a ship off the Cape Colony in South Africa."[12] The cosmopolitanism of much mining, for all the sense of global brotherhood it sometimes fostered, included clear social and ethnic boundaries. As Mary Ellen and Ralph grew to maturity, doctors, schoolteachers, stationmasters, ministers, local landlords, and colliery managers and owners peopled the local elite. Miners did not, but those who laboured deep underground, such as Ralph, were at the top of the industrial workforce; those engaged elsewhere near the rim of the pits, such as Richard Spear, received lower status and pay. Such hierarchies generated conflict, but mutual dependence on successful resource extraction and respect for tough labour also prompted "cordial and even friendly" relations across social and economic divides.[13]

Whereas the British Midlands demanded girls and women for the Victorian age's bustling mills and factories, the collieries of Northumberland and Durham privileged men and boys. Their coin was not for women, especially after their legal exclusion from underground labour in 1842. Mothers, wives, sisters, and daughters nevertheless remained indispensable.[14] Marriage and families created economic partnerships, with female labour replenishing and maintaining male wage-earners. At home, women and girls were never off shift. In the two- to four-room row cottages that lacked indoor toilets, running water, or furnaces, characteristic of mining villages, they hauled water and fuel, cleaned, washed, cooked, gardened, kept pigs and poultry, preserved, sewed, shopped, and nursed relatives and boarders. Their workplace hazards included domestic violence, repeated pregnancies, high levels of infant mortality and morbidity, and poor nutrition, in effect counterparts to the industrial deaths, diseases, and injuries of miners.[15] Women like Mary Ann and Mary Ellen had good reason to value their own sex.

Mining settlements in north Britain expected wives to stay home, but single women, whose domestic labour was not entirely absorbed by kin, might compete for pitiful remittances, most often in household service and, less commonly, in teaching and dressmaking. However, they were not encouraged to become the era's independent New Women. Their ambitions were firmly directed to subsidizing their families and, soon enough, to wedding locally, birthing a new generation, and sustaining husbands and sons in their contribution to the nation's industrial might. As a recent history of the region confirms, "it was a matter of pride for miners that their wives did not take on paid work outside the home."[16] Such was the expectation for Mary Ellen.

When they fled north, the Spears, like many economic exiles, met an uncertain reception. In the 1830s and 1840s, Northumberland and Durham mine owners had imported Cornish and Devon strikebreakers, whom local workers roundly condemned as "black jacks" or "Blackleg Miners." "Bootleg Miner," a popular ballad originating in an 1844 lockout in Seaton Delaval, near where the Spears would settle and Mary Ellen would marry, expressed English tribalism and targeted class treachery. Its lyrics, sung into the twenty-first century, hailed the righteous strikers:

> Across the way they stretch a line,
> To catch the throat and break the spine
> Of the dirty blackleg miner.

Equally significantly, the song celebrated the fact that

> There's not a woman in this town-row
> Will look at the blackleg miner.[17]

Indeed, Northumbrian women had a rowdy history of supporting their menfolk against the bosses, a tradition that would aid them in other forms of political protest.[18]

Conflict between Northumberland miners and southern interlopers, like that between British and Chinese migrants in BC mines, simmered for decades. In 1865, mine owners predictably turned to newcomers to crush a strike in Cramlington, the heart of the county's collieries.[19] Ethnic hatreds were never, however, inevitable. "Bootleg Miner" concluded with both a death threat and an invocation of class solidarity:

> So join the union while you may.
> Divvin't wait till your dying day,
> For that may not be far away,
> You dirty blackleg miner![20]

During the drawn-out Cramlington contest, many Cornish miners opted to honour picket lines and join the Northumberland Miners' Mutual Confident Association, which had been established in 1864 and was soon renamed the Northumberland Miners' Association (NMA).[21]

Like most newcomers to the northern coalfields, Dick Spear left few records. Only after his daughter became a noted Canadian politician did memories surface of him as a deputy overman, effectively a safety supervisor, in Cramlington, and "one of the canniest men that ever 'stepped in leather shoon,'" alongside similarly rare acknowledgment of his wife's piety and devotion to Methodism.[22] Evidently, the couple joined an émigré contingent that increasingly sided with native Northumberland miners, even as it preserved its own cultural distinctions. The latter could be important, as some contemporaries credited the Cornish with more advanced gender relations: "They had none of that feeling, still strong in the north, that a man has amply performed his share of the marriage compact when he has handed over to his wife the bulk of his earnings. They did not shame to help their wives to wash, or even to cook."[23] Such egalitarianism benefitted ambitious consorts. Marriage did not bar Mary Ann from commitments to church and temperance. Her daughter, Nellie, as she was familiarly called, was encouraged to use the "great ability" that she demonstrated as a pupil at the Cramlington Colliery School.[24] Such support laid the base for Mary Ellen's confidence and insistence on equality.

However, before her marriage and for some time afterward, the future BC cabinet minister shared her parents' near invisibility in the historical record. Only at odd moments did she surface as a teacher, though it remains unclear whether she taught solely at Primitive Methodist Sunday schools or in the local primary school, where promising senior students sometimes apprenticed. In any event, the 1881 English census identified her as a teenage seamstress living with her parents. This respectable occupation gave Mary Ellen some personal experience of waged employment while providing useful preparation for a future as a wife, mother, and activist. In an age when most clothing was made at home, her superior sewing skills would allow her and her family to assert propriety and even style, as attested by repeated Canadian reports of the elegance of her dress. Such talents facilitated the *embourgeoisement,* or adoption of middle-class habits and presentation, that would form an essential part of her later political and social capital. In tight-knit communities, potential sweethearts found plentiful opportunities to show their charms, sartorial and otherwise, in Methodist chapels, cooperative stores, temperance societies, and popular lectures. Like many colliery village girls, Mary Ellen found a local husband in her late teens.

The Smiths

Born on August 8, 1858, Ralph Smith was working in the pit at the Hartley mines near the Spears' home by age eleven. By the late 1870s, he had gained a local reputation as a lay Primitive Methodist preacher, an advocate for the cooperative movement, and an activist miner. The 1871 English census placed his family in Holywell, Northumberland, described two years later as "an old-fashioned country village" near the North Sea, boasting two collieries, albeit one near exhaustion.[25] Ralph's father, Earsdon-born Robert, had roots in rural labour, but he was employed as a coal hewer. He and his wife, Irish-born Mary (her maiden name is unknown), produced four sons – John, Robert, Ralph, and Mathew – the first three identified in the 1871 census as miners and the fourth as a student. Two girls – their daughter Mary and foster-daughter Sarah A. – were both "scholars," perhaps at the Primitive Methodist Sabbath School in Holywell. Twelve-year-old Sarah carried the surname Riddle (sometimes given as Riddell or Riddel). Like John, the eldest Smith child, and unlike his siblings, she came from the county of Durham, which lay to the south of Northumberland. The 1861 census records an Irish-born Riddel family in that county, with a daughter of her name. Perhaps they were kin to Ralph's mother. Sarah's presence a decade later in the Holywell household may well reflect a need for more domestic hands or even family tragedy, since relatives sometimes rescued orphans from bleak asylums or workhouses.

Close ties were further affirmed in 1880, when Ralph and Sarah wed in the nearby seaside village of Tynemouth. They soon became parents to Mary Elizabeth (1881–1944), born at Bates Cottages, Holywell.

Conditions were far from ideal in the "fifteen tenements with sixty inhabitants and a limited privy accommodation." Smallpox, diphtheria, and other diseases visited frequently.[26] Childbirth often injured women, which may explain why Sarah was dead by 1882. Soon enough, she was largely forgotten, glimpsed only in a rare document, such as the 1905 BC marriage licence for her daughter, Mary Elizabeth, and John Carr (c. 1880–1918). For the most part, however, Mary Elizabeth was publicly linked with her stepmother, Mary Ellen, who quickly eclipsed Ralph's foster sister and first wife.

Marriage and Domestic Life

On February 10, 1883, nineteen-year-old seamstress Mary Ellen Spear espoused the recent widower and miner for the East Holywell Mining Company in the Primitive Methodist chapel in North Shields.[27] She immediately became mother to toddler Mary Elizabeth and probably lodged in the same cottage where Sarah's short life had ended. Such substitutions were commonplace. When death stole wives and mothers, their inputs had to be quickly replaced if offspring were to survive and breadwinners to earn. Such tragedies underscored life's fragility and the value of kin, church, and community.

The Smith village, Holywell, was described as far from a "clean place," suffering from "a want of drainage, and a deficiency of sanitary arrangements." The dismal housing awaiting the young wife suggested routine neglect by the lord of the manor, the conservative Duke of Northumberland. As an 1873 article in the *Newcastle Weekly Chronicle* stated,

> To speak plainly, it is very far from what it ought to be ... Each house has two rooms, a large kitchen on the ground level, and a cold dismal garret of the same size above, which is reached by the accustomed break-neck ladder. The pantries project from the rear of the cottages ... Privies and ashpits there are none.[28]

Although their home in Bates Cottages (or East Holywell) might have been somewhat superior to much working-class housing in Britain's industrial cities, it remained cramped and dependent on public water taps until the later 1890s, well after the Smiths had departed. Digestive and respiratory ailments flourished, as did typhoid, scarlet fever, measles, and whooping cough. Ever-present slag heaps and smoke threatened breathing, and the pigsties common in back gardens added to dirt and pollution. Porcine contributions, like those of chickens, rabbits, and gardens, nevertheless mainstayed family diets as well as adding to the chores of household life.

Such domestic settings kept colliery wives, mothers, and daughters hard pressed to keep families presentable and healthy. Pervasive community oversight nevertheless fostered high standards of housewifery and the commonly observed "cleanliness and brightness of the houses" on miners' row.[29] Difficult to miss was the message that female industry and talent buttressed respectability and provided proof of superior morality. Women like Mary Ellen readily measured themselves by their public reputation for excellent housewifery. Pride in hard work well done bolstered women's claims to fair dealing in personal relations and much else. Relatives and neighbours did more than set high standards for housewifery. Their networks, strongly dependent on women's friendships and kinship, supplied critical assistance in childcare, budgets, and managing husbands. The nearby presence of the birth families of Mary Ellen and Ralph was likely to be useful, all the more when the babies arrived.

Relatively high wages, opportunities for sons in the pits, and the shortfall in waged labour for women encouraged fertility. Company housing in many villages also sometimes put larger households at the front of the queue.[30] Whatever the cause, the young Mrs. Ralph Smith, unlike her own mother, produced children in rapid succession. Richard William (1885–1925), Robert (1885–1927), and Ralph Gladstone (1887–1963) quickly joined their half-sister, all their names invoking the previous generation and blood ties, not to mention William Ewart Gladstone (1809–98), the grand old man of British liberalism and long-serving prime minister. They crowded the cottage, where the 1891 English census also listed Ralph's brother, twenty-seven-year-old Mathew, as resident. Although Mary Ellen had led a somewhat protected life as a daughter, she soon had to worry about making ends meet. In the mid-1880s, her parents and brother, William, joined the Cornish diaspora's continuing search for better prospects, first in the American western states, San Francisco, and perhaps Grass Valley, California, and then in Nanaimo, British Columbia. Their departure could only have made life tougher for kin left behind.[31]

The Smiths' last child, John Wesley (1893–1960), was not born until the family had relocated to Nanaimo. Perhaps the gap in childbearing between 1887 and 1893 was due to miscarriages, a special danger for women who continued to work hard during pregnancy. It might also reflect efforts to regulate fertility, to bring it in line with limited resources. Given Mary Ellen's appearance of robust health throughout much of her life, birth control seems likely. Certainly, discussion of its value was commonplace among the British reformers whom the Smiths favoured. In his *Principles of Political Economy* (1848) and *The Subjection of Women* (1869), the influential Liberal theorist John Stuart Mill typically endorsed family limitation as a condition of women's emancipation and progress in general.[32] Though contraceptive options remained limited and sometimes illegal in both Britain and Canada, the couple could only benefit from an "upsurge of commercial literature in the 1890s which publicized sex manuals, contraceptives, and abortifacients."[33]

For the ambitious Smiths, fertility and domestic relations in general were further informed by Victorians' growing idealization of family life overseen by industrious, moral, and respected wives and mothers, the female counterpart to the male aristocrats of labour who have fascinated historians of the working class.[34] In particular, the Methodism that anchored their lives (and inspired the name of their last-born son) embraced a familial culture that assigned a prized role to women, and its ideals, sometimes embodied in the cult of true womanhood, permeated both private and public life. Whereas the "balance of power" in matters from wages to diets routinely favoured men, companionship became an increasing ideal in many working-class marriages,[35] perhaps aided in Mary Ellen's case by her Cornish roots. By the close of the nineteenth century, some women built on that regard, as well as older traditions of working-class family solidarity, to assert their right to respect and to a role in public life.

Although they were always a minority in mining villages, as elsewhere, female activists often stood in solidarity with other women who devoted themselves solely to their own households. They might be regarded as odd or extraordinary, but many were admired for their courage and diligence. Such approval underlay the region's emerging support for female preachers in Methodist chapels and as office-holders in the cooperative movement and in local government.[36] Even community champions, however, were required to meet domestic expectations and to prioritize their families, just the identity that Mary Ellen would later publicly espouse as a maternal feminist. This stance would help her secure invaluable approval when she campaigned for suffrage and other reforms in Canada. In contrast, as he climbed socially, her politician husband would have difficulty in maintaining claims to a working-class male identity and, with this, support from organized labour.

Public Life and Self-Improvement

Miners, like fathers and husbands in other occupations, met the primary requirement for their sex in generating income and not drinking or gambling it away. Despite or because of pervasive agreement about men's obligations, the pits fostered "a hypermasculine culture centered around the trade union, working men's club, allotment, and football field."[37] Women were encouraged to "treat men like kings" in exchange for their wage packet.[38] If crowded housing, endless domestic chores, and frequent pregnancies shortened all tempers and lives, men could escape to pubs or inns far more readily than women. Holywell boasted the Fat Ox and Half Moon, just down the road from the Smith home. Such commercial spaces offered men drink, gambling, and companionship, but they also hosted discussion of public issues, from cooperatives and unions to electoral candidates. Wives more frequently relied on gatherings associated with homes, chapels, the local primary school built by pit owners and dubbed "a handsome edifice," or Seaton Delaval's cooperative store.[39]

Religion, notably for the Smiths in the form of Primitive Methodism, was a powerful presence in everyday life, strongly associated with "well-kept homes and well-run households," where women were upheld in expectations that men would turn over their wages.[40] Local chapels encouraged self-help, individual restraint, and personal improvement at home and at work. Evangelical itinerant preachers, both male and female, spread national and global networks of faith and activism. Little in personal or political life escaped their scrutiny. In particular, Methodism armoured many miners in demanding a better deal from employers and governments, even as it communicated two sometimes contradictory messages: on the one hand, worthy men and women should be industrious and dutiful; on the other, they should challenge unfairness and corruption.[41] In other words, respect and position had to be earned; abuse, whether by bosses or men, justified demands for remedy. The era's radical class and gender politics resonated with those principles.

To spread their activist message, Methodists, mostly men but a few women too, were trained in public debate, committee work, and fundraising. Teaching in the chapel Sunday school, as Mary Ellen did, regularly demonstrated female competence and respectability, but churches occasionally offered their distaff members opportunities for greater service. In 1891, a female lay minister from Newcastle, the metropolitan centre just down the coast, joined Ralph in rallying coal village congregations, and she was not alone.[42] For the most part, however, men dominated Methodism's public ranks. By the 1880s, Ralph Smith stood out as a promising candidate for leadership. The local newspaper typically applauded him for inspiring attentive audiences in special Sunday services to large congregations in the United Methodist Free Church at Seaton Sluice.[43] The talented young miner appeared to be following in the footsteps of Thomas Burt (1837–1922), an influential local MP (1874–1918) who lectured regularly in the Methodist chapels and schoolrooms of Bates Cottages and Holywell.[44] Local success encouraged Ralph to dream of training for full-time ministerial employment. However, the responsibilities of a growing family and his own chronic respiratory problems doomed that future, though he retained his determination to spread a gospel of individual and collective salvation.

Even as Methodism cultivated confidence and courage among ambitious miners, it found allies in the higher ranks of Victorian society. Many local land holders, colliery owners, business people, and professionals shared its faith in the promise of self-improvement. Their diverse contributions to community projects, ranging from land and buildings to heating, insurance, and scholarships, aimed to cultivate orderly habits and demonstrate responsible leadership.[45] In colliery villages, repeated evidence of elite engagement reminded beneficiaries of possible cross-class solidarity, not to mention the need for gratitude. Before the appearance of the welfare state, this potential assistance supplied a significant basis for social cohesion, even solidarity.

Yet if the gifts of the powerful were hard to miss, advancement in colliery communities depended above all on individual effort by workers and their families. Education was increasingly central to their hopes for a better future.[46] On the one hand, state schooling gradually improved. The Elementary Education Acts of 1870 and 1880 offered girls and boys under thirteen basic training and levels of literacy and numeracy that typically outstripped those of their parents. Many miners nevertheless took for granted that sons would apprentice in early adolescence in their own relatively well-paid occupation.[47] Bright girls like Mary Ellen, for whom no pit jobs existed, whose mothers were not weighted down with childcare, and who might aspire to teaching, sometimes stayed on longer in school. Such opportunities could pay dividends when young women negotiated their own marital relations with less literate and numerate pitmen. Ultimately, like Methodism, schooling delivered mixed messages. It integrated working-class pupils into a national culture that encouraged deference to authority, even as it could recognize academic talent, develop skills, and open doors for the imagination, better employment, and challenges to the status quo.[48]

In any case, the relatively short stay of many youngsters in schools meant that auto-didacticism and adult education were critical bolsters to ambition.[49] Itinerant booksellers recruited buyers for the growing output of Britain's democratizing presses, with their mass-market "classics for the masses." Texts from literary greats such as William Shakespeare and John Milton joined those of newcomers such as Alfred, Lord Tennyson, Thomas Carlyle, Christina Rossetti, Samuel Taylor Coleridge, Emily Bronte, and Charles Dickens, many of whom would be cited in later speeches by both Smiths. History and politics attracted a popular readership that was trying to make sense of the world. Northumberland mining households could appraise their own hard lives in reading popular exposés, such as Andrew Mearns and William Preston's *The Bitter Cry of Outcast London* (1883), which condemned poverty as a product of human greed.[50]

They might not have had much in their pockets, but the Smiths were inspired by the great debates of their age. In Canada, a cartoonist would later single out Whig historian and politician Thomas Babington Macaulay (1800–59) as an ongoing spur for Ralph. Macaulay's opposition to universal suffrage would have given him pause, but his idol could be applauded for defending popular education, anti-slavery, the civilizing mission of the British Empire, and Jewish political emancipation. Ralph likewise encouraged friends to discover "inspiration in the pages of the older economists," particularly Herbert Spencer (1820–1903), whose writings on self-reliance he had consumed as a young man. Unfortunately, nothing is known about Ralph's views of Spencer's shift from pro- to anti-suffragist.[51]

The Smiths and their village contemporaries did not have to depend on their own purchases for stimulation. The lectures, reading rooms, and libraries of local Mechanics' Institutes and mutual improvement societies, including the Ancient Order of Foresters, which Ralph later fondly remembered,[52] offered scientific and technical texts as well as cherished fiction. From the 1880s on, Cambridge, Oxford, and Durham Universities offered science, literature, and philosophy extension classes to miners, supplying further opportunities for the talented and determined.[53] One enthusiastic instructor hailed

> the sturdy intelligence of the pitmen, their determined earnestness, the appreciative and responsive way in which they listened, the down-right

straightforwardness of their speech ... I am persuaded that in the Northumberland and Durham district the pitmen are ripe for a scheme that will bring Higher Education and Culture within their reach. The financial difficulty is the only serious one.[54]

Albert Grey, the progressive Liberal MP for Northumberland South (1880–85) and then Tyneside (1885–86) and future governor general of Canada (1904–11), lobbied for Cambridge classes as part of his commitment to cross-class collaboration. Whereas ties to mine owners and managers and aristocratic and middle-class philanthropists sometimes incurred suspicion, just as they might in local schools, educational initiatives reflected widespread investment in the principles of *Self-Help*, an 1859 bestseller written by Samuel Smiles.[55]

Elite support was critical since the Northumberland Miners' Association (NMA) had few resources to subsidize additional schooling for its members. Nor, as the father of a growing brood, did Ralph have money to spare. In 1886, even the minimal tuition fee for the extension lectures on "Work and Energy" offered near Bates Cottages would have been hard to find.[56] Ralph was remembered, however, as a student of coal mine engineering and other technical studies that helped win promotion and respect.[57] Caring for young children and housewifery meant that Mary Ellen was unlikely to contemplate such opportunities, which were in any case directed at men. When much later she moved in Vancouver's suffragist circles, where the University Women's Club held pride of place, she would keenly feel the lack of extended formal education.

One of the Victorian age's most powerful sources of edification, however, welcomed both sexes and all classes for self-improvement. Temperance groups, such as the International Order of Good Templars and the Bands of Hope associated with Primitive Methodist chapels, swept the pit villages with popular "weekly meetings, fund-raising concerts, interclub visits, and annual summer concerts."[58] Although later identified with prohibition and middle-class efforts to discipline male workers, temperance campaigns stressed radical messages of individual redemption, moderation for all classes, and self-respect. Like many Britishers, Ralph and Mary Ellen Smith became resolute teetotallers, convinced that sobriety and discipline determined life's outcomes. That conclusion was shared by many in the so-called labour aristocracy of skilled workers.[59]

Sobriety lay similarly close to the heart of another powerful inspiration to self-improvement. Predating the insistence of Karl Marx and Friedrich Engels on class conflict, a surging cooperative movement promised empowerment to ordinary folk. Early apostles, such as the utopian socialist Robert Owen (1771–1858), insisted that shared production and consumption could override the divides of class, and indeed sometimes of gender, en route to social progress and justice. In 1869, this vision inspired Britain's first Cooperative Congress in London. Six years later, thirty-one cooperatives in Northumberland and thirty-nine in Durham, many in colliery villages, testified to its widespread appeal.[60] By the 1880s, the British movement had enrolled some half a million members and by the First World War more than 3 million, with strongholds in the Midlands and the north. Ralph and Mary Ellen supported the Northern Section, which recruited almost a third of Northumberland and Durham's total population.[61] By the early twentieth century, the movement had outpaced the combined enlistment in the British Labor Party and its socialist rivals.[62]

Northumberland cooperative stores led in consciousness raising about sharing in the fruits of capitalism. Winning members' loyalty with lower prices, accurate weighing, safe products, and dividends, they left previously often dominant company stores in the dust. By the time Ralph and Mary Ellen were adults, co-ops' often impressive buildings stood alongside Methodist chapels, mechanics' institutes, and union rooms "as a symbol of the miners' growing interest in both the principle and the practice of self-help."[63] Whereas men controlled the vast majority of executive positions in cooperative societies, women, as family shoppers and, frequently, financiers, proved ardent supporters.[64] In 1883, the creation of what became the Women's Cooperative Guild introduced what has been termed a "relational" feminist agenda, which "argued for public roles and voices for women in order to help them perform their traditional duties as wives and mothers." Essentially a version of the domestic ideology more commonly known as maternalist feminism,[65] this philosophy – much like Methodism – legitimated respectable activism for women such as Mary Ellen. They could remain proud of domestic pursuits, even as they questioned the profits and the brutality of capitalist competition. As the thoughtful mother of young children, Mary Ellen supported her husband's forays into local cooperative politics as a way of assisting the family and improving the community.

In October 1890, Ralph demonstrated his mastery of key movement arguments in a well-received public lecture titled "High and Low Dividends," a controversial subject as co-ops struggled to balance books and principles.[66] At much the same time, he joined the board of directors of the Seaton Delaval Co-operative Society.[67] In 1890, he ran for election to the Northern Central Board, and though he was defeated by a more seasoned activist, he was chosen as a local delegate to the Twenty-Second Annual Cooperative Conference of Great Britain and Ireland. Held in Glasgow's monumental city hall that May, this historic assembly of mighty and more humble cooperators took the young miner beyond England's northeast, probably for the first time.

In the lectures and the crowds in attendance, Smith glimpsed a far bigger stage than that he knew. Lord Rosebery (1847–1929), the conference president, chairman of the London County Council, great Whig landowner, and later Liberal prime minister, set out a creed to unite otherwise warring classes in the industrial age. His well-received keynote address began persuasively, suggesting that he was present "to listen and to learn." Linking cooperatives firmly to Christian socialism, Rosebery argued that

> it is not so many years since movements of a social character – of a socialist character or Socialist character – were regarded as anathema ... and Fourier, St Simon, and Owen were words of ill-omen and ill-favour in the eyes and in the nostrils of the country. But now the case is widely altered ... Much is included in the word socialistic which is not merely unobjectionable but desirable ... We cannot – public men cannot, statesmen cannot afford to disregard the solid mass of adult and intelligent opinion which you represent ... We hear much of the jealousy of the working classes ... If co-operation can remove that jealousy it will be a great advantage to the State ... It is an evil for the State not to be able to recognise leaders among the working classes.[68]

Deftly separating Liberal-Labour MPs Thomas Burt, Henry Broadhurst (1840–1911), and John Burns (1858–1943) from all the prophets of class conflict, Rosebery suggested that a politics of conciliation and prosperity would be ushered in by cooperatives and, not so incidentally, the Liberal Party.

Rosebery was followed on the podium by another Liberal, Lord Aberdeen (1847–1934), also a grandee of Scotland, later governor general of Canada, and a feminist, like his influential wife, Ishbel Marjoribanks Gordon (1857–1939), the founder of the National Council of Women of Canada. Aberdeen proclaimed the "great cause" of cooperation as the solution to the "urgent" problems of poverty and industrial conflict.[69] The congress's vision of a radical new world of human collaboration and self-betterment aligned closely with intellectual influences surrounding the Smiths in their pit village. For the next twenty-five years, that Scottish convention loomed particularly large in Ralph's life story. At his death in

1917, it was remembered. In Canada, he had to surrender his hopes for the cooperative movement, but he harboured his faith in its spirit.

For the ambitious miner, regional class politics sometimes fed the same vision. Northumberland and Durham produced powerful Whig aristocrats, often dubbed "friends of the people," with long traditions of service as Liberal MPs. Like Lord Aberdeen, such magnates sometimes linked Canada to a heritage of aristocratic duty. "Radical Jack" Lord Durham (1792–1840) and Albert Grey were similarly outspoken governors general, for 1838–39 and 1904–11 respectively. Champions of an expanded franchise, such authorities seemed to counter the inevitability of class conflict.[70] One of Ralph's personal heroes, long-time Northumberland MP Thomas Burt, cherished the northeast's great Whig families, praising them as

> the Reformers of their day, and they fought bravely and disinterestedly for the liberties and for the political enfranchisement of the people when those without votes had few friends and helpers among the rich and powerful. In the Greys and the Lambtons of Northumberland and Durham afforded splendid examples of Whig noblemen who had for generations championed the claims of the poor and the political outcasts when these were voteless and voiceless, politically, in the land of their birth.[71]

High regard could be mutual. Earl Grey, Canada's former governor general, once described Burt as "the finest gentleman I ever knew."[72] The shift of the late Victorian British royal family into a "cult of benevolence," though not, with rare exceptions, into the suffragism endorsed by Aberdeen and Grey, likewise encouraged optimistic workers to anticipate mutual respect from elite reformers.[73]

Well-published industrial conflicts in Britain during the years that the Smiths were sorting out their own views sometimes offered the same lesson of mutual aid while confirming links to radical non-conformity. Victorious strikes by East End London match girls and dockers in 1888 and 1889 mobilized a broad band of public opinion. Allies among Britain's middle class and aristocracy, such as noted feminist writer Annie Besant (1847–1933), progressive Liberal MP Charles Bradlaugh (1833–91), Catholic Cardinal Henry Edward Manning (1808–92), and the Aberdeens succoured unions that contested brutal conditions and pitiful wages. Still closer to home for the Smiths were the benefits of cooperation evident in the Northumberland and Durham Miners' Permanent Relief Fund. Instituted in response to the 1860s' underground disasters, it presented the edifying spectacle of accident insurance managed jointly by mutually attentive miners and colliery owners.[74] The Northumberland Coal Trade Joint Committee, of which Ralph was a member, was in the same spirit.[75]

For decades, the Northumberland Miners' Association embodied the regional sinews of Methodism, self-education, temperance, and co-operation.[76] Insisting upon a "manly independence," the NMA demanded respect and equality in the course of achieving a universal male franchise for which it mounted a massive demonstration of pitmen, their wives, and children in Newcastle in 1872.[77] Its liberal-labour, or labourist, radicalism was informed by "continual contact with the sympathetic middle-class radicals" and "the long standing alignment of middle- and working-class reformers dedicated to the parliamentary system."[78] Those allies constituted the left wing of the great reform coalition that the Liberal Party marshalled under Gladstone. The first general secretary of the NMA, William Crawford (1833–90), who had entered Hartley Coal Mines as a boy, preached as a Primitive Methodist, and campaigned for co-ops, became an MP in 1885. His successor in the NMA was the like-minded Thomas Burt, who was elected a Liberal-Labourite in 1874. Burt survived to be dubbed the "Father of the House of Commons."[79] Almost a half a century later and some halfway around the globe in Vancouver, BC, Nicholas Thompson (c. 1853–1934), a former president of the city's Board of Trade and a native-born Northumbrian, invoked Burt's long shadow when he mourned the loss of Ralph Smith, dead at less than sixty years of age:

> In the old days in Northumberland he was ever working in the interests of the underdog. I remember his fight in the interests of compulsory education, the extension of the franchise to workingmen, the co-operative movement and other activities that were in the interests of the working classes. He was an associate of Tom Burt and other famous Labor men and throughout his long career from the time when he went to work in the mines at 11 years of age, he has never deserted his principles.[80]

Emblematic of the alliances embedded in the era's radical liberalism, Burt presented an 1881 petition from his Bates Cottages constituents to the House of Commons. It endorsed a petition launched by Liberal MP Charles Bradlaugh, demanding that he be permitted to take his parliamentary oath as an atheist.[81] The broad-based reform faith was similarly asserted when, in an 1884 speech to some five hundred Bates Cottages miners, Liberal MP Albert Grey endorsed proportional representation "as more just and equitable."⁸² In the same spirit, Burt addressed the Seaton Delaval Co-operative Society on "co-operation, temperance and education" as the key principles of social progress.⁸³ Many miners were convinced that "the interests of capital and labour could be balanced through bargaining on the basis of trade union strength and good will on both sides."⁸⁴ They rallied to Britain's New Liberalism, set forth by theorists such as John A. Hobson (1858–1940) and politicians such as David Lloyd George (1863–1945), with their faith in an "organically evolving human community" in which the state guaranteed a social minimum and class conflict was avoided.⁸⁵

Before the First World War, such convictions made Northumberland "one of the most successful sites of the Lib-Lab alliance and of consensus between employers and employees."⁸⁶ Even when socialist and social democratic alternatives to Britain's long-standing two-party system gradually emerged, a pervasive gospel of self-help, personal responsibility, and respectability grounded in Methodism and the cooperative movement buttressed the NMA as a "bastion of liberalism."⁸⁷ This was the steady inspiration for Ralph, whom a Canadian Presbyterian minister later lauded as hurling "with such destructive effectiveness into the socialistic camp, the doctrine of the individual will."⁸⁸

Influence never travelled in one direction. To attract increasingly self-conscious workers, many of whom were enfranchised after the Third Great Reform Act of 1884, the Liberal Party had to be proactive. In exchange for resisting more revolutionary doctrines, it offered the expanded electorate prospects for political, industrial, and social improvement. Democratic progress might be slow but its promise, unlike that of more revolutionary doctrines, was inevitable and bloodless. Very tellingly, *The Speaker,* a leading proponent of progressive liberalism, declared in January 1892 that "the Liberal party has reached a point at which the consideration of the claims of Labour takes precedence over all others."⁸⁹

Cooperation among the classes was not the only cause hanging in the balance. Like workers, women were increasingly mobilizing in demands for a better life. A threatened war between the sexes supplied the era's gender equivalent of class conflict. Liberal feminists argued that cooperative partnerships of women and men were similarly essential to peace and progress. When the legendary Burt praised his wife (and cousin) Mary Weatherburn (1842–1926), with whom he had ten children, as a "daughter of the people," someone "in complete sympathy with my public work" and a "brave and loving helpmate," he located his class politics firmly within a familiar tradition, that of marital solidarity in mining villages and mutual respect fostered by Methodism. Such declarations associated principled working men with women's right to respect and equality.[90] In the mid-1880s, the Northern Counties Women's Liberal Associations (WLA) for Northumberland, Durham, and Yorkshire, part of a national federation numbering some fifty to sixty thousand members, asserted the possibility of cooperation between reform-minded women and men.[91] WLA meetings in Mechanics and Temperance Halls and Methodist chapels throughout the region tapped overlapping loyalties of class and gender. This message clearly resonated with the self-conscious Smiths, who would become one of Canada's power couples in liberal-labour politics.

Yet for all its advocacy of class and gender cooperation, liberalism proved an uncertain ally. Its political parties readily regarded both workers and women as noisy and obstreperous, believing that they would not reliably submit to party discipline and that they would expect to have input into policies and positions claimed by elite male power brokers.[92] National leaders, such as William Gladstone and Herbert Asquith (1852–1928) in London and Wilfrid Laurier and William Lyon Mackenzie King (1874–1950) in Ottawa, displayed indifference or hostility to many reforms, including women's representation in Parliament, a stance that sowed much disillusionment with liberalism. That letdown, however, was only in its infancy when the Smiths set off for Canada.

Just days before their departure in September 1892, Ralph Smith spoke to the Bates Cottages Debating and Mutual Improvement Society. His speech, titled "Disestablishment and Disendowment," criticized the privileges enjoyed by the Anglican Church. In probably his last public engagement before closing the door on British politics, he placed himself firmly in a non-conformist radical tradition of righteous protest. The local Anglican vicar, whose support subsidized the society, mounted a spirited rebuttal, but Ralph trounced him without apology. In the following months, the society continued to advance an independent course and a progressive agenda, staging a model parliament with working-class MPs and sanctioning woman suffrage.[93] By then, however, the Smiths had set their sights on improving themselves and Canada.

The coal-mining communities in which Ralph Smith and Mary Ellen Spear came of age largely trusted that the radical politics of liberal-labourism represented a realistic option for self-conscious workers. Rejecting socialist dismissal of class cooperation as politically irresponsible, believers insisted that "their own proletarian origins and direct practical experience of industrial life" made them superior guides to a transformed politics and that a sympathetic elite could be enlisted as allies.[94] That faith appeared especially confident during the late 1880s, King Coal's boom years. Very soon, however, Britain's pit families faced wage cuts and deepening hardship.[95] Slowly, the Lib-Lab ship foundered upon the shoals of rising industrial conflict, Irish nationalism, woman suffrage, and elite intransigence. After its creation in 1903, the British Labor Party increasingly carried the political hopes of organized miners in Northumberland, as elsewhere.

In September 1892, the Smiths set sail for Canada, hoping to restore Ralph's health and acquire assistance from the Spears who had settled in British Columbia. By that time, the "well known public man" and his respected partner had developed a politics of resistance to capitalism's depredations,[96] to counsels of class warfare, and to male abuse of power. They took pride in hearing Ralph acclaimed as a "radical leader" of the Bates Cottages Debating and Mutual Improvement Society and seeing Mary Ellen rewarded with "a gold mounted bracelet" for her service as a "leader of the children and an organizer of concerts for the Methodist chapel." The ardent liberal-labourite left the farewell gathering of admiring neighbours with an conclusion that surely resounded with his wife: "I do not want to go to heaven yet, for I want to do all the good I can for humanity."[97] As it turned out, Canada would provide a far brighter stage for both Mary Ellen and Ralph to realize the ambitions that Britain's colliery villages had first nourished.

2
Replenishing the Empire, 1892–1900

In September 1892, Mary Ellen, Ralph, and their young children headed off to join what has been termed the "settler revolution" that scaffolded the rise of the "British World" before 1939.[1] While coal mining and the Industrial Revolution fuelled global ambitions, arrogant claims to Indigenous lands in far-off corners of the globe affirmed the supremacy of what has been labelled "Britannicization."[2] As transplanted evangelical Britons, the Smiths shared the Dominion of Canada's taste for the Old Testament in its claim to rule: Psalm 72:8 – "He shall have dominion also from sea to sea, and from the river to the ends of the earth." That omnipotence would be tested in British Columbia, the "West beyond the West."

In making a new home on the edge of the Pacific Ocean, the ambitious newcomers embodied an imperial politics of gender, race, and class. Escapees from Britain's shores cherished diverse dreams,[3] with many migrants taking for granted their right to better their families and the world at large. That evolving mission had both feminist and anti-feminist implications. White women's role in creating "civilized" British space would empower and constrain them even as it largely marginalized others.[4] As the Smiths arrived in Nanaimo, racial lines were hardening. While Pacific Coast tribes continued their resistance and remained essential to the coal, agricultural, and marine economy, their dispossession was taken for granted by the imperially minded. Nanaimo itself was founded on land belonging to the Snuneymuxw First Nation, acquired via a Douglas Treaty of 1854. As Jean Barman chillingly describes, the Indigenous presence in urban British Columbia was being actively erased.[5] The

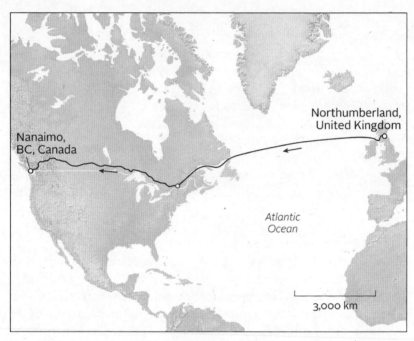

From Northumberland to British Columbia, 1892. | Cartographer Eric Leinberger.

Chinese increasingly replaced the First Nations as the decisive racial other, suspected of harbouring their own imperial claims to supposedly empty frontiers. British settlers likewise negotiated the meaning of class. Ambitious workers, like the Smiths, and the Spears before them, intended to extend their fortunes with insistence on superior intelligence, morality, and industry. In that process, they claimed the respect and authority often denied them at the heart of empire and sometimes scorned members of their own class who stumbled at the tests of superiority. Though rarely acknowledged, their enhanced prospects depended on "inequalities sown by the settler state."[6] Indigenous land and labour, and Asian rivals, subsidized White working-class as well as elite newcomers in the Last Best West.

To Replenish the Empire and Britannicize the World

In late summer 1892, the Smiths journeyed to Liverpool, the departure point for many British and European emigrants. From this "Gate of Empire,"[7] migrants typically followed their dreams to the United States, but a significant minority chose Canada and other dominions in what has been termed "an act of patriotism." The Smiths followed the Spears in a pattern of chain migration that contributed to significant population growth in the Vancouver Island coalfields from 1887 to 1892.[8]

Despite the financial strain of Ralph's ongoing respiratory problems and four children aged ten and younger, the couple paid their own way, asserting their status as preferred immigrants. On September 15, 1892, they embarked on the passenger steamer *Vancouver*.[9] Launched at Glasgow in 1884, it had recently been rebuilt so that the Dominion Line could fulfill its contract with Ottawa to maintain a regular line of steamers to promote immigration between Liverpool and Quebec City or Montreal.[10] The Smiths were among 153 "English" and 75 adult "foreigners" and 261 children.[11] Many immigrant ships were uncomfortable, but this vessel boasted dining saloons, electricity, attractive furnishings, an absence of livestock, and promenade space for the second- and third-class clientele in which it specialized.

When they reached Montreal on September 26, 1892, the Smiths joined some 31,000 arrivals to Canada that year. This number, a significant drop from 82,200 in 1891, reflected an economic slowdown that persisted until the end of the century. Anticipating hard times, many newcomers promptly departed for southern climes. Not so the Smiths, who stalwartly headed west on the recently completed Canadian Pacific Railway (CPR) main line. Again, they voyaged respectably, eschewing the immigrant cars that carried most single men and poorer wayfarers. Indeed, the continental trip, helped by extravagant CPR publicity, was already a significant tourist attraction, notably the transit through the Rocky Mountains, celebrated as the Canadian Alps. That adventure, so alien to the dark polluted colliery villages, heralded a different future.

The overland trip terminated in Vancouver, where the CPR was a leading employer and landowner, unwittingly introducing the Smiths to the significance of railways for politics, patronage, and corruption in their new home. The city's main train station proved a relatively modest overture to an imperial outpost where immigration was dominated by bachelors in quest of quick cash on the resource frontier. In 1891, Victoria, the capital of a province that had been created in 1871, had a population of some 16,841, but Vancouver was home to 13,709. Most of its residents were Canadian-born, though some 3,600 came from the British Isles, 1,400 from China, 1,200 from the United States, and 500 from Europe.[12] Allocated small reserves, the dwindling Indigenous community was on the defensive. An overwhelmingly Protestant city, with powerful Methodist congregations, Vancouver would soon become British Columbia's major metropolis, but economic difficulties throughout the 1890s encouraged immigrants to shift to Seattle and San Francisco. Some two decades later, the Smiths would return to Vancouver as it boomed, but their immediate future lay sixty kilometres across the Strait of Georgia, whose name inserted an earlier British monarch into an Indigenous landscape.

Canada's Newcastle of the Far West

Their destination was the city of Nanaimo, known as the Newcastle of the Far West.[13] It had been incorporated in 1874, twelve years before Vancouver, and lay some quarter of the way up the east coast of Vancouver Island. Tiny Newcastle Island lay immediately offshore. Christened after the famous Northumberland coal city so familiar to the Smiths, its signal of an omnipresent imperial realm would have been a cheerful reminder of home ties. In 1892, Nanaimo was the freight and distribution centre for central Vancouver Island.[14] The second-fastest-growing city in British Columbia, it boasted in a self-conscious salute to empire that its port provided "safe anchorage for craft of every description, from a canoe to a line of battle ships."[15] Sidestepping its origins in a Snuneymuxw village (although "Nanaimo" was an anglicized version of the tribal name) and Indigenous employment in coal mining,[16] the settler city aimed to provide the province's industrial engine even as Victoria laid claim to political leadership and Vancouver to financial and commercial majesty. In 1891, Nanaimo and the surrounding area had a population of 18,229; by 1901, it would be 27,198.[17] The much smaller central city census sub-district, where the Smiths would live, was dominated by the British-born, with other White residents from the United States, Continental Europe, and the rest of Canada, particularly Nova Scotia. Only seventy-nine Chinese people lived within its borders. Like Indigenous women and men, they were shunted to the margins. The city's leading land developer, the New Vancouver Coal Mining and Land Company (NVCMLC), refused to sell land to either group. Men were in the majority, especially among Asians, a "maleness" that further defined them as outsiders in an imperial province that lionized Old Country couples. In 1854, the *Princess Royal* had brought British mining families to Nanaimo. Like that contingent, settlers such as the Smiths were to guarantee peace, order, and good government. In 1877, BC legislation finally caught up with its UK counterpart of 1842 by prohibiting women in the mines, thus affirming the pervasive ideal well summed up as "male publicness and female reproductiveness."[18] White households headed by skilled breadwinners supported by proper wives and promising offspring were to civilize and dominate the imperial frontier.

Whereas coal miners, like loggers and fishers, embodied admired masculine physicality, female wage-earners once again lacked comparable élan. British bride ships, notably the *Tynemouth* and the *Robert Lowe*, which had docked in Victoria during the 1860s, captured continuing preferences: ideal women were to marry, rear children, and support male ambition. Disrepute dogged alternatives. Mary Ellen would have been appalled to discover that her former employment as a dressmaker was "commonly used as an occupational disguise among prostitutes," with Nanaimo possessing "an inordinate number of unmarried female dressmakers between the ages of 18 and 35 in 1891."[19] The path to female respectability and authority in White households ran inexorably through marriage and housewifery. As a wife and mother with four children, Mary Ellen was right on track for public approval.

Mary Ann, Richard, and William Spear guided the newcomers. In Britain, both families tenanted a few rooms, but by 1891 Nanaimo prided itself on being "essentially a city of homes," with "nearly every miner and laboring man having a comfortable house of his own, or else purchased from the New [Vancouver Coal] Company on a long term of payment."[20] As a skilled hewer from Britain's northeast, with close links to similar workers in the NVCMLC pits, Ralph slipped readily into the local labour aristocracy, a man from away who would expect to be treated with respect.[21] The Spears lived in the heart of the city at 20 Milton Street, near "Cornish Town," where they could listen to Cornish-language recitations at the local Methodist church.[22] The Smiths quickly moved nearby to 171 Machleary. Mary Ann Spear's contributions to the Methodist community and the Woman's Christian Temperance Union (WCTU) soon proved important assets for Mary Ellen, though the birth of her last child, John Wesley, in 1893 and the care of a large household kept her busy. The decade nevertheless saw her gradually move to assert a public presence in the city and to travel around Vancouver Island and occasionally to the mainland and as far afield as California.

As Mary Ellen guaranteed domestic well-being, Ralph remained the family's dominant representative in the world at large. Richard Spear's employment for the NVCMLC, just down the road, opened doors. The newcomer was immediately connected to that company first as a worker and soon as the agent for its approved union. The career of Mary Ellen's brother, William, as a music teacher, choir leader, and retailer of musical instruments was also significant, confirming that ambitious progeny could look beyond the pits.[23] No Spear or Smith offspring ever worked underground for any extended period, and they benefitted from lengthier schooling than most miners' sons. In the same spirit, many hewers treated their own hard toil as little more than "an occupational way-station" and turned readily to "small businesses, artisanal occupations," and farming.[24]

By the end of the nineteenth century, the Smiths and Spears resided together on Milton Street, though without Mary Ann, who had died at home after a fall in December 1895. Ralph had transitioned from miner to miner's agent and provincial politician. Mary Ellen and Mary Elizabeth kept house. The eldest son, Richard, had become a dry goods clerk, and Robert, Ralph, and John were students. Their resident Spear grandfather was still a miner. On hand to add to family income and demands was the hewer Mathew Smith, Ralph's brother, who boarded with kin like many bachelors. Filling out the household was the live-in servant, Annie Wright. An Anglican who had emigrated from Britain in 1893 at the age of twenty, she helped with caring, cooking, cleaning, shopping, gardening, and sewing. Meanwhile, William Spear, who had married in 1891, lived nearby with his wife, Elizabeth. She was the daughter of R.P. Edwards, a Methodist general merchant and prominent member of the Independent Order of Odd Fellows, a mutual aid society.

Close to this family enclave were many neighbours also hailing from north Britain. That community was extensive enough to support a Tyneside Society, for which Ralph Smith became first president in 1896.[25] Mary Ellen also asserted ties to the Old Country. By 1900, she was reciting at concerts in the Nanaimo Athletic Club in honour of Robbie Burns and presenting a "Scotch Reading" to St. Andrew's Presbyterian Church.[26] The Milton Street community was nevertheless diverse, as indicated by its nickname of Finn Town, a testament to the lure of mining jobs for other newcomers.[27] Neighbours also included the Lebanese peddler Michael Saba, whose person and products supplied further reminders of the broader world in which Nanaimo intended to flourish.[28]

Steamships conveyed residents regularly to Victoria and Vancouver, and the Esquimalt and Nanaimo Railway offered links south to the capital and eventually north to Port Alberni. The growth of the port, mines, gasworks, telephone system, waterworks, electric generation, shipyard, sawmill, foundry, leather and shoe factory, and breweries promised good jobs for White male teenagers and men. The core of economic life nevertheless centred on the collieries, where wages compared favourably with those in Nova Scotia, the heart of Canadian coal production.[29] As in the Old Country, domestic service, dressmaking, and teaching provided far fewer and less well-paid options for girls and women. The 1898 Act respecting the Nanaimo Electric Light, Power and Heating Company, Limited, banned Chinese and Japanese people from working for the company, a measure that, like efforts to deny them mining jobs, codified the pervasive racism of the day.[30]

The ambitious colonial enclave laid the groundwork for economic prosperity for its preferred community. Branches of the Bank of British Columbia and the Dominion Post Office Savings Bank tapped the savings of the provident of either sex. The Nanaimo Building Society and a rival eastern building society encouraged hopes for homeownership. The 1887 revision to the province's 1873 Married Women's Property Law potentially empowered the most fortunate of the fair sex to invest in land, as happened in Victoria at the end of the nineteenth century.[31] In a related, and similarly limited, improvement, the 1873 Municipal Elections Act enfranchised "femes sole," both spinsters and widows, who met the property and age qualifications. Soon afterward, the municipal franchise was extended to all qualified men and women over age twenty-one, regardless of marital status. The *Nanaimo Free Press* nevertheless presented civic government as relentlessly male.[32]

Although the Smiths never seem to have secured a profitable footing in real estate, they resided far more comfortably than they had in Bates Cottages. They shared in the modest rewards of the co-operative store operated by the Nanaimo Equitable Pioneer Society (NEPS). Founded in the mid-1880s, the downtown store connected public-spirited residents and incorporated space for a dressmaker and her apprentices, while the NEPS hall hosted meetings of the Knights of Labor, a progressive group active in the city. Here on British Columbia's settler frontier, prospects seemed bright for the cooperation the Smiths had prized in Britain. The edge of empire, however, failed to rise to the challenge.[33] As Ralph reported to his British comrades, there was ultimately "no co-operation in Canada." He judged its citizens as lacking "the spirit of personal enterprise, the principle of an intelligent socialism without depriving an individual of the development of the personal authority and power." From Ralph's perspective, cooperation's weakness in his new home encouraged irresponsible socialists.[34]

If cooperatives faltered, newcomers profited from the region's agricultural, hunting, and marine bounty.[35] This promised household comforts and a significantly healthier diet than that available in British colliery villages. Household gardens and poultry runs were augmented by venison, salmon, and herring, and diverse fruit, vegetables, and dairy goods were produced by local farmers, who might well be former miners. Healthy prospects were displayed at the Nanaimo Dairy Agricultural and Horticultural Fair, which opened in 1894. Its prizes for farm products, many produced by women, and also for "Ladies' Work," a category that included upholstery, linens, knitting, and plain and fancy needlework,[36] only confirmed the wisdom of immigration. Ralph might have arrived in Nanaimo "a dying man," as he put it, but the region's advantages helped him find "that treasure, health," which allowed all the Smiths to put down roots in their new home.[37]

Well-being and upward mobility were similarly demonstrated by Mary Ellen's emergence as an attractively dressed matron. In Nanaimo, she applied her old skills as a seamstress to a new realm of unprecedented public engagements. Even as her husband began to add "esquire" to his name and her brother declared himself a "professor" of music,[38] both proof of social aspirations, Mrs. Ralph Smith used dress to present herself as a "lady" who could pass muster in polite society. Musical pursuits helped her carve out a prominent position. In 1897, Nanaimo's Haliburton Street Methodist Choir performed at the local Opera House, presenting a sacred cantata titled "Joseph," written by Boston composer John Astor Broad. The part of the queen was sung "charmingly" by Mary Ellen.[39] Such accomplishments asserted both Smiths' right to share space with more privileged contenders for respectability and power.[40]

An Improving Community

Nanaimo might have been a small town on the imperial frontier, but it prided itself on moving with the times. The Smiths confidently joined that process, bringing from north Britain "a populist gospel of social duty, moral uplift and physical improvement" that "laid stress" in Canada, "as elsewhere across the British world, upon ethnic solidarity: 'Britishness' was to be the building block of a more efficient, better-disciplined as well as more mobile society."[41] Nanaimo's main newspaper, the frequently liberal-minded *Free Press,* regularly updated residents on social movements and improvements around the globe, from the 1893 franchise victory in New Zealand to the tactics of liberal-labour hopefuls in Great Britain. Prominent visitors were equally on display to inspire and educate. In the mid-1890s, Nanaimo welcomed Herbert Booth (1862–1926), the son of the Salvation Army founder and its commandant for Canada; the Aberdeens, Canada's viceregal couple; and Pauline Johnson (1861–1913), the dominion's "Mohawk princess," as evidence of the empire's religious and political sway. On city streets, Salvation Army "lassies" offered instructive reminders of women's claims to moral and public space, whereas the charismatic Lady Aberdeen was well known as a suffragist and a leader of Britain's Women's Liberal Federations and Canada's own National Council of Women.[42] As the *Free Press* lamented, "she is necessarily precluded from taking part in any question that can by any pretense be alleged to belong to the domain of party politics," but "it ought not to be a question of party politics to affirm that a woman is a suffering being, nor should the Governor-General's wife be debarred from insisting upon the natural corollary of that fundamental truism." It noted approvingly the Aberdeens' "wholehearted devotion" to one another and their children,[43] accomplishments associated with the modern marriage of equals, similarly espoused by the Smiths.

Pauline Johnson provided other inspiration. Taking to the stage at the Nanaimo Opera House under the patronage of the Smiths' Wallace Street Methodist congregation, she was welcomed as "the poet representative of the Redman of this continent." Her always popular public professions of imperial loyalty drew an enthusiastic following, even as her messages about Indigenous heroism and talent went largely unappreciated.[44] Although Ralph was later apparently offered a position with Indian Affairs by the Laurier administration, and his wife occasionally lectured on BC tribes, both remained publicly indifferent to the growing apartheid inflicted on Canada's First Peoples. Such indifference took racial superiority for granted, and as Fred Burrill rightly concludes, "a white working class formed in opposition to Indigenous peoples easily transitioned to anti-Chinese and anti-Black and other racist ideologies."[45]

The city's reform-minded newcomers focused instead on improving life for people much like themselves. In concerns typical of the Victorian age, they paid considerable attention to public health. The prevalence of outdoor privies and the absence of a public sewerage system, condemned by the Smiths' doctor and the local medical officer, Robert E. McKechnie (1861–1944), as "the greatest menace to the public health," helped keep disease and death a costly presence.[46] The year in which the Smiths arrived saw a serious outbreak of smallpox, and measles, scarlet fever, whooping cough, diphtheria, typhoid, cholera, and pneumonia and other respiratory ailments struck regularly. Their tally, even among the prosperous, preoccupied mothers and wives, who were Nanaimo's first line of medical defence. Injuries from mining operations likewise wreaked havoc. While Ralph struggled with lifelong chest ailments, his father-in-law survived common industrial injuries. In 1893, as a shot-lighter (someone who placed and detonated explosives in the mines), he was "slightly injured by falling rock."[47] In a 1896 report, the BC Ministry of Mines listed him as "severely injured about the body by being thrown from and jammed by a run of loaded cars."[48]

In 1876, pervasive health threats had prompted Nanaimo "ladies and gentlemen" to fit up cabins for the sick and dying, overseen by a matron. Accommodation soon expanded to include general, surgical, and private wards, a morgue, and operating rooms, presided over by both a male steward and a matron.[49] A maternity ward was notably absent until 1900, since births, like most care giving, generally occurred at home, as was true for John Wesley Smith. Only in 1893 did the local Hospital Board publish notices that it was "prepared to receive Female Patients," who would "receive the best medical treatment and competent female nurses to attend on them."[50] By 1895, Mary Ellen had joined the new Ladies' Committee in raising money for a female ward, and her mother served as the WCTU superintendent of hospital work.[51] Regular community fundraisers, together with donations of food, linens, and comforts, supplied in the main by women, augmented intermittent funding from coal companies, local businesses and societies, government grants, and modest fees. In early 1900, even as Ralph explored provincial and federal politics, Mary Ellen took on the vice-presidency of a new women's auxiliary that aimed to secure a better financial footing for the hospital.[52] Later that year, on behalf of Nanaimo ladies, she welcomed Lady Minto (1858–1940), the wife of the governor general, to open the "recently instituted Female Wards."[53] Such opportunities helped her keep up with Ralph's march into public prominence as a liberal-labour advocate and politician.

Just as in Ladysmith, the small colliery town established in 1898 just south of Nanaimo, the women's hospital auxiliary constituted one of the city's leading societies. In both instances, a membership of miners' wives and the local middle class operated "relatively autonomously and independently in the public sphere" and exercised "considerable influence over decisions affecting the day-to-day life of the community without having to compete with or be subordinated to the demands of men."[54] From their strategic location at the heart of a modern gospel of good health, they embodied a common female, sometimes feminist, politics that helped energize a diverse women's community. Their often intimate contact with the morbidity and mortality associated with mining inspired some auxiliary members to support unions, resist evictions, and challenge the Dunsmuir family, local mine owners with origins in north Britain and a habit of using police and troops in aid of low wages, poor housing, and union busting.[55] Her volunteer efforts for the city hospital confirmed Mary Ellen's credentials as a worthy partner for an ambitious representative of BC workers. Uncommented upon was the organizational experience that could be put to good feminist use in improving the lot of her sex.

Healthcare was always prominent but far from the only inspiration for regional reformers. Despite the crowing of municipal boosters, Nanaimo was plagued with moral and physical temptations. Pubs "did a roaring trade on Saturday night with beer a nickel a glass, and a lot of the men would get drunk to drown out their troubles and come home and sometimes would beat up the wife and kids."[56] Drunkenness enraged the progressively minded *Nanaimo Free Press*. In March 1892, it condemned "a regular drunken brawl in the vicinity of the 'Devil's half acre,'" which involved both women and men "shouting, swearing and screaming."[57] A few months later, just after the Smiths arrived, the newspaper censured a Mrs. H. Thames, who lived in the same neighbourhood. She was described as "in command, wielding an axe as the sign of her power, to the unmistakable terror of Mr. Thames." Far from a BC equivalent of Carrie Nation (1846–1911), the notorious American hatchet-wielding prohibitionist, Thames was charged with "keeping a disorderly house" – in other words, a brothel – and "with a breach of the Indian Act."[58]

Sexual misconduct served as a recurring target for worthy citizens. In October 1895, Ralph Smith played the organ at the YMCA Hall for a Methodist minister who defended an equal moral standard for both sexes, in these years termed "the white life for two," and attacked local bar-owners and pimps as "the Knights of immorality." Unlike the staunchly high-minded, if near-moribund, local Assembly of the Knights of Labor, such reprobates "made it easy for men to gratify vicious propensities simply because they had inherited them."[59] Demands that men do better met stiff resistance. In August 1898, "keepers and inmates of houses of prostitution" appeared before the police court and were fined accordingly, but, as was typical, the court turned a blind eye on their male clients.[60] As ever, girls and women bore sexuality's costs. In the spring of 1896, Nanaimo learned of a newborn baby girl who had been wrapped in a potato sack and abandoned in the harbour. Her married but deserted mother, an immigrant from Finland whose son worked for the Dunsmuirs, was struggling to support other youngsters. Ultimately, after her name was dragged

A 1905 view of Nanaimo, with the Odd Fellows Building and Emerald Stables in the foreground. | A1-32, Nanaimo Museum.

through the mud, the Provincial Court judge, Montague Tyrwhitt Drake (1830–1908), a former politician who had proposed enfranchising women provincially in 1883, suggested community sympathy in recommending only twenty-four hours' imprisonment for infanticide.[61]

Such tragedies fuelled progressive efforts to aid impoverished women and children while scandals associated with police toleration generated further enthusiasm for legal controls on immoral behaviour.[62] In 1896, the city passed a wide-ranging By-Law Relating to Public Morals. This outlawed swimming "without a proper bathing suit covering the body from the back to the knees"; "indecency" in person, writing, or pictures; "houses of Ill fame"; "swearing or immorality"; "drunkenness and vagrancy"; "gambling"; "begging"; the "sale of intoxicating liquors, tobacco or cigarettes to minors"; and "cruelty to animals," including "the fighting or baiting of any bull, bear, badger, dog, cock or other kind of animal whether domestic or wild."[63] Nanaimo was to be made very good even as it became, far from coincidentally, more resolutely White and British.

Churches stood at the forefront of the moral crusade. As in Britain, Methodists were notably organized and outspoken. Upon their arrival,

Mary Ellen and Ralph channelled much energy into their neighbourhood congregation at Wallace and Franklyn Streets, but they became well known in other Protestant settings as well. Ralph made regular appearances as a preacher. In a typical sermon asking "Are We Owners or Stewards" of the world's goods, he drew on the New Testament Gospel of Timothy to urge good deeds and generosity.[64] Like many of Canada's labour leaders, he possessed "an evangelic cast of mind" that readily embraced "personal moral regeneration" as the solution to all problems.[65] Both Ralph and Mary Ellen enlisted with progressive social gospellers in Canada's relatively new Methodist Epworth League.[66] In October 1896, Ralph gave a talk titled "Culture of the Human Being, Physical, Mental and Moral," in which he urged the cultivation of character as the "true test of our status," even as Mary Ellen celebrated dedication to "Duty."[67] Although the Epworth League has sometimes been associated with efforts to remasculinize Methodism in the face of congregations composed heavily of women and children, Mrs. Ralph Smith appeared confident in her assertion of female merits. She became distinguished for forthrightly assuring listeners of both sexes that God intended them to be "courageous," "decisive," "observant," and "energetic." As she argued, Christianity guaranteed "the highest civilization, the best manhood and womanhood."[68] During Wallace Street's 1898 Easter Sunday service, Mary Ellen sang Handel's aria "He Was Despised."[69] A few days later, she expanded on that musical testament to Christ's humility and poverty in a speech to the Epworth League that condemned "people of means" for ignoring community duties. "Thank Heaven," she observed, "the Gospel can be spread by the untried efforts of the poor. It is not dependent on any class." She finished by citing English poet Elizabeth Barrett Browning (1806–61) as an inspiration. Browning's epigraph, "The sweetest lives are those to duty wed," conflated a good woman's "life of charity and marriage" with commitment to reform and social justice.[70]

Close linkages among Nanaimo's evangelically minded settlers inspired ecumenical appearances before YMCA audiences. In a lecture entitled "What Christianity Has and Is Doing for the Toiler," Ralph praised Jesus as championing the labourer's "honest claims." Without such divine influence, capitalists "would be worse still." Equally importantly, the Gospel taught "the rights of labor," freed slaves, and elevated women. Socialism could not match Christianity in teaching "the State its duty to its subjects" and fostering "a grand brotherhood amongst men," making "each man his brother's keeper."[71] Even in Nanaimo the Good, however, such enthusiasm was contested. In a letter to the *Free Press*, the self-dubbed

"Freethought" retorted that advances for women and civilization owed nothing to "barbarous religion" – such progress was due solely to the extension of "mental liberty and scientific knowledge."[72] Ralph remained unapologetic, denying that true Christianity ever justified "the divine right of kings and priests."[73] If newspaper coverage and audiences are any indication, his views prevailed, at least among the public-spirited community that he admired. By 1895, the local YMCA had elected him president.

The Smiths' familiar advocacy of reform adjusted well to a city filled with newcomer groups devoted to personal and collective improvement. Most, such as the YMCA, the Ancient Order of United Workmen, the Independent Order of Foresters, the Independent Order of Odd Fellows, and the Knights of Pythias, enrolled male Protestants while providing auxiliary opportunities for women. In April 1893, even as she was pregnant, Mary Ellen was giving recitations for the YMCA.[74] In 1897, Ralph was elected vice grand master of the Independent Order of Odd Fellows, a fraternal group that provided sickness benefits to male workers.[75] He hailed "the advantages to be derived by organization of kindred societies, which embodied the same principles as the Orangemen, viz: equal rights to all."[76] Mary Ellen was not eligible for Odd Fellow benefits, but she took her part in its Rebekah auxiliary. During its fundraisers, she performed at the Opera House "as an elocutionist of marked ability," raising money for Victoria's Protestant Orphanage, since no such institution existed in Nanaimo.[77] In the same spirit, she became an officer for the Companions of the Forest, the female ancillary to the Foresters.[78] Such Masonic groups proclaimed allegiance to community service, but their exclusion of Catholics continued a long-standing sectarian or tribal politics that provided ample preparation for chauvinism with regard to Indigenous and Asian communities.

While their contributions helped sustain male congeniality, many women mobilized on their own behalf as well. Zeroing in on men's abuse of alcohol and its damage in violence and poverty, the WCTU enrolled large numbers.[79] The provincial union had been founded in Victoria in 1883 by the charismatic American leader Frances Willard (1839–98), with direction from local women, notably Methodists. Far from coincidently, that initiative was closely followed by the introduction of the first woman suffrage resolution in the BC legislature. By 1885, Canada's national WCTU president, Letitia Youmans (1827–96), was rousing the coal city. Initial growth was slow, but in 1894 British Columbia "received the Dominion 'prize banner'" for its ten local unions and 5,909 members;

with the assistance of a Vancouver organizer, an outpost sprang up in Nanaimo.[80] Until the appearance of the Political Equality Leagues in the 1910s, the WCTU was the province's leading champion of women's suffrage and political rights. Consciousness raising in Nanaimo was one beneficiary.

Ralph returned the favour of Mary Ellen's support for his endeavours by giving WCTU lectures and highlighting the importance of temperance to Nanaimo's Reform Club platform in the 1894 provincial election.[81] In 1895, the local movement was sufficiently flourishing to host the provincial WCTU convention and to join in successfully lobbying the BC Methodist Conference to approve female enfranchisement. Though caring for young children and aging parents meant that Mary Ellen could not match the range of Ralph's activism, by mid-decade she was hosting monthly WCTU mothers' meetings at their home, performing as a musician at local fundraisers, and helping to establish a Loyal Legion of Young People as a WCTU auxiliary.[82] By 1898, when she had been elected an officer of the City Union, she was widely admired. Tasks of the branch secretary, such as the sale of the fund- and consciousness-raising volume *The Beautiful Life of Frances E. Willard*, could be undertaken in the midst of an active household.[83] In the run-up to Canada's national prohibition plebiscite in September 1898, the "fluency and earnestness" of her presentations confirmed local prominence in a cause close to many women's hearts.[84] Whatever its heights, her oratory failed to sway most male voters in either Nanaimo or Victoria. Although British Columbia and Canada ultimately produced a small favourable majority, the Liberal government deemed the national result too close to justify federal implementation of prohibition. That bitter disappointment spurred the WCTU to redouble agitation and to prioritize women's vote as the key to progress. Like other BC towns, Nanaimo soon benefitted from mock parliaments, such as the 1900 spectacle held in the school room of the Wallace Street Methodist Church.[85] For many reformers, temperance and suffrage were inseparable.

When it came to improving the community, the Smiths paid close attention to public education. Their youngsters profited from an expanding free, non-denominational, and coeducational elementary and secondary system. Before the First World War, a booming school-age population, which included all five of their children, required more buildings and teachers. In a representative expression of progressive politics, the Reform Club's Workingman's Platform for the 1894 provincial election singled out education as a compelling good.[86] The president of the Mine Workers and Mine Laborers Protective Association (MWMLPA) identified "his ability to 'give my little girl education' as one of the preeminent tests of his standard of living."[87] Not all newcomers, however, invested equally in schooling. Some miners maintained Old Country practices of sending their sons into the profitable pits as early as possible. Indeed, the employment of boys at Canadian coal mines, most between thirteen and sixteen years of age, "reached its peak during the first decade of the twentieth century, when over 1,200 boys laboured at any given time."[88] Whereas the Nova Scotia pits hired more youngsters than did British Columbia, the latter's hostility to adult Chinese miners weakened "legal restrictions on child labour."[89] Ultimately, the prospect of pit wages helped explain why older boys did not match girls' numbers in senior school classes. Non-White youngsters faced different exigencies. Indian girls and boys were directed to the nearby segregated reserve mission day school or to the Kuper Island Industrial School some twenty miles south of Nanaimo. The latter readily inspired despair, leading to acts of arson in 1895.[90] Segregation was also affirmed in 1897, when the BC Public Schools Act denied Chinese residents the right to vote for school trustees.[91] Such practices further instructed the Smiths in the racial politics of their new home.

Although Mary Elizabeth Smith's schooling history has not been found, girls in general often moved through school more quickly and with better marks than boys.[92] Such demonstration of excellence occurred, ironically enough, alongside persistent barring of women from the city's senior teaching appointments.[93] Gender fairness nevertheless had defenders. School trustee and soon MLA Dr. Robert E. McKechnie rejected a "proposed exclusion of female teachers" as "retrograde" and stressed women's success in the professions and in universities.[94] When Ralph followed his friend on the school board in 1897, he likewise championed female ambition in education and employment. White girls, though not students from Indigenous and Asian communities, deserved a fair deal.

Coal Companies and Unions

Most Nanaimo improvers expected the region's coal pits to underpin progress. Mary Ellen and Ralph had good company in this belief. Their faith in progressive elites was evident in their friendship with McKechnie, who would serve as one of Ralph's pallbearers in 1917. A graduate of McGill's medical school, a resident of Nanaimo's so-called Nob Hill, and eventually long-time chancellor of the University of British Columbia, that Ontario migrant served as a physician for the NVCMLC and for a time as a local MLA.[95] The NVCMLC, owned by British investors and run under the relatively benign eye of the resident manager, Cornwall-born Samuel Matthew Robins (1834–1920),[96] had pride of place in the city. The company favoured family-based machinists, carpenters, locomotive engineers, and miners, encouraging its employees to live nearby with their wives and offspring and to commute on trains that ran from the pits to the wharves, where most output proceeded to the United States. Robins, who resided locally in an "ornate and cosy villa," was not publicly contradicted when he asserted that during "his management and administration of the company's affairs he has never uttered nor received from his employees a single angry word." The fact that wages were "paid uniformly in hard cash, and with unfailing regularity,"[97] did much to cement his popularity, as did the company's recognition of the MWMLPA, its exclusion of Chinese workers from the pits, and its gifts for schools, the hospital, and the cemetery. As Robins told the 1902 federal Royal Commission on Chinese and Japanese Immigration into British Columbia, a (White) man should be paid wages "upon which he can live respectably and support a family respectably."[98]

Although the NVCMLC never escaped industrial injuries or criticism, its reputation benefitted from contrast with its major Vancouver Island rival.[99] Nearby excavations in Wellington, Ladysmith, and other small communities were dominated by Canadian Collieries, owned by the Dunsmuirs, whose intractable labour relations included active hostility to unions, tenancies rather than homeownership, evictions during strikes, and the use of Chinese labour to undercut other wage-earners. In effect, Ralph and Mary Ellen had travelled halfway around the world to confront supposedly responsible capitalists (the NVCMLC) and their ugly twin (Canadian Collieries).

During the 1890s, coal-mining politics were deeply influenced by two events: in 1887, the NVCMLC operations experienced the worst mining disaster in Canadian history; and in 1890–91, workers at the Dunsmuir mines staged a disastrous strike for the eight-hour day, recognition of the MWMLPA, and Chinese exclusion. The 1887 explosion killed 150 miners, leaving still more widows and orphans. Commonly illiterate (in English), Chinese workers were blamed for faulty placement of explosives. That tragedy's bitter aftermath prompted Richard Spear to join his brother colliers in demanding that Asians be excluded from the diggings.[100] A commemorative monument on Milton Street, near both the shaft and the Smiths' house, would list only the White miners who died in the explosion, firmly installing them as the foremost victims of capitalist greed.[101] In condemning Asian competitors, hewers rejected Dunsmuir and company's "unambiguous statement of contempt for what the émigré British miners valued most: their hard-earned skills."[102] That rejection resembled feminists' anger at patriarchy's commonplace trivialization of female labour and their own insistence on dignity and respect.

During the 1890–91 strike, the Dunsmuirs resorted to blacklisting, evictions, and the provincial militia. Two obvious outcomes were the November 1890 Nanaimo meeting of British Columbia's first Provincial Labor Congress and the election of Tully Boyce as its president. An Irish American, Boyce was a local activist miner and officer of the MWMLPA whom union-busters dubbed a fearsome "Molly Maguire," effectively an industrial terrorist, but who left little record.[103] Denied recognition by Canadian Collieries, the MWMLPA organized mass petitions for Chinese exclusion and endorsed the election of sympathetic politicians, including the miner Thomas Keith (1863–1918), who would mentor Ralph. By the late nineteenth century, Nanaimo had emerged as a key site in the mounting conflict between Canadian labour and capital.[104] In particular, it provided a milieu in which labourism, described by historian Craig Heron as the era's "political expression of a distinct layer of the working class – the skilled workers in manufacturing, construction, and mining," would get a hearing and begin to detach "workers from their traditional party allegiances."[105] Ultimately, however, liberalism proved a sturdy survivor not readily displaced by the rise of more radical alternatives.

More than race and class conflict was on display during industrial confrontations. The 1890–91 strike demonstrated the frequently close ties between diverse politics of resistance. For instance, a Belgian immigrant, Naomi Poulet (about whom little is known at present) led the remarkable March for Female Suffrage, which linked the brutality of capitalist operations such as Canadian Collieries with women's subordination in public life.[106] Unionists and feminists could be at odds, but mutual sympathy surfaced regularly during the Smiths' long association with BC coalfields. The conclusions of working-class suffragists during a 1912–14 Ladysmith strike against Canadian Collieries echoed down the years:

> Do you think if the women of the province had the vote and elected representatives to the house that they would allow those men not to care whether ... our menfolks had to work where they were risking their lives every minute? No they wouldn't. Women are different. They wouldn't ask how much will it cost to make the mine safe. They would say those men who toil way below the earth's surface must be protected.[107]

Brutal capitalists should fear women as well as unions.

Partnerships were a tactical response to the corporate terrorism of reactionary mine owners. In the 1890s, the MWMLPA, the scarred veteran of harsh industrial defeat, sought allies in the Workman's Party, the Reform Club, and liberal-labourism. It signalled its commitment to that strategy by choosing Ralph, then a pit timberman, as its first salaried officer, paying him a monthly wage of ninety dollars plus mileage.[108] The MWMLPA was so shaky from its failure to unionize Canadian Collieries that its meetings regularly lacked quorums, but Ralph came to its rescue. A "brilliant Orator and debater, the Astute Diplomat, the wise General," he could ensure "a magnificent and triumphant victory."[109] Citing "reason, conciliation and arbitration" and Lord Rosebery, Ralph rallied workers to alliances with good capitalists "who recognized the right of labor to be fairly remunerated to the extent, at least, of making itself able to live respectably." Setting himself apart from socialist rivals, he insisted that "trades unionism would not make every man equal. It could not do so and it should not aim to do so ... Trades unionism wished to give every man an equal chance."[110] Such populist views were despised by Canadian Collieries, which refused recognition of the union and fired its members. The invoking of a far-off Liberal aristocrat and British prime minister (1894–45) meant nothing to company owner James Dunsmuir (1851–1920), who would become premier in 1900.

Contemporary socialists, like some historians subsequently, soon condemned Ralph as little more than a coal-mining Uncle Tom for the NVC-MLC, in effect collaborating in the oppression of his own community.[111] That assessment resembles accusations by socialist feminists that liberal women's acceptance of capitalism colludes in the subjugation of their sex. Whatever their merit, such allegations commonly underestimate both resistance to dominant class and gender regimes and pervasive approval of a political gradualism that depended upon cooperation between labour and capital and between women and men. Ultimately, as John Belshaw argues of Nanaimo miners, "the legacy of the British collier on Vancouver Island was not one of monolithic radicalism nor even Labourism; instead it was one of conflicting inclinations which were as politically divisive for labour on Canada's West Coast as they were in Britain."[112] Miners and feminists struggled with competing remedies for their own oppression. Ralph and Mary Ellen's choice of class and gender collaboration remained deeply divisive, but so too were the more hard-nosed politics of critics farther on their working-class and feminist left.

For all their disagreements, most BC gradualists and revolutionaries were united in condemning Chinese rivals. Throughout their lives, Ralph endorsed exclusion and Mary Ellen did no better. As late-nineteenth-century immigrants, both absorbed the prejudice that did so much to define Nanaimo and British Columbia as an imperial frontier. Intolerance was nevertheless never straightforward. The Smiths always faced a conflict between racism and their professed liberalism and Christianity. They conceded, although no more than in passing, the common humanity of the Chinese and other negatively racialized communities, particularly if they were Christian converts who accepted British superiority. Ultimately, however, the Smiths sidestepped the humanitarianism and a possible politics of inclusion, which historian Kenton Storey identifies as a significant experiment on Vancouver Island a few decades earlier.[113] Like most contemporaries, the Smiths believed that racial hierarchy was naturally or divinely ordained, an assumption reinforced by much scholarship of the day.

Ralph's emergence as a union leader in one centre of Canadian industrial conflict attracted attention beyond the province. In 1896, the *Toronto Globe* hailed him as a veteran UK labour leader, ranged against dangerous socialist agitators.[114] The *Ottawa Journal* singled out his virtues: "He earns his living as a miner and preaches the Gospel whenever the opportunity presents itself. He is an ardent labor man, and is carrying the gospel of labor into the legislative halls of his province, where it can be used most effectively."[115] The Trades and Labor Congress of Canada (TLCC), founded in 1883 to mobilize craft unions, spotted a saviour. A heroic British lib-lab miner could help it consolidate loyalty beyond central Canada and reap political benefits. Ralph in turn hoped to gain support for Chinese exclusion and to advance the agenda of cooperation that he had imbibed in Northumberland. In 1896, he was elected TLCC vice-president and in 1898 president, an office he held until 1902.

Mary Ellen was little mentioned in coverage of Ralph's meteoric rise within labour circles. In fact, she was invaluable. In her, Canadians, like Nanaimoites, could embrace a woman strongly rooted in the working class – a miner's daughter and a miner's wife – who could compare favourably with "lady" partners of the nation's male elite. When she joined Ralph in Winnipeg as he became the TLCC's first Western president, Mary Ellen was on her way into the national spotlight.[116] A labour lady, she embodied the promise of the New World for ambitious newcomers and imperial settlers.

The Turn to Provincial and Federal Politics

That trajectory was further ensured by Ralph's enthusiasm for politics. Barely a year off the boat, he successfully opposed American annexation in a debate at the Wallace Street Methodist Church.[117] In February 1894, he praised British miners turned Lib-Lab MPs in Westminster, and in the next month he urged workers to join farmers and middle-class progressives in the Nanaimo Reform Club.[118] In April, running as a candidate in the BC election, he declared himself a liberal-labour reformer:

> I come before you as a wingman, a miner, one of yourselves ... I am opposed to the conduct of the present Government ... Take its great sympathy with monopoly, its railway policy, its giving away of public lands free of taxation ... The far-reaching influence it had on the prospects of the laboring community could not be calculated ... The legislation of the present government was not such as a working man could support.[119]

As Craig Heron recognizes, Ralph Smith was representative of skilled workers who championed "parliamentary democracy," along with proportional representation, votes for women, the abolition of the Senate, and "the sweeping away of all property qualifications and election deposits."[120]

In 1894, Ralph could not afford the two hundred dollar candidate's deposit, which was paid by the Reform Club, but he immediately proved formidable in debate and, alongside Mary Ellen, a musician who could stir a crowd.[121] He attacked the sitting MLA, John Bryden (1833–1915), a Dunsmuir son-in-law and Canadian Collieries manager, for "interests [that] were with the capitalist class" while nevertheless praising his suffragist sympathies. Rejecting disparagement of his own newcomer status in British Columbia, Ralph insisted that

> he had always endeavored to make himself conversant with the affairs of the Province, and particularly with the requirements of the working classes. He was a law-abiding citizen, and as such had a perfect right to seek to represent the district ... He was by no means a socialist, but he wanted an equal chance to get at the wealth of the country ... He reminded his hearers what labor representatives had done in England, and urged them to be true to their own interests and return to Parliament those who would fight their battles and not seek to add to the strength already possessed by the capitalist class.[122]

The recent immigrant invoked former British Liberal prime minister William Ewart Gladstone, demanding temperance policies to make it "easy to do right when it was hard to do wrong."[123] Such arguments failed to sway a majority of voters, but Ralph attracted notice. An otherwise skeptical provincial premier pronounced him "one of the most polished speakers he had ever had the pleasure of listening to."[124]

For the next few years, Ralph focused on union work even as he maintained political enthusiasm. In an 1895 debate at the Wallace Street church, he endorsed federal Liberal leader Wilfrid Laurier on the Manitoba Schools Question, and he remained irrepressible in demands for "anti-Mongolian" or anti-Chinese policies.[125] In the June 1898 provincial election, he again tested the voters. Celebrated as "a leader working men may well be proud of," he won South Nanaimo as a Labour candidate, with Liberal support.[126] In Victoria, he learned legislative lessons as he watched a new premier, Charles Semlin (1836–1927), struggle to corral unruly MLAs who had long eschewed the firm party lines that helped discipline Ottawa parliamentarians.[127] In the turmoil, labourites sometimes wielded influence. Indeed, the period before the 1900 election has been said to "set a new direction in public affairs, one less animated than its predecessors by the interests of leading businessmen and large property holders."[128]

Nor was labour the only hopeful group. Suffragists too glimpsed opportunity. In February 1899, Ralph introduced a female franchise bill, and McKechnie, now a minister without portfolio, as well as husband of a Nanaimo WCTU leader, presented a suffrage petition.[129] During second reading of the bill, Ralph was cheered for defending the intelligence of women and condemning both the Chinese and "aboriginal people" for subordinating them. Likewise applauded was his declaration that it was "a poor argument, of having kept her from the enjoyment of political rights, to blame her because she does not know how to use them."[130] His bill, supported by the three miner MLAs, failed by fifteen to seventeen but would, it was suggested, have been successful if one legislator hadn't unintentionally voted against it. A tied result would have allowed the Speaker of the House, an avowed suffragist, to cast the deciding ballot.

Legislative instability forced another provincial election in June 1900. The appearance of the first BC socialist candidate signalled a new competitor for workers' votes, but Ralph rode to success in Nanaimo City. Now the "unofficial leader of the Independent Labor Party," he demanded the eight-hour working day, the union label, public ownership of utilities, and Chinese exclusion.[131] Confirming divisions among miners, James Dunsmuir, whom Smith attacked as a "capitalist tyrant," won South Nanaimo.[132] From June 1900 to November 1902, Dunsmuir reigned as premier. His embrace of railways, corporate handouts, and Chinese labour, like the government use of the militia against strikers in Steveston canneries during the summer of 1900, curtailed Ralph's hopes for early progress in Victoria.[133] Even as some sympathizers dubbed Ralph "the recognized head of the labor forces in the Province,"[134] he looked across the Rockies to Ottawa.

In early 1900, Ralph worked with the dominion labour commissioner to promote conciliation in the Kootenay mines.[135] That September, he became the labour representative on the federal royal commission to investigate Chinese and Japanese immigration to British Columbia. He also took time to sanction British engagement in the South African War. In December 1899, he preached a sermon to the Wallace Street Methodists, titled "Peace and Warfare as Introduced by the Lord Jesus." The latter might have been surprised by his conclusion: "Through warfare, whether carried on by the individual or the nation; whether it be mental or physical, we attain character, civilization, and all the blessings which come with it, and peace at the end."[136] Jingoism was reaffirmed when Ralph joined other MLAs to demand that British Columbia "furnish a company of mounted men" to serve in the Transvaal. His position on the war allied him with such Liberal imperialists as Lord Rosebery and against such notable anti-war critics as the Lib-Lab MP Thomas Burt, otherwise his inspiration.[137] It also distanced Ralph from many Canadian labour radicals and portended his support for Canada's involvement in the First World War.

The Smiths were united in their views of the South African conflict. Mary Ellen inspired a crowd at the Nanaimo Opera House with a recitation to benefit the "wives, sweethearts and kids" of British troops in South Africa.[138] In the same spirit, she was hailed as the "talented lady" who stood "draped in flowing folds of white, with the Union Jack descending from her shoulders in graceful festoons" to deliver verses by her contemporary, Nobel laureate Rudyard Kipling (1865–1936). Her "crowning feature of the entertainment" produced "a rain of silver upon the stage."[139] Mary Ellen needed no lessons in patriotism or rallying a throng.

As national TLCC president, Ralph asserted his independence as a provincial MLA when he addressed Vancouver unionists in May 1900: "No government is likely to carry radical legislation unless it is urged on by those interested and appears almost naturally inclined to treat the capitalist better than the laborer." He added that he saw little "distinction between the results achieved by a Tory or Grit administration" in Ottawa. The Laurier majority had "done something in the interests of labor, but so far has not done anything in regard to the Chinese question, and it is doubtful if what it proposes to do will be sufficiently drastic to secure what is necessary in the interests of white labor." Workers needed their own representatives.[140] He nevertheless admitted to voting Liberal federally in 1896, because he felt "that party works in the best interests of the workingman."[141] As an "independent labor man," he did "not believe in obstruction, criticism and opposition as the proper policy, but rather in the policy of construction, advice and education as the best way to advance the interests of the working class in parliament."[142] Such words presaged his jump to Ottawa's parliamentary stage.

In November 1900, the TLCC backed its president's Independent Labour candidacy in the federal constituency of Vancouver, which included Nanaimo. In a sign of growing doubts about his loyalty to workers, however, Victoria's Labour Council declined to recommend him, and the *Nelson Miner* warned, "Ottawa is the grave of countless labor reputations."[143] Nonetheless, Ralph was elected, winning just over 42 percent of the popular vote, with the remainder split almost evenly between the Conservative and the "straight" Liberal candidate. He soon reassured Wilfrid Laurier, who replied with "sincere congratulations."[144] Smith's choice reflected Canadian Liberals' flirtation, on the Gladstonian model, with "a coalition of diverse ideological tendencies" that could offer "a recognized place for organized workers alongside the francophones, farmers, Catholics, and corporate capitalists."[145]

Ralph's 1900 electoral triumph found almost a match on the distaff side of the Smith team. In the same month, Mary Ellen emerged as the star of the fortieth anniversary gala of the Wallace Street church. Her "humorous selection, a satire on the law and legal phraseology," revealed the comic turn that would be her stock-in-trade as a suffragist. Equally effective, and in contrast to Ralph's deep bass, was her "quiet gentle voice." Nanaimo's Liberal-Labour lady renounced "the shouting vigorousness of this hurly-burly age" and appealed "to the deep and the quiet in human nature."[146] Here was a reassuring femininity to partner Ralph's collier masculinity. The talented duo was on its way to Ottawa, proof it seemed of British workers' opportunity to scale the heights of settlers' evolving dominions.

3
From Nanaimo to Ottawa and Back Again, 1900–11

The first decade of the century, which Wilfrid Laurier famously proclaimed as belonging to Canada, once again tested the Smiths. Though still smarting from the conflict and disarray of British Columbia's last non-party governments and tormented by the rise of socialism among the miners, Ralph took his lib-lab politics to Ottawa, with the support of the Trades and Labor Congress of Canada. That trajectory lasted slightly more than a decade. In 1911, stymied as a federal Lib-Lab and defeated as a straight Liberal MP, he would return to the Pacific Coast for a renewed assault on provincial politics. Mary Ellen's flight path remained linked to her husband's, but it was neither so dramatic nor so painful. It was, however, equally instructive. Her children's growing independence, like her husband's Ottawa experiment, provided greater opportunities to demonstrate talents that could pass muster on stages well beyond the Nanaimo Opera House. Just as Ralph's election as the Liberal MP for the federal constituencies of Vancouver and then Nanaimo (as electoral boundaries shifted) allowed him to test Canadian prospects for New Liberalism, Mary Ellen's instruction in Ottawa politics and charming of its elites moved her from the periphery of Canada's feminist politics to an elevation from which she could dare its provincial heights after his defeat.

Baseline Nanaimo

The word "Nanaimo" did not figure in the name of the federal riding won by Ralph in November 1900, but the city remained his launching pad during his years as an MP. In the first decade of the twentieth century, its growth stagnated, although mining employment and coal production continued to expand until the 1920s.[1] Of course, that future was not immediately evident to residents who treasured loftier ambitions. Nanaimo seemed to be a hub of promise, and an extensive network of kin and allies rooted the Smiths in a life that remained significant. Like the Northumberland mining villages earlier, the BC city might have been on the wane, but its influence persisted.

In 1901, forty-four-year-old Ralph and thirty-seven-year-old Mary Ellen were living with Mary Elizabeth aged nineteen, Richard and Robert aged fifteen, Ralph aged thirteen, John Wesley aged seven, and Richard Spear aged sixty-two. Ten years later, they were still together, except for Mary Elizabeth. In November 1905, she married John Carr, a miner for the NVCMLC, in the Wallace Street church. The unusually early 6:00 a.m. ceremony was unpretentious, with only one attendant each – the bride's, her cousin, a Miss Brenton from Vancouver – and breakfast was held at the Smiths' Milton Street home. The couple then caught the 8:20 a.m. train for a Victoria honeymoon.[2] They would return to live modestly in Nanaimo and later in the provincial capital, after Carr left mining for a position in the federal post office, probably expedited by his MP father-in-law.

Though unmarried and almost twenty when Ralph became an MP, Mary Elizabeth is not visible in the Ottawa press and only rarely, usually at church-related events, in Nanaimo. Like that of many older daughters, her role probably emphasized domestic support in a hectic household, with younger siblings, busy parents, and sometimes a woman hired by the day for general work. Her husband was the only miner to join the family, and, revealing of that group's shifting loyalties, he would be active with the Western Federation of Miners, the American rival union loathed by Ralph. John Carr nevertheless attested to kin feeling in endorsing Ralph's re-election efforts.[3]

All the Smith children attended Nanaimo schools and performed in amateur musical pursuits. As newspapers tell us, the sons visited Ottawa intermittently from 1901 to 1911, sometimes staying for lengthy periods or for breaks from school or employment. Only Robert and, possibly, John Wesley (known as Jack) pursued schooling in the east after Ralph became an MP. Robert, who accompanied survey parties marking the international boundary between British Columbia and Alaska in 1906,[4] was the most academically successful, graduating from the University of Toronto and completing legal studies at Osgoode Hall. In 1911, as a law student, he campaigned for Ralph on Vancouver Island and was rewarded by local Liberals with a gold chain and watch.[5] His brother Richard explored opportunities, probably as a surveyor, in the Cariboo. By 1906, Ralph Smith junior was employed as a Nanaimo waterworks collector. A year later, he was reported as entering "a wholesale house in Vancouver," probably in sales.[6]

The family gradually disinvested from the Newcastle of Canada, though their official home remained on Milton Street until Ralph's 1911 political setback. By then too, Mary Ellen's brother, William Spear, and his growing family had relocated to Vancouver, where he took employment as a choirmaster and music teacher. Other relatives were also sometimes visible. In 1902, Mary Ellen visited England during the coronation of Edward VII and returned with a nephew, Joseph Smith (d. 1957), who lodged with the family for a time. Later, he too would move to Vancouver.[7] Ralph's younger brother Mathew remained in Nanaimo to work as a janitor for the school board. Household labour associated with such kin explains why Mary Ellen advertised for girls to do general housework.

During these years, Ralph attempted to reposition himself economically out of the working class, an aspiration that could only confirm the suspicion of socialist detractors. In February 1901, he joined Conservative MLA and future BC premier Richard McBride (1870–1917) on the board of trustees of the BC Permanent Loan and Savings Company. Located in Vancouver, this firm instigated an association with provincial business interests that continued until his death. For her part, Mary Ellen demonstrated a financial confidence that exceeded that of most housewives, miners' daughters or wives, or indeed women generally. When investors across the country were left unsecured with the 1905 collapse of Ontario's York County Loan Company, she marshalled local victims, like herself, in an effort to win compensation.[8] Nanaimoites, many of whom had lost their "entire savings," entered "the fight with Mrs. Ralph Smith in the lead."[9] Such initiatives suggested an ambitious couple's determination that capitalism could be called to account and made to work for all citizens.

Just as he had as an MLA, the new MP worked to build up support in his constituency. Post-election life was full of events, such as assembling with other Foresters in high-profile festivities that included a political speech and a tour of the NVCMLC mine.[10] Methodism, with its enthusiasm for music and good works, continued to supply a substantial anchor in community outreach and moral endeavour. When Parliament was not in session, Ralph regularly lectured for Wallace Street's Epworth League on topics such as "the cultivation of one's own natural powers" and "trust in God."[11] He could also be found before other congregations, debating "fundamental principles of Christianity" and the meaning of faith.[12] By 1904, he was president of the broadly Protestant BC Lord's Day Alliance, campaigning against Sunday employment, and in 1909 he represented Nanaimo at the provincial Methodist Conference.

Ralph also let voters know that he remained a firm supporter of female enfranchisement and public health reform. City suffragists applauded him and their socialist MLA James Hawthornthwaite (1863–1926) for their loyalty. One explained the sympathies of their elected representatives by suggesting that "there is no city on the coast in which we would get a larger vote for woman suffrage, per capita, than Nanaimo."[13] Ralph applied lessons learned back east to the city's ongoing sanitation problems. Ottawa's debates over health failures encouraged him to make public "comparisons with regards to our sewerage system with alarm, as do many other citizens ... [who identified the] danger of an epidemic from defective sewerage."[14] Such interventions buttressed Ralph's claims to be a vigilant parliamentarian and an up-to-date reformer.

While her husband worked his constituency and toured the province and the country in aid of left-wing liberalism, Mary Ellen performed the necessary chores to keep the family name before Nanaimo electors: as the *Free Press* reported, "the duties of a parliamentary member [are] being borne in no small measure by his wife."[15] Even when both she and Ralph appeared together, she did not stand in the shadows. In 1905, while he oversaw a benefit concert given by the city's Football Club, she was front and centre as an elocutionist.[16] When he defended Methodism against proposed church union at the Wallace Street church, she was equally notable in emphasizing women's influence in the world.[17] The *Cranbrook Herald* applauded his 1907 after-dinner speech to the Nanaimo Odd Fellows, while also singling out his good fortune at having "a wife who has brains, wisdom and tact. Possessing an attractive appearance, a most interesting conversationalist, being both a pleasing talker and an attentive listener, she makes friends and admirers wherever she goes, and must be a tower of strength to Mr. Smith in his political life."[18] Ralph's absences meant that Mary Ellen often flew solo. Many of her contributions as an organizer, speaker, and singer centred on the Methodist church, but her reach extended to the Native Sons of BC, the Athletic Club, the Presbyterian church, the Boys' Brigade, and concerts for injured miners.[19] She also kept up her work for the WCTU, still the local bastion for suffrage. When the principal of the Nanaimo High School promoted the cause, she typically acknowledged male support: "She had recognized every day the importance of woman's influence in the world; men were more broadminded than they used to be, and in proportion women should rise to the occasion and keep step with their progress."[20]

Still close to Mary Ellen's heart as well was the Nanaimo Hospital Auxiliary, the city's most prestigious women's group. She remained its president and frequent "mistress of ceremonies" in a continuing social round, whose purpose was essentially fund- and consciousness-raising about public health. In 1903, she was congratulated at the auxiliary's conversazione for dispelling "the stiffness which always marks the commencement of such an entertainment." In a characteristically light touch, she teased "the husbands of the members of the Auxiliary," describing them as "honorary members" whose services could be counted on. She encouraged everyone to "turn themselves loose and have a good time" with "cards, board and table games, ping pong, songs, recitations and refreshments."[21]

Mary Ellen's genius as a hostess was rewarded. In 1904, in recognition of the "ladies for their noble efforts in the cause of humanity," she was asked, as auxiliary president, to dedicate the new hospital ward, with its "3 semi-private rooms for 6 female patients; elevator; operating room and recovery room."[22] MP Ralph stood at her side to add that

> the moral standard of a community could best be estimated by the consideration given to institutions for the aid of the distressed. The hospital was not representative of any faction or creed, but stretched hands of sympathy to every member of the community ... The time was approaching when the legislatures would be compelled to recognize such institutions as of national importance.[23]

The hospital remained, as it had begun, a powerful local emblem of the cooperative effort that should engage reformers of both sexes. Despite Ralph's nod to inclusiveness, however, Indigenous and Asian patients were expected to go elsewhere.

The reform ideals of the age were similarly on display during a September 1906 visit of Governor General Albert Grey and his wife, Alice Holford (1858–1944). The *Nanaimo Free Press* applauded the liberal-minded Grey as "not a snob," "broad-minded," and "unaffected." These qualities were widely understood as lacking in James Dunsmuir, now BC lieutenant governor, who, with his spouse, Laura Surles Dunsmuir (1858–1937), joined the Smiths in welcoming the Greys. Dunsmuir's vanity could only have been injured when Grey complimented Ralph on the "scene" presented by the operations of both the NVCMLC and the city hospital. Nanaimo's mayor tread on the same toes when he described the governor general as a "friend of the Northumbrian miner" and of the "great movements of conciliation and co-operation."[24] In the decades-long warfare between miners and the Dunsmuirs, that skirmish of 1906 clearly went to the former.

Partisan politics always lay close to the surface of commitments. In 1904, Mary Ellen joined as treasurer in establishing Nanaimo's Laurier Liberal Ladies' League.[25] A still important alliance was signalled when the league met a few weeks later in the "rooms of the Labor Party."[26] In 1907, as her sojourns in Ottawa lengthened, the league reminded her of its appreciation by sending "a gold brooch of exquisite design, beautifully studded with pearls." That gift enabled the *Ottawa Citizen* to salute her as a "leader socially," as well as "one of the best informed women on matters political in the Dominion today." Although Ralph received a present too, there was little doubt as to who prompted the recognition.[27] Mary Ellen was a vital part of Liberal success on the coast.

Ottawa's New Fields

Ralph retained his federal seat in the elections of 1904 and 1908, and Mary Ellen accompanied him to Ottawa for parts of many parliamentary sessions before his defeat and that of the Laurier government in September 1911. The world of Canada's capital was very different from that of Nanaimo. Ralph's claim to being the nation's foremost labour leader gave the Smiths a certain cachet, especially at the beginning, but as sojourners with limited income and few social connections who came from a region regarded as both remote and eccentric, they started at a disadvantage.

In the early twentieth century, Ottawa, like Nanaimo, had essential links to a resource frontier, in the former's case timber. In many other ways, however, the two cities were very different. As the national capital, Ottawa experienced substantial growth. In 1901, it was already much larger than Nanaimo, with 27,442 male and 30,198 female inhabitants, a gender split quite different from that of the BC mining town. In Ottawa, many women worked for pay before marriage, even as they encountered familiar prejudice in wages, conditions, and promotion. Segregated and dominant in the lower ranks of the expanding civil service, they were highly visible. Other differences also mattered. Over half of Ottawa

RALPH SMITH, M.P.,
MEMBER FOR VANCOUVER ISLAND.

Ralph Smith, 1902. | J.A. Cooper, Men of Canada (Toronto: Canadian Historical Company, 1902), 296.

residents were Roman Catholic, Anglicans formed the largest Protestant denomination, and Methodists and Presbyterians were minorities. Similarly unfamiliar were the French Canadians, who made up about half of the population.[28] As representatives of Britannicization, the Smiths showed little interest in the survivors from an earlier European empire, and Quebec never shone as part of the Canadian future that they envisaged. The tiny number of Asians in Ottawa provided a further reminder that politics on the Pacific were very different from those in the heartland of Canadian liberalism.

Countering the unfamiliar was the operation of nation-wide ethnic, religious, and progressive networks. In 1902, Ralph would have been at home as a settler booster in addressing the city's St. George Society "in a highly patriotic vein," celebrating Canada's future as "the greatest of

Britain's colonies," and speaking on trade union ideals to the local ministerial organization.[29] In the same spirit, he later addressed a downtown Methodist church to predict "the future of the grand empire of Canada" and to dismiss "the red man who did nothing to open up its riches." Indigenous Peoples, like Asians, were never credited with the industry that underlay claims to a fair deal from meritorious British workers such as himself. And as always, Christianity laid the foundation of a great future. Ignoring contradictions between rhetoric and reality, he finished "with an appeal for equality and justice to all, and sat down amid much applause."[30] Exclusions from the national imaginary were taken for granted.

A generation of Ottawa reformers would have offered common ground in the Smiths' search for remedies for urban ills. They had special cause to cheer efforts to improve public health. Ralph was regularly ill in Ottawa, and in 1911 their eldest son, Dick, suffered a "very serious attack of typhoid fever," requiring full-time nursing by Mary Ellen.[31] Local feminists such as Ella Webster Bronson (1846–1925), wife of a powerful Liberal politician and timber merchant and a long-time leader of the Local Council of Women, typically campaigned for causes familiar to British Columbians, such as domestic science instruction, libraries, and public health. In a testimony to her prestige, the "culmination" of Bronson's work was healthcare for women, notably the Ottawa Maternity Hospital.[32] Her elite circles were not, however, readily accessible to occasional visitors such as Mary Ellen, all the more so because she could muster nothing like the Bronson fortune.

In contrast to support for hospitals, the movement for female enfranchisement was far less prestigious. Recent work by Tarah Brookfield suggests that Ottawa was not greatly or at all in advance of Nanaimo in suffrage activity.[33] Nevertheless, by the time the Smiths arrived, Ottawa had "established a burgeoning suffrage community under the motto 'For the taxes we pay, And the laws we obey, We want something to say.'" Such emphasis on taxation invoked a rather more economically independent group of female activists, with more female wage-earners and professionals than Nanaimo. The Ottawa Equal Franchise Association included influential imperial representatives such as Miss Belfrage Gilbertson (1882–1977), private secretary to Governor General Grey. The well-known progressive sympathies of that luminary would have armed her well as she joined the capital's feminist activists. The city also regularly hosted visits from Montreal and Toronto suffragists, who anticipated setting in motion a national network.[34] This broad community welcomed Mary Ellen as a parliamentary wife and a western activist.

Ultimately, of course, the Smiths were wayfarers. For much of their tenure in Ottawa, they joined the itinerant parliamentary crowd that typically tenanted hotels and apartments when the House met and left when it shut own. For politicians, the city was often an episode in a career, and their main commitments, and often their wives and families, lay elsewhere. Like many others, Ralph, particularly in the early years, was often alone in Ottawa, and he and Mary Ellen budgeted carefully as they moved from location to location. Ottawa could not match their social and economic investment in Nanaimo. It did, however, encourage their taste for public life and influence.

Whatever funds they possessed and wherever their chief loyalties lay, the female kin of parliamentarians were expected to entertain in order to assure influence. A busy round of dinners, parties, and bridge games staged essential networking opportunities. In 1907, the Smiths secured rooms in the fashionable Russell Hotel, dubbed "the capital's great meeting place and central promenade,"[35] a move designed to position them as advantageously as possible. Whenever she was in Ottawa, Mary Ellen presided over "at homes" during regular hours every month. Exchanges on such occasions could win and lose friends and causes. As one astute and caustic contemporary explained, "While the parliamentarians perform 'promises and Pie Crusts,' the wives have their own play – 'Petticoats and Power.'"[36]

Writing as Amaryllis in *Saturday Night Magazine,* the feminist journalist Agnes Mary Scott (1863–1927) exercised the capital's female muscle.[37] Born in 1841, Zoe Lafontaine Laurier, the wife of the prime minister, may have seemed a little old lady in the eyes of many newspaper commentators, but she was a formidable player. Her preference for "women's society" and her choice of company in endless card games and musicals mattered.[38] As Sandra Gwyn argues in *The Private Capital,* "in other Canada cities, ladies were relegated to knitting by the fireside, or entertaining themselves over teacups. But in turn-of-the-century Ottawa, ... women were actually allowed, even encouraged, to wield influence."[39] Its social circles proved a productive setting for a former seamstress who could dress to impress and whose passion for music won the ear and perhaps the heart of Zoe Laurier. Mary Ellen proved a popular addition to fashionable entertainments, and the wife of the prime minister supported her protégée in well-attended gatherings hosted at rental suites. Zoe's public hostility to English suffragists, whom she condemned in 1910 as "indecent and unwomanly," insisting that "it is unheard of for a woman to compete with masculine superiority,"[40] seemed not as significant as her social power and susceptibility to Mary Ellen's personality and musicality.

Yet if Sir Wilfrid Laurier's spouse acted as an influential cultural arbitrator, he was Ottawa's dominant force. Few observers of any political persuasion could resist the well-practised charm of the long-time Liberal leader and prime minister (1896–1911). The drama critic for the *Toronto Star* summed up the appeal that quickly captured both Smiths. Laurier, he said,

> swung in a great romantic orbit of political sentiment ... We never had a statesman who could smile so potently. Never one with such a mellifluous music in voice, such easy grace in his style, such a cardinal's hauteur when he wanted to be alone and such a fascinating urbanity when he wanted to impress a company, a caucus or a crowd ... The Romist whom Orangemen admired, the Frenchman who made an intellectual hobby of British democracy, the poetic statesman who read Dickens and re-read in two languages Uncle Tom's Cabin and sometimes played the flute, and the Premier of a bilingual country who had a passion for the study of the war which emancipated the negro, was the kaleidoscopic enigma of Canadian public life.[41]

This charismatic parliamentarian, somewhat like the compelling, if far less pulchritudinous, Gladstone in Britain, became "nearly all things to all men" and was in the process "effortlessly attractive to women."[42] In 1910, he told an audience in Lacombe, Alberta, that women should stay at home to create "a country of happy and contented homesteads" and "to inspire their husbands and brothers to take an active and intelligent interest in civic and national affairs."[43] Perhaps his Old World charm helped the women in the audience to listen attentively or even succumb to his suggestion of backstage influence. Ultimately, for the Smiths, Laurier's allure, not to mention his promise of patronage, apparently outweighed his indifference to the cause of either labour or women. Their long-standing faith in sympathetic and well-meaning aristocrats and capitalists made the former Northumbrians especially susceptible to the "sunny ways" of Canada's seductive Liberal chieftain.

Ralph Smith as Labour Activist and MP

When Ralph came to Ottawa, he was already celebrated. He joined a few Lib-Lab MPs in Ottawa, proof it seemed of opportunity for the talented and the industrious and the promise of left liberalism's expanding tent. In 1902, Ralph attended Edward VII's coronation as a Canadian representative, and he and Mary Ellen toured their old home during the trip. The Northumberland press praised him as a man of "thorough-going, sterling honesty" who deserved to go far.[44] Ralph visited British labour leaders such as John Burns, Thomas Burt, and Keir Hardie (1856–1915), and claimed "a large stock of new ideas which will be utilized to the advantage of the labor cause in this country." Despite such posturing, legislative results rapidly disappointed.[45] When mainstream liberalism proved a feeble reed, Canadian unions had good cause to scrutinize socialist and social democratic alternatives. During his first term in Ottawa, Ralph was deserted by Canada's TLC and by Nanaimo miners, with the latter voting in 1903 to affiliate with the socialist Western Federation of Miners. Ultimately, Canada's Liberals never matched the recurring, if always limited, enthusiasm of their British counterparts for the labour movement and self-conscious workers.

Although Ralph was never a particularly active speaker in the House of Commons, he criss-crossed Canada to spread the gospel of conciliation, cooperation, and parliamentary democracy. He urged workers to resist strikes and socialism and to approve federal initiatives such as the Conciliation, Railway Labour Disputes, and Industrial Disputes Investigation Acts as solutions to industrial conflict.[46] In presenting the case of picketing Montreal longshoremen in 1903, he typically defended their right both to organize and to strike. According to the *Ottawa Journal*, he went on to argue,

> There were unreasonable men in the labor movement and unreasonable men in the capitalistic movement, and it was the duty of the government to mediate between them. Compulsory arbitration was impracticable, but the government should have power to initiate some sort of compulsory investigation and effect a conciliation of contending interests if possible. If a scheme of arbitration was adopted he would like to have an assurance that the employers would accept the awards. At present, it would be found that labor accept the awards far oftener than capital.[47]

As always, collaboration, not revolution, promised the greatest gains. Skeptical BC socialists lined up to jeer, a response that later scholarship largely justified.[48] Ultimately, Ralph's inability to secure even a federal law in support of a union label to guarantee that certain government purchases were produced by unionized labour suggested that Canadian Liberals remained, at best, "referees rather than committed protagonists" in industrial struggles.[49]

In the spirit of his idols in the Westminster Parliament, Ralph nevertheless persisted in calling for a gradualist agenda. To this end, he stood in the House in 1908 to recommend an old age annuities bill, which empowered fraternal and religious societies and employers to provide funds, as well as the incorporation of cooperative societies to carry on wholesale and retail businesses. In 1910, Laurier added him to a special committee to investigate old age pensions.[50] Spurred by labour dissent and New Liberal thinking, with its hopes for the conciliation of workers through state moderation of capitalism, Britain had introduced old age pensions in 1908. Under Laurier, Canada was determinedly tardy, and Ralph could not force the pace. Only intense pressure from progressive forces and the threat of a minority government produced a national old age pension plan in 1927.

Laurier was in sync, however, with his British counterparts in resisting female suffrage. Like many European liberals, he believed that female voters were likely to be reactionary and a pawn of churches. In Ottawa, just as in British Columbia, Ralph became a rare suffrage ally, and he arrived with a reputation that feminists intended to exploit. In 1909, the Toronto Suffrage Association urged him "to continue his praiseworthy efforts for the enfranchisement of women."[51] Ottawa's Equal Suffrage Association welcomed him to oversee public meetings and demanded that he introduce enfranchisement bills.[52] In 1911, it arranged for him to chair a gathering for the British suffragette Emmeline Goulden Pankhurst (1858–1928), already an active recruiter among miners in north Britain.[53] Much like British Columbia's MLAs, however, Liberal and Conservative MPs rejected mobilization for female enfranchisement. In the end, Ralph proved minimally engaged as a suffragist on the floor of the House. His failure did not go unnoticed. In 1909, the *Ladysmith Chronicle* concluded caustically, "Just about election times Ralph Smith was strongly in favor of extending the franchise to women. Now he is quietly occupying his seat in the House of Commons, and he implores the ladies to possess their souls in patience – that the time is not ripe to move on their behalf. Alas, another case of misplaced confidence!"[54]

Many British Columbians were likewise disappointed when Ralph failed to stop Asian immigration. Though a notorious champion of exclusion, he had to present Laurier's limited restrictions as the half a loaf that was preferable to none at all.[55] He did, however, join a national chorus of disparagement of other potential newcomers to the dominion. When the

Salvation Army proposed an immigration scheme that targeted the British poor, he denigrated its potential clients as members of the "drunken and immoral classes."[56] Ultimately, for a man insistent on a meritocracy of talent, a common racial background offered no guarantee of quality citizens.

Despite Ralph's uninspiring parliamentary record, persisting disarray in BC Liberal ranks kept him a prospect for leader, and ever-present rumours predicted his return to unify liberal and labour forces.[57] One high point for such speculation occurred in 1902–03, when he backed the Provincial Progressive Party, a BC expression of the British Liberal experiment with the "Progressive Alliance" to bring workers under liberalism's big tent.[58] Indifference from most Liberals and distrust from organized labour quickly torpedoed that proposal. In 1910, the *Prince Rupert Optimist* speculated that Smith would move to Vancouver as a Liberal organizer endorsed by Laurier, who was fed up with the fractured provincial wing. The article concluded its reflection on Ralph's suitability by saying that he was "in fact no more a labor member than Sir Wilfrid himself."[59] Ralph's own frustrations, combined with those of Canadian Liberals who clearly didn't know what to do with him, fuelled ongoing gossip about his candidacy for alternative employment as a cabinet minister for labour, the BC lieutenant governor, a senator, the immigration commissioner to Great Britain, the federal commissioner for the Yukon, or perhaps most extraordinarily, superintendent of Indian Affairs for British Columbia.

Ottawa's Liberal insiders never bailed Ralph out. The sanctimonious William Lyon Mackenzie King, the sometimes left-leaning Liberal who became deputy minister of labour in 1900,[60] labour minister in 1909, Opposition leader in 1919, and prime minister in 1921, first met Ralph in 1901. His diary entry for January 30 of that year dismissed the cigar-chomping Ralph as "first & foremost a 'politician'" with little real commitment to workers, a clear case of the kettle calling the pot black. On September 30, 1901, when it had become obvious that Laurier would never appoint Ralph to a Labour portfolio, King admitted Ralph's "shrewd & rather sound judgement in dealing with men but biased from one point of view."[61]

Mary Ellen had early star standing in Mackenzie King's diary. When she called at his office, shortly after a visit from Ralph, King declared, "I was perfectly charmed with her, never before have I been so surprised in any woman. She is bright, clever, pretty, well informed, talked in a straightforward & sincere manner, is exceedingly natural and she is something of a politician, wh.[ich] she certainly is. She quite won my heart, both for herself & for her husband." The Smiths were immediately invited to dine with King and his best friend, Henry Albert Harper (1873–1901). After extended conversation, including Ralph's proud observation that Mary Ellen would "hold her own with any of them here," King reported on October 1, 1901, "I see where Ralph Smith's future is made for him, he is sure to remain at the front & rise. This woman [would] make any man. She is the sort that makes a man call halt; wait till we see more like her."[62] Typical of King's recurring enchantments, such admiration did not last. Few women could compete with his own *amour-propre*.

Some five years into his Ottawa tenure, enough apparent intimacy survived for Ralph to share with King his dream of a Senate seat, with "the means to educate his boys, three of them were ready to go to college now, one wished to study for the ministry, the other law, it was hard not to be able to send them."[63] Ultimately, however, an appointment to Ottawa's second chamber was too valuable a gift for a man who could not deliver working-class voters. Even an extraordinary wife could not beat the odds. In time, when Mary Ellen took her own place at the political table, King would again prove faithless. The Senate would receive neither husband nor wife into its august membership.

In the 1904 federal election for the new riding of Nanaimo, Ralph surrendered his claims to be anything but a partisan Liberal. The disillusioned *Nanaimo Free Press* abandoned him, stating that "a vote for Mr. Smith as things stand today is a vote against Government ownership and a vote for the Grand Trunk Company and a line built by Mongolian labor with the money of the white workers of Canada."[64] Socialist rivals, such as James Hawthornthwaite,[65] who had succeeded Ralph as the local MLA, kept him on the defensive, but enthusiasm remained sufficient to return him to Ottawa. In the 1908 federal election, Hawthornthwaite almost defeated his former friend, who was saved by voters from the Esquimalt naval base, with its long-standing conservative sympathies.[66] Even so, Ralph could not combat the odour of betrayal, as summed up by Canada's first Labour MP, Winnipeg's Arthur Puttee (1868–1957). In 1908, Puttee wrote that "no man felt more bitterly disappointed over his treachery than myself, who was on the spot at Ottawa and witnessed his undoing and consequently the fading away of the immediate prospects of labor becoming a force in the Dominion parliament."[67] In this same year, Ontario's only Labour MPP, Alan Studholme (1846–1919), wrote to Hawthornthwaite that Smith had betrayed Lib-Lab hopes in Ottawa.[68]

In 1911, Ralph ran for re-election as an unrepentant Liberal loyalist committed to the party's platform of a reciprocal lowering of trade tariffs with the United States. Invoking Britain's old investment in free trade against Canadian party rebels, such as the "Toronto 18," who thundered about threats to national sovereignty and manufacturing posed by the loss of tariff protection and greater American competition, he attacked the Canadian Manufacturers' Association as "the most selfish institution in the country."[69] In the course of transplanting himself to the dominion, Ralph had retained the liberal "free trade convictions of the British working class" and rejected Tory claims of the danger posed by American industry to Canada's traditional imperial allegiance.[70] He was equally enthusiastic in endorsing Laurier's proposal to establish a Canadian navy, a creation that might benefit his constituents in Esquimalt, the long-time Pacific home of the British fleet. Such arguments did not suffice. The *Vancouver World* summed up the pervasive disillusionment:

> What Ralph Smith may have to say on the subject of reciprocity or any other matter is of very little interest to wage-workers in British Columbia. But when he starts out parading under the guise of being a working class representative ... it is time to register a protest ... At the last general election this was amply demonstrated by the vote of the miners, who went two to one against his treachery. But with the aid of a few misguided farmers and the members of the navy at Esquimalt the Liberal machinery managed to pull him through ... He will never again be re-elected on any political ticket in British Columbia. He couldn't be elected as doorkeeper in any union in Western Canada.[71]

Claims of "never" are always dangerous. Ralph remained a force in BC politics, even as his wife moved increasingly to the fore.

Mary Ellen's Rising Star

Soon after Ralph became MP, Mary Ellen began regular trips to Ottawa, becoming Nanaimo's "second MP," as Laurier joked.[72] Style was as significant as substance. In Ottawa, a stranger with labour antecedents could expect to be soundly scrutinized for faux pas. As she sought allies for her husband and herself, Mary Ellen put herself on display on an intimidating scale. In Nanaimo, people already admired her as a proud mother, Methodist activist, talented elocutionist and musician, and wife of a leading unionist and political reformer, but in Ottawa she had to begin again to win friends and influence. In April 1902, a great state ball hosted by

Governor General Lord Minto at Rideau Hall, dubbed the "Event of the Season," suggested that official Ottawa found the newcomer at least sartorially acceptable. Amid partiers, who included "representatives in Ottawa from every constituency in Canada as well as from many foreign countries, with their wives and daughters," Mary Ellen was spotlighted. Her outfit, a "New York gown, lace and spangled net, orchids," did not let her down among the "handsomely gowned ladies and gallant men."[73] That approving moment inaugurated a decade's worth of press coverage that depicted a clever woman who knew how to dress for success. As she variously wore "chiffon satin with gold and silver appliques," a "gown of blue net over silk, amethysts and pearls, bouquet of roses," a "lovely gown of opalescent sequins over pale pink silk embroidered with sequins and cut steel," and a "handsome gown of pale blue satin striped filet net, fashioned empire, and trimmed with lace applique," the former seamstress passed muster with Ottawa's highest ranks.[74]

In 1902, she was mentioned by name among the guests at a "ladies' luncheon" hosted by Frances Mary Scott (1855–1939), daughter of Richard Scott (1825–1913), sponsor of the 1878 Canada Temperance Act, and Mary Ann Heron (1833–1905), an accomplished singer and activist in the National Council of Women.[75] Such gatherings, repeated regularly throughout parliamentary sessions, introduced Mary Ellen to a network of reformers who frequently counted suffrage, as well as prohibition and public health, among their causes. They provided the foundation for unprecedented prominence and assisted her elevation in BC feminist circles.

Mary Ellen exhibited approved talents in presenting teas, bridge parties, and luncheons ranging from the simple to the lavish. Perhaps the highpoint of her success occurred in April 1908, when she hosted a remarkable afternoon card party much praised for its originality and its salute to imperialism. Ten bridge tables named after British forts – Sheerness, Gibraltar, Malta, Aden, Singapore, Hong Kong, Port Arthur, Esquimalt, Halifax, and Quebec – were adorned with tiny flags that had to be captured by the winners. Guests included the spouses of leading Liberal MPs – Lady Laurier, Mrs. Frank Oliver (Harriet Dunlop, 1863–1943), Mrs. Clifford Sifton (Elizabeth Burrows, 1861–1925), and Mrs. Robert F. Sutherland (Mary Bartlet, 1858–1923).[76] A year later, Mary Ellen was again congratulated for "an attractive and enjoyable tea" attended by Lady Borden (Laura Bond, 1861–1940), the wife of the Conservative leader, as well as a gaggle of Liberals, including Mrs. Sifton and Mrs. Oliver. The latter, wives of prominent cabinet ministers, poured tea and coffee in auxiliary roles to the event's star player.[77] Networking possibilities for "the charming wife of the member of parliament for Nanaimo" were likewise evident in 1911 at "one of the most enjoyable teas of the season." The long list of guests included the veteran Ontario feminist Dr. Elizabeth Smith Shortt (1859–1949), wife of Adam Shortt, a leading New Liberal.[78] It remains unclear how Mary Ellen managed such costly self-presentations and entertainments. Perhaps the dresses and accessories were loaned or rented? Perhaps Liberals or friends came to her support? Perhaps the Smiths went into debt? Whatever the explanation, they helped secure the couple's popularity in Ottawa.

By 1904, Mary Ellen had come to the attention of Margaret Graham (1870–1924), a feminist founder of the Canadian Women's Press Club (1904), former Presbyterian missionary teacher, and journalist for the *Montreal Star*.[79] The result was a gushing article sold as special to the *Vancouver World*, which had no equal in the coverage of any other parliamentary wife from the West in these years. Graham began with the familiar story of the young miner-preacher in north Britain. Ralph's "wise and happy choice" of Mary Ellen as wife (his first marriage was conveniently forgotten) was a windfall "both for his own sake and for the sake of the labor cause which he has since made his own, and to which he is today in the House of Commons devoting talents of no mean order." Though Graham gave no hint of her subject's own preparation for the role, she declared that Mary Ellen

> has long taken a deep interest in economic problems, an interest that impels her to lend a hand in the solution of these ever present problems. Indeed, I know few women better able to discuss disputed matters between master and employee with that calm judicial mind unbiased by sentiment, which is commonly supposed to be a monopoly of the sterner sex ... Her knowledge of labor conditions everywhere, particularly in Canada, and of the especial needs of the working men of her own province cannot but be an immense inspiration and help to her husband and to the constituency ... a thoroughly progressive westerner and as loyal a Canadian as though she had chosen this fair land for her birthplace.

Here was a full partner for Ralph, indeed effectively a political operator in her own right. Though "full of sympathy for the men who toil, she is yet able to see and judge from the employers' standpoint as well and does not allow our woman's heart to blind her to the mistakes of labor organizations whose short-sighted methods too often destroy the object striven for." Mary Ellen's personal knowledge of coal miners' wives and children and her "strong desire to be of service" were exactly what Canadian women needed. Public service in no way threatened her femininity. As her children became adults, she remained "essentially a home lover and home maker ... able to keep in touch with the larger world outside, to enter with sympathy into her husband's political career." The breadth of her mind was disguised, in effect made agreeable, by the "charm of a frank, friendly and wholly unaffected manner," and enhanced by her "unfailing memory for faces and names."

The paragon was also modest. When asked "whether the progress of society would be advanced by her active participation in politics," Mary Ellen seemed disingenuous in expressing herself

> as having more faith in woman's consciousness of, and an effort to live up to, the influence she now possesses, rather than in the securing of more privileges or rights. By using rightly the wide far-reaching influence which is now hers, woman will accomplish more for her own sex and for the race than by becoming a voter and politician. When women thoroughly realize that they already possess the substance of power, they will not be so insistent about their right to the shadow.

Like her subject, Graham finessed the controversial question of suffrage:

> Just here I would like to say to my women suffrage readers: Although none of the wives of our legislators whom I have thus far met are what one would term "suffragists," that is, they neither want equal suffrage nor do they believe that it would greatly benefit society in general, yet you must not consider them as unqualifiedly opposed to giving a vote to the women who want it.

Exactly what such poppycock translated to in the real world, readers could only wonder.

Graham completed her reassurance with the droll proposal that Mary Ellen "qualified for a pension from the Carnegie Hero Fund." She had first met Mary Ellen in dressmakers' rooms. Was it not, she asked readers, a "severe test of heroism" to answer questions "about labor problems in British Columbia, the education and training of children, woman suffrage and kindred subjects while being fitted into a gown?"[80] The need for such sycophancy, with its sidestepping of Mary Ellen's employment in Northumberland, suggests persisting dangers for independent and intelligent women. Patriarchal and class society required deception and camouflage. By the end of the Ottawa sojourn, as she perfected the performance applauded by Graham, Mary Ellen had won plaudits as the acceptable face of suffrage. It was said that "the sheer force of her personality" secured Ralph "friends in both political parties."[81]

Nor was labour presumed to be Mary Ellen's only field of expertise. As a representative of British Columbia, she gave at least one lecture for Methodists on "the customs and lives" of the "Indian, Japanese, and Chinese peoples" on the Pacific Coast.[82] For a woman with little formal schooling and knowledge of the reality lived by non-Europeans, the status of expert was extraordinary. It was not, however, atypical of the pretensions of Canada's settler community. In contrast, few disadvantaged groups got the public opportunity to express their views on themselves or on those who sought to dominate them. That exclusion was obvious during Laurier's last tour of British Columbia in 1910. As Mary Ellen served him tea, he kept "Chief Mathias, son of old Chief Joe," waiting for an interview to set out grievances about settler land grabs. Claiming fatigue, he cavalierly drove off with Mary Ellen and others. Not so much of a gentleman or lady then.[83]

Yet, even as Mary Ellen worked hard for acceptance in Ottawa, her endorsement of both the vote and the WCTU set her apart from the vast majority of parliamentary wives and high society. In April 1907, she joined with sister Methodist Amelia Roe Gordon (1853–1933), the WCTU's evangelistic superintendent and chair of the National Council of Women of Canada (NCWC) committee on the suppression of the White slave traffic,[84] to outline the wrongs against their sex. Gordon urged the "good strong women of the Dominion" to serve their less fortunate sisters, a call that would have resonated with Mary Ellen, but associating herself with such a well-known campaigner against sexual violence was brave for a woman whose working-class origins could well have raised questions about her own respectability.[85] Gordon, a "woman of some note throughout Canada for her oratorical abilities," who visited Nanaimo during a 1908 proselytizing campaign with her husband, "one of the leading attorneys of Ontario," was nevertheless a reassuring figure in the global moral reform network in which Mary Ellen had long enlisted.[86] Gordon's courage must have helped strengthen Mary Ellen in enduring open insults to her sex, such as the BC legislature's 1907 cancellation of Victoria's municipal franchise for women.

In Ottawa that year, Mary Ellen and Gordon took the Twenty-third Psalm as their starting point in reviewing what every woman needed for well-being and fair treatment: namely, "education; the right to earn her own living; the right to her own wages; the right to own property; the right to make contracts; personal liberty; to possess her own children; [and] to claim a fair share of property accumulated during marriage." At the close of the assembly, Mary Ellen deplored conditions facing British Columbians and celebrated New Zealand's 1893 enfranchisement of women. While reckoned as generally in agreement with the suffrage arguments of their forceful speakers, the audience repudiated British militants, preferring to commit to "a quiet unostentatious study of the subject." Guests included two other wives of Liberal parliamentarians, Mrs. Laurence and Mrs. Sutherland, whose opinions (and first names) went unreported. Unlike Mary Ellen and Gordon, they never left the shadows of feminist campaigns or of their husbands.[87]

The selection of Mary Ellen Smith for Ottawa suffrage keynotes acknowledged her eloquence, but it likewise reflected the weakness of local activists. As late as 1908, Ottawa's Local Council of Women remained divided over female enfranchisement. When some members, led by the WCTU, organized a meeting chaired by Ralph Smith to challenge timidity, the Local Council of Women (LCW) president denied advocacy.[88] Although the Great Cause was "talked of quietly for some time" by various members, who held "informal, but never official, conferences," the LCW feared the cost of partisanship.[89] Mary Ellen, however, remained resolute. In 1909, she again presented a detailed defence of enfranchisement "in a scholarly and eloquent manner" to the city's Equal Suffrage Association. A well-attended meeting of both sexes at the new Carnegie Library took note as she pointed to queens such as Elizabeth I, to the 1848 Seneca Falls American women's rights convention, to a future world filled with "women telegraphers, school teachers, plumbers, plasterers, paperchangers, saloon keepers, workers in iron and steel, clergy, textile workers, journalists, veterinary surgeons," and to enfranchisement in New Zealand, Denmark, Finland, and Australia. She dismissed opposition as no more than "pride of predominance and prejudice."[90]

By the year of that talk, 1909, Mary Ellen was confident and well known enough to challenge the status quo by writing an article for the *Western Methodist Recorder,* the official publication of the BC Conference of the Methodist Church. Published out of Victoria, the *Recorder* highlighted the social gospel views, including support for female enfranchisement, of progressive members.[91] As a long-time leader in the women's auxiliary of her church, Mary Ellen could feel right at home. Her article, first presented as a talk to the Wallace Street Epworth League, summarized ideas that she would repeat on returning to British Columbia. She began by identifying the franchise as a "burning" issue. If it had ever been a joke, it was no longer. Educational, economic, and legal changes had prepared the ground for progress. Lingering resistance was rooted solely in "the organized selfishness of human nature and the pride of predomination." Opponents merely employed "the old stale argument" used "against the admission of the Jews, the Catholics, and the Dissenters to power, namely that they are not fit for the privileges sought." Men had made a "house of dolls" for women, presumably a reference to Henrik Ibsen's 1879 feminist play, *A Doll's House,* and then complained of female frivolity.

"Justice and logic, precedence and experience" demolished reactionary arguments. History's lessons told the true story. Great monarchs such as Britain's Elizabeth and Victoria, Austria's Maria Theresa, and Spain's Isabella fully rose "to the responsibility of rulership." Smith pointed likewise to jurisdictions where enfranchisement had already positively affected political life and new electors turned out in good numbers. Female office-holders on English school and poor law boards were already skilfully addressing social and economic problems. Moreover, as tax-payers, women deserved the right to determine governments. Even if, "for the sake of argument," they were not men's intellectual equals, "do not the humblest and feeblest as well as the most gifted enjoy the same civil rights?" In fact, women were "dissimilar" to men but "not inferior." And "the proper sphere for all human beings is the largest and loftiest to which they are able to attain, and this can only be ascertained by liberty of choice." Women deserved better than being ranked with "lunatics and imbeciles." As voters, they would be "steadied by political responsibility, and by the important moral education which such responsibility carries with it." Nor was the franchise sufficient. Office holding mattered as well, for "to be represented by others no matter how intelligent, sympathetic or trustworthy can never be a substitute for the mental and moral development involved in the exercises of personal responsibility." Mary Ellen concluded by setting her standard "on the ground of justice and expediency, on the self-evident and indisputable principle that every class should be endowed with the power to protect itself." Once political equality was won, men could no longer ignore female interests, and female voters would develop a greater "public spirit" since "narrowness of view, local coloring of judgment are best cured in men or women by participation in wider interest."[92]

Mary Ellen's "Franchise for Women" was noteworthy in its explicit demands for both justice and expediency and its reminders of the importance of training and self-government. This classically liberal document was equally significant for its blind spots. Asians and First Nations were conspicuously absent. Mary Ellen, like Ralph and the vast majority of their peers, excluded such outsiders to the settler project from the rights they demanded for White women. Not surprisingly, contradictions abounded. If the practice of political equality elevated both women and men, as she insisted, why should any group be denied its benefits? How were racial exclusions any better than those imposed historically on Jews, Catholics, and Dissenters with whom such liberals sympathized? The article offered no answer. Nor did the Smiths.

Back to the Coast but beyond Nanaimo

In 1911, Sir Wilfrid Laurier was still reckoned "by far the most popular man in the country."[93] It did not suffice. The September 21 election returned 131 Conservatives, a gain of 49 seats, 85 Grits, a loss of 48, and 3 independent Conservatives. Only 1 Labour MP was returned, Alphonse Verville (1864–1913) from Quebec. All 7 BC seats went Tory. Despite being "counted a certain win" by his party, Ralph and the Liberal machine were swamped.[94] For the next half decade, federal opportunities evaporated.

The Smiths deserted Nanaimo within weeks, suggesting that the prospect had been on the horizon in case of a rout. Early in December 1911, Ralph declared his "intention to engage in real estate and general brokerage" and to move to First Avenue in the Vancouver middle-class suburb of Kitsilano.[95] Most of Nanaimo, including the Conservative mayor (soon appointed to the Senate by Prime Minister Robert Borden), had not supported Ralph, but the city nevertheless feted him. At a good-bye gala, Mayor Albert Planta (1868–1952) complimented the defeated candidate as having "acquitted himself with credit to himself and to the people he had represented." He then moved quickly to single out Mary Ellen: "One could not think of Mr. Smith ... without thinking of Mrs. Smith who by her charming personality was respected all over the city and all who had the pleasure of meeting her feel sure Mr. Smith has in her an estimable wife and a very able helpmate."[96]

Ralph got the last public word. Like many politicians before and after, he attributed his move to family responsibilities. He was leaving for the Lower Mainland to "make a home for my boys already residing there." In addition, he claimed, rightly enough, to be following "hundreds of other men," who saw "a wider scope in Vancouver." He promised nevertheless always to honour Nanaimo as the town where he had recovered his health and as the birthplace of his youngest son.[97] Though not asked to comment, Mary Ellen could have added that she too had thrived, all the more so as pregnancies came to an end in Nanaimo, that she likewise would devote herself to her family, and that she also glimpsed a bigger stage. That story engages the next chapter.

4
Boom, Bust, War, and Death, 1912–17

Mary Ellen and Ralph returned to British Columbia just as the Laurier economic boom crested. The 1911 political defeat was bitter, but they proved irrepressible in repositioning themselves. With its diverse progressive networks, Vancouver encouraged ambitious feminists and Liberals in expectations of settler entitlement. By 1913, dreams had crashed against a nation-wide recession and fell farther with war in August 1914. Although recovery was visible by 1916, benefits were compromised by wartime losses, corruption, and speculation. Hard-won victories that autumn, including a majority in a provincial suffrage referendum and the return of a Liberal government to Victoria, nevertheless revived dreams. Ralph's long-awaited acquisition of a portfolio, albeit in a provincial cabinet, and Mary Ellen's ascension to the heights of the BC suffrage movement appeared to realize the promise of emigration from Northumberland's dark pits.

Boom-times and Bad-times in Vancouver

In Vancouver, Mary Ellen and Ralph lived in Kitsilano, a relatively new middle-class neighbourhood. From then on, except for spells in Victoria, notably at the Empress Hotel after Ralph's election in 1916, they would reside permanently in various Kits locations. This community was well connected by public transit to the downtown business district and to Liberal and feminist circles in the West End, Mount Pleasant, and South

Vancouver. Nearby too, in testimony to the close ties that sustained many migrants, lived Nicholas Thompson (often called Nicol). A childhood friend of Ralph's, he had not only founded the BC Chamber of Mines but also become a leading member of the Liberal Party and a businessman with ventures from mining to salmon canning. Moreover, in 1917, Thompson became British Columbia's federal fuel controller.

While the economy surged, Ralph explored business possibilities, often in association with Thompson. In 1912, he was elected president and secretary of the city's Federal Investment Company.[1] Two years later, the *Canadian Engineer* reported that he would be the new superintendent for the Monarch Colliery in Taber, Alberta, recently purchased by a Vancouver syndicate, and *Henderson's Greater Vancouver City Directory* described him as a manager for N. Thompson & Company.[2] In the months before the outbreak of the First World War, Ralph joined "well-known Vancouver business men," again including his boyhood buddy, in promoting the B.C. Steel Works.[3] Such ventures assumed that the boom-times would last and testified to Ralph's determination to improve his economic fortunes. Such hopes were widespread. For example, they were shared by Ernest Winch (1879–1957), future founder of the Socialist Party of Canada and later an MLA for the Co-operative Commonwealth Federation. A British-born bricklayer, Winch tested the boom as a building contractor, but creditors foreclosed on his dreams.[4] That fate did not befall Ralph, though his projects appear to have left him little better off.

Mary Ellen's relocation did not involve obvious commercial prospects. Her attention focused on domestic, social, and political re-establishment. Proximity to the recently constructed Kitsilano Methodist Church (later the Crosby United Church) at Second Avenue and Larch Street linked her to a familiar progressive network, but the new community also presented opportunities in more conservative women's groups. Mary Ellen's inclusion, at least on some political occasions, in the upper echelons of society was signalled by what she wore at an autumn 1912 reception for Canada's viceregal couple, the Duke and Duchess of Connaught – a dress made of "ashes of roses brocade with handsome garnitures of bugle and crystal lace."[5] Less than a year later, she organized a chapter of the Imperial Order Daughters of the Empire (IODE), presided over the Women's Canadian Club (WCC), and worked for the Pioneer Political Equality League (PPEL). In this, she was joined by feminists such as British immigrant tailor Helena Gutteridge (1879–1960) and former teacher and social worker Laura Marshall Jamieson (1882–1964).[6] As activists with working-class origins, Mary Ellen and, even more so, Gutteridge, a suffragette from the militant Women's Social and Political Union, were hard to match in any other large Canadian city.

The BC IODE was closely associated with Lady Janet McDonald Tupper (1858–1935), leading matron of the Lower Mainland. Its acceptance of Mary Ellen heralded its slow expansion beyond society's top drawer, treasured since its founding in Montreal and Toronto during the South African War.[7] An eventual IODE regency (this term for the presidential post invoked monarchist sympathies) fitted nicely into the Smiths' hopes for social mobility and faith in cross-class cooperation. Links to Canada's Liberal elite were evident in the leadership of the WCC and the Smiths' hosting of Saskatchewan premier Thomas Scott (1867–1938) and his wife, Jessie Read Scott (c. 1869–1932). Work with the PPEL affirmed the Smiths' orientation to liberalism's left and familiarity with more radical feminists. The overall result nested the newcomer in a broad settler community with impressive female activists.

As a veteran political wife, Mary Ellen, with limited paid help, cemented ties through an active "at home program" that was regularly covered in the society pages of local newspapers.[8] Guests came regularly from Vancouver, Nanaimo, and Victoria, but the couple proved a magnet for a range of Canadian and international visitors, whose presence confirmed their social status. If politics (and music) supplied incentives for such social networking, so too did family ties. Mary Ellen oversaw time-consuming duties that did credit to Ralph and herself. In a typical gathering in 1913, she welcomed her future daughter-in-law, Katherine Winnifred Johnson (nicknamed Kitty, d. 1951), and her mother, members of a respectable Nanaimo merchant family. Mary Ellen dressed the part of a middle-class lady, in a "costume of pale grey satin charmeuse with an overdress of ninion trimmed with silver bands and embroidery." Her two guests of honour confirmed their superiority in "white net and white satin with flowered ribbon banding" and "white satin with overdrape of black minimum."[9] A few months later, Kitty and Robert Smith married in Nanaimo. A Victoria magazine described the bride as "particularly well known in musical circles" of Nanaimo and the groom as "a partner with a well-known [law] firm" in Vancouver.[10] After honeymooning, they lived close to Ralph and Mary Ellen, and Robert emerged a coming man in Liberal circles.[11] Mary Ellen had already introduced her daughter-in-law to Ottawa society, and now she did much to ensure that Kitty found a comfortable perch in Vancouver.

Although Robert attracted special note as a potential heir to his parents' liberalism, most family members rarely surfaced in public records. In 1916, his brother Ralph Gladstone married Inness Ogilvy (b. 1892), whose Presbyterian family lived in Kitsilano and whose mother was active in the war effort.[12] Ralph worked as a salesman in Vancouver. Meanwhile, Richard, the eldest son, worked for a time in Regina as a night operator for the CPR. The youngest, John Wesley, serving with the Vancouver Seaforth Highlanders, was wounded in France in 1917 and was awarded the Croix de Guerre. Mary Elizabeth remained in Victoria with her husband, that city's assistant post-master. Mary Ellen's father, Richard Spear, died at the Smith home in December 1913 and was buried next to his wife in Nanaimo.[13] Mary Ellen's brother, William, lived on Vancouver's North Shore, where he worked as an organist and choir director. In 1915, his son, Sergeant Edgar Spear, returned from France suffering from shellshock and the effects of gas.[14] Though commonly overlooked, such kin supplied demands and comforts, particularly for women, who led in managing ties.

As demonstrated by Ralph Smith's dalliances with corporate affiliations, Vancouver was afloat with risky speculation offering the "hypnotic promise of instant wealth."[15] Between the end of the nineteenth century and the beginning of the First World War, its population quadrupled to over 100,000, as it filled with ambitious migrants.[16] When the Smiths arrived in Vancouver, about a third of its residents were British-born, and White settlers from the United States, Canada, and western Europe were in the ascendant. That community remained rife with racism, though this may have diminished during the war, given that Japan and China, not to mention India, were Canada's allies in battle and in filling labour shortages at home.

Unchanged, despite the military service of Indigenous soldiers, was hostility and ignorance regarding First Peoples. It is easy merely to note the public silence of Ralph and Mary Ellen, all the more when they left limited records about those displaced by British newcomers determined to rule and replenish the earth. Vancouver between 1911 and 1917 nevertheless offered significant reminders of how Indigenous Peoples framed the options and politics of the Smiths. On the one hand, Coast Salish bands were forcibly removed from Stanley Park and False Creek, both only a stroll from the Smith residence. Ralph and Mary Ellen gained unearned benefits from the transformation of these two purloined spaces into expressions of imperial aspirations.[17] At the very least, Ralph's speculative real estate ventures made him an interested spectator on profits garnered along the city shoreline.[18]

Another pertinent reminder of an Indigenous history lay with Mohawk-English writer and performer E. Pauline Johnson, who rented a West End flat during the last years of her life. Widely celebrated as embodying Canada's special, that is to say supposedly superior to the American, relationship with Native Peoples and its claims to a heroic, if safely distant, Indigenous past, Johnson was renowned, notably among the city's female patriots and literati, who eased her slow death from breast cancer.[19] Despite Johnson's high visibility, which included publishing in the local press and the appearance of her best-selling *Legends of Vancouver* (1912), Mary Ellen seems to have left no observation on her neighbour. The press coverage of the writer and performer's elaborate civic funeral in March 1913 made no mention of Mary Ellen, although the Women's Press Club, the Pauline Johnson Chapter of the IODE, and the WCC all sent wreaths.[20] While not an open suffragist, Johnson left personal bequests to a handful of Canadian activists, including Nellie McClung and WCC president and Vancouver General Hospital Women's Auxiliary activist Harriet Oille Banfield (1863–1959).[21] Like the stolen land, the so-called Mohawk princess, as with more modest exemplars of Indigenous talent such as sometime Vancouverite, Cree recitalist Frances Nickawa (1898–1928),[22] informed the settler stage on which both Smiths performed. In contrast, the seemingly innocuous Better Baby Contests initiated by the LCW in 1913 placed the British "race" front and centre in the century that was to be Canada's. Its exhibits of supposed perfection flaunted the eugenic ideal of British and northern European stock.[23]

Twentieth-century Vancouver consisted of increasingly segregated space. Indigenous and Asian residents were assigned the margins, and by 1914, "80 per cent of the members of Vancouver's social register – composed almost entirely of the city's business leaders and their families – lived in Shaughnessy Heights," a posh district south of Kitsilano.[24] In boom and bust, newcomer society sorted itself into a hierarchy of privilege. Before 1900, a handful of generally more established families claimed the pinnacle. The Terminal City Club and the Vancouver Club, both restricted to men, signalled prominence, but the former was less exclusive. Its members, Ralph among them, were less likely to be Anglicans or university-educated and more likely to be involved in "real estate and resource promotion enterprises, in financing speculative schemes through the many trust and loan companies that flourished in the prewar period."[25] In contrast, the Vancouver Club trumpeted old money. Its families, most of them far from self-made, included such notables as Sir Charles and Lady Janet Tupper who capitalized on eastern connections, in their case to a Nova Scotian Father of Confederation and Conservative prime minister, as well as wealth gained in the exploitation of British Columbia.

The similarly top-drawer Henry (1856–1931) and Marie Isabella del Carmen Beattie Bell-Irving (1862–1936) asserted status linked to Scottish and Caribbean money, as well as profits from the resource sector. No female Tupper or Bell-Irving stood out as a suffragist or a reformer. Their lives largely enshrined consumption, pretension, and, usually, offspring. Even philandering husbands rarely unsettled respectability's facade.[26]

Below the Tuppers and Bell-Irvings stood others, such as the John Wallace de Beque Farrises, whose self-importance originated with the Atlantic Canadian middle class and subsequent male professional and political success in British Columbia. John Wallace (1878–1970), a future Liberal attorney general, joined both the Terminal City and the Vancouver Clubs. The Farris matron, Evlyn Fenwick (1878–1971), who moved to Vancouver in 1905, affirmed rank in founding its University Women's Club (UWC) two years later. A committed Liberal, she was neither an early nor an ardent suffragist, and she dismissed Mary Ellen as pushy and far too much a feminist.[27] In face of a womanizing spouse, Evlyn would eventually retreat into maternal obsession. Such women often populated the group whom Nellie McClung condemned as "gentle ladies" in thrall to comforts and self-regard.[28] Certainly, the pretensions of the UWC were sometimes seen as out-and-out snobbery. That critique appears close to the heart of a Vancouver book club that was formed in 1913 and dedicated to "the development of literary talent among its members," who believed that academic degrees were not the only proof of intellectual merit. Its first meeting was held at the home of an executive member, Mary Ellen Smith.[29]

In stark contrast, a few middle- to upper-class women, such as university-educated Helen Gregory MacGill (1864–1947) and Laura Marshall Jamieson, developed a vision of a more just world. Veterans of struggles to make a living, both were passionate suffragists who eventually became Juvenile Court judges.[30] Vancouver also welcomed settler activists from elsewhere who never matched the social credentials of its elite. The American social democrat Susie Lane Clark (1875–1956) arrived in 1907. A former member of San Francisco's first suffrage group, she was married to and then divorced from a Canadian printer. Six years after coming to Vancouver, she presided over the Woman's Suffrage League in Mount Pleasant, a neighbourhood associated with "the artisan or moderately well-to-do class."[31] Unlike high-tone Shaughnessy, it pulsed with enthusiasm for voting reform. In 1911, another powerful recruit – Helena Gutteridge – arrived directly from Britain's Women's Social and Political Union, which was captained by Emmeline Pankhurst. Representing the Tailors' Union on the Vancouver Trades and Labor Council (TLC), the redoubtable Gutteridge founded the BC Woman's Suffrage League.[32] Although none appear to have been intimate friends, MacGill, Jamieson, Clark, and Gutteridge all campaigned alongside Mary Ellen. In 1911, diversity and teamwork underpinned the efforts of women's clubs to establish the Vancouver Women's Building, a meeting centre that would be unmatched elsewhere in Canada and a confirmation of broad feminist networks.

In the immediate pre-war years, the suffrage cause developed new momentum. For years, the movement had been led from Victoria. *The Champion* magazine, first published by that city's Political Equality League in 1912 but soon favoured by suffragists province-wide, featured a White guardian of her sex on its cover, even as it affirmed an inclusive agenda:

> This League stands for no one religious Creed, no one Political Party, no one Social Class; all shades of opinion unite in its membership, on the elemental basis of justice, honour and chivalry, under the banner of Woman Suffrage.
>
> Believing, as we do, that every human being is sent into the world for the service of humanity, we regard the vote as the symbol in political life of the individual expression, as the key in social life to a wider and more direct usefulness, as the opportunity in national life for full and responsible citizenship.[33]

Despite the bold declarations on the cover – the Latin "FIAT JUSTITIA," or "Let there be justice," and "The Woman's Cause Is Man's," a quote from "The Princess," the famous poem of British Poet Laureate, Alfred Lord Tennyson (1809–92) – activists in the BC movement for women's equality struggled for a hearing. As late as 1915, Gutteridge despaired about "the lack of interest displayed by the women themselves."[34]

Change, however, was under way. Vancouver's inclusion on the international feminist circuit, with appearances by speakers such as Nellie McClung, Charlotte Perkins Gilman (1860–1935) from the United States, and Barbara Wylie (1862–1954) and Emmeline Goulden Pankhurst from Britain, spurred consciousness of a global crusade and the desire not to be left behind. The city's aspirations were signalled in 1913, when Mrs. Janet Kemp (1864–1960), vice-president of the Vancouver LCW and co-founder of the local Women's Forum in 1910,[35] replaced Victoria's Helen Maria Grant (1854–1937) as president of the Provincial Political Equality League. Other portents included endorsements of suffrage by the British Columbia Federation of Labor (BCFL) in 1912 and the provincial Social

"The Woman's Cause Is Man's," *The Champion*, December 1913.

Democratic and Liberal Parties a year later, as well as a barrage of legislative petitions and bills and the creation of the Vancouver Progressive Club on the Liberal left. In contrast, the Socialist Party of Canada and its organ, the *Western Clarion,* remained contemptuous of suffragists. The Vancouver movement nevertheless built linkages across party and doctrinal differences. That hard-won alliance became an inspirational politics for Mary Ellen, as indeed it was for her husband in trying to muster progressive support.

The commonplace insults of votelessness and what often seemed to be deepening legislative hostility stiffened suffragist unanimity and resolve.[36] In 1913, the Vancouver LCW and various Political Equality Leagues received a desperate plea from the northern settler women of Fort George, who protested the extension of the local red-light district. Smith, MacGill, and others took up their cause to condemn the Conservative government for permitting "tolerated vice."[37] At much the same time, an amendment to the Public Schools Act changed school board voting eligibility from any British subject to "any person being a male British subject," even as revisions to the Guardianship of Infants Act threatened maternal rights.[38] The documentation set out in Helen Gregory MacGill's popular (and later much reprinted and updated) 1913 pamphlet, *Daughters, Wives and Mothers in British Columbia and Some Laws regarding Them,* supplied still another spur to action. In January 1914, *The Champion* applauded Gutteridge for coordinating city suffrage societies in a Parliamentary Committee, praised Victoria's male voters for endorsing female enfranchisement in a referendum, and ridiculed Premier Richard McBride's insistence that female voters threatened "the welfare of the nation."[39] The *Vancouver Sun's* satirical cartoon "Too Proud to Speak" captured suffragist anger at McBride's continued obstruction. The onset of the First World War diverted some feminist energy into patriotic undertakings such as the Red Cross,[40] but the distraction was far from total. Growing distress, obvious male incompetence, and pride in women's wartime accomplishments soon reinvigorated franchise struggles.

The trade unionist Gutteridge was an unusual suffragist, but the number of female wage-earners was growing in Vancouver. Servants remained in great demand, encouraging middle-class women's support for a city crèche or daycare and domestic employment bureau,[41] but Vancouver resembled Ottawa more than it did Nanaimo. Diverse jobs in stores, offices, factories, teaching, nursing, and journalism supplied a subject and a constituency for political action. Sympathetic presswomen were especially invaluable, as they "reported events, analyzed arguments, and

"Too Proud to Speak"

It Is Assumed That Premier McBride Is Not In Favor of Woman Suffrage.

"Too Proud to Speak," *Vancouver Sun*, February 24, 1913.

advocated points of view which allowed women greater latitude inside and outside the home" and extended the "sisterly solidarity" of the Canadian Women's Press Club.[42] An expanding war effort increased the numbers of female workers but did little to alter discriminatory wages and conditions.[43] For remedy, Vancouver's hard-pressed women drew on a pre-1914 history of unionizing as telephone operators, store clerks, waitresses, and laundry and garment workers.[44]

Women who were allied to male unions supplied other reminders of cooperation's benefits. The feminist sympathies of the United Mine Workers' Auxiliary in Ladysmith during the Great Strike of 1912–13 reflected progressive ties among the province's diverse women.[45] Vancouver groups, such as the WCTU, the YWCA, and the LCW, drew on an intermittent but persistent record of aid to female workers, often linking economic vulnerability to sexual exploitation. One poem, titled "Shame!," in *The Champion,* justified militancy by exposing the plight of "girl workers, taught to sweat/By toll of vice their wage's lack," in effect driven into prostitution.[46] In the winter of 1914–15, the LCW sponsored a Women's Employment League and set up a cooperative toy factory and labour bureau. When feminists persuaded city council to take over the latter, Vancouver acknowledged for the first time "a continuing obligation" to jobless women, even as it determined "to discourage as many future requests as possible."[47] In this charged context, fierce debates about wage-earning fired suffrage meetings.

Vancouver's male unemployment and unrest, which always generated most official concern, sometimes terror, supplied further inspiration for reform. Deskilling, a highly competitive labour market, and an unstable resource economy, all made worse by employers' use of scabs, imported labour, the police, and the militia, kept industrial relations at a boil. Workers for the local building trades, who initiated a general strike in 1911 in the face of a "concerted attack by employers on unionism,"[48] regularly resisted exploitation, and hostility deepened with wartime inflation and profiteering. Much discontent was channelled through the Vancouver TLC and its newspaper, the *BC Federationist,* but it also flowed through the province's feminist and socialist circles.

Overlapping feminist, unionist, and socialist communities of dissent were rarely unanimous, but they encouraged broad progressive sympathies, which helped put suffragist reformer Louis D. Taylor into the mayor's office in 1910. A "strong Liberal, who openly identified with the interests of working men," Taylor won TLC commendation for policies that included the eight-hour day and the exclusion of Asians from city jobs.[49] Victories were never secure. Taylor lost to pro-business candidates in 1912 and 1914 only to be returned in 1915. In the 1912 provincial election, anti-union and anti-feminist Conservatives eliminated the Liberals, including Ralph Smith, who ran in Vancouver at the top of his party. Progressive hopes rested with the victory of two Socialist Party candidates.

In January 1915, the *Vancouver Sun* and the *World* sponsored a mock election to test the temper of the times. Readers were given their choice of nineteen candidates. Conservative prime minister Robert Laird Borden (1854–1937) and Liberal leader Wilfrid Laurier topped the poll, but Nellie McClung, the nation's best-known suffragist and a regular BC campaigner, came third. A few months later, Mary Ellen introduced McClung to the WCC as "known and loved by every Canadian of high ideals" and as "a noble woman, wife, and mother."[50] Such women were at least men's match. By 1916, suffrage societies believed that they stood at a historic turning point, when "the old order socially and industrially has given place to the new." The war confirmed that "this is not an age of brilliant statesmen, it is rather one of scheming politicians." Perhaps a "strictly non-partizan and non-sectarian" BC movement could overturn the disastrous old order.[51]

Richard McBride's successor as premier, William John Bowser (1868–1933), feared a future foretold in the 1915 defeat of Manitoba's anti-suffragist Conservatives, which was engineered in part by McClung. In 1916, he sought salvation in the direct democracy of a referendum: the people, or rather male voters, would determine whether to accept female enfranchisement, thus letting his administration off the hook. That referendum, accompanied by another on prohibition, would be held simultaneously with the provincial election. Suffragists protested strenuously, arguing that rights gained in such a manner might similarly be later rescinded. Some urged a boycott, but ultimately most supported a Provincial Women's Suffrage Referendum Association, which emerged to campaign for a positive result.[52] Their task became harder when the *BC Federationist* went sour, denouncing suffrage as a plot by "the master class."[53] Such betrayal did not, however, silence Helena Gutteridge. In addition, the referendum campaign offered further opportunities for cross-party collaboration. In support of the provincial referendum association, Mary Ellen toured British Columbia in a Model T Ford, along with suffragist and future Conservative MP Leon Ladner (1884–1978).[54]

In September 1916, the BC Liberal Party capitalized on widespread discontent, winning thirty-six seats and 50.0 percent of the vote; Conservatives took only nine seats and 40.52 percent. Ralph triumphed as a straight Liberal in Vancouver, while the also victorious Nanaimo miner Parker Williams (1873–1958), who ran on the socialist ticket, soon absconded to the Liberal left.[55] Other winners included John Wallace de Beque Farris, the elite lawyer who had defended unions and the claims of pioneer Mabel Penery French (1881–1955) to membership in the BC bar.[56] The suffrage referendum passed by 43,619 to 18,604.[57] Vancouver recorded 63 percent support for suffrage, but in Ward Two, an East Side working-class neighbourhood, 61 percent of voters turned thumbs down. Ultimately, the Liberals introduced a suffrage bill, which received Royal Assent on April 5, 1917, making British Columbia the fourth Canadian province

"As It Should Be," *Vancouver Sun*, March 30, 1917.

to enfranchise White women (and, more incidentally, Black women). In a typical expression of unexamined racial privilege, the *Vancouver Sun* featured a cartoon in which Miss [Indigenous] BC conferred the franchise on the province's White women.

Immediately after the election, Vancouver's female reformers, including Gutteridge, MacGill, and Smith, founded the Voters' Educational League to bury party differences and to link British Columbians, led by female voters, in aid of "a new race and a new humanity."[58] The league denounced the party system and the selection of candidates by "a small controlling and selfish interest." To include "the best brains," party discipline should yield to "many shades of opinion."[59] As the league exemplified, wartime

British Columbia explored alternatives to political partisanship. The remedies of recall and proportional voting further tantalized many citizens, even as conservative hopes to contain democracy thrived.

Ralph Smith, BC New Liberal

For all the lure of his business adventures, Ralph could not resist politics. Within weeks of his return to the coast in 1911, he was wooing the electorate and invoking British efforts to link middle- and working-class voters in a New Liberalism of unemployment insurance, old age pensions, and workmen's compensation.[60] On the executive of local and provincial Liberal associations, he called for such programs, with the critical addition of female enfranchisement, which still divided Liberals in Britain.[61] By the March 1912 provincial election, after originally demurring, he accepted nomination in Vancouver's multi-member constituency and roared into action against Premier McBride for toadying to corporate interests in resource industries. Invoking Britain's David Lloyd George, Ralph insisted that "the Liberal party can only live when it stands and fights for radical principles. If the Liberal party in this province is as radical as it should be there will be no use for a Socialist party."[62] During a campaign speech to Kitsilano's Methodists, he framed a familiar theme in referring to Ralph Waldo Emerson's 1841 essay "Self-Reliance" and John Stuart Mill's "Individual Liberty" (1859), as well as to the Duke of Wellington and Sir Walter Scott: "While it is true that human beings are not born to equality and just as true that they have not equal chances ... no human being ever became anything great without persistent effort."[63]

Topping Vancouver's Liberal ticket, Smith was hailed by partisans as "a most valuable acquisition to the fighting line" and as the "Great Smith."[64] Wearing "the white flower of a blameless life," he could be taken for the BC version of British labour leader John Burns, standing for the "rights of the people" against the corporate "grafter."[65] Ralph spared time to denounce socialists, whom he accused of helping to keep McBride in power, even as he slew Tory dragons with "comedy touches, mimicry and withering sarcasm."[66] In retaliation, the conservative *Western Call* mocked a "badly wrecked" Liberal Party, where contending factions included "extreme disruptionist, anarchist, [and] opportunist" radicals, who were supposedly determined to separate Canada from Britain.[67]

Although McBride's Conservatives swept Vancouver in 1912, Ralph led all Liberal candidates. As usual, the *BC Federationist* was eager to print his obituary: "a Judas to labor" and a "well known has been."[68] The socialist *Western Clarion* called for an undertaker to bury "the Liberal's last hope otherwise known as a friend of labor."[69] Ralph was unrepentant. He next rallied provincial Liberals in Saskatchewan and defended Laurier, attacking Borden's Conservatives for naval and immigration policies that suited London better than they did Canada. The empire was best maintained by "freedom, elasticity," and "affection."[70]

In 1913, Smith carried on efforts to reposition the Liberals. Political Equality Leagues heard regular appeals from him.[71] The Liberal Party, he insisted, championed suffrage not for political advantage but because women were "human beings," who like the "poor and weak" in general needed the ballot. However, he denounced militant British suffragettes for inciting prejudice.[72] He repeatedly toured the province, spreading the liberal gospel. In Golden, he welcomed socialists and announced that his party should become the Liberal-Democratic Party. Thus united, socialists and Liberals would drive Conservatives and imperialists "out of the plush seats into the cold cosmos."[73] Reactionary Grits, on the other hand, should find another home.[74] Only "a great democratic combination" could defeat McBride's Tories.[75] Many working-class activists derided such proposals as opportunistic.

During the first half of 1914, Ralph continued to criticize Conservative naval policies federally and resource development provincially. Britain's "constant and permanent reforms" under Prime Minister Herbert Asquith and his chancellor David Lloyd George were better inspiration.[76] By May, Ralph was president of the Vancouver City and District Liberal Association. Partisanship, however, had limits. He joined local Conservative MP Henry Herbert Stevens (1878–1973) to denounce the Indian migrants on board the *Komagata Maru,* a ship that had entered Vancouver harbour in a bid to challenge Canadian immigration laws designed to exclude arrivals from British India. Invoking a moral and public health threat, he contended that such Asian "anarchists" required "obliteration of party distinction."[77] His June election to the presidency of the Provincial Progressive Club produced no backtracking on racism.[78] Ralph was seemingly oblivious to obvious contradictions in a speech delivered to the Central Methodist Church: "It is not patriotism to hate your brother because he was born in a different country. True patriotism is to lead him to higher and nobler ideals and to show him that your country can give him more freedom than his own."[79]

The declaration of war in August 1914 renewed Smith's calls to end party politics,[80] but they lacked credibility. His October address,

Ralph Smith, 1916. | J.M. Bengough, "Popular Profiles," *Vancouver World*, September 9, 1916.

"The War: Its Causes and Results," delivered to the Vancouver City and District Liberal Association, typically credited British Liberals with "the removal of the tyranny of capitalism" and the "liberty and democracy we enjoy today."[81] He also condemned civil service appointments for prioritizing Conservative loyalty over competence.[82] He closed the year by reiterating that "the great reforms of England, the cradle and upholder of freedom for the people, were won by and through Liberal principles." They required "evolution," not "revolution."[83] War abroad only deepened the need for change at home.

In 1915, as Premier Bowser succeeded the far more popular McBride and the economy faltered in the midst of political scandal, Smith's attacks mounted. By March of that year, he had emerged as one of Vancouver's "Smashing Six" Liberal candidates for the next provincial election.[84] Despite such hyperbole, his party was in disarray. Former premier and Ralph's long-time foe Joseph Martin (1852–1923) led the opposition to any "fusion of the Liberals and the Socialists and labor party," proposing Tory allies instead.[85] Ralph tried to enlist working-class voters with demands to intern German and Austrian immigrants who were employed in BC coal mines.[86] Again, he urged anti-progressive party members to make way for socialists and even sympathetic Tories.[87] Such appeals rankled sterner partisans, who lined up as "enemies of Ralph Smith in his own party."[88] His calls for cooperation were just as unpopular with the *BC Federationist,* which dismissed him as a "cheap Liberal."[89] Opposition leader Harlan Carey Brewster (1870–1918), however, joined Ralph in advocating a "new Liberalism" for all citizens, including women.[90]

Within the party, campaign financing scandals undermined efforts to pivot left or maintain a united front. In Vancouver, a so-called purity squad attacked elite corruption, and Ralph insisted that he was "no rubber stamp" for party bosses.[91] Divisions deepened when the Conservative government brandished its 1916 election referenda on suffrage and prohibition. Ralph declared himself "non-partisan" in opposing the former, as suffragist leaders had rejected it, and in supporting the latter because activists had asked for it.[92] The Liberals ultimately entered election season "Not a Happy Family," with rumours that Smith would lead an "independent Liberal ticket."[93]

For all the in- and out-fighting, much press attention was favourable. The *Vancouver Standard* hailed Ralph as the city's "most valiant radical," the father of a son who was fighting on the Western Front, and as having won over "many Liberals, Independents and Conservatives."[94] The always irrepressible Smith invoked far-flung battlefields in firing "volleys of verbal shrapnel and high explosive" against squirming Tories.[95] He was praised as a veteran of "the 'Nanaimo' school of politics, much the most turbulent in this province, and which has the virtue of killing off those not lusty enough to survive its exacting requirements." Equally widespread was agreement that Ralph had "the great advantage of a helpmate who is as keenly interested in public matters as he is, and who is equally effective on the platform."[96] His starring performance in a victorious campaign did not guarantee him a reward. Even with a massive government majority, he remained *persona non grata* among many senior Liberals repulsed by his history with the labour movement, his anti-corruption campaigns, and his undoubted tendency to hyperbole. Only at the last minute was he named minister of finance.[97] Like all cabinet ministers in this period, Ralph had to be re-endorsed in a by-election. He won it easily, but his colleague Attorney General Malcolm Archibald Macdonald (1875–1941) fought a hard battle as he dodged charges of venality from "independent" Liberals.[98]

The new finance minister set to work immediately. In a "Get Together" dinner at the Hotel Vancouver with the business top brass, he declared his intention to clean house. Backed by Premier Harlan Brewster, he sought out "accountants of national and international reputation" to scrutinize the previous administration. Entrepreneurs were told to embrace "high ideals" in protecting "the interests of all the people."[99] He announced that the civil service would be investigated by the federal civil service commissioner Adam Shortt (1859–1931), a Queen's University political economist and influential purveyor of Canada's New Liberalism.[100] "British Columbia's patronage-cursed system" was in his sights.[101]

As it turned out, Ralph Smith did not have time. In some two months, he would be gone. In the weeks before his death, however, he cemented his reputation as a clean broom when he informed Richard McBride, now the province's agent-general in London, that his operations were to be audited.[102] An interview with military recruiting officers in mid-January 1917 offered a final exercise in patriotism. Smith stated bluntly "that any young men in his department without physical or domestic disability must either join the military or leave the service."[103] If necessary, he intended to assist recruiters.[104] The audit confirmed New Liberal sympathies, and the endorsement of military service revealed alienation from the BCFL and socialists such as Ginger Goodwin, the radical miner and union organizer who would be shot and killed as a war resister in 1918 by the Dominion Police (a precursor to the Royal Canadian Mounted Police).[105]

Mary Ellen Moves into the Limelight

When Mary Ellen left Nanaimo, the *Free Press* expressed the hope that she would discover "another sphere of influence for her kindly and thoughtful personality."[106] Its wish was granted but not by accident. In Vancouver, she remained Mrs. Ralph Smith, the talented partner of a man on centre stage, someone who superintended family and social relations. Now, however, liberated from caring for young children and playing the parliamentary spouse, she flew solo more often. Just as Ralph fought to extend liberalism, Mary Ellen evangelized for respectable feminism, a suffragist who was first a good mother and wife and then a gifted organizer and platform performer.

She nourished the distinct but closely linked reform constituencies that distinguished Vancouver: the first was a diverse assemblage of women's organizations; the second consisted of provincial and federal Liberals and some of Canada's most determined socialists. Labour activists figured in her mix of backers, but their numbers appeared to drop as she climbed socially. Her leadership in the rising tide of women's autonomous groups nevertheless ensured serious consideration by the Liberal Party, which hoped to secure female loyalists. Among many feminists, she managed to attain the credibility that her husband found increasingly hard to mobilize in labour circles. Might Mary Ellen be a better prospect for recruiting new voters to the Liberal standard?

She maintained her commitments to Methodism and the WCTU. The Kits Methodist Church, with its Epworth League and Woman's Auxiliary, replaced Wallace Street for meetings and speeches. However, church membership appeared to be a diminishing force in Mary Ellen's public life, a decline that coincided with British Columbia's continuing ascent, or descent, depending on one's sympathies, into secularism.[107] In 1914, she reminded WCTU members that Frances Willard had concluded "that if she had the years to live over again she would fight for the emancipation of women instead of temperance." Mary Ellen introduced herself as having been a suffragist since "she was knee-high." The franchise meant justice and peace.[108] Her memberships in various groups, from the IODE, the WCC, and the LCW to various franchise associations, the Women's Forum, and the Consumers' Club, sustained broad engagement in the women's movement. In October 1912, now on the Women's Forum executive, Mary Ellen highlighted a favourite theme: female wage-labourers deserved suffragist support since "everything depends on what we do for the masses; with them we will rise or fall."[109] That duty of care prompted the Pioneer PEL, for which she served as vice-president, to demand that Premier McBride add "clerks, accountants and all such helpers, male or female, whether in financial, industrial, mercantile, or other similar pursuits" to the mandate of a proposed commission on labour.[110] When the *Vancouver Sun* solicited her views in the autumn of 1912, she prioritized organizing for women and added the responsibility to Canadianize "the stranger within our gates," a reference to the 1909 volume of that name written by Methodist minister James Shaver Woodsworth (1874–1942). Organized women should integrate foreigners, or at least "the different white nationalities," as part of the "onward march of civilization."[111]

Mary Ellen's 1913 contributions to what she termed "divine unrest" included speeches for Protestant, franchise, and Liberal groups.[112] A talk to Grandview Methodists saw her extolled as "one of the cleverest women speakers in Vancouver, if not in Canada," and a local Epworth League lauded her condemnation of "repression and suppression" and "taxation without representation."[113] An autumn meeting of the Equal Franchise Association had her emphasizing "the spiritual nature of women's revolt" and casting enfranchised Australia and New Zealand as models of "righteousness, justice and liberty, for which their British forefathers had fought and died."[114] Enthusiasm swept Liberal gatherings where she starred in membership drives, the antidote for the dismal electoral results of 1912. This "moderate" and "talented lady" was to awaken "sleeping" members.[115] A mass Liberal picnic in July 1913 cheered her reassurance that the franchise would make her sex not "one whit less womanly."[116] Maternally minded voters could tackle child custody law, which she termed a "disgrace to civilization." Applause greeted her denunciation of a Conservative assembly that ignored women and children.[117] Fraser Valley gatherings welcomed her as an apostle of "moderate action," of "education" not "revolution."[118] South Vancouver received a similar message, albeit with the proviso that pent-up women had "lots to say."[119]

She assured listeners everywhere that if women got the vote, child labour would be ended – "no babies will toil."[120] In September 1913, she addressed the Liberal Party's affiliate, the Progress Club, the first time it had "entertained a body of ladies (and a baby) at its weekly luncheon." Once more, she linked feminism and liberalism as products of history. The former materialized because of "the introduction of machinery, which drove industry from the homes and compelled women to go out into the world to earn their livelihood." And, like liberals, feminists fought prejudice for the greater good. They needed no "hatchets or bombs" to cooperate with, but never rule, men.[121]

Whereas hosts were often women's and mixed groups, some of Mary Ellen's audiences were described as being composed mostly of men. An attractive and bantering advocate of moderation, she was hard to beat.[122] As she told Vancouver's civic ratepayers, "The newspapers are calling militant suffragettes arsonettes now. I am an arsonette, but of a slightly different type. I am in sympathy with arson to this extent, I would like to burn from the hearts of men the prejudice against women's suffrage."[123] Elsewhere, as "the only lady speaker," she drew "prolonged applause" in placing feminism and liberalism in civilization's vanguard. What men made of her suggestions to share domestic and national housekeeping went unrecorded.[124]

When the Labor Temple staged a suffrage debate on November 17, 1913, Mary Ellen was the obvious choice to pit against the Oblate priest William Patrick O'Boyle (1875–1949) of Holy Rosary Cathedral. Chaired by Ralph, the event had to turn hundreds away. In "rare form," both speakers offered "ready and racy humor" to the gratification of their own "strong followings." O'Boyle condemned feminists as socialist threats to family government. Mary Ellen retorted that inequality was the real problem: woman wanted "not to usurp man" but "to insist on her rights as a human being."[125] Whereas some commentators judged the result a dead heat, suffragist Susie Lane Clark slammed O'Boyle as "either uninformed" or a believer in the "exploiting and subjection of women."[126] Helena Gutteridge was equally angry: "We live in an age of hard facts, not an ideal dream land."[127]

During the months before the declaration of war, as Conservative governments in Ottawa and Victoria remained obdurate, Mary Ellen barnstormed the Lower Mainland.[128] In February 1914, her essay "The Woman's Place in Modern Life," published in *The Champion*, argued that "the right of one age is the wrong of the next." It pointed to China as a notorious offender, "a great nation sunk in the slough of despond" because of "its reverence for customs which had outlived their usefulness." In the smaller, more efficient homes of the modern world, duties could be done "collectively," and female voters would ensure that "more broad-minded, liberal and tolerant" policies were established.[129] At the annual meeting of the Women's Forum, where she and Laura Jamieson joined the board, she denounced a recent inquiry's glossing over of women's wages. Nor did she spare clubwomen: they should have "tabulated facts and figures" to dispute the claims of "the manufacturing and mercantile interest." Mary Ellen also warned that prostitution would blight San Francisco's 1915 Panama-Pacific International Exposition: "It rested with every woman to see that her neighbor got as much protection as she demanded for herself."[130] At the meeting of the Political Equality League, she welcomed Belgian feminist peace advocate and WCTU leader, the Baroness de Lavelaye.[131] Less controversial were her duties the next month as judge at a best baby show.[132]

The August 1914 declaration of war did not trigger any immediate recalibration from suffragists. As Susie Lane Clark observed in the *BC Federationist*, "A great many people seem to think that suffrage has been relegated to the background on account of war conditions. To thinking people, however, it is apparent more than ever that women should be enfranchised, and while assisting in this calamity as much as possible, women will still insist on having their political rights."[133] The conflict's initial exacerbation of unemployment only confirmed the need for a feminist agenda. By October, Smith had joined Gutteridge and Jamieson in championing the Women's Employment League and Labor Exchange.[134]

Feminists nevertheless slowly adjusted their arguments to address the war's unfolding tragedy. In a November speech to the Kits WCTU, Mary Ellen foresaw that the conflict would produce "a greater gain in democracy, people of rank mingling with those of most humble station" and "an enormous extension of the sphere of women's activities." Better still, she trusted that "the women of the nations involved would all band themselves together and intervene in an attempt to put an end to warfare."[135] That wish evoked the unsuccessful call for "continuous mediation" by American social worker Jane Addams (1860–1935) and Canadian academic Julia Grace Wales (1881–1957) in 1914–15.[136] Addressing the LCW, Mary Ellen condemned spending on war rather than on children, insisting that "if the motherhood of Germany could have spoken the day before the war broke out, Germany would not now be at war with any nation."[137] As she became convinced of the ignominy of the "Hun," however, Mary Ellen demanded nothing less than the enemy's total defeat. She would not join the Women's International League for Peace and Freedom, one legacy of war resistance embraced by Addams that soon found resonance in the hearts of a handful of Vancouver suffragists such as Laura Jamieson.

By early 1915, the war's unmet welfare needs were attracting greater attention. Mary Ellen joined multi-party speakers in appeals for the Canadian Patriotic Fund, a voluntary relief effort to support military families. Her speeches for the Red Cross were likewise often non-partisan, and she collaborated with other suffragists in linking remedies for wartime evils to the Great Cause. In April 1915, the PPEL hosted a fundraiser to help South Vancouver's poor, during which "diminutive maidens clad in white, and wearing little caps and sashes of the suffrage colors, sold homemade candy in tiny purple white and green baskets which they carried around in trays and which sold like the proverbial hot cakes." Applause greeted Mary Ellen's blunt question as to why charity was necessary. The remedy was clearly presented in *How the Vote Was Won,* a one-act play that followed her speech.[138] In the same spirit, on "Frances Willard Day" in 1915, Smith warned that the Elections Act Amendment Act, then under consideration in Victoria, posed a threat to the municipal vote.[139] A few weeks later, Liberals heard her declare that exclusion from the franchise was all the more "unfair" since "our women were big enough when war was declared to call a truce for the time being."[140] Such arguments sometimes produced detractors. Though a frequent admirer, the *Nanaimo Free Press* denounced "pet theories" about the payoffs of enfranchisement.[141] From such perspectives, the distraction of suffrage could only undermine the war effort.

As dreams of a quick war crumbled, suffragists increasingly renounced silence on the vote as the price of patriotism. The Grandview Liberal Association heard Mary Ellen's reminder that though "good women" were treated like "Indians, idiots and Chinamen," their addition to the electorate would "purify the national life."[142] In May 1915, she joined LCW stalwart Margaret Griffin (d. 1918) and Evlyn Farris to create the city's first Women's Liberal Association (WLA), an initiative that Farris later tied to a frustrating interview with McBride. Their reward was a "black and white" promise from Brewster of suffrage legislation.[143] Such explicit Liberal partisanship provoked concern and skepticism. Because WLA meetings were held in the afternoon, one writer to the *Vancouver Sun* suggested that they targeted "the leisure class" and "shut out completely the wage-earning element." Warning that a female "socialistic party" might emerge, that critic further urged "women from all walks of life" to organize without reference to party."[144] The WLA generally sidestepped such concerns. In June, during an afternoon meeting that welcomed a letter of support from Nellie McClung, it asserted its confidence in the Liberal Party.[145] A few days later, Mary Ellen stressed "the usefulness of women's political associations."[146] The WLA's potential for recruitment to the cause was clear when Evlyn Farris confessed, "I never belonged to any suffrage society myself. I've been too busy rocking the cradle to think of helping to rule the world. But I would be glad to have a vote. I think women with their votes can do a great deal of good."[147] Ultimately, the WLA agreement to send representatives to the male Liberal association suggested that it was walking a fine line when it came to women's independence.[148]

Even as the WLA harnessed suffragist energy, many loyalists stuck with the Political Equality Leagues and other suffrage clubs for which Mary Ellen remained a popular speaker. She was part of the feminist team that won a "Full-Dress Debate in Kitsilano." During the event, the noted antisuffragist Almroth Wright (1861–1947), author of *The Unexpurgated Case against Woman Suffrage*,[149] was consigned in absentia to the "dark ages." Justice required that women have the vote, not the demeaning position of "cajoling" men for influence.[150] Introduced by Gutteridge a few days later at the Labor Temple's People's Forum, Smith described moving to the "land of freedom with only one river to ford – the river of prejudice" against women. To that end, she applauded Lloyd George's introduction of equal pay for equal work in British munitions factories.[151]

Claims to non-partisanship, or at least to no formal party links, grew more popular as Canadians gained wartime reasons for disillusionment. The BC Consumers' League, which declared some four to five thousand members by April 1915,[152] abounded in suffragists. Mary Ellen became an early officer. Dodging old-line allegiances, the league claimed to be "in the interest of no class" in fighting inflation and price gouging and urging the purchase of BC goods.[153] Smith similarly used opportunities, such as an address to the American Women's Club, to express concerns broadly shared among settler residents: foreigners needed to be assimilated to ensure "a new race with a wonderful vigor." Audiences understood that her appeal "to cherish the meanest flower that blooms, and the highest stars in the sky" did not extend to Asian, African, or Indigenous Peoples.[154] She also found allies in outrage that British wives and mothers could not vote, whereas foreign-born men could.[155] Although *The Champion,* and Vancouver and Victoria newspapers, approvingly covered suffragist and feminist campaigns in Asia, racism regularly bulwarked the activist assumptions of White supremacy in Canada.

By 1916, casualty reports, enlistment failures, and war profiteering were fuelling mounting chauvinism. Even as socialists and the BCFL remained deeply critical of the war effort, Mary Ellen joined Liberals and Conservatives to help launch the Greater Vancouver Recruiting League. It largely ignored warnings against "indiscriminate white feathering," which aimed to shame men of military age not in uniform, or the need for "caution and judgment."[156] The same month took her to Ottawa WCC meetings, where she urged easterners and westerners to unite in "sacrifices for the greatest Empire the world has ever known."[157] Women's growing mobilization in multiple efforts slowly brought results. A nominee of women's groups –

Mrs. Irene Hawkins Moody (1879–1958) – was elected to the Vancouver Board of School Trustees. A widowed philanthropist and author, Moody had graduated from Ontario's Alma College and Boston's Curry School of Expression. She was never a prominent suffragist.[158] She nevertheless benefited from endorsement by the WLA and by Mary Ellen, then president of both the WCC and the Women's Forum, who put women's rights on the agenda in chairing the latter's all-candidate mayoralty meeting.[159] In February 1916, when celebrating Manitoba's suffrage victory, Smith was lauded as "one of the pioneers of the movement in the province, and who has probably done more missionary work in British Columbia in the cause ... than any other person."[160] That same year, she became regent of the IODE's Malaspina Chapter, affirming conservative allies. Such suffragist momentum was ignored by Premier Bowser, who rejected the arguments of a February suffrage delegation, even after reassurances that not all its members were Liberals.[161]

During the autumn election of 1916, when the Bowser Conservatives tried to reposition themselves via the strategic deployment of the suffrage referendum, few British Columbians were swayed, and Mary Ellen went to the forefront of the Liberal campaign, moving "her audience to laughter or tears at will" as she took "several hard cracks at the Bowser government." Ridiculing the referendum as a Tory "life preserver," even as she gambled that it could be won, she stood firmly on the Liberal left. Her endorsement of longstanding reform demands for the introduction of "the initiative, the referendum and the recall" as the means for strengthening voters and "put[ting] the fear of God into the heart of a politician" told the same story.[162] She condemned the Tories for diverting women from patriotic work into a referendum campaign. As the mother of a son "in the trenches," she demanded "the onward march of democracy."[163] When she went east to attend the IODE national convention, she affirmed her party credentials in the hot and heavy battles of British Columbia by a visit to the Lauriers.[164] She emphasized the intimacy of the connection. Sir Wilfrid met her train at "an early hour." He looked well and so did his wife, who despite her blindness knitted "constantly for the soldiers."[165]

Though never less than a fierce Grit, Mary Ellen positioned herself within a patriotic common front in aid of the war effort. When Emmeline Pankhurst visited in June 1916 to promote military recruiting, Mary Ellen led the WCC and the Pioneer Political Equality League in assembling the city's great and good. Now a self-professed British Tory, Pankhurst justified a halt to suffrage agitation by warning that a civilization "based on right and justice" lay in the balance.[166] She also fed familiar hopes, suggesting that "class distinction and prejudices" were "being thrown aside" on the battlefields.[167] A few days later, Mary Ellen used a Liberal rally to celebrate Pankhurst's "grace and charm" even as she refused to defer the suffrage cause.[168] As she repeated elsewhere, her politics remained "straight woman's suffrage and equal franchise." The referendum was nothing more than an effort "to chloroform the women of the province."[169] But even as Mary Ellen regularly claimed the high ground of non-partisanship, her Liberal allegiance was never far away, and a Nanaimo suffragist tried to set her straight, insisting that she had "made the grave mistake of confusing Woman's Suffrage with party politics." Women were free "to campaign with and for any party," and partisanship threatened their enfranchisement.[170]

In the end, disagreement about the best way to advance the Great Cause did not deter celebration of the Liberals' September 1916 election victory. The BC Equal Franchise League joined the Vancouver WLA at a luncheon, which drew congratulations from activists across the country. Mary Ellen hailed the election result as ensuring citizenship for women, and UWC president Laura Jamieson welcomed the end of "the winter of discontent."[171] The *Toronto Globe* congratulated Mary Ellen, "well-known in Toronto," and the "charming and girlish" Evlyn Farris for "outwitting" politicians while not neglecting "a child, nor a husband, nor a household duty."[172]

Party partisans, in turn, were quick to mobilize to recruit newly enfranchised voters. In December 1916, Farris took to the Victoria stage with Premier Brewster to urge her sex to "organize along the lines of the two great parties, preferably the Liberal" and, only too revealingly, to "be content to work day and night in the humblest capacity while others took the credit." Above all, "talk of a woman's party" should be abandoned. Only "cooperation and comradeship and co-working as in the home" brought "moral or material" advancement. Not surprisingly, Brewster agreed, embracing "team-work from now on in British Columbia. It must no longer be the two sexes at odds and unequal."[173] Soon enough, as the next chapter suggests, the former Conservative premier Bowser would make the same pragmatic calculation about the utility of wooing the new electorate. Both old parties would discover that non-partisanship could not be wished away. Interest in political alternatives flourished. Feminists were after all well acquainted with the fickleness of both Liberals and Tories.

Death Intervenes

When Mary Ellen celebrated partnership, her first thought was of Ralph. On February 12, 1917, her ally in love and politics died at age fifty-eight. She and sons Robert and Ralph reached his side in Victoria, but Richard could not arrive in time from Regina, and John Wesley was lying wounded in an English hospital. Pallbearers at Ralph's public funeral in Vancouver included Nicholas Thompson, his childhood friend and president of the Vancouver Board of Trade, and his long-time intimate and doctor Robert McKechnie, as well as Charles Tupper, who as a Conservative MP had been a parliamentary colleague during Smith's first term. Impressive as his send-off was, Ralph died a far poorer man than those pallbearers. His estate, most of it in real estate and life insurance, amounted to $31,150, with debts of $23,000.[174] Politics had been his passion, but it did not make him wealthy, and Mary Ellen would have to budget carefully.

Obituaries saluted a self-made and God-fearing man who had risen from mining pits to high office.[175] A few contradicted all evidence in applauding his "retiring nature."[176] The BCFL and provincial socialists would have questioned the *Ottawa Journal's* claim that "the labor men lost a loyal and sympathetic friend," but the *Vancouver Sun* offered a balanced assessment in describing Ralph as "known far and wide as a man of aggressive spirit in support of whatever he believed to be right."[177] Perhaps Ralph would have been most pleased by the conclusion of the *Vancouver World:* "He belonged to that distinguished school of public men who have worked themselves up by sheer native brain-power and industry to high rank in the service of the country and of which the Rt. Hon. John Burns [in Britain] is perhaps the most distinguished example."[178] A subsequent scholarly assessment by Mark Leier was equally accurate in observing that Ralph Smith's real importance for British Columbia, and indeed for Canada, lay in his representation of "a trend of reformism that has too often been ignored."[179] Liberal-labourism, in whatever proportion the balance lay, was a critical component in the evolution of parliamentary democracy and, as Craig Heron has persuasively argued, of "trying to keep alive the legacy of 'liberty, equality, and fraternity.'"[180] So too, if commonly forgotten, was liberal-feminism, for which Mary Ellen was British Columbia's pioneering legislator. Ultimately, however, the "limited nature of Liberal sympathy for democracy" in both Britain and Canada curtailed alliances with organized labour and feminists.[181]

Many commemorations singled out Ralph's partner in life and politics. A Vancouver writer emphasized her loyalty and assistance as "one of the beautiful chapters in the history of this province."[182] The Conservative-leaning *Vancouver Province* saluted her as "a constant helpmate" and "a gracious hostess on many public and private occasions." Her husband's pride "found expression in many playful allusions from the public platform as well as in myriad tendernesses in private."[183] The *Victoria Times* identified "a woman of great talent as a thinker and speaker ... especially in relation to women's rights and the suffrage."[184] The *Vancouver World* acknowledged her as "one of the best known leaders of the greater women's organizations in Canada."[185] Readers might well have wondered about the future of this paragon. Mary Ellen, still hailed as Mrs. Ralph Smith, would soon answer.

5
Independent Liberal Lady? 1917–20

By 1917, in the midst of a war that left over sixty thousand Canadian dead in a population of fewer than 5 million, Canadians were at fisticuffs over conscription, war profiteering, the Union government, prohibition, post-war re-establishment, feminism, and much else. Reformers and reactionaries alike were shaken by the Russian Revolution of 1917, the influenza pandemic of 1918–19, with its Canadian death toll of some fifty thousand, massive demobilization after the November 1918 Armistice, and the 1918–19 wave of general strikes. Against that deeply unsettled backdrop, Mary Ellen Spear Smith entered the BC legislature.

A "World Aflame": British Columbia and Canada

The blood and mud of the First World War has been hailed as forging Canada and Newfoundland, but it was equally powerful in fostering division, that between French and English Canadians being only the most obvious. Newspapers and magazines filled with the names of dead, missing, and wounded and crowded with battles lost and won fired emotions and tempers. People lived daily with war's terrible toll. In February 1917, Lieutenant Jack Smith was unable to attend his father's funeral, kept away by injuries that turned out to be lasting. In October 1918, Mary Ellen's nephew, Lieutenant Reginald Gordon Spear (c. 1895–1918) of the Forty-Sixth, known as the "Suicide," Battalion, died of his wounds in France. Like other Canadians, British Columbians did not share equally when it came to hardship, and the aftermath of the war did not alter that brutal reality. In attempting to realize her hopes for a better world, Mary Ellen walked a political minefield.

By 1917, the Canadian economy was booming due to wartime demands. As in previous and future economic cycles, this meant riches for a few and tough times for many. In terms of purchasing power, real wages peaked in 1915, bottomed out between 1919 and 1920, and then rose until 1924.[1] Inflation undercut gains, and federal fuel and food controllers had limited effect. In 1917, the average increase in the cost-of-living index hit 17.9 percent.[2] Bosses blamed unions and wages, while workers blamed monopolies and profiteers. Everyone denounced middle-men.[3] Misogynists upbraided modern women, supposedly addicted to trivial pursuits, and housewives were urged to join the front line in monitoring prices, conservation, and consumption. Feminists challenged new voters to heal an injured world. In the midst of turmoil, maternal activists could sometimes "claim political space and justify behavior that would otherwise be regarded as transgressive."[4]

Women's free labour in initiatives such as the Canadian Patriotic Fund, the Red Cross, the YWCA, the NCWC, and the Women's Institutes enabled inexperienced and overburdened governments to manage the war. Families at home and servicemen and nurses overseas depended on their fundraising, including major war bond campaigns, and voluntary organization of food, clothing, and goods.[5] As Canada tried to maximize productivity and recruiting, responsibilities for planting, harvesting, and livestock fell increasingly to girls and women. Like those elsewhere, many Vancouver students and other young women became "farmerettes" for seasonal crops in the Fraser and Okanagan Valleys.[6] Others served as military nurses or took jobs in finance, industry, the professions, and retail. Many fled domestic service for a better life. Whatever the contribution, women's toil outside homes raised fears of social breakdown, unanchored men, and delinquent offspring.

Female workers, with the exception of nurses, did not appear in chauvinistic propaganda that featured women as "practical patriots," "soldiers of the kitchen," all-sacrificing mothers and wives, and "moral guardians of society."[7] Better baby contests still overseen by women's clubs and occasionally judged by Mary Ellen told the same story. Students at Vancouver's all-male Technical School typically encountered courses and instructors who took for granted that men were the rightful "worker-citizens" and women no better than interlopers in the labour market.[8] In the same spirit, feminism's claim to equality was routinely trivialized.

In many minds, only domesticated womanhood could ensure social stability for the family and the nation. Mary Ellen's determined promotion of the revolutionary doctrine that economic inequality fuelled "conflict between men workers and women workers" faced fierce opposition.[9]

Other quarrels also festered. Unemployment spurred xenophobia about residents whose origins lay in enemy countries and Asia. With demobilization, veterans' and workers' groups dominated by the British- and Canadian-born demanded preferment. As they faced bosses eager to cut wages, organized labour and the left blamed capitalists for putting profits before respectable male workers.[10] The July 1918 shooting of BC socialist and anti-conscription miner Ginger Goodwin by the Dominion Police conjured up class war.[11] The August 1917 introduction of a federal income tax that terrified the rich, without offering them much serious hurt, incensed "those who had called for conscription of wealth and equality of sacrifice."[12]

The Spanish flu further diminished public confidence. Some four thousand BC victims highlighted community deficits. Vulnerable paid, but more often unpaid, female caregivers worked on the front line just as they would in the COVID-19 pandemic little more than a century later. Like injured veterans, flu victims spurred demands for health and welfare reform.[13] Mary Ellen visited ravaged homes and linked the suffering to low wages and inequality in general.[14] Popular anger grew as governments failed to control profiteering or prices while wages and working conditions deteriorated. Strikes in Vancouver, Victoria, and Prince Rupert, often in sympathy with the 1919 Winnipeg General Strike, drew on commonplace frustration.[15] Challenges to the status quo in turn produced blowback from self-proclaimed patriots. Vancouver strikers out for justice went toe to toe with Union Jack–wearing Citizens' League defenders of the status quo in business and government.[16]

Women stood on both sides of the confrontations. One "Plain Working Woman" told *Vancouver World* readers that "labor is now trying to overthrow the tyrannical dollar, and put life in its place."[17] A feminist, later an Independent candidate in the 1920 BC election, disagreed: "I am a strong believer in unionized labor and I do know that better wages, better working conditions and shorter hours are brought about through their organizations ... steady, constructive means ... But the leaders here seem keen to destroy all that labor has accomplished and bring about chaos."[18] The Vancouver LCW rejected general strikes as acceptable remedies to admitted ills, and the visiting Emmeline Pankhurst warned that Bolshevism, "class war," and strikes menaced democracy.[19] Mary Ellen pointed out that men had fought for "democracy, right and truthfulness" and thus expected "a more equal distribution of the good things of life."[20] Post-war reconstruction had brought a reckoning. In a climate of "strikes, lock-outs, [and] bickerings," female voters would, she anticipated, inject "real balance" into industrial life.[21]

Canadians generally agreed that the organization of capital and labour was in tatters. The federal Royal Commission on Industrial Relations, created in April 1919 and popularly known as the Mathers Commission, proposed collective bargaining and industrial democracy, as did the Canadian Women's War Conference in March. So too did the September 1919 National Industrial Conference, applauded by Smith as "momentous."[22] *The World Aflame*, a popular American feature "photoplay" viewed by union, business, and political attendees at the latter conference, linked anxious Canadians to global industrial unrest, even as it relied on a stale fantasy of a heroic businessman with a daughter romantically involved with a worker.[23] While her feelings about the film itself are unknown, Mary Ellen too trusted in prospects for capital-labour cooperation. Such optimism would be hard put to survive the savage anti-unionism of the post-war decade.

In these unquiet years, returning soldiers supplied an additional volatile element.[24] Many veterans, welcomed "with flag-waving and speeches full of promises, soon felt a deep sense of rejection."[25] Their associations, variously opposing and supporting labour or business, and, still more, prospects of soldiers' parties unsettled political calculations at every level. As governments faltered, women, like "fatherhood and employment," were expected to "decontaminate" and "resocialize" men trained in warfare.[26] That pressing duty easily stole the stage from women's rights.

Elections mirrored divisions. Pro-reform Liberals won the BC contest in the autumn of 1916, but they soon split over remedies for social and economic tragedies, and the government faced charges of corruption and patronage. Federally, the December 1917 so-called khaki election, judged the most bitter in Canadian history, proved a battle royal. Tory prime minister Robert L. Borden went to the country with a Unionist coalition (formed in October 1917) that included a powerful crew of pro-conscription Liberals (known as Liberal-Unionists). Laurier rallied followers, notably but not only in Quebec, who feared that compulsory mobilization would split the country. Before election day, Borden stacked the deck by passing the Military Voters Act and the Wartime Elections Act. This legislation allowed the overseas military vote to be distributed in a way that favoured the government; disenfranchised numerous citizens, notably conscientious objectors and many voters with origins in now enemy countries; and enfranchised close female relatives of servicemen, who were assumed likely to support conscription. Borden won the election with 56.93 percent of the popular vote and 153 of 235 seats. Eight-five Liberals were returned, sixty-two of them from Quebec. British Columbia returned no Liberal MPs, and Labour was shut out entirely. The quick introduction of military conscription confirmed divisions. Feminist suspicions about a Borden-led administration that had long opposed women's enfranchisement (as indeed had the earlier Laurier regime) centred on the Wartime Elections Act, which was widely viewed as no more than a cynical effort to manipulate women in aid of the Conservative Party.[27]

In the aftermath of the federal election, unhappy voters in British Columbia and Canada condemned partyism and reviewed the remedies of non-partisanship, recall, and proportional voting long proposed by would-be reformers of the parliamentary system, including the Smiths.[28] Many feminists credited women's groups, such as the NCWC, the IODE, the WCC, and the Women's Institutes, with the potential to cleanse politics, even as they feared their manipulation by political parties (as with the Wartime Elections Act), their frequent earlier failure to prioritize suffrage, and the absence among their ranks of representatives from "women in industry."[29] Everyone waited to see whether women's clubs would mobilize female voters as a new political force. Some observers saw a portent of the future in the June 1917 victory of Louise McKinney (1868–1931) of the Non-Partisan League in Alberta's provincial election, the first in which women could vote. Would that WCTU veteran, the first woman elected to any Canadian legislature, usher in a new era of parliamentary reform? *Everywoman's World* saluted McKinney's "non-partisanship." Here were both "the type of woman by whom other women wish to be represented" and "opposition to the giant evils that have grown up under the party system."[30] *Maclean's Magazine* prophesied that "political 'heelers,'" (a commonplace term for corrupt and sycophantic politicians and their followers) would at long last receive "a cool reception."[31] In October 1917, *Everywoman's World* featured Nellie McClung, Canada's "most representative woman," rejecting all parties in favour of a principled non-partisanship that would rescue the nation.[32]

In the midst of their own turmoil, Canadians tried to make sense of the world's slow march to female enfranchisement. Britain's December 1918 election, the first in which women (over age thirty) could vote, was scrutinized as it returned a Liberal-Conservative coalition under Liberal Lloyd

George and one female candidate, Constance Markievicz (1868–1927), a champion of Irish independence from Sinn Féin, the Irish republican and social democratic party. In a foretaste of Canadian experience, political parties urged British women "to vote as proxies for their male relatives, and their own wartime experiences were largely marginalized."[33] Asked to comment on the UK election, Vancouver's female leaders ignored the successful Sinn Féiner but revealed much about their own hopes and fears. The president of the New Era League emphasized the "injustice" of the failure to elect more women, women's lack of experience in politics, and men's lack of appreciation of women's contributions. Juvenile Court judge Helen Gregory MacGill observed a British electorate unwilling to abandon parties. The visiting president of the Winnipeg Women's Civic Forum argued that voters "want nothing of the old parties or the new sectionalism, pacifism nor Bolsheviki tendencies of the labor party" and attributed the Liberal-Conservative coalition victory to the support of Pankhurst's Women's Party.[34] The president of the Women's Conservative Association credited new voters with "common sense," but the LCW president saw better prospects for women achieving gains through their own organizations' pressure on politicians. For her part, Smith deplored British conservativism and indifference to women's "heroism and sacrifice" while praising Lloyd George as an "anti-Bolshevist" who had "a programme of sane, sound reconstruction."[35]

The United States provided other opportunities for reflection on women's political future. Although Montana elected suffragist Jeannette Rankin (1880–1973) as the first woman to the House of Representatives in 1916 and the national Nineteenth Amendment on women's right to vote was ratified in 1920, the broad-ranging Equal Rights Amendment, first proposed in 1923, remains unratified in 2021. Internationally, President Woodrow Wilson refused to approve female enfranchisement as part of a post-war settlement, and the League of Nations, after its founding in 1919, did not require it of member states. The Canadian press's regular updating on franchise struggles around the world left little doubt that the battle for equality was unfinished. This troubled landscape set the stage for Mary Ellen's campaigns in 1917 and 1918.

The 1917 Federal Election

New and excluded female voters stood near the centre of the 1917 federal contest. Feminists broke ranks over the Wartime Elections Act, Union government, and conscription, ending a fragile politics of cooperation in the Great Cause and the war effort in general.[36] Mary Ellen once more sought common ground. Within days of Ralph's death, she communicated that message to the Vancouver Women's Building broad-based board of directors. By April, she had succeeded Lady Tupper as regent of the Vancouver IODE.[37] Everywhere she stressed "unity and the burying of bitterness and controversial feeling in order that all may do their utmost to win the gigantic struggle for the Allies."[38]

British Columbia's April 1917 enfranchisement was widely understood to mean that women (at least Whites) would vote on the same terms as men and that they would be a force in the upcoming federal election. As an executive member of the Women's Liberal Association and the IODE, Mary Ellen pushed resolutions that demanded both the conscription of wealth and the selective conscription of men.[39] Until the fall of 1917, she joined Conservative and Liberal speakers in officially non-partisan win-the-war rallies.[40] Her campaign attacks on the Hun and anti-conscription Quebecers made her virtually indistinguishable from Unionist Liberals and Conservatives.[41] During a gathering of two thousand women at Vancouver's Orpheum Theatre, described as "cast[ing] to the winds all creeds, all political and social barriers," she attacked military "slackers" and "speculators who reaped profits at the price of blood."[42] Mary Ellen next stood with Conservative Opposition leader William John Bowser and leading Liberals during a mass meeting at the city's Horse Show Building, where the audience cheered her demand for "the conscription of man-power, the conscription of wealth and the conscription of woman-power."[43] The *BC Federationist* condemned the speakers for illogic and hysteria but spared Smith, whom it commended for suggesting that "we should do our duty as we see it, and not as others want us to do it."[44] In September, she joined old friend Nicholas Thompson as a delegate sent by the Vancouver Win-the-War Committee to a mass meeting at the capital's Royal Victoria Theatre.[45] By then, even the new premier, Brewster, was reported as a possible candidate for Borden's Union government.[46] Canadian Liberals grappled with hard choices as they watched their British counterparts form a wartime Coalition government, which included Conservatives and representatives of the Parliamentary Labour Party, in 1915.[47]

Ultimately, however, old loyalties held firm for Mary Ellen, as they did for Brewster. In August 1917, she was selected as a delegate to the Winnipeg conference of western Liberals (though she failed to attend), which endorsed Laurier.[48] Her friendship with Zoe and Wilfrid, as well as her trust in Canadianization for assimilating non-British settlers from Europe, kept her at odds with Conservatives. Addressing a local primary school with a multicultural student body, she declared that "all nationalities" would vote to keep Canada "the best country."[49] She remained deeply suspicious of the Wartime Elections Act's disenfranchisement of so-called enemy aliens, seeing it as no more than a ploy to steal votes from Laurier.[50] More influential still was her opposition, like that of most BC suffragists, to its restricted female franchise, proof positive of Conservative iniquity.[51] Smith first paraded her final colours far from British Columbia. In October 1917, she attended Ottawa conferences on welfare, tuberculosis, and public health; addressed the Ottawa Women's Club and the Montreal Political Educational League; and renewed partisan friendships.[52] Liberal election rallies heard her express "indignation that women born under the Union Jack should be numbered with the aliens." She nevertheless presented herself as a supporter of the citizenship and voting rights of loyal foreigners.[53] Why, she asked, was Borden failing democracy when "the boys in the trenches are fighting for the rights of people individually and collectively ... fighting for the individual rights of the women as well as the men"?[54] She insisted that "no one party and no one section had any monopoly on wanting to win the war."[55] Although some Vancouver observers still counted her as a Unionist mere days before the election, the orthodox *Canadian Annual Review* stated that she was a rare woman among the Laurier Liberals.[56] In fact, there were many. One Toronto feminist applauded such partisans for *Everywoman's World,* and when that ambitious periodical polled readers "of every class and rank, and in every part of the country," it declared that "conscription is defeated!" by six to one.[57] Also notable was the refusal of the Vancouver LCW, dominated by Liberals, to endorse the Union government and everything it represented in terms of Conservative opposition to women's rights and more progressive politics in general.[58]

When British Columbia returned only Tories in the 1917 election, Grits went into a tailspin much like that of Bowser's Conservatives after their 1916 provincial defeat. Political rage, combined with daily reports of war casualties and profiteering, fed pervasive disillusionment with the status quo. The *Vancouver World* condemned all "political machines" as selfish, "vicious," and indifferent to the era's "new conscience." It concluded that women were especially disenchanted.[59] They in turn had plentiful company in returning soldiers and labour activists.[60]

The 1918 By-Election

Within days of Ralph's death, Vancouver seethed with gossip about who would replace him in the necessary by-election. The *Province* found early interest in a female contender but little in a "woman's party." The president of the Women's Conservative Association called for a "compromise candidate," whereas her counterpart with the Mount Pleasant Suffrage League favoured a non-partisan woman "to bring in a great deal of legislation on behalf of women."[61] At the grassroots, "thousands and thousands of Vancouver women" registered as voters.[62] In December 1917, the *Victoria Colonist* reported that women now made up at least eighteen thousand of the forty-four thousand names on the new voters' list.[63] The stage seemed set for a history-making changing of the guard in political life.

For months, Mary Ellen appeared to be headed for the Liberal nomination. The way, however, was not straightforward. Worried as he was about attracting female voters, Premier Brewster was beset by bitter party divisions and corruption scandals that made him nervous about political innovation that might undermine allegiance.[64] Like many in his and other parties, he wanted female support without having to sacrifice male candidates or domination of policy. New voters were preferably assimilated into existing organizations to serve as effective handmaidens to male politicians. Men determined to hang on to power were not the only advocates of defanging female challengers. In March 1917, Brewster's ally Evlyn Farris demonstrated determination to keep her sex in line when she instructed the Nanaimo WLA to affiliate with the local Liberal men's group. An independent "woman's association" was not the future she preferred.[65] In May, Vancouver Liberals patted themselves on the back for including "some of the strongest and oldest suffragists in the city, whose political skill, clever speaking and devoted service have been a source of strength to us," and they applauded McClung's rejection of a woman's party.[66] Many women Liberals nevertheless wished to seize the moment for greater independence. In June 1917, the Vancouver WLA nominated Mary Ellen, with Judge Helen Gregory MacGill seconding the nomination, on the very day that it unanimously adopted Smith's resolution demanding "selective conscription of men" and of the "wealth, money and resources, labor and service of every man and woman" so that "all may equally do their duty."[67] Its initiative was paramount in placing Mary Ellen on the Liberal ticket in the forthcoming by-election.

Soon, however, the battles of the federal election campaign overtook the WLA nomination. By October 1917, during a trip to Ontario, Mary

Why Not a Woman and an Independent?

There are 46 men representatives in the Legislature, Liberals and Conservatives.

Twelve of them are lawyers, five are doctors, four are soldiers.

Between them they look after the interests of the Liberals, the Conservatives, the lawyers and doctors and soldiers.

There is no woman representative and no independent in the Legislature.

Why not a woman, and an independent at that?

MRS. RALPH SMITH
Independent candidate representing the enfranchised women and the independents of the city of Vancouver

TONIGHT

Hear Mrs. Ralph Smith at Orange Hall, corner of Gore Avenue and Hastings Street

Chairman—EX-ALD. JAMES RAMSAY

Speakers—Mr. G. Roy Long, Mrs. J. W. Bryan and Mrs. Ralph Smith

Also Big Meetings in the Labor Temple on Saturday Night — Speakers to be announced later

"Why Not a Woman and an Independent?" *Vancouver Province*, January 18, 1918; *Vancouver Sun*, January 18, 1918.

Ellen was signalling ambitions, reported in the Vancouver press, that reflected widespread disillusionment with partisan politics, not to mention the divisions among Liberals.[68] Asked about running as a straight Liberal, she responded,

> Personally, I don't feel perfection lies with either party, and while I am a good Liberal, I feel that there may be times when I may not see eye to eye with the leaders of the party, and I should want to feel free to act according to my convictions ... I was fortunate in having a husband who was quite sure of his principles all the time, and I've had no reason to doubt his wisdom, but I know that when I run there will be many Conservatives among my supporters – men and women who want to see the provinces made right for the women and children.[69]

A non-partisan ticket, reminiscent of Ralph's Lib-Lab search for cross-class alignment, corresponded to the sentiments reported in a survey by the Saskatchewan Equal Franchise League. Asking "well-known Canadian women" about their political affiliation, it found that most, including McClung, preferred non-partisanship.[70] By the end of 1917, such sentiments prompted a *Vancouver Sun* editorialist to recommend that all parties accept Mary Ellen's acclamation in the by-election.[71]

When he heard of Smith's intention to run as an Independent, John Wallace de Beque Farris, Vancouver's Liberal "godfather," was nonplussed:

> Well, it certainly does take a woman to start something ... I would find it personally very difficult to oppose Mrs. Smith. If Mrs. Smith had sought and received the endorsement of the party in the regular way my support of her would have been unquestioned. The course which she has adopted, however, makes the situation, to say the least, somewhat unusual.

The Liberal government deserved better: after all, it had enfranchised women, legislated equal guardianship of children, and appointed a female superintendent to the Girls' Industrial School and a female Juvenile Court judge (Smith's formidable ally, Helen Gregory MacGill).[72] Farris was nevertheless later confident enough to reassure Chilliwack Liberals that after "Mrs. Ralph Smith has talked to them in her independent-with-Liberal-tendency-spirit, the fair sex will know how to vote."[73] In his posh home, hostility was more evident. Evlyn spurned any hint of a "woman's party" as "contrary to the idea of the family, the foundation of the state."[74] Whereas magistrate MacGill told Bowser that she endorsed Mary Ellen,

Mrs. Farris detected a trespasser in a "male arena," someone with too much self-regard and too committed to feminism.[75]

In early January 1918, the unrepentant Smith unleashed her platform as a "free woman," a loaded term in the liberal, and larger political, lexicon.[76] Targeting dissident voters, she presented independence as the antidote to a fractured political culture in need of new blood. She told electors,

> My late husband and myself had common ideas of political reform. I could have no higher idea of service now ... My life has been spent in doing what I could for the communities in which I have lived; the highest opportunity for service is in the legislature, where the reforms we talk of can be crystallized into law ... [I am] going to Victoria as a free woman ... I stand as an Independent – independent of both parties – believing that women can best serve their own and the public welfare by not allying themselves with either side.

Her first plank was a "minimum living wage for women workers," and the remainder, with the addition of a plank for veterans, similarly invoked an agenda straight from the pre-war women's movement.[77] British Columbia's leading labour newspaper, the *BC Federationist*, immediately acknowledged "one of the foremost and energetic workers for woman suffrage during the past twenty years" but cautioned about overestimating the power of a single MLA. Much public education was needed, and workers would do better to put their faith in the Minimum Wage League.[78] The province's leading feminist weekly jumped in equally quickly but without reservations about Mary Ellen:

> We are proud to endorse her, first for herself, as she is first, last and always a woman. Secondly, because she is a woman who will make a capable representative, as she has always stood for her sex and tried to raise the standard of citizenship. She is pre-eminently fitted for such a position, having shared her husband's experience in public life in this Province for over twenty years, thus gaining a knowledge of public affairs that few women have been privileged to enjoy.[79]

A week later, it added that veterans had less claim than women to Ralph's old seat and suggested that the Great War Veterans' Association (GWVA), whose president became Mary Ellen's chief opponent in the by-election, was little more than a stooge for the Bowser Tories.[80]

With the New Year, the campaign heated up. Describing herself as a "people's candidate," Mary Ellen denied that she was a stalking horse

Electors, Attention!

Have the women done their part in this war? Mrs. Ralph Smith gives the electors of Vancouver the first opportunity to recognize the women. Read carefully Mrs. Smith's announcement and platform.

To the Electors of Vancouver:

Some six months ago I was approached by leading citizens and asked to run in the forthcoming provincial election, either as an independent or as a People's candidate. At that time I was not sure whether I would run or not, so waived the question, as there was not an immediate election in sight. Since then I have been frequently asked the same question, and now when the time for a decision has come my answer is "Yes." My husband and myself had our own ideas of reforms, and possibly I could not have any higher idea of service to the people I have lived amongst for over a quarter of a century than to take his seat, providing the people want me. My life has been spent in trying to do what little I could for the communities I have lived in and the last and highest place is where one can get legislation to put into force reforms long talked of but still waiting realization. Women have been enfranchised and I feel I can best serve the people (if elected) by going to Victoria a "free woman," doing my best to secure the best possible legislation for women and children and supporting to the best of my ability any good measures that may be introduced in the best interests of the province, by whomsoever introduced. I have the time and opportunity to devote to such a cause, and if the platform below appeals to the electorate and they decide on election day that I am to be their representative, I ask no greater honor at their hands.

I have many friends, for which I am thankful, and if they feel they can conscientiously support me I shall be gratified, because by so doing they give me the chance to work for what I have long believed in and think a necessity to the happiness and well being of the people of this province.

I stand as an independent and am independent of both parties, believing that women can best serve by not being allied with either side, and the support of any and all friends I shall be glad to have, and will try as far as is humanly possible to discharge my duties faithfully if I am the choice of the people on January 24.

Following are some of the principles which I shall strive for:

1. Minimum living wage for women workers.
2. Supervision of workshops and factories to ensure healthful conditions for women and girls.
3. Equal pay for women with men for equal work.
4. Pensions for dependent mothers.
5. Education and reform of juvenile delinquents.
6. Organized assistance to enable returned soldiers to become agricultural settlers or to acquire training for technical careers.
7. The bringing into force of the Civil Service Act with provision for enabling invalided war veterans to qualify for indoor positions in the civil service.
8. Proportional representation for multiple constituencies.
9. Strict enforcement of the Prohibition Act with necessary amendments.
10. Provision of an adequate system of technical training to fit young men and women for vocational work.

"Electors, Attention!" | "To the Electors of Vancouver," *Vancouver Sun*, January 6, 1918.

for the Liberal Party, declaring, "as far as Mr. Brewster and Mr. Bowser are concerned, neither 'B' makes any difference to me ... I shall, despite my liberal training and tendencies, support whatever good measures come before the legislature without regard" to party.[81] City newspapers ran quarter-page ads, featuring her photograph and the question "Why Not a Woman and an Independent?" These explained her victory would offset forty-six male MLAs, including twelve lawyers, five doctors, and four soldiers.

A journalist captured the disorder of BC Liberals abashed by Smith's momentum:

> Like Caesar's Gaul, the Liberal party in this city is divided into three parts, which parts more or less overlap. First of all there are the old-line Liberals, who are Liberals first, last and always ... [who] last month cheerfully immolated themselves on the party altar in the federal election. Then there is the reform section, the men who demanded a clean party or no party at all ... There are also the Unionist Liberals, some of whom separated themselves from the old-line Liberals, while the rest consisted of the other wing, who went over to the Unionist cause by a very large majority ... The problem of the government supporters is to get all these factions together and also to secure the allegiance of the women Liberals who are inclined to favor Mrs. Ralph Smith.[82]

Nor were left-leaning Liberals necessarily onside. James Conley (c. 1875–1950), a former president of the BC Progressive Club and member of the party's Provincial Executive spied a corrupt cabal hiding behind Smith's skirts.[83] Other objections were voiced by long-time party maverick and former premier Joseph Martin. Now a British MP (1910–18) and perhaps anticipating Lady Astor's run for her husband's UK parliamentary seat in 1919, he suggested that transferring a man's position to his wife was reminiscent of aristocratic privilege. Attorney General Farris agreed that Smith ought to run as a Liberal but reckoned it best not to enter a government candidate against her. She could attract a broad swathe of liberal-minded voters, without offering a focus for discussion of government scandals.[84] Ultimately, Liberals and Conservatives of both sexes sat on Smith's campaign committees, a testament to political pragmatism, if not feminism.[85]

Meanwhile, female activists had their own disagreements. Buoyed by the recent federal victory, some Unionists considered intervening in the by-election. An early January 1918 gathering wanted "either another lady or a returned soldier," a "fusion" candidate, not a suffragist who was dismissed as a closet supporter of the provincial government.[86] Ultimately, the group decided to stick to federal matters,[87] but some champions of Borden's Union government, such as suffragist Janet Kemp, president of the Mainland Association of Wives and Mothers of Soldiers and Sailors, insisted on opposition to Smith, preferably by a soldier, "one who has been over the top and has been wounded." If such a candidate was not forthcoming, Kemp threatened to be her group's nominee and was further supported by the Wives, Widows and Mothers of British Heroes Association.[88] Irene Hakwins Moody (1879–1958), the Unionist sympathizer and chair of the Vancouver School Board, was canvassed for candidacy but declined.[89] Provincial Conservatives were similarly at odds, with many concluding that opposing British Columbia's first female candidate "would be a tactical error."[90] Bowser, now the leader of the official Opposition, faced his own divided female partisans: some maintained suffragist loyalties to Smith, whereas others condemned her as a Laurierite. Many scorned conventional candidates, preferring a veteran or a patriotic woman.[91] Bowser sought a solution that would not enflame divisions nor cast his party as out of sync with demands for a better politics.

Veterans who eyed the seat were also fractured. Early to appear was Sergeant-Major James Robinson (c. 1855–1933), DCM, who proposed to run as an "independent returned soldier candidate" and a critic of Brewster's policy on veterans.[92] The Comrades of the Great War, allied to the Vancouver TLC, nominated its own president, former private R.H. Young.[93] Labour voters were denied a more familiar alternative when W.A. Pritchard (1888–1981), defeated in the 1917 federal election as a socialist, failed to file his nomination papers in time.[94] Ultimately, Sergeant Walter Drinnan (c. 1877–1949), president of the local GWVA, became the main military, and effectively the Unionist/Conservative, candidate.[95]

The open convention that chose Drinnan was "the first in which the ladies had taken part as voters in their own right."[96] They constituted about half of delegates, many from the Mainland Association of Wives and Mothers of Soldiers and Sailors and the Wives, the Widows and Mothers of British Heroes Association. Equally revealing was the presence of longtime anti-suffragist Clare FitzGibbon (1862–1933), better known as the journalist Lally Bernard. An imperialist and leader of the recently established Good Government League, she claimed that women's war work and "the thrill of pride with which she discovered her name on the voters' list" had converted her to the franchise. She demanded that women forego partisanship and be "guided" by the GWVA.[97] Drinnan took the high road, assuring the convention "that he would always remember that Mrs. Smith was a lady and the mother of one of his comrades." Robinson conceded the field but not without knocking Mary Ellen for "basking in the sunny smiles of Sir Wilfrid Laurier."[98] Elsewhere, she was accused of "fox-trotting," effectively flirting with, conscription and being an improper choice for military families.[99] She was even charged with accepting money to defray Ralph's funeral costs and from the scandal-ridden Pacific Great Eastern Railway.[100]

The "free woman" proved no pushover. Her campaign posters hammered unrepresentative government, a long-standing left liberal leitmotif. In targeting gender, she extended the claims for democracy.[101] A large Labor Temple rally enjoyed her laceration of the "demagogic" Clare Fitz-Gibbon. Claiming the support of many women's groups, Smith declared that women "had not asked for the franchise for the purpose of voting and letting it end there, but to send their own representatives to ask for better laws for women and children." She dealt deftly with Drinnan: "I am not against the returned soldier. Would I be against my own flesh and blood and relations? Women who stayed behind have gone over the top, too, I tell you. And it is the women who have been over the top and who would have given their own sons willingly had they had them." In short, women were as meritorious as veterans.[102] At the Finnish Hall, Smith continued her attacks. Rejecting FitzGibbon's charge that she was anti-soldier and that her platform was outdated, she presented the minimum wage as a cure for "the antagonism that exists between the sexes today."[103] She lauded mothers' pensions as "women's magna carta."[104] Why shouldn't the government "bear some of the cost of bringing up and educating children that the mothers have borne for the benefit of the state?" "Feeble-minded children" similarly required action. Like soldiers, new voters would benefit from a "woman's viewpoint" in the legislature. Claiming that Toronto newspapers had misrepresented her arguments, she insisted "that any alien who was not fit to vote should be interned and put on the land to produce foodstuffs." Finally, she rejected Oriental immigrants and stated that she had never had "any dealings with one in a quarter of a century in British Columbia," a comment that, if true, testified to Nanaimo and Vancouver's pervasive segregation.[105]

An audience of some two thousand at the Hotel Vancouver saw Mary Ellen flanked by the city's progressive elite. A Methodist minister who "handled" Conservatives "without gloves" came to her defence: she was a "splendid specimen of cultured, capable, high-minded womanhood in the public and private life of this province" and a "noble" mother,

Mary Ellen Smith, New Year, 1918. This rare headshot portrait of Mary Ellen Smith, which presents her as both decorous and feminine, was likely commissioned for her candidacy in the 1918 by-election. AM427-54, 289-046, City of Vancouver Archives.

"abundantly capable of looking after the best interest of the men who have fought and bled alongside her own sons [sic] in the trenches of Europe." Mary Ellen next renewed her attack on FitzGibbon and the Good Government League, denying claims that she had used women's groups as "stepping stones" to power.[106] She threatened to launch legal proceedings against the "canard that she had received $25,000 from the Pacific Great Eastern Railway for her campaign" and relished the applause greeting her declaration that "no corporation, nor party, has any strings on me." Women in politics would ensure that "those who make statements have got to produce the goods or apologize."[107]

Mary Ellen's oratory was supported by a quarter-page *Vancouver Sun* advertisement from the United Suffrage Societies. Stressing the long struggle for the vote, it condemned FitzGibbon as "a persistent opponent of reforms." No one had fought harder, "longer or more consistently than Mrs. Ralph Smith, whose name is a household word for her service for social and political reform." The United Suffrage Societies rejected the Good Government League's right to "speak in the name of or advise" women.[108] In response, a league ad depicted Mary Ellen as a tool of "Laurier, the arch-enemy of conscription," with a platform "stolen from the different women's organizations she has used for her own advancement." It declared "our women's cause [is] safer in the hands of Sergt. Drinnan, and the men he represents."[109]

On the eve of the by-election, after "one of the keenest campaigns in the history of Vancouver politics," the *Vancouver Sun* predicted Smith's victory:

> She has been as ready in attack and defence as any of the male candidates of past campaigns. The opposition has not been held in check in the least by reason of a woman being in the field. Nor has Mrs. Smith asked for any consideration on account of her sex. She has explained that as the women now have equal rights with the men, they must expect to fight their own political battles against or with the men, and neither ask nor expect quarter. And such has been her course while the male politicians favorable to her have asked and been refused by the privilege of going upon the platform and fighting for her ... She has made a valiant and splendid fight against the best efforts of the old Bowser machine.

The *Sun* dismissed Walter Drinnan as little more than a dupe of the Conservatives, many of whom were predicted to vote for Smith.[110] The final count gave 9,356 ballots (and all eight wards) to Smith, 6,112 to Drinnan, and 467 to the candidate for the Comrades of the Great War.[111] The result was both personal endorsement and proof of "the impatience of the electors with the old-line party leaders and organizations."[112]

Smith's victory, like those of Louise McKinney and Roberta MacAdams (1880–1959) in Alberta in 1917, prompted the *Toronto Globe* to spy a new politics: "These women members of Parliament did not abuse opponents, but only the bad customs that have debauched the political life of Canada for generations ... They have trusted the people, and their faith has been justified."[113] In Vancouver, the by-election victor was welcomed. As Ralph's partner, she was no neophyte: the *Vancouver Sun* pronounced that "she will be thoroughly at home in the local legislature."[114] Some

WOMEN IN PUBLIC LIFE

It is going to make an awful lot more work for the staff.

"Women in Public Life," *Vancouver Province,* January 16, 1918.

observers could not resist making attempts at wit. The *Grand Forks Sun and Kettle Valley Orchardist* observed, "She has the reputation of being an eloquent speaker. Being a woman, this is, of course, a[n] inherited gift and not an acquired art."[115] The *Vancouver Province* cartoon "Women in Public Life" revealed a similar discomfort in welcoming newcomers to the political stage.

BC suffragists, however, left no doubt of their elation. Campaign volunteers presented Mary Ellen with a "gold medal held on a diamond bar bin" and spoke confidently of

> a great victory for the women of Vancouver, as we have proved beyond a doubt that an intelligent public, backed by the power of the ballot, can have anything they want ... We are fortunate in having as our representative, a woman so well versed in the political affairs of Canada, both provincial and dominion. A knowledge of this kind does not come by inspiration but by deep study, and our member has worked for woman's freedom for very many years; she has left the beaten path and blazed the trail. We believe that the woman's point of view will be of great help in solving the problems that confront our members at the present time.

They recalled a bitter past when suffragists who met "gibe[s] and jest[s]" from legislators had nevertheless persevered in

> studying conditions and investigating the true state of affairs, and we came to the conclusion that we would do everything in our power to put an end to this injustice and gain a franchise ... This was only British justice. Now we have attained our object, and there is this difference between those who opposed us so bitterly and ourselves – that they are going and we are coming. In fact, we are here now.[116]

James Hawthornthwaite, Ralph's old foe and the Socialist Party of Canada winner in a Vancouver Island by-election held at the same time, joined Helena Gutteridge, president of the Minimum Wage League, and Susie Lane Clark, president of the New Era League, to toast Smith as long "working in the interests of labor." Clark, reported as "rather grim in her mention of men," declared that "the question of women today was as great as the returned soldier question or any other problem."[117] She told *Sun* readers that "we are only on the threshold of great things" and that women would at last find the province "a safe, good place to live in, move in, and have their being in."[118] The irrepressible Mary Ellen heartened supporters by claiming a future in which "she would be able to help to better conditions for women and girls ... the dream of herself and her late husband."[119]

In Victoria, suffragists led the celebration. The LCW presented the new MLA "with a handsome floral ship covered with white carnations and violets." The idea for the ship dated from some two decades earlier, when it was intended as a gift to the premier who introduced suffrage.[120] Maria Grant, chair of the Victoria LCW Citizenship Committee, presented it to Mary Ellen in honour of the "truly wonderful realization of our dream, our hopes and our labors of the past 32 years."[121] For all such exuberance, hostility was never far away. Less than two months later, Hawthornthwaite disparaged "old women" and "pink tea artists," terms of sexist opprobrium with respect to women's age and preference for meeting over tea rather than alcoholic, or more manly, degustation, who were trying "to make people good by act of parliament."[122] His warning to women to curb their demands to improve men was only too clear.

A Reform Agenda, 1918–20

On February 11, the Independent MLA nevertheless thrilled well-wishers at a reception at British Columbia's neo-baroque legislature. On March 1, her maiden speech was conciliatory but firm: "I come with no chip on my shoulder and no sword in my hand to take off any one's head, but to secure the best legislation I can in the interests of my sex." She warned that "if any of the members were not pleased to see [her] ... they would have to put up with it." Proclaiming herself a "mother protector," she provoked "merriment" in remarking, "I do not think there are many who do not know where I stand on the man question." Evading queries as to "whether she was to be Radical, Socialist, Independent, Suffragette, Conservative or Liberal," she promised to deliver a "woman's viewpoint."[123] As always, Smith sharply distinguished her stance from the "sex war" that was commonly invoked to smear suffragists, declaring,

> Do not, however, imagine that I forget the men; but when we legislate for men and women alike we shall have a better understanding in our community. Since woman received the suffrage man has come to realize that his wife knows as much as he does ... Woman has no monopoly of the virtues ... but with the goodness of woman united with the manliness and character of men we will have that sympathetic understanding which will make the world a better place to live in.

Her supporters did not want "a woman who could be made a door-mat." She promised, "I can go the Liberal party one better. I am an out and out democrat."[124]

Press commentators noted Smith's self-assurance as the "leader of the newly franchised sex" and her expectation that other MLAs "would stand behind her ... in the interests of the mothers and children of the Province."[125] While sitting in the legislature, she sometimes knitted, an activity that journalists judged much more "profitable" than male MLAs' habit of "smoking in the members' room."[126] Her first "historical pair" of socks raised ten dollars for patriotic societies,[127] confirming her adroit use of stereotypes to counter fears about free women. John Sedgwick Cowper, the progressive Liberal MLA who sat next to her in the legislature, described her tactics:

> Always armed and armoured with a sweet smile, a sense of humor and her native womanly dignity, Mrs. Smith sat through every session early and late without for a moment ever feeling out of place, or for a moment making any of the other members feel embarrassed.
>
> "She's a real good fellow; one of the very best," declared a prominent opposition member to me in the midst of an all-night session. He had been one of the most steadfast opponents of women suffrage, not to mention women in Parliament ... As a trailblazer and a mountain mover, the women of Vancouver are to be congratulated on their choice of Mrs. Smith as their pioneer legislator.[128]

A later meeting of the Vancouver Liberal Association gave Mary Ellen the chance to tell her own story of how she worked the legislative boys' club. In 1918, she had congratulated John Oliver (1856–1927) upon becoming premier. He thanked her and suggested that she looked "good enough to kiss," to which she replied, "It's up to you John." She told her listeners that she wouldn't reveal what happened next, and they broke into laughter, joined by Oliver.[129] Less accommodating of gendered norms was her casual surrender of a hat in the legislature (wearing hats at indoor public events was customary for respectable women) and her preference for press use of "woman" rather than "lady" in referring to her.[130] As a too often unwelcome pioneer, Mary Ellen juggled accommodation and resistance.

A sense that political currents were running in feminists' favour pervaded 1918. The *Western Women's Weekly* set out expectations: "Men are proud of strong men. Women should be proud of strong women ... Like a girl with two beaux, we could keep both political parties guessing ... If women divide into political parties ... they will become submerged in the party machine ... The franchise would be as good as lost."[131] *Everywoman's World* called women "to arms," arguing that post-war reconstruction depended on them and proposing a "Canadian Women's War League," with "no politics, no nationality, no religion – except indeed, that which is centred in the good that may be done for fellow-creatures."[132] It singled out the "Mothers of Consolidation" at Ottawa's 1918 Women's War Conference. From "all walks of life," they had come "laden down with statistics and a plenitude of common sense."[133] In actual fact, the conference was unsurprisingly unrepresentative, missing both labour and minority group women.[134] For all its appealing proposals of equal pay and a federal children's bureau, it proved little more than a government ploy to seduce female activists. By 1919, Prime Minister Borden showed his true colours in dismissing calls for a female delegate to the Versailles Peace Conference, concluding, "I cannot see any possible advantage in selecting representatives from [the women's] societies ... I do not know of any work they could do."[135]

In British Columbia, feminists faced other challenges. Less than a month after Mary Ellen's maiden address, Premier Harlan Brewster, who had added middle class and labour concern about the social needs of working people and women to the settlers' preoccupation with development, was dead.[136] His successor, John Oliver, was a personally conservative Delta farmer, whose distrust of labour was heightened by the 1919 wave of strikes and who showed no sympathy for feminists at any time.[137] Although the Liberals treasured the title of the province's party of reform, they required ongoing inducement to deliver it. Historian Robert McDonald credits Vancouver's "outstanding women activists" for providing the spur. Smith and allies such as MacGill, Jamieson, and Gutteridge lobbied to shift British Columbia from the classic liberalism of the nineteenth century, with its emphasis on competitive individualism, to the new, "more collectivist and statist" liberalism of the twentieth.[138] In 1919, this produced legislation for the equal guardianship of children, the suppression of venereal disease, the necessity that mothers consent to the marriage of their underage children, the maintenance of deserted wives, the minimum wage, and mothers' pensions, all mobilizing state engagement in women's well-being.

Mary Ellen knew she was riding a wave, telling the Vancouver Kiwanis that "every government loves the women now."[139] Counting on the usefulness of public education, she accepted the *Vancouver Sun*'s invitation to write on "social and economic conditions in so far as they affect the position of her sex."[140] Her 1918–20 *Sun* articles took on "the sacred responsibility of mothering the nation" through proposals for "united action, steady perseverance, [and] intelligent co-operation."[141] Always optimism's apostle,[142] she pleaded for conciliation and mutual understanding between sexes and classes. The war should serve as a catalyst, a demonstration of "the indestructibility of human ideals" that would produce "a new world order," one dedicated to "unity and action on the basis of our faith in the gospel of goodwill the Master preached." Only the "fellowship of free peoples or the league of nations" could "justify the sufferings and sacrifices of the last four and a half years."[143]

Smith's columns condemned reactionary trends. Now that women "knew what a pay cheque means," they would not return to the past and the "old-fashioned idea that women were created for the purpose of marrying."[144] The war had proven their "aptitude in nearly all kinds of work" and justified "progressive thinking."[145] Vancouver's introduction of female police officers was a step in the right direction.[146] "Living wages" for teachers was another.[147] She denounced the poor pay and long hours for nurses, whose value the flu pandemic had highlighted.[148] The collection of more accurate statistics, a demand regularly expressed by New Liberals, would generate policy that enabled women to support both themselves and their dependants and would ultimately curb dissension between the sexes.[149] Without reform, celibacy and small families for White settlers would become the norm. In the occasional column, Mary Ellen also questioned the "traditions, conventions and prejudices" that assigned sole responsibility for home labour to women: it was time "to stop theorizing about what women's place ought to be and take notice of just what woman's place actually is." She foresaw "room at the top for women," who no longer had to marry. When they chose to wed, they would be better wives and mothers.[150]

Her *Sun* articles were equally insistent about democracy. Citing free education and the abolition of slavery, Smith argued that "intelligent agitation," born of discontent, could save the world.[151] A good Methodist, she believed that democracy "was ordained by a Higher Power than our own."[152] Holding another federal election under the terms of the Wartime Elections Act would be a catastrophe. In the midst of "the chaos, disorder and the upheavals of the day, the returned soldier problem, the women in industry problem," all (White) women needed "an equal opportunity to express their opinion."[153] Ultimately, "the people must rule."[154] In contrast, "badly disrupted" revolutionary Russia offered no guidance.[155] Democracy could be reformed without violence, and Smith stressed rising global support for suffrage. Hard experience nevertheless made her warn that "women must never forget that eternal vigilance is always the price of liberty."[156] She also reassured the fearful that the desire of female voters for a "lasting peace" did not entail "disruption" of their domestic role or threaten their "womanliness." Omitting mention of her own antipathy to

At home in her modest apartment in Kitsilano, in the 1920s, Mary Ellen appeared to embody comfortable maternalism. | AM54-54: Port N31, City of Vancouver Archives.

Asian newcomers, she singled out Mrs. Sarajin (Sarojini) Naidu, Indian political activist, feminist, and anti-imperialist, as proof of women's capacity to redeem the world and demanded that Canadians appreciate "the value of our franchise."[157]

The new MLA firmly directed female voters to undertake key duties, such as the assimilation of the White foreign-born. Canadians should match Americans in "making it compulsory for every boy and girl to salute 'Our Flag' on entering the school grounds."[158] Despite employers' pressure for cheap labour, governments should maintain racial exclusions and scrap "bonusing" for immigrant agents. She endorsed female inspectors to safeguard immigrant women who arrived to take up domestic service and the higher standards "in the interests of both employer and employee" set forth by the Canadian Council on the Immigration of Women, on which she represented British Columbia.[159] She similarly underlined child and maternal welfare.[160] Warning about the war's removal of fathers, Smith felt that delinquent youngsters would benefit from probation officers who were "drawn from our convalescent soldiers."[161] She praised the US

Children's Bureau and urged the creation of a similar Canadian agency.[162] Suggestions that the world needed a "better brand of us" showed her enthusiasm for eugenics, the attempt to improve the human species by restricting the fertility of those deemed inferior, and her assumption that "fit" was almost synonymous with "White." Women needed to be trained "to feel that maternity is a privilege."[163] Family life was, however, "sapped" by many mothers' desperate search for wages.[164] She foresaw solutions to such problems in the 1919 BC commission on state health insurance, maternity assistance, and mothers' pensions.[165]

Capital-labour relations were similarly central to Smith's public education efforts. As a BC MLA, she boosted local companies as remedies for unemployment and outside profiteering.[166] She commended certain businesses, such as Imperial Oil of Canada, for progressive labour policies, which revived practices "when master and man worked side by side and if any difficulty arose both were in a position to judge the question on its merits, view it from their own angle, and decide wisely." Cooperation meant a "Wider Brotherhood" but paternalism went unmentioned.[167] Like many New Liberals, Smith advocated capital-labour partnerships such as Britain's Whitney Councils.[168] Subject to public scrutiny, like the federal inquiries embraced by her husband, such employer-employee councils would foster "co-operation and community action."[169] Smith's trust in corporations was nevertheless conditional, and she argued that female consumers had a right to oversight.[170] For example, in describing her tour of an Alberta abattoir, she demanded regular inspection.[171] Stressing that the high cost of living bred "distrust and mistrust," she called for restrictions on profit.[172]

In the midst of the general strikes in the Canadian west in 1918–19,[173] she warned that the war had only postponed tackling industrial ills. Now, it was time to focus on "bread and butter and a living wage." Although passions were understandably high,

> the Canadian workingman is not a Bolshevist. He is too straight a thinker for that. He knows that wrongs can be righted more effectively and more enduringly with the ballot than with the sword. He is as much opposed to the dictatorship of the proletariat as to the tyranny of the plutocrats. The people are insisting on elemental rights. The good nature of the people has been sorely tried for nearly five years. We have in Canada well-fed-profiteers who waved flags, cheered lustily when the boys marched off to war, and who at once returned to their offices to mark up the price of flour or coal; and immediately shout because members of a union want better conditions.

Canadians deserved a reconstruction that would include female enfranchisement; workers' right to organize; federal laws on working conditions, hours, and wages; and a minimum wage for women and children. National policies should also place "land in the hands of those who cultivate it," wipe out illiteracy and profiteering, raise "taxes on incomes and not on the necessities of life," and ensure "government ownership of railroads and other utilities."[174] She lamented the National Industrial Conference's failure to demand a minimum wage for women.[175] Ongoing "chaos" occurred because ills had not been addressed "intelligently and fearlessly." Working women supplied the benchmark for better standards for all.[176]

Although Mary Ellen prioritized reform of the industrial relations of the sexes and the classes, like many Canadians she succumbed, albeit infrequently in public, to the romanticization of rural life. This helps explain her trust that agricultural programs could return veterans to useful lives on the land.[177] More particularly, she applauded the Federated Women's Institutes, with which she was associated, for fostering city-farm cooperation.[178] She nevertheless remained practical enough to warn would-be women emigrants from the United Kingdom that good land was expensive and agricultural labour demanding.[179] Rewards required hard work and some capital.

Regularly looking abroad, Mary Ellen's columns likewise confronted the "birth throes of a new world order, in which national purposes have fallen into the background, and the common purposes of enlightened mankind have taken their place." The League of Nations, like the Whitney Councils, represented "the principles of fellowship, freedom and fraternity." "Men and women, fearless and strong," could carve out "a policy of progress" together.[180] Commonplace prejudices once again informed Mary Ellen's views of what was best. While praising Japanese and Chinese suffragists in Asia, she didn't extend sympathy to her own shores. As was the case for so many of her contemporaries, her worries about immorality often centred on Asian men.[181] Alongside Edmonton suffragist Emily Ferguson Murphy (1868–1933), she blamed Chinese outsiders for the traffic in narcotics.[182] Her enthusiasm for eugenics and fears about the feeble-minded were grounded in the same pervasive bigotry.[183]

Mary Ellen took her ideas to the legislature and around Canada. Careful to present herself as more than a single-note politician preoccupied with so-called women's causes (such as mothers' pensions), she regularly defended veterans, resource development, and a progressive stance in international affairs.[184] In April 1918, as Canadians watched the unfolding of the Russian Revolution and strikes and protests around the world, she showed the path to reconciliation by seconding a motion that called for pensions for disabled soldiers to ignore rank since "social differences are repugnant and inimical to the national welfare."[185] American and Canadian women were urged "to stamp out 'snobocracy' on this continent." As publicly minded citizens and soon-to-be elected politicians, they should unite in a neighbourly campaign to welcome and assimilate previous "outsiders" in a melting pot that would "actually melt and amalgamate." Snobocracy was ultimately "the slyest alien enemy of democracy, doubly dangerous during our period of joint reconstruction, feeding the red fever."[186] In the same spirit, she protested Polish anti-Semitism and favoured the establishment of a Jewish state in the Middle East.[187]

For all her recurring claims of independence, Smith remained loyal to the BC version of New Liberalism, which created Canada's first Department of Labour (1917) and the Land Settlement Board (1917), appointed MacGill as judge of the Vancouver Juvenile Court (1917), and introduced the Equal Guardianship of Infants Act (1917), the Civil Service Act (1917), the first public health nursing course in the British Empire (1919), the Act to Fix a Minimum Wage for Women (1918), the Deserted Wives' Maintenance Act (1919), the 1920 Legitimation Act (applying to children of parents who later married), and Mothers' Pensions Act (1920). Despite the significant limitations of such interventions, women and children, workers, and veterans reaped unprecedented rewards. Countering such gains was the male-dominated legislature's refusal to grant women longstanding demands for dower rights as widows and an enforceable interest in family property. In many ways, reforms, useful as they might be, merely shifted part of the cost of women's ongoing subordination to a male state.[188] Most remained to be paid in hard coin by victims. Patriarchal rule was only curtailed, not abolished.

Scholars have carefully examined the BC minimum wage and mothers' pensions legislation of these years, stressing their limitations and failings.[189] Both were far from inclusive: The minimum wage legislation omitted many occupations, and mothers' pensions were not available to Asian or Indigenous women. Both ignored the real cost of living. In his survey of western Canada, sociologist Bob Russell rightly observed that "'fair' wages [were] largely reserved for men, while minimum wages were deemed sufficient for women."[190] While more generous than in many jurisdictions, BC mothers' pensions did not stave off suffering. As she surveyed the program, Mary Ellen was not naive. As she put it, pensions amounted to no more than a "half loaf," but they were also "better than no bread, and I am sure there will be no turning back ... We have only just got the vote, and we must work hard to get many more things we want."[191]

Prospects for improvement, however, were waylaid by many factors, including the decade's heightened conflict over federal-provincial jurisdiction. The labour legislation recommended by the new International Labor Organization (ILO) set up a major field of battle: it called for "freedom of association; reasonable minimum standards of wages; the 8-hour day and the 48-hour week; one day's rest in seven; abolition of child labour; and equal pay for women doing work of the same value as men."[192] On the one hand, BC Liberals wanted to demonstrate their sympathy for workers and internationalism. On the other, they preferred that someone else pay the costs, all the more so when corporate lobbyists condemned such legislation as a threat to their competitiveness. A series of federal-provincial conferences failed to resolve disagreements over jurisdiction, and progress was stymied until after the Second World War.[193]

In face of contesting arguments, the Oliver administration struggled to present itself as a principled procrastinator. In 1920, the *BC Federationist* called the government to account when it torpedoed an eight-hour-day bill from an Independent but labour-identified MLA.[194] On this occasion, Mary Ellen was not present in the legislature due to illness – whether strategic or otherwise is unknown. She did, nonetheless, support the government's postponement of such initiatives. She looked to Ottawa to take the lead. Such caution, much like Ralph's investment in Laurier's slow-go preferences, cost her dearly in union circles.[195] Eventually too, it would bolster Tory attacks on her credentials as a liberal-labour lady.

The introduction of a measure of minimum wage and mothers' pensions nevertheless helped many women and offered overdue recognition of their paid and unpaid labour. Even inadequate advances required unrelenting pressure from activist women and unionists. When Mary Ellen introduced a minimum wage delegation in March 1918, Premier Oliver responded with a telling warning. He declared his support for "revolutionary legislation" but cautioned that "the matter was largely in the women's own hands as voters." Victoria could not go "faster than the people who paid the taxes would allow it to travel."[196] The new MLA struggled to inspire a sufficiently powerful lobby to keep government attention. She urged the labour movement to consult with her so that "she would be equipped in the best way to make the fight for this legislation."[197] Gutteridge, fearing pressure from the "many large establishments" whose wages were so low that women couldn't "keep themselves

"Striving for 'Mothers' Pensions,'" *Vancouver Sun*, February 15, 1920.

decently," argued that "had it not been for Mrs. Ralph Smith there would have been no action."[198] Neither woman stopped championing equal pay for equal work and insisting that "women are their sisters' keepers."[199]

The introduction of mothers' pensions likewise required steely will. Smith lamented that unwed women had to rely on discretionary provisions that often left officials with the power to determine eligibility: "May God forgive us for brand[ing] a mother who has not gone through a marriage ceremony [as] different [from] ourselves."[200] She promised that just "because I am satisfied today does not indicate that I will not agitate for more tomorrow."[201] Women should be "prepared to stand together for each other" and to reject calls to return to their pre-war status.[202] Smith attempted to build support through her own membership in a daunting raft of organizations. The NCWC, which during and immediately after the war tried to mobilize new voters, was a particular enthusiasm. In April 1919, its president visited Vancouver to stand alongside its BC vice-president and urge support for its Woman's Platform, suggesting that its "broad lines" offered something to all women.[203] Smith wanted its some 400,000 members to enlist wholeheartedly in reform, particularly welcoming young women, and saw "no limit to their possibilities."[204] In return, she promised eastern activists western support.[205] In the same spirit, she endorsed political campaigns in Ontario, applauding a call by the Ottawa Woman's Club for "humane legislation."[206]

On occasion, Mary Ellen's brave face faltered. Like many suffragists,[207] she worried about women's weakness. In March 1919, she denounced self-hatred, "especially when allied with party bias," and warned that

> if women are going to divide into the old parties ... and carry on in this same picayune party spirit, then of necessity women in parliament, to be effective, must line up with one or other of the old camps ... We, who worked for suffrage, always hoped that at least for a time until they found their political feet, women voters would remain independent ... and would go single mindedly after the things for which women have struggled unsuccessfully as nonvoters for years and years.[208]

She nevertheless clung to hope, asserting that "many, many women in B.C." did "place principle before party and the public good before party advantage." This had produced results in social legislation, and there would be more, including old age pensions, a provincial bureau of public health, dower rights, and university training of nurses.[209]

Mary Ellen's other approach to sustaining reform impetus targeted male allies and fears. To put it bluntly, she buttered up the boys, in effect engaging in a female version of the posturing and horse trading that regularly coloured political life.[210] This sometimes took courage. In April 1918, she won over a hostile Victoria crowd of veterans. Credited as scoring "a bigger victory" than any "in the exclusive region of the house itself," she faced down "heated" protests, insisting, "I'm not a politician. I'm a woman and a soldier's mother. I'm not afraid of man or devil." Her "fairness and defiance" delivered the audience, all the more when she slammed Ottawa for mistreating veterans. The sympathetic *Vancouver Sun* spied "a personal victory," declaring that "the returned men had found a mouthpiece."[211] A political meeting in Enderby, North Okanagan, under the auspices of the Women's Voters' League, exemplified Smith's tack with legislators. The evening began with the league president charging Premier Oliver and the legislature with hostility to the sole female MLA. A British coal miner before he was a Delta farmer, Oliver took offence. Noting that he had "known Mrs. Ralph Smith some thirty years," he insisted that she was "appreciated by his ministers, and all members of Parliament, regardless of political creed." Taking to the stage, Mary Ellen offered a healing touch of "good cheer and encouragement" and "duty." Semi-humorously, she observed that "next to woman, man is the dearest thing the Lord made. We marry him, we live with him, and we must learn to vote with him. By this co-operation, she felt confident women would find little difficulty in getting any legislation desirable and fair."[212] The same vision informed a manuscript (unfortunately lost) that she apparently took to California movie producers in the spring of 1920. It dealt with "industrial conditions and the problem of uniting capital and labor for the common welfare." The story opened with the "dismissal of women munition workers" from an iron and steel plant immediately after the Armistice and closed with cooperation and a "pretty love story."[213]

Only rarely did Smith let her guard slip. During her first month in the legislature, she admitted that "it was not an easy thing being the only woman," but she claimed rewards, as women were "at last recognized, and she was happy to feel that the women throughout the province had a woman whom they could confide in and write to."[214] She was more forthright during a visit to Alberta Women's Institutes: "You women in

Alberta are fortunate in having a government that stands by you as we in British Columbia have not."[215] As scandals involving liquor, railways, and elections tarred the Liberals, and popular votes fizzled for labour, socialism, and feminism, challenges to patriarchs and capitalists would become harder still.

6
From Hope to Disillusion, 1920–28

In 1920, a premier's kisses might have intimated that women were welcome in British Columbia's first election after the Great War, but far more seductive than John Oliver's lying lips in securing at least the pretense of listening to a feminist champion was "our Mary Ellen's" headlining Vancouver polls. Betrayal of that promise came in many forms. Women, workers, and Liberals thwarted hopes for a fair deal in politics. But disappointment ran both ways: as a veteran MLA, Mary Ellen would dishearten many progressive voters. This chapter charts her trajectory from the heights of her 1920 election triumph to her controversial and brief tenure as a cabinet minister, the 1924 provincial contest in which she barely retained her seat, and the uninspiring years that followed before she again tempted the electorate in 1928.

THE DISAPPOINTING DECADE

In the 1920s, women discovered the true meaning of post-war reconstruction's high talk of a fair deal. Few in British Columbia's expanding metropolitan communities lived precisely as their mothers had, even as life remained largely unchanged in rural and remote areas and on the province's hard-pressed Indian reserves. Only a handful anywhere could or wished to experiment with the sexual autonomy and material abundance projected in the contemporary image of the flapper. The double standard flourished, and so too did the criminalization of much birth control. Mary Ellen's recurring advocacy of divorce equality brought no relief in its reminder of an unfinished feminist agenda.[1]

Gender, enmeshed in class and race, divided Canadians. Persisting high levels of maternal and infant mortality and the absence of legal provision for dower or community property kept most women preoccupied with survival, as did flawed minimum wage legislation, mothering with inadequate state pensions, exclusion from better jobs and wages, meagre old age pensions after 1927, and dealing with pervasive racism. Limited options and particularly intense engagement in family life easily fostered narrow loyalties and prejudices. The chilly reception granted feminists and the prevalence of domestic violence bolstered the gendered status quo. Bedecked with silk and feathers in the society pages, members of the BC elite paid little attention to pleas from suffragists such as Mary Ellen that they care for their "sisters." Like other Canadians, too many British Columbians capitulated to the "dope" (the meaningless flattery and kowtowing to idealized womanhood) that Nellie McClung so firmly condemned in her best-selling book *In Times Like These*. Despite calls for women's platforms and political agitation, female voters resisted mobilization and all parties exploited female volunteers. Although a post-war flurry of female candidates surfaced in municipal, provincial, and federal elections, most linked to women's groups, victories were rare. Exceptions came largely in contests for school and library boards.[2] Vancouver did not produce its first female alderman until 1937 – the suffragist Helena Gutteridge, who represented the social democratic Co-operative Commonwealth Federation (CCF). Feminists learned to grieve the pervasive failure to use the vote to secure reform.[3] As British Columbia's solitary female MLA, Mary Ellen bore the weight of unrealized expectations.

Despite having attained the franchise significantly earlier than women, male workers did little better in placing people like themselves on city councils or in provincial or federal legislatures. When the Great War's "world fit for heroes" failed to materialize and the decade's Red Scare intensified censorship, deportations, and demonization of radical critics, many men sought compensation in ruling at home, sometimes with their fists, and in masculinized public spaces, from the beer parlour and the shop floor to the union hall and the party meeting. Few heeded advocates of industrial, socialist, or communist action or feminist dreamers of "brave women and fair men."[4] Between the 1920 and 1924 BC elections, support for labour and socialist candidates dropped from 16.15 to 5.04 percent of the popular vote.[5] By mid-decade, "labourism had collapsed as a significant force in Canadian politics."[6] Only the Great Depression, with the CCF's capture of seven of forty-seven seats in the 1933 BC election, shifted significant numbers to the left.

For believers in representative democracy, liberalism proved deeply disheartening. In British Columbia, the Liberal Party was mired in battles over prohibition, railway development, civil service reform, campaign financing, social and economic legislation, and women's rights. Restive women, workers, and farmers (who formed their own provincial party in 1917) shrank the 1916 Liberal majority in the December 1920 election. The Oliver government was even weaker than it seemed since it "had put up persons who were in fact Labour, Soldier and Farmer candidates."[7] An uncertain economy and rising pressure from the right, including the Conservative-dominated Provincial Party after 1922, further dimmed reform prospects. Oliver's preference for fighting federal Liberals over "better terms" for the province was distracting. In 1924, all party leaders failed to win their seats on election day, and the Oliver government became a minority relying on independent Liberals and Labour.

In a bitterly partisan legislature, the independence that Mary Ellen had staked out in the 1918 by-election proved shaky. Just as Helen Gregory MacGill warned, her lack of party affiliation diminished her effectiveness.[8] Although Oliver experimented with pivoting left by extending workman's compensation benefits, few Liberal or Labour MLAs recognized the claims of the distaff side of the province. Oliver died in 1927, but his successor, John Duncan MacLean (1873-1948), whose brief term has been labelled "the twilight of the gods,"[9] struggled to deliver a reform agenda that went beyond the federally initiated old age pensions.

Ottawa Liberals, led since 1919 by Ralph's old colleague William Lyon Mackenzie King, a supposed expert on industrial conciliation, occasionally seemed more suited to gender and class partnership, which partially explains Smith's temptation to move to the federal stage. Like the BC political elite, however, King balked at strong women. In any case, his party was torn between former Unionists and Laurier loyalists, between French and English, and between corporate and more progressive Liberals. The farmers' parties that won Ontario and Alberta elections in 1919 and 1921 and fifty-eight seats as the Progressive Party in the 1921 federal election (including five seats in British Columbia) boded political realignment. King set out to seduce Progressive MPs and three Labour MPs as "Liberals-in-a-hurry," even as he reassured his right wing.[10] Brief Conservative success in 1920-21 and 1926 under Arthur Meighen was not repeated after some Progressives turned Liberal-Progressive in the 1926 election that returned King as prime minister. Old age pensions were one result of King's dance of accommodation. In the face of federal political turmoil, British Columbia, with its internecine rows, kept the federal party cross. Whatever their differences, however, politicians in neither Ottawa nor Victoria saw women or workers as significant enough to merit the justice demanded by feminists and labourists. Liberal inability to coalesce behind a reform agenda provoked a few suffragists, such as British Columbia's Laura Jamieson, to consider socialist, labour, and communist parties, which spurned old Lib-Lab accommodation. Federally, more radical Progressives and Labour MPs, notably the suffragist James S. Woodsworth and the first female MP, Agnes Macphail, left the Progressives to form the Ginger Group. In 1933, it provided one basis for the creation of the CCF. For all the promise of the 1920s, only fragments of a fair deal made it past mainstream defence of privilege.

In the midst of the political struggle, Mary Ellen juggled family demands. Her son, Captain Jack Wesley Smith, suffered wartime injuries, which left him sometimes under her care.[11] Happier was his wedding in 1923 to Mabel Catherine Quesnel, a Vancouver debutante and neighbour of Mary Ellen, who lived with her widowed mother.[12] Family losses darkened these years. In 1925, pneumonia killed Richard William, aged thirty-nine, a telegraph operator based in Prince Rupert. He left a widow and two children.[13] Some two years later, Robert died. Aged forty-three, he was a graduate of Osgoode Law School, a member of both the BC bar and the Vancouver Club, a Unionist-Liberal and then mainstream Liberal, husband of Nanaimo's Kate Johnson, and father to two young children. Bob was a stalwart campaigner for his mother, and his resemblance to Ralph, "not only in features and general characteristics, but in his attainments and ready wit,"[14] deepened the blow. Mary Ellen was increasingly bereft.

"O What a Pal Was Mary": The 1920 Election

Right from her 1918 election, doubts multiplied about Smith's independence. The *Cranbrook Herald* was typically dismissive in describing the WCTU member's refusal to endorse prohibition, a long-standing feminist cause, and her acquiescence in the 1920 prohibition referendum gambit that tried to put voters, not the government, in the hot seat (reminiscent of the Conservative 1916 suffrage referendum).[15] When heckled, she explained that "you couldn't legislate against human desire." Voters themselves had to commit to self-discipline, and the community had to supply alternatives to drink.[16] The *BC Federationist* became acerbic about her retreat to mainstream liberalism, mocking her "blarney" in introducing "Honest John" Oliver as a "wonderful man" who had "given his whole life to his country," a view entirely "in line with the premier's opinion of himself."[17] The *Montreal Gazette* was kinder in describing her modus operandi:

> On the public platform Mrs. Smith has an easy, breezy manner. Blessed with a splendid figure and a fine delivery, a ready wit and a rare gift for repartee, she can hold her own in any gathering, and has all the old-time politician's ability to turn the subject deftly when an awkward question is put ... She knows every trick of the stage speaker, carefully studies her audience, takes advantage of every opening, but withal does this so naturally that her very art appears only artlessness. Particularly clever at telling stories.[18]

In making sense of Smith's conduct, we need to remember that conciliation and cajolery, sometimes termed "women's wiles," are familiar tactics in class and racial, as well as gender, hierarchies. She applied time-honoured tools to a political caste system that feared independent women. Of course, what might be a strategic accommodation for long-term advantage could smack of toadyism or even become the genuine article. Beyond soft-soaping Oliver and other heavyweights, Mary Ellen pursued early suffragist advice to juggle multiple "suitors," another strategy hardly restricted to women. Soon after her 1918 win, Mary Ellen boasted of alternatives of federal seats in British Columbia, the Prairies, or Ontario, a clear call for BC Liberals to treat her better.[19]

Familiar support and surviving family members, not to mention limited funds, nevertheless anchored the new legislator in British Columbia. She relied on Vancouver's broad progressive networks in which the Women's Liberal Association joined socialists and labour activists in sanctioning proportional representation, and suffragists worked with unionists in causes from health to education.[20] Prospects on the Pacific appeared preferable to those on the federal level when the Progressives and Tories complicated life for Prime Minister King. Yet, if non-partisanship had worked well in 1918, it stumbled in a legislature where Conservatives became the chief foe and Liberals seemed open to persuasion and came courting. Mary Ellen's decision to return to the Liberal fold was all the easier when female activists lost the shared purpose of the Great Cause. A feminist journalist reached a common conclusion: since women "do not stand together as men do," their best bet was to clean up the old parties.[21] That idea was strengthened when New Liberalism promoted "government social programs" as a solution to "pressure from the left, increasing urban and factory problems, the chaotic nature of capitalist production, and evident class conflict."[22] In the autumn of 1920, Mary Ellen announced that she "couldn't oppose a Government who had done so much for the women of this province."[23] She immediately topped Vancouver's Liberal nomination slate.[24]

In the election of December 1, 1920, three women joined the field of twenty-eight candidates for the city's six seats. Mary Ellen ran against Edith Louise Patterson (c. 1891–1980), a Conservative lawyer, and Esther Margaret Biddle Crosfield (c. 1886–1968), "widow" and Independent from the Women's Freedom League.[25] Both were much younger than Smith, and they lacked her prominence in activist circles. Male challengers included John Wallace de Beque Farris for the Liberals, Bowser for the Conservatives, and future Winnipeg MP James Woodsworth for the Federated Labour Party. Much press attention focused on Smith and Patterson. The latter "spoofed" the incumbent on her age, while claiming most "humane legislation," including women suffrage, for her party.[26] Mary Ellen retorted by recalling Bowser's hostility to suffragist delegations, dismissing Patterson as "too young" and "not knowing," and citing the beneficiaries of Liberal policies.[27] The exchange about age led some observers to detect a stereotypical "cat fight" or "eternal jealousy."[28] Bowser drew on another cliché to effectively undermine his Conservative acolyte by musing publicly that "Miss Edith" would fall to "Cupid" and be lost to the party.[29] The *Western Women's Weekly* magnanimously described all three female candidates as "women of energy, force of character, culture, and ... a clear understanding of public affairs," adding, "of course they have a peculiar fitness to represent women and look after their affairs and those of children, a highly important thing neglected when the female part of the community was unrepresented in the legislature."[30] It also approved of the Federated Labour Party's Women's Committee.[31]

Other suffragists rose to Smith's defence, dismissing Patterson as woefully ignorant.[32] Representatives of the New Era League, the Political Equality League, the WCTU, the LCW, and the King's Daughters allied with sympathetic male reformers in her interest.[33] That crowd ignored a feminist critic, Mary Insley Corse. A champion of the Women's Labour Leagues and Federated Labour Party candidates, Corse was a member of the Calgary Women's Labour Council and a former member of that city's school board. She caustically dismissed Smith's "reported remark" that she had "'lots of legislation in my mind.'" This, said Corse, "was somewhat nebulous and she hoped the hon. member would get it off her mind before election day or she might forget it."[34]

Perhaps to undercut invidious comparisons with the youthful Patterson, Mary Ellen soon refashioned herself for the flapper age, exchanging "Mrs. Ralph Smith" for "Mary Ellen Smith" and sometimes just "Mary Ellen" or even "Our Mary Ellen."[35] Apparently "the sonorous title 'Mrs. Ralph Smith, M.P.P.' [sic]," intimidated young women. Due to the name change, according to the *Montreal Gazette,* working-class "shop girls and stenographers felt that 'Mary Ellen' was a chummy kind of person, a lovable woman and one whom they could implicitly trust," a persona that won her many votes.[36] Whatever her moniker, the suffrage veteran cudgelled the Conservative chief, charging him with paying a young stenographer in his law office less than the minimum wage.[37] Tory malfeasance required correction, not kowtowing to acolytes such as Patterson. Tough talk aside, Smith also knew the value of the velvet glove. The St. Andrews' and Caledonian Society was predictably seduced by her "inimitable recital of Scottish stories, intermingled with nicely chosen sentiment lauding Scottish spirit and ideals."[38] Platform popularity kept her vying with Premier Oliver and Opposition leader Bowser "for the honor of having made the greatest number of speeches," and her visits to Liberal constituencies became a "triumphal progress."[39] Her star power clearly disturbed Oliver. Whenever possible, he resisted giving her credit, preferring to applaud Farris for the new laws regarding women and children.[40] A party advertisement in the *Vancouver World* typically left Mary Ellen unmentioned.[41] Another in the *Vancouver Sun,* titled "Women's Rights – without Restriction," did the same.[42]

On election day, the Liberals held on to power but lost seats province-wide, with both Oliver and Bowser tumbling. The party dropped to 37.9 percent of the popular vote and twenty-five seats; the Conservatives rose to 31.2 percent and fifteen; the new Federated Labour Party won 9.1 percent and three; independents took 10.8 percent and three; and the People's Party garnered 0.38 percent and one.[43] Mary Ellen, however, topped the Vancouver poll with 8.66 percent of the vote and secured more votes than any other candidate in BC history to that point. The next five victors in the multi-member constituency were all Liberals, followed by Bowser with 5.75 percent. Margaret Crosfield took 2.06 percent, Patterson 4.73, and Woodsworth 3.68. Smith thanked city women and workers for their support and the press "for the spirit of fairness."[44] The

"Polled the Largest Vote Cast for Any Candidate in the History of B.C.," *Vancouver Province*, December 2, 1920.

long-time labourist ideal of "social equality and honest toil as the basis of social worth" seemed in sight, at least for settler women.[45] The *Western Women's Weekly* hailed the victory of a "capable representative both in the matter of judgment and experience and as a womanly woman, a mother and a citizen" who had pushed "progressive and humane legislation."[46]

Worldwide curiosity greeted the defeated premier's salute of his triumphant candidate. Celebrating at the Hotel Vancouver, Oliver kissed Mary Ellen "with a resounding smack" as the Veterans' Band played the popular song "Oh What a Pal Was Mary."[47] Though quickly "reproved" by the purity-minded, he defended himself by saying that "the kiss was a duty not a sin."[48] Oliver's enthusiasm was matched by another Liberal, who "publicly proposed marriage" to Smith and offered $3,000 to demonstrate that "he could support her properly."[49] The *BC Federationist* added to the comedy with a satirical poem, "When John Kissed Mary Ellen":

When John kissed Mary Ellen,
On those lips so chaste and fair,
A softer heart to politics,
Was given then and there.
And though John blushed his hardest,
Of shame there was no trace,
And he can still his grandchild
Look bravely in the face.
Chorus:
When John kissed Mary Ellen,
The fairest of the fair,
Oh? A softer heart to politics
Was given then and there.

But when the winsome Ellen
Comes with her bills so bold,
With increases for the widow
And pensions for the old,
How can our dear old Johnny
(For he said he is not slow)
As her pouting lips are tempting
Return a naughty no!
— Chorus

And should Johnny e'er refuse her
What agony he'll feel,
When those rosy lips are stiffened,
And she turns her dainty heel?
How his "want-of-money" pleading
Will banish all his bliss
When Mary Ellen tells him
She'll go and Bowser kiss.
— Chorus[50]

Mary Ellen's sexualization, and the double-edge of her use of femininity, was confirmed when the *Ottawa Journal* wondered if she had "kissed her way into a Cabinet position."[51]

Progressive and Reactionary Causes, 1920–24

During her second term, Mary Ellen kept a busy schedule despite the recurring bronchial ills that beset her like so many refugees from British mining villages. Since the Victoria legislature normally had brief sittings, she remained based in "modest quarters" in a Kitsilano apartment house on Point Grey Road.[52] That unpretentious site was matched by her humble perch in the legislature, at the rear of the government caucus, buried in a sea of male faces. From there and Kits, she oversaw the needs of workers, women, and children, the settler project, and the New Liberal state. Ultimately, however, cabinet membership often preoccupied Mary Ellen, her contemporaries, and the subsequent memory of her.

As the Liberals and BC budgets stumbled, Mary Ellen struggled to defend the legacies of the 1916 election victory against hostile MLAs, overwhelmed administrators, and resurgent reaction. With limited resources and few legislative partners, she faced not only outright foes but a public, including women's groups, female clients, and the labour movement, that demanded an accounting.[53] Her exhausting round of women's and community organizations aimed to raise consciousness and support. When allies proved in short supply, discouragement lurked. During a 1922 speech to the Vancouver Women's Forum, she expressed regret for

A lonely figure on the left, c. 1920. Identifiable by her white collar, Mary Ellen is third from the left. | G-06230, British Columbia Archives and Records Service.

"the lack of co-operative spirit among women's organizations" and urged unity "in the things that matter." Politics needed "fearless" women and men.[54] Despite that or perhaps because she was praised as one of the "men" who were making British Columbia, she insisted that a women's platform was more necessary than ever.[55] Like most feminists, Mary Ellen placed local struggles in the context of an ongoing global battle for equality. When she received an invitation to visit from suffragists in Cape Town, South Africa, she endorsed their cause as part of a shared crusade.[56]

"'Men' Who Are Making B.C.," *Vancouver World,* September 21, 1921.

As beneficiaries and costs spiralled, the Oliver administration shifted mothers' pensions, the cause with which Mary Ellen remained identified, to the Workmen's Compensation Board; dismantled oversight by female volunteers; and stiffened eligibility criteria. While Conservatives targeted still supposedly wasteful operations, defenders of pensions saw worthy applicants and condemned male politicians and administrators for finding "money for automobiles and such and for reclamation schemes and other interest-bearing projects" but not for mothers. They contended that "only women can thoroughly understand the needs of women."[57] Mary Ellen insisted that women were better at handling budgets than bureaucrats while rebuking a future Conservative cabinet minister, denying that he had "women's interests at heart."[58] Writing to the province's attorney general, Alexander Malcolm Manson (1883–1964), she characterized pension administration as "not satisfactory to put it mildly" and lobbied for an investigation and an arena "where women & their friends who claim they have had a wrong deal can be heard." She warned that opponents of pension cutbacks were in fact "bona fide Liberals" who merited attention.[59] Manson was little moved, writing to the pension administrator that "we have nothing to fear from criticism on any individual case" and suggesting that taking "some steps to cut the ground from under the feet of the complainers" might be a good idea.[60] A year later, in 1924, Smith again alerted Manson to women's discontent with pensions and with employers' undermining of minimum wage protection. She offered to talk to the "most aggressive" critics and warned that they had to be faced.[61] Her "vigorous" opposition, alongside women's organizations, to the loss of a female probation officer in Vancouver sent the same message:[62] female oversight was essential to effective state initiatives.

The minimum wage came under similar assault as businesses stoutly defended pitiful pay. Smith's hopes had to rest with the introduction of a men's minimum wage in 1926, but the intent of the latter was far from progressive: it was to deter employers from paying Asian men less than either White men or women.[63] In any case, all workers remained responsible for initiating grievances, and many groups, such as farm and domestic labourers and teachers, never gained even limited protection. When Mary Ellen received Vancouver TLC protestors, who included Gutteridge (now Mrs. H. Fearn), she could do little more than agree that "minors, learners and apprentices" were badly served, direct them to the Minimum Wage Board itself, and promise support.[64] The 1921 introduction of the Maternity Protection Act, which prohibited women's employment for six weeks after childbirth but left them without income, was part of a parcel of protective labour legislation proposed by the ILO. Other laws, however, did not come into effect without matching enactments in other jurisdictions. The Maternity Protection Act itself was toothless since it lacked mechanisms for enforcement. Although British Columbia's introduction of unimplemented ILO measures has been judged "impressive," it was ultimately meaningless, an outcome that the government understood, as did the Opposition and the labour movement.[65] Despite growing "gender jitters" about threats to male breadwinning, however, Smith never stopped calling for equal pay for equal work.[66]

Her sex's economic vulnerability similarly lay behind Smith's appeals to women's groups to lobby for equal access to old age pensions.[67] She also reiterated demands for dower and community property laws, but the government fought any "imperil[ling of] men's liberty," and British Columbia remained the sole province without dower legislation.[68] Other efforts similarly aimed to bolster women's finances. The 1922 Children of Unmarried Parents Bill promised to compel child support from fathers.[69] The costs of domestic well-being were recognized in her endorsement of the University of British Columbia (UBC) public health nursing program (1920), the 1921 Royal Commission on Health recommendations regarding health insurance and maternity benefits, and the government's acquisition of Tranquille Sanatorium in 1921. Mary Ellen also continued demands for a "single standard of morality" and for divorce equality.[70] In 1921, despite pressure and the clearing of the public gallery, she refused to leave her legislative seat during discussion of venereal disease, the costs of which feminists had long demanded should not rest solely on women.[71] In 1922, she won a minor skirmish about her sex's capacity to confront immorality when she joined MacGill and the WLA in forcing the Liberal convention to endorse women's jury service.[72] She then had to gird herself to repeat the same battle in the legislature: fatigue with male intransigence could not have been far away.[73]

Recurring failures to extend state protection of women and children necessitated familiar band-aid remedies. In 1922, debate about the plight of the unemployed prompted a female delegate to the Vancouver TLC to ask Mary Ellen, "Are we going to stand idly by and see these children starve?" Responding, "We certainly are not," Mary Ellen immediately wired Ottawa and was promised $50,000 by the local Conservative MP "to help feed the children of South Vancouver."[74] The *British Columbia Labor News* reported approvingly that "with all her faults, Mrs. Ralph Smith loves the children," though it disparaged Oliver as "a crabbed specimen of humanity."[75] Sometimes, the maternal MLA could make a difference in Victoria, as when her insistence that "there are no illegitimate children, only illegitimate parents" did much to secure legislation legitimizing offspring after their parents married.[76]

The long-settled British immigrant found broader support in defending White British Columbia. During these years, many of her interventions entailed an anti-modern and racialized narrative, in which women were especially responsible for fending off the "twentieth century inventions and attractions" that threatened "the future of our race."[77] Even as she remained a discreet advocate of birth control, she championed eugenics, suggesting that controlling the reproduction of the "feeble-minded" would limit degeneration within European and other communities. White supremacy similarly required the prevention of miscegenation, especially between Chinese men and British women.[78] In 1923, the New Era League organized a mass meeting in Victoria, which applauded her insistence that "the Oriental is one of the greatest menaces today. You will go out on the street after this meeting and see them riding in their limousines. Most of us will take a street car. I am not so sure they are not using drugs as a means to debase the white race."[79] With their soiled sexuality, female addicts and the mentally inferior (often seen as one and the same) became the antithesis of the responsible White womanhood that was to be protected by mothers' pensions and minimum wage legislation.

Smith continued to support the Canadianization of European newcomers, but she also spent months in 1923 touring the United Kingdom for the federal Department of Immigration and Colonization, attempting to attract new immigrants to Canada. Settlers from the Old Country remained her ideal.[80] At home, she urged audiences "to get an Imperial viewpoint" and to welcome Britishers "for the sake of Canada."[81] Although she was lobbied on behalf of post-war Britain's supposed "surplus" women, she rejected that demeaning designation.[82] She also advised prospective arrivals to be well prepared for a new world that demanded toil and energy. Like many recruiters before her, she targeted female candidates for domestic service to shore up respectable Canadian homes and White dominion.[83]

Mary Ellen's efforts to boom British emigration soon got her into trouble with an old constituency. Accusing her of misleading workers, the *BC Federationist* declared that "unemployment and destitution" existed in British Columbia and that her government "has ignored or refused to take the only steps possible to relieve the misery of the working class in the last great west, where men starve in the midst of plenty, and where the natural resources and the workers are exploited for the profit of a ruling class which has no God, no sentiment, and only greed."[84] She retorted, "I am not ashamed of Canada and I make no apology for it. I do deplore the backdoor kickers," or ignorant people, "who retard the country's progress."[85] Smith's growing breach with labour was highlighted when she enthused about "British capitalists." Her UK tour had included a reception from the mayor at Newcastle, near her old home, and a welcome from the former viceregal couple, the Aberdeens, as well as George V and Queen Mary. She reassured the dubious that her trip had revealed "an almost unanimous view among people of all classes that a more equitable distribution of population throughout the empire would mean greater prosperity for all."[86] She also repudiated claims that the fate of new immigrants was destitution.[87] A long corporate history of using foreign workers to undermine Canadians did nothing, however, to reassure labour doubters. In contrast, Winnipeg's Edith Angell Hancox (b. 1874), another working-class refugee from Britain's harsh realities, turned to the Communist Party in her condemnation of the exploitative imperial colonization programs in these years.[88]

New Liberalism, a key pillar of Smith's post-war politics, was one response to skeptics. The election of reform-minded politicians would harness capital for the collective good. Mary Ellen campaigned for sympathetic candidates across the province, into the Prairies and beyond, notably Ontario.[89] Although the latter would not produce a female member of provincial Parliament until 1943, Smith's endorsement helped Nellie McClung enter the Alberta legislature in 1921.[90] Women everywhere remained her core constituency, but she made veterans a particular concern, especially the wounded, like her son Jack.[91] The New Liberal state was to create jobs and provide relief when the economy failed.[92] Her enthusiasm for UBC, improved facilities for juvenile delinquents, and schools for the blind, deaf, and the feeble-minded was driven in part by the promise of employment in construction and related fields, as well as trust in the benefits of better education.[93] She drew on her own history as a miner's wife to demand that the modern state resolve consumer and cost-of-living problems. During the winter of 1920–21, she backed public protests about the price of coal and the "injustice to the ordinary consumer," demanding a public inquiry into "the chief necessities of life."[94] The same spirit informed her opposition to the regressive personal property tax and her preference for the provincial income tax as the means of generating revenue for state programs.[95] Her advocacy of oil development and an iron and steel industry assumed gains in both employment and taxes.[96] Hopes for revenue similarly encouraged her support for the state sale of liquor, when she split from the WCTU, and for "Buy BC" consumer campaigns.[97] Her agreement to delay the implementation of ILO labour legislation until other provinces acted was a concession to business fears of rivals with lower labour costs. Unsurprisingly, this stance further damaged her relations with unions, which spied subservience to corporate interests.[98]

In a decade still shell-shocked by the killing fields of Flanders, Mary Ellen's support of international peace and the League of Nations expressed the internationalism that was characteristic of New Liberalism, even as it remained closely associated with female reformers and confirmed the maternalism expected of a female MLA.[99] In joining "No More War Demonstrations" alongside the Quakers, the University Women's Club, the Women's International League for Peace and Freedom, the New Era League, the Federated Labour Party, and the Theosophical Society, Smith affirmed the broader progressive networks on which her political life depended. Their vitality remained essential as well to New Liberalism's willingness to tame capitalism. Ultimately, however, the Liberal Party's progressive flank in Canada, as in Britain, was "very much in the minority."[100]

Battle for a Cabinet Position

Smith's policy efforts during her second term attracted less attention than her battle for a cabinet post. With her 1920 victory, suffragists anticipated her appointment to cabinet as proof of "woman's political progress."[101] Their hopes were bolstered when Vancouver partisans demanded better cabinet representation for the city. Rumours circulated that Smith had been promised a high-ranking position when she ran under the "straight Liberal banner."[102] After the election, the prize appeared to be the legislative Speakership, but allies deemed that this would constitute a loss of "significance and usefulness," for all the furor it sparked about suitable hats.[103] Demands for recognition of Mary Ellen focused on a "new department of social service," which would handle the "enforcement of the Minimum Wage law, labor laws, factory inspection, mothers' pensions and social legislation generally." Opponents countered by insisting that BC legislation permitted only "eight salaried" cabinet ministers,[104] spoils that not so incidentally were already divided up among the boys. By February 1921, as both "indignant suffragists" and their foes bombarded Oliver, Mary Ellen had stopped attending the Liberal caucus, in what was described as an "open breach with the premier."[105] The cabinet was evidently split, with Farris in particular named as opposing her elevation.[106]

When Mary Ellen snubbed the backbench, her principles were questioned. An editorial in the previously sympathetic *Vancouver Sun* charged that "Mrs. Ralph Smith is boldly out to get an office for herself even at the cost of splitting the Government, bringing the woman vote into ridicule, and delaying the consideration of important legislative claims. She is no worse than other members who are barking about their claims to jobs."[107] Only after much pressure and much public and apparent personal confusion as to what exactly was offered did Smith emerge in March 1921 as a minister without portfolio, stipend, staff, or the right to join cabinet meetings, in what one newspaper called the premier's "little shell game."[108] Another observer declared that Oliver intended to "be master in his own family" and that he "holds the same views with regard to a woman minister that old fashioned husbands did in regard to their wives. They would give them neither authority to exercise, nor money to spend – a deprivation for which the modern woman finds little compensation in occasional osculatory outbursts."[109] This hollow victory, reported around the world, enshrined Mary Ellen as the first female cabinet minister in Canada and the British Empire. Alberta's Irene Marryat Parlby (1868–1965), who likewise took up a cabinet post in 1921, summed up the reality: "Minister without Portfolio is a stupid position."[110]

The trinket soon lost its shine. Cabinet remained deeply divided about elevating Smith.[111] In response, she launched a charm offensive. At Ottawa's Chateau Laurier in the spring of 1921, this "middle-aged woman with a charming and well modulated voice" announced her pleasure in public life and suggested "that the men in the government of British Columbia are willing to listen to women and to the demands of women not only sympathetically but practically."[112] She was, however, already looking at seemingly greener pastures. When the 1920s produced demands that the Canadian Senate admit women, Mary Ellen, like Alberta's Emily Ferguson Murphy, the instigator of the 1929 Persons Case, became a prospective candidate. In August 1921, the *Vancouver Sun* editorialized that

> Mrs. Ralph Smith has the interests of women at heart. She thoroughly understands the machinery of government and her field of activity and opportunities for good work would be greater in the Canadian Senate than in holding a complimentary season ticket to the meetings of B.C.'s Cabinet. With a few women of Mrs. Murphy's and Mrs. Smith's stamp on its benches, the Senate would soon become more than a refuge for retired political workers.[113]

In September, the New Era League, "British Columbia's most important women's organization," passed a resolution favouring Smith's appointment to the Senate by a "large majority."[114] The *Vancouver Sun* endorsed Mary Ellen as an "exceedingly well-informed woman of magnetic personality."[115]

By September, as the option of a Senate seat faded, Mary Ellen turned her attention to the House of Commons. She publicly considered a run in the federal election of December 6, 1921, against H.H. Stevens, the Conservative MP for Vancouver Centre: "I am prepared to abide by whatever will be in the best interests of our country. I have done my best at Victoria. If they want me at Ottawa – if in the fight for better conditions, for better treatment of our soldier boys – if they want me to help frame better immigration laws – well." She also raised the prospect of tackling discrimination against women in divorce law, an area of federal jurisdiction.[116] Ultimately, inducements to try for Ottawa were insufficient, with the *BC Federationist* sniggering, "Well, we wish her luck! If she can rectify the defects of capitalism a desperate ruling class will write her name in the scroll of fame."[117]

Fearful of losing its star and its link to female activists, the jittery Provincial Liberal Committee contemplated what the *Vancouver Sun* termed "the bribe of a place in the Oliver cabinet with full power over a department and a minister's salary if she will now turn her back on public opinion and refuse to serve the women of Canada at Ottawa." The same article blamed Oliver and Farris for denying Smith, the recipient of over five hundred letters a day, the "power to carry out the great work for which she was elected."[118] In a letter to Prime Minister King, a Liberal activist suggested that the "Farris machine" had engaged in "misrepresentation and fraud" in promising "full cabinet rank" to Smith if she relinquished her plan of running against MP H.H. Stevens.[119] At the beginning of October, even as she endorsed Vancouver mayor Robert H.O. Gale (1878–1950) as the federal Liberal candidate, Smith assured allies that "she hoped to go to Ottawa in the not distant future," either for the city or for "her late husband's old constituency of Nanaimo."[120]

In November 1921, the long-simmering conflict flamed out with Smith's resignation from cabinet. She did not go quietly. Stressing the promise of a ministry for women and children, she said she could not accept responsibility for "the acts of the government without being in a position to criticize or advise." Being "without portfolio" was to act "as a sort of fifth wheel on the political coach, a superfluidity." She would not remain "an ornament or a wallflower." She nevertheless kept the door open, telling the *Vancouver Province* that her "retirement from the cabinet did not mean her withdrawal of support from the Liberal party and the Oliver Government." Noting that she would vote as her conscience dictated, she raised the possibility of a "new woman's party": "Oh, it's moving and moving fast ... Our aim is to have women all over Canada independent of party, so that in seeking legislation affecting women and children particularly it may not be necessary to deal with party factions and compromise ourselves. The women must not be under the domination of any political party."[121] Smith's dramatic secession triggered daylong "messages of congratulation by telephone and telegraph," hailing her for keeping "trust with the women electors."[122]

For many suffragists, Smith's action was nothing less than "a protest from the womanhood of British Columbia against public wrongdoing." Even her Unionist opponent in the 1917 federal election, Janet Kemp of the Widows, Wives and Mothers of British Heroes Association, agreed: "I am glad and I am proud." WLA president Bertha Grace Kidd Menzies (1871–1954) announced, "I knew she was resigning her portfolio because there was nothing in it for her. She had her resignation written out two months ago."[123] Others linked Smith's resignation to cutbacks to mothers' pensions, improperly administered by "strange gentlemen" without commitment to women and children while Mary Ellen bore the "blame for maladministration."[124] The *Vancouver Sun* approvingly quoted a comment from Nancy Astor, Britain's irrepressible Tory MP, that male politicians "belonged to the days of Noah."[125]

Mary Ellen's resignation apparently owed something as well to general caucus unhappiness with Oliver's "dictatorial tendencies." Even as she headed for the door, many men were said to be disenchanted. Harry G. Perry (1889–1959), the Liberal mayor (1917–18, 1920, 1924) and MLA for Fort George, told Oliver that "the caucus system is ... contrary to all democratic principles, a relic of the early days of parliamentary Government ... It chokes and stifles the intellect and ideas of its adherents ... [It is] a dictatorial rule of a minority within a minority."[126] Dissension festered for months, with the premier only slowly reining in his MLAs.[127] Whether because of cowardice, discretion, or hope for reward, no other rebel, however, publicly joined Mary Ellen. Some observers nevertheless charged her with being no better than other politicians. As the *Cranbrook Herald* put it, "'Honest John Oliver'" may have been "a veritable prince of jugglers," but she was "a close second" in claiming to both criticize and support the government.[128] The casual disrespect of many MLAs for "old girls" in public life went largely unremarked.[129]

Although Smith dreamed that her resignation might help Canadian women achieve beneficial legislation without compromising themselves,[130]

Mary Ellen Smith is a Home Woman

A terrifying figure. | *Lethbridge Herald*, May 26, 1928.

her hope proved illusionary. Henceforth, despite regularly barnstorming the province on behalf of the Liberal Party, she left little legislative mark. The party brass trusted her even less than before. In the summer of 1923, having been told that the government "is going to clip my wings," she wrote to Attorney General Alexander Manson to complain: "I have done more for the government than any member of the House, and got less from them than any member." By contrast, any "man who gets ugly & hard to manage gets pretty nearly anything he goes after." Manson disagreed, chiding that the cabinet "is most anxious that you should be well treated, not only as a Liberal, but as the one woman Member of the

House." He grumbled, however, that she had "resigned from the Government at an extremely critical time" without consulting "some of us who thought we were your personal friends." As a result, "You certainly injured yourself ... The rank and file of the Party are not prone to forget the incident."[131] What Manson ignored was that neither Smith nor women in general had reason to trust the Liberals, or indeed any party. A cartoon in the *Lethbridge Herald*, which suggested that other MLAs were terrified by Mary Ellen, was no more than poorly conceived comedy.

Signs of further perfidy came soon enough. In the spring of 1922, Smith and other insurgents had to defend the women's and left Liberal groups of Vancouver from the threat of dissolution by the provincial party brass. The president of the WLA predicted that "if women and progressives were removed, Liberalism in the city would be dead for a half century at least."[132] A visit from Ottawa Liberals that summer was clearly designed to mend fences. King's cabinet ministers "gallantly" joined in "pouring tea and cutting ices at the reception given by the executive of the Women's Liberal Association in honor of them and their wives." Such "chivalry" was matched by local bigwigs, an effort publicly described as "much appreciated by the members of the fair sex." It is unlikely, however, that the latter approved of the sequel when "the members of the male sex assumed full charge of the function."[133] Next year, the attack on affiliated groups resumed, with most women again resisting "expulsion" from the Vancouver City and District Liberal Association. The WLA president announced that she would "not allow the men to accomplish the act of disbanding the women" for "no good purpose" and that the women would not be "domineered" by the men, who were endeavouring to seize hard-won gains.[134] The survival of the women's group barely masked continuing hostility.

In early September 1922, stories circulated of offers to Smith of the post of provincial secretary with responsibility for "one or two small sub-departments of special interest to women."[135] When the BC Liberal convention met in Nelson, however, a "new unity" was proclaimed by the party leaders. Mary Ellen was awarded the sop of a first vice-presidency of the provincial association.[136] Her continuing reservations surfaced in a March 1923 speech to Vancouver's New Era League, during which she said that women required an independent platform. Citing the Canadian Senate, rather than the BC legislative body, she lamented that "there is still something in the male mind that thinks woman's brain is inferior." With equal access to education, women challenged such calumnies. She urged no surrender but agitation "to make the men of the government broaden the scope of the old age pension" and support "equal wage for equal service."[137]

The uphill battle was confirmed a few months later in a speech given by Attorney General Manson to the New Era League and the local Political Equality League. He claimed that women had "arrived" in public life with "higher ideals and finer instincts" than men but too often relied on their "women's intuition." Although he believed that "woman attained her highest and best in the home," he smarmily allowed, in the spirit of the "dope" condemned by McClung, that "women will bring something else to public life that men cannot – the spirit of service." To do this, they should ally with a party and not sit "on the fence." The press reported that his remarks were "warmly received by the women." Since his listeners included Laura Jamieson, who had already ditched the Liberals in favour of the Federated Labour Party, and the rebellious Smith, the actual response was probably closer to nausea.[138] Indeed, less than a week later, Mary Ellen urged the Business and Professional Women's Club to defend "the laws on the statute books of the province for which the women have fought long and hard."[139]

Though she toyed with the possibility that her prospects might be better with the federal Liberals, Mary Ellen had little reason for optimism. In June 1923, the first National Federation of Women's Liberal Clubs was launched in Ottawa before "over 100 Liberal members of the House of Commons and Senate," together with "their wives and daughters." The organizing committee, which included Smith, heard King declare that "group government," a reference to farmers and labour that might well have included women, was "a bad idea." Only liberalism would liberate "individuals or members of a collective group from those obstacles in the way of *his* progress in business, in education, or in *his* social and personal life." King's message was contradicted by a head table populated by male cabinet ministers (and perhaps their unmentioned wives) but few female party activists. No Liberal female legislator, not Smith, McClung, Saskatchewan's Sarah McEwen Ramsland (1882–1964), nor Manitoba's Edith McTavish Rogers (1876–1947), got the honour of inclusion.[140]

Diminishing Returns: The 1924 Election

Despite a relatively strong economy, the June 1924 provincial election confirmed the divisions that beset BC politics. In 1922, unhappy Conservatives had joined a few Liberals in the new Provincial Party, the so-called Shaughnessy Crusade. Two years later, it ran almost a full slate. Premier Oliver irritated his party's left wing with patronage practices that the more idealistic Brewster had earlier condemned. Ultimately, however, both mainstream parties had much in common, notably a commitment to railway expansion (with attendant patronage), Asiatic exclusion, and rising levels of government debt.

During the run-up to the election, the Liberals were sullied with charges of venality involving the Pacific Great Eastern Railway and government liquor sale while bills to implement ILO labour legislation stalled until other jurisdictions acted. Uncertainty about federal-provincial jurisdiction similarly clipped calls for health insurance and maternity benefits.[141] Poor headway on progressive hopes kept Mary Ellen all the more reliant on female loyalists for a boost. An executive member of the Women's Auxiliary of the Great War Veterans' Association went public to assure friends encouraging her to enter politics that she had every confidence in the "social reform" efforts of the government and "the high qualifications of Mrs. Ralph Smith."[142] In rejecting political candidacy, she ignored the strain of serving as the sole representation of suffragist hopes. No wonder Smith sought and campaigned for other female Liberals across Canada.

In the riding of Vancouver City, party advertisements urged, "Vote for the Oliver Six – and Prosperity." The ads praised "fearless fighting" Oliver for bringing honesty and prosperity to British Columbia, and instructed voters, rather curiously, to disregard "personal and political sentiment" and cast their ballots in "their own best interest."[143] Smith stood at the top of the party list alongside two other familiar faces, Farris and the lawyer and military veteran Ian Mackenzie (1890–1949).[144] These veteran MLAs were now joined by business notables – Christopher MacRae (1873–1938), the head of the Alberta Lumber Company; Charles Woodward (1842–1937), president of Woodward's Department Store; and Brigadier-General Victor Odlum (1880–1971), a financier. The selection of these three men indicated the party's shift to the right, much like the British Liberal Party in a December 1923 election. In that election, some more progressive Liberals had responded to the change by entering the Labour Party, which formed a minority government under Ramsay Mac-Donald (1866–1937) in January 1924.[145]

In British Columbia, a Liberal campaign pamphlet titled *Some Plain Facts about the Oliver Government* oozed smug satisfaction with male-run operations. Smith was mentioned just once – as the "mothering MLA."[146] The party nevertheless counted on her to invigorate its campaigns. As Mary Ellen reminded cabinet minister Dufferin Pattullo (1873–1956), the

Conservatives would be competing for crucial female voters.[147] Another minister, M.A. Macdonald, reported to Premier Oliver that "there is no reason why, with Mrs. Smith as a private member we shouldn't do better than our opponents among the women voters." His elaboration was far less positive:

> So far as her own position is concerned ... when she looks into the political mirror she sees only her own reflection. Her action in resigning, and doing so in the middle of a Dominion Election [1921] where attacks on the Provincial Government at that particular time were the chief arguments against the Dominion candidates in Vancouver, was most unjustified.

Smith's utility ultimately kept her a necessary evil, though Macdonald cautioned that she should never be more than a minister without portfolio.[148]

The maverick MLA's reach nevertheless extended beyond Vancouver. She was "inundated with wires and letters from interior candidates" in Princeton, Penticton, Keremeos, Kelowna, Salmon Arm, and Kamloops.[149] On the hustings, Mary Ellen made the case for reform, defending mothers' pensions and social security initiatives as "worth every cent." She quoted "the journal of the Trades and Labor Congress of Canada, which declared that the Oliver government had done more for labor than any government in Canada."[150] The new Provincial Party considered her worrisome enough to target her with cartoons titled "Amours of Oliver," which progressive Liberals deemed "licentious."[151] More significantly, she again faced competition from other women for Vancouver's six seats.[152] Emma Wood Scott (1854–1942), long-time WCC, LCW, and Unionist activist, carried the Conservative banner. Jessie Hall (1872–1949) of the Native Daughters of BC and the board of the Victorian Order of Nurses, stood for the Provincial Party.[153] Priscilla Janet Smith (1879–1954), a Methodist activist and Victorian Order nurse, did the same for the Canadian Labor Party, an advocate, like its British model, for gradualism and a foe of "working-class liberalism and conservatism."[154] A "battle of the tea cups" ensued among the female aspirants for a Vancouver seat, though Priscilla Smith, described "as one of the trump cards of the Labor campaign," announced that the "nearest she expected to get to a tea cup during the campaign would be at her meeting with the union waitresses."[155] In Victoria, long-time activist Mary Gertrude Graves (d. 1929) ran for the Canadian Labor Party.[156] And in Creston, Annie H. Foster, Nelson's first female alderman,[157] represented the Provincial Party.

The magisterial historian Margaret Ormsby later summed up the election as "a revolt by the masses against the caucus system, against machine politics and against the spoils system."[158] The Liberals took five of the six Vancouver seats: Woodward with 5.97 percent of the vote, Odlum with 5.28, MacRae with 5.15, Mackenzie with 4.99, and Mary Ellen with 4.88. The sixth seat went to Andrew McCreight Creery of the Provincial Party, who garnered 4.78 percent. Among the defeated candidates, Hall fell with 4.61, Farris with 4.44, Bowser with 4.12, Wood Scott with 3.84, and Priscilla Smith with 3.20.[159] Oliver went down in Victoria. Until the mail-in ballots were counted, Mary Ellen seemed to be in trouble.[160] When her victory was finally confirmed, the *BC Federationist* mentioned her UK "joytrip" as a federal recruiter, during which she had misled potential immigrants, and trusted that she understood her low election numbers as a reprimand for the jaunt. The paper nevertheless branded her "one of our number" and suggested that she write to "justify herself." It further intoned, "In our opinion, if she does not redeem herself during the coming session, her political future looks very black indeed."[161]

That epitaph was disputed. Allies hailed the now "senior member for Vancouver City" as coming through "with flying colours," bolstered by "her breezy humor, her tolerance for the opinions of others, her smiling acceptance of what knocks come her way in the ordinary course of human events."[162] Writing for the *Edmonton Journal*, a feminist stated that Smith had won "a notable victory" in difficult conditions. She took

> things as they come, the bad with the good, without whimpering. She is so full of grit that she has to be helpless before illness will make her stop working. Trifles never annoy her, she remains serene and optimistic in the face of endless interruptions ... [She is] equally popular with both men and women ... a real home-maker ... the robust, buoyant type, with large blue eyes, well modelled features and light brown hair, – now touched with grey ... and a well set up figure.[163]

In the near future, Smith would need all her reserves of serenity.

The Liberal hold on British Columbia was tenuous. The party had won 31.34 percent of the popular vote and twenty-three seats, but the Conservatives had taken 29.45 percent and seventeen, the Provincial Party 24.16 and three, and the Canadian Labor Party 11.30 and three. Scholars disagree about the meaning of these divisions. Some conclude that "the Liberals' enthusiasm for reform diminished in the 1920s because the political challenge came from the right rather than from the left."[164] Others emphasize a progressive renaissance, with an emerging Liberal agenda of extended workman's compensation, additional funds for UBC, public school reform, old age pensions, health insurance, and maternity benefits.[165] A leading historian of BC politics, Robert McDonald, agreed with the older conclusion of political scientist Martin Robin that Oliver's administration suffered from "acute political anemia" but spied reform's post-1927 reflowering under his successor John Duncan MacLean.[166] He ultimately concluded, however, that the dominant Liberal story was the saga of "scandal related to patronage and the politicization of administration."[167]

As they strove to retain power, BC Liberals scrutinized Ottawa's tumultuous politics, where King stalked farmers and labour and bitterly fought Conservative chieftain Arthur Meighen. During federal elections, British Columbia remained largely in the Conservative camp, ensuring that Mary Ellen was regularly wooed to take down H.H. Stevens, the Vancouver Tory MP.[168] Though she spoke against him, she resisted nomination. Contemporaries gossiped that she was waiting for a call to the Senate.[169] When King stumped British Columbia, he gave her hope, praising her as the fine widow of a fine man and an exemplar of post-war women who "had stepped into public life with their intuitive perception of the welfare and interests of the home and family." Men, he promised, "welcomed that new influence."[170]

Losing Progressive Momentum

In fact, the years after the 1924 election showed little sign of welcome. Female activists were increasingly sidelined in face of reactionary influences such as the Ku Klux Klan, which appeared in both Vancouver and Victoria, the ongoing bigotry of settler society, splits within the labour and feminist left, and the aging out of influence of suffragists. As she watched the darkening portents, Smith urged women to defend their gains: only "acknowledged support" could empower an MLA to do "what was desired."[171] However, according to at least one satirist, she too often evoked another time:

> There is such an air of aloofness about her as she sits in her place, such an indication of undeveloped efficiency, such an increased femininity by reason of there being no other woman there, nobody of comparison. She

has become this last two sessions the living embodiment of Leonardo da Vinci's famous Mona Lisa, the lady with the enigmatic smile. The smile that seems to say, "Ah, you'd laugh, too, if you only knew."[172]

For more radical activists, speaking through Vancouver's *Canadian Labor Advocate* and, soon, the *Labor Statesman,* Smith was of little or no interest: in their rare consideration of women, they turned to socialist and social democratic feminists such as Rose Henderson (1871–1937) and Laura Jamieson.[173] On the other side of the political spectrum, an observer from the Conservative *Vancouver Province* dismissed Smith as giving "no trouble": in fact "no political butter has ever melted in the eloquent mouth of the lady member for Vancouver."[174] If Mary Ellen had once posed a threat to the status quo, she had lost that power.

After 1924, Mary Ellen's causes in and out of the legislature remained aimed at women and children, affirming settler entitlement, and championing liberalism. Charities such as the Salvation Army fundraiser for Vancouver's Grace Maternity Hospital called upon her frequently for the band-aid solutions to inequality that were always needed.[175] In league with Judge MacGill, she championed boys' and girls' industrial homes, probation, the children's aid society, and Juvenile Courts. She made occasional forays into an old feminist issue, tax reform, notably women's liability for poll taxes.[176]

Smith's closest identification remained with women's rights as mothers and workers. The cost of mothers' pensions far exceeded estimates, and Mary Ellen was often in the hot seat of unredeemed expectations. Would-be pension recipients counted on her for help and readily reproached her if they were unsatisfied. One wrote, "I thought Mary Ellen Smith would help the Vancouver widows out better than she has done, but she does not care since she was elected." The answer, that "Mrs. Smith is doing everything in her power to help such cases as yours, and I would suggest that you telephone to her and see if she cannot be of some assistance to you," offered slight consolation.[177] Smith had opposed the removal of oversight by female volunteers, but her hopes increasingly focused on condemning municipalities' avoidance of responsibility for the poor.[178] She warned that desperate wives who should be supported under the Deserted Wives' Maintenance Act contributed to the overload on mothers' pensions. Though she conceded that restrictions on government assistance to mothers "frequently caused hardship," she insisted that "they had been included to counteract an abuse of its privileges by some unscrupulous beneficiaries." Ultimately, BC mothers' pensions remained "the most merciful" in in the world. Cautioning that the Treasury was not "bottomless," she urged increasing the value of property that beneficiaries might hold without penalty and imprisoning fathers delinquent in support of their children.[179] When she joined the Select Committee to Investigate Workmen's Compensation and Mothers' Pensions, she was interested in provision for appeals, exactly what female supervision had allowed in the early pension program. The absence of women in key roles made male MLAs' referral of mothers' pensions cases to her as "the only woman member" all the more galling.[180]

Mary Ellen was similarly on the spot for the defects in minimum wage legislation. That proverbial "half loaf" covered few occupations, ignored the cost of living, and required victims to initiate complaints against their employers. A female factory worker who attended a TLC meeting typically blamed Smith for the law's exclusion of women piece workers.[181] With very limited influence on the administration of women's minimum wage, Smith shifted her attention to the professionalization and unionization of workers in domestic service, still the largest area of female employment. She urged "a large gathering of household workers" to compare themselves to nurses and to take pride in uniforms. She was not alone. Vancouver's TLC president promised his support. Mary Ellen's backing for household science at UBC was part of the same attempt to upgrade an occupational ghetto.[182]

A more significant effort to intervene in the labour market was Smith's 1927 bill to allow the hairdressing and beauty services industry, dominated by women and rapidly expanding in response to the new fashion for shorter hair and the commercialization of beauty regimes, to regulate itself independently of male barbers. In 1924, the latter had won legislative protection for their professional status, but this had expressly excluded women. The opposition of the barbers and disinterest of other MLAs – a reflection of their general lack of respect, often hostility, for female labour – doomed Smith's bill. In 1929, the Hairdressing Association again approached Victoria, this time with the support of labour-affiliated MLAs and the barbers.[183] The resulting legislation confirmed segregated work spaces, with (male) barbers serving male customers and (female) hairdressers serving women, boys under seven, and "men being fitted for wigs."[184] By then, however, Mary Ellen was no longer an MLA.

Settler Assertions

As a seasoned legislator, Mary Ellen continued to embrace special entitlements for the British community while acknowledging the contribution of other worthy Europeans: "The people of Italy, Germany, Scandinavia and other European countries have brought with them their art, folklore, traditions and culture, and are a great asset to growing Canada."[185] While she largely snubbed Indigenous Peoples, she increased her attacks on Asians as workers, employers, and dispensers of drugs who imperilled British dominion. In 1923, she defended the Women's and Girls' Protection Act, which in its original form barred Chinese-owned laundries and restaurants from hiring White or Indian women, and in late 1924 she sponsored Bill 24, which prohibited the employment of Chinese men and White women servants in the same household. It was nicknamed the Janet Smith Bill, in reference to a Scottish nanny who had been murdered in the Vancouver mansion of a rich couple, supposedly by Wong Foon Sing, one of their Chinese servants.[186] Although the legislative gallery applauded and local Scottish Societies decorated MLAs' seats with heather, support ebbed away. The *BC Federationist* accused Smith of favouring "idiotic legislation," insisting that "our quarrel is not with the unfortunate Orientals who happen to be seeking their bread here. Our quarrel is the same as theirs – with capitalism."[187] Since the bill clearly tread on federal jurisdiction, the *Vancouver Province* spied grandstanding by the lady MLA.[188] In Victoria, more progressive clubwomen worried about losses for female workers and condemned "the unfairness of the apparent assumption that an Oriental was the guilty party in the case in question." They "pointed out that British law was based on the acceptance of the innocence of a defendant until he or she was proved guilty."[189] After Wong Foon Sing had been kidnapped, tortured, and subsequently released by vigilantes, he was tried for murder, but the case collapsed for want of evidence. The strongest denunciation came from the BC Chinese community, whom Smith ignored.[190] When her bill was dropped, she took consolation in raising public awareness of the supposed Asian threat to White employment and morality.[191]

Segregation and surgical sterilization of the supposedly mentally unfit joined Asian exclusion and job bans in her defence of settler society.[192] She showed those sympathies as a member of the Dominion Board of Mental Hygiene, but she was not unusual in her endorsement of intervention. A series of reports from the provincial Royal Commission on Mental Hygiene took the same stance in these years.[193] Institutionalization of so-called abnormal children and adults was deemed necessary so that "the English-speaking peoples would maintain their position of supremacy on which the peace and prosperity of the world depended." She congratulated Washington State for having "the courage" to introduce a bill for the sterilization of "mental defectives."[194] Her sympathies for eugenics owed something to traditional labourism's "strong belief in advancement according to merit – meaning, implicitly, through manual or mental proficiency and honest labour."[195] Casualties of mental impairment and drug addiction lacked such virtues. The protection of "the race" likewise inspired her well-publicized demands for flogging of both female and male drug dealers, who similarly threatened British superiority.[196] The growing prominence of such reactionary proposals in the arsenal of British Columbia's sole female MLA corroded all claims to advanced politics.

Liberalism

Despite battling with Liberal apparatchiks and politicians, Mary Ellen refused to move left, as suffragists Laura Jamieson and Susie Lane Clark had done. She relied on Liberal support for institutions such as UBC, the Tranquille anti-tubercular hospital, schools for the blind and the deaf, asylums for the mentally ill and feeble-minded, and reformatories to offer the best deal available, as had been the case with mothers' pensions and the minimum wage. Funding infant social security became a gnawing preoccupation. The extension of the Pacific Great Eastern Railway to Prince George,[197] like the fostering of a BC iron and steel industry, would put cash into the pockets of workers, businessmen, and governments. Development would help fund old age pensions, for which British Columbia passed enabling legislation in 1927, while reducing the number of applicants who required their means-tested aid. Liberal enthusiasm for efficiency was a further way of maximizing resources. The Town Planning and City Manager Bills she introduced in December 1925 aimed at curbing patronage and corruption.[198] Smith's zest for boosting BC business sometimes led to strange bedfellows. Her 1925 New Year's wish to offer "every encouragement to industries ... to meet world competition" saluted ex-premier Richard McBride, an anti-suffragist, as "the father of the slogan, 'If you can't boost, don't knock.'" Rather extraordinarily for a politician who had long claimed a distinctive mandate, she ignored women, children, and workers in her message.[199]

More obvious was Smith's continuing service to the Liberal Party, for which she took on the provincial presidency and rallying the faithful across British Columbia. Many of her speeches appeared designed to deflect criticism and disappointment, as in 1925 when she told Ottawa's Women Liberals that "not one Conservative Government ever had the nerve to undo a law put on the statute books by Liberals."[200] She ventured into the anti-suffrage fortress of Quebec. Speaking before the Montreal Reform Club for federal Liberals, she eulogized Laurier and condemned Arthur Meighen's Conservatives "for the national debt, the difficult immigration situation and the general dissatisfaction among the returned soldiers." The rights deficit of Quebec women triggered a feminine charm offensive. To "general hilarity," she teased her dinner table-mate Liberal premier Louis-Alexandre Taschereau (1867–1952), suggesting that he had been "flirting" with her and that she could do "a lot with this premier if I lived in your province."[201] The response of hard-pressed local suffragists is unknown. Certainly, the anti-feminist Taschereau found no reason to reconsider votes for women.[202]

Much of Mary Ellen's party service in these years was largely ceremonial, as in 1927 when she entertained the wives of other Liberal MLAs.[203] A Nelson rally for the new premier, John Duncan MacLean, typified her modus operandi. After accompanying a soloist, she played "old time favorite songs in which the entire assembly joined."[204] Charming the men, however, was becoming a stale narrative, and BC skeptics increasingly scorned such spectacles. One *Vancouver Province* columnist played with the meaning of a familiar tune, "Coming through the Rye," based on a poem by Robbie Burns (1759–96), while expositing traditional misogyny, in dismissing the former WCTU member as she endeavoured to rally voters in Nelson, where alcohol, as elsewhere, remained a constant of political life:

> She realizes the futility of all political reasoning and decides to reach the hearts of the people through her gift for music. It is a charming picture ... Intuition is the thing and Mrs. Smith's intuitions are correct. At the recent convention of the British Association for the Advancement of Learning it was shown that women's intuitions are always more lucid than those of man and for the reason that women are less blessed with the reasoning faculty. Let us hope that her vigor of attack and pianistic skill ... in rendering 'Coming Through the Rye' was not intended as a subtle hint upon campaigning methods in that sanctified borough.[205]

Even as she kept up assistance to the Liberal Party, Mary Ellen could not hide her growing disappointment with post-suffrage politics. She was not alone. Many Liberal women had hoped that Mackenzie King would "give women a real place in the councils of the nation." They had anticipated that federal patronage appointments, which had always gone to male party loyalists, would now be allocated to women as well.

Jobs on Ottawa's Tariff Board, for example, were considered appropriate, and overdue, recognition of women's talents as "practical economists."[206] Activists lobbied for the appointment of Smith, but the board remained all-male, which critics judged "a breach of promise to the women of Canada." When neither Meighen nor King's administrations selected women for any "lucrative government position," outraged observers warned that "politicians of all stripes will pay for breaking promises to the women voters."[207] Punishment did not come. Instead, women found themselves receiving little more than baubles for service and competence. In 1928, amid renewed rumours that Mary Ellen would enter the BC cabinet, which set "political tongues a-wagging,"[208] she became a one-day replacement for the House Speaker, the first time that honour had gone to a woman in the British Empire or Commonwealth. Observers who were oblivious to misogyny described it as the "final step in the emancipation of women."[209] Dismal prospects were not restricted to any party. In 1927, Conservatives met in Winnipeg with 360 accredited female delegates, but "matters important to the women were never allowed to reach the floor of the convention," and efforts "to form a national sisterhood of Conservative women" collapsed.[210]

As the 1920s closed, Mary Ellen and many female Liberals were losing patience. In November 1927, over a hundred Vancouver women created "a women's Liberal organization of an educational nature." Named the Laurier Club, after the defunct anti-suffragist, what it had to offer postwar women was far from clear.[211] More significant was the emergence in 1928 (with origins in 1923) of the National Women's Liberal Federation in Ottawa. Its divisions – between east and west, between French and English, and between those who warned of female separatism and those who embraced it – revealed the difficulty of mobilization.[212]

As one of the two surviving Liberal women provincial legislators (the other was Manitoba's Edith McTavish Rogers), Mary Ellen was the unanimous choice for the first president of the National Women's Liberal Federation. Her acceptance speech did more than hint at dissatisfaction:

> There was a feeling throughout the country that the women were being chloroformed. But we refused to react to the anaesthetic. I did not want the presidency. But now that I have it and that you have set up the machinery to make this a permanent organization I am going to stay until that machinery is in smooth running order, and I shall welcome criticism. From now on we women want to go on record as being constructionists.[213]

Critical feminist onlookers were less optimistic. The new federation lacked representatives of the "wives of laboring men, factory and store workers, the armies of stenographers and other business women ... and farm women."[214] Such exclusions had already undermined the National Council of Women. What could Mary Ellen, a miner's wife and daughter, who had arrived in Nanaimo in 1892, offer as the flapper decade ended? That question preoccupies the next chapter.

7
On the Margins, 1928–33

Although the 1924 election contest was often gloomy, its 1928 counterpart destroyed what little remained of first-wave feminist hopes for a justice revolution in British Columbia. The Liberal Party was voted out of office, and Mary Ellen failed to take the riding of Esquimalt. It was the long-time fiefdom of Charles Edward Pooley (1845–1912) and his son Robert Henry (1878–1954), her family's old adversaries as the henchmen of the Dunsmuir coal barons. Compromised suffragist and liberal-labour dreams found no safe harbour among a BC electorate betrayed by misogyny, nativism, and class politics. A monument to blighted expectations, Mary Ellen continued her slide from the political centre stage as liberal-labour's not always predictable "old lady," or that "old cat," as she was christened by the Pooley crowd. Familiar causes, such as mothers' pensions and reform liberalism, hung on, as did her hopes for political election or appointment, but British Columbia's most famous lady was deeply wounded, bereft of most of the progressive allies who had returned her in triumph to Victoria in 1918. This last chapter charts that stage in a feminist, settler, and liberal-labour trajectory that marooned a former working-class woman as a historical curiosity for almost a century.

Testing Times

Between 1928 and 1933, progressive British Columbians found plentiful cause for discouragement in shambolic politics, economic collapse, and surging misogyny. The October 1929 stock market crash was the sign of worse to come. British Columbia's per capita income dropped by nearly half between 1929 and 1933. Although women's jobs and low pay had rarely been sought by men, female wage-earners, particularly wives, were regularly scapegoated for the ills of the times. Public relief, which scorned both unemployed single women, who were expected to embrace domestic service, and single men, who were directed to federal and provincial relief camps, proved no bulwark against distress. Desperate for jobs, refugees from other hard-hit regions, often young men but a few women too, fuelled fear and bitterness at the failures of Canadian governments and the glaring and widening gulf between rich and poor. The shrinking tax base, the bankruptcy of municipalities such as North Vancouver and Burnaby, and the growing popular protest (often associated with the Communist Party) against work camps, evictions, and police brutality set the stage for rising dread of revolution and demands for new solutions.

All parties struggled to confront the emerging disaster. On the left, the Canadian Labor Party (with its briefly united communist and socialist front) challenged working-class liberalism and conservatism as well as capitalism, but it formally disappeared in discord over Asian enfranchisement at the end of the 1920s. Meanwhile, the Canadian Communist Party struggled to mobilize more than a minority of workers after its founding in 1921. In 1933, shortly after Mary Ellen's death, the BC section of the Co-operative Commonwealth Federation (CCF) appeared as another "effort at labour political unity" and it warred internally about a common front with Communists.[1] After the November election, the CCF formed the official Opposition, with seven seats and 31.53 percent of the popular vote. It became the future of the province's parliamentary left and the nightmare of Conservatives and Liberals, when they were not obsessed with Communist bogeymen.

The Conservatives under Simon Fraser Tolmie (1867–1937), British Columbia's only Métis premier (though that genealogy largely slid under the public radar), were well placed to take the 1928 election, but internecine feuds made them vulnerable.[2] Their prioritization of corporate interests between 1928 and 1933 helped ensure that they would never again form a BC government. As the Tories flailed in confronting the Great Depression, provincial Grits, like Mary Ellen, scrambled to mount an alternative, but the party remained factious, splitting once again between progressives and reactionaries. In November 1933, Dufferin Pattullo, no friend of feminism or veteran lady MLAs, emerged with the "Little New Deal" (evoking the contemporary agenda of US president Franklin D. Roosevelt) to form a majority government with thirty-four seats and 41.74 percent of the vote. Vancouver Liberal Helen Douglas Smith (1886–1955), who had been defeated in 1928, was returned as the sole female MLA.

Federal politics were equally contentious, but the timing of elections, 1930 and 1935, put Tory prime minister R.B. Bennett in the hot seat for the worst of the decade. He had little to offer the unemployed, ensuring that no government of his persuasion would reappear in Ottawa until 1957. In the July 1930 election, British Columbia returned seven Conservative and five Liberal MPs, contributing to the 135 to 89 Canada-wide result. Nine female candidates ran in that contest: three Liberals, one Progressive, two Farmers, one Independent Conservative, and two Independents. None stood in British Columbia, where a woman would not run federally until 1935. The Progressive Party continued to disintegrate, with its more radical members allied to the parliamentary Labour group and then the CCF led by James Woodsworth. Bennett's pyrrhic election victory freed King to slither left in hopes of outflanking the CCF, but by then death had removed Mary Ellen. In 1935, Martha Munger Black (1866–1957), who earlier slandered Smith in the 1928 provincial campaign, replaced her husband, a Conservative Yukon MP, in the House, where she joined the veteran Agnes Campbell Macphail. The Senate remained a male preserve until Alberta's Famous Five scored a Privy Council decision in 1929. King appointed a wealthy Liberal activist, Cairine Reay Mackay Wilson (1885–1962), in 1930 and Bennett a Conservative, Iva Campbell Fallis (1883–1956), in 1935.

Commonly ignored as a contribution to the progressive malaise of the later 1920s and early 1930s was the sideswiping of suffragists. Although they possessed a wealth of talent, few got the nod from major parties or winnable constituencies. Some persevered in trying to influence mainstream politics, but repeated disappointment taught hard lessons, and something like an activist fatigue understandably dogged a generation that had grown old in suffragist campaigns. A handful of hardy survivors turned to labour, socialist, and communist alternatives; more continued to seek satisfaction in women's independent organization, where familiar options such as the University Women's Clubs and the Local Councils remained popular. A few focused on often progressive efforts from the Business and Professional Women's Clubs, the Women's International League for Peace and Freedom, and the Pan-Pacific Women's Association. In none was Mary Ellen the acknowledged leader she had once been. Her absence from the front ranks of the era's organized women confirmed her growing marginality to feminist politics.

Sending women home. | "The Confessions of a She-Politician," *Maclean's Magazine*, June 1, 1922.

Maclean's, self-described as "Canada's National Magazine," conveyed the taken-for-grantedness of prejudice and male entitlement in Smith's last decade. In 1922, it published an article that would rightly be derided as "fake news" a century later. Accompanied by the cartoon above, "The Confessions of a She-Politician" purported to be a "startling admission from the pen of a successful feminine politician, known in several Canadian provinces." The anonymous author claimed to be a reasonable suffragist. Certainly not one of the "agitating variety," she was properly thankful to the good men who conferred the franchise and was only anxious to share the burden of government. She claimed to have been brought to her senses by a stint in provincial office, which had taught her that it was "a grave mistake for women to rush into political life." She confessed to succumbing to the "feminine mind," prone to "awandering" when serious matters were at hand. She absolved the male sex of responsibility for the tiny numbers of women in political office and smeared women as largely frivolous and inept. Denounced as uninterested in candidates' "qualification or preparation for office," clubwomen were parodied as little more than defenders of their "social standing" and toadies to "male relatives." That behaviour explained their sex's political failure.[3]

Feminist critics of such misinformation were outraged. In time for Dominion Day, teacher M. Ada Dickey of Pembroke, Ontario, took direct aim. Concluding that the "purpose of *Maclean's Magazine* was (if it had one) … to insult the women of Canada," she cast doubt on the gender of the author. In any case, that writer was a "coward," purveying no more than the "anti-suffrage" views of "the days gone by in English, United States and Canadian third-rate publications."[4] A few months later, after consultation with Canada's six other female legislators, Alberta MLA Nellie McClung challenged the "she-politician." She went straight to the heart of editorial integrity:

> I do not doubt for a moment that a lot of people would be glad to think that the women in politics are just as shallow and insincere as the writer of this article evidently is, but even that fact does not establish the truth of her assertions, and the point at issue is this: the writer of this article IS NOT one of the women politicians of Canada.[5]

The editor remained unrepentant. He conceded that none of the six female legislators had written the piece, but he refused to recant. In listing them, he deliberately emphasized their relationship to men – "Miss Agnes McPhail, Mrs. Arthur Rogers, Winnipeg, Mrs. L.C. McKinney, Claresholm, Alb., Mrs. Harvey Price, Grande Prairie, Alb., Mrs. Walter Parlby, Alix, Alb., Mrs. Ralph Smith, Victoria, B.C., and Mrs. H.S.L. McClung, Edmonton." The article remained, as it does today on the *Maclean's* online archive, apparently a searing testament to women's inadequacy and self-hatred.[6]

Maclean's returned to the same mean spirit in February and March 1929. Its "Letters of a Woman M.P.," purportedly written by a Miss Clarice McAllister, MP, for the non-existent riding of Seebach, Ontario, clearly targeted Agnes Campbell Macphail. Running for the United Farmers of Ontario, Macphail had won her seat in the 1921 federal election, and Canadian publications had conspicuously neglected her, but now *Maclean's* lampooned her as singularly superficial and pretentious.[7] Its fondness for women-blaming was further reaffirmed just months after Mary Ellen's death. This time, however, it employed a female writer, Dora M. Sanders. She denounced women who refused to be free and stated that female Canadians were no more than a "subject race," more submissive than ever to male rule. "The vote is superfluous to them, because they have other, better, more practiced ways of getting what they want," as "the weaker sex – dependent, devoted and indispensable."[8] Such pontifications typified the steady drip, drip, drip of political discouragement that mounted in Smith's last years. The 1930 Liberal campaign poster, showing a radiant White Miss Canada above the phrase "The Gates Are Mine to Open," was no more than a fanciful expression of the "dope" damned by McClung as sedating women, as well as a typical example of the racialized sexual double entendres that haunted treatments of public women.

"Vote Liberal," campaign poster, 1930. This stereotypical representation of Canadian womanhood favoured whiteness and beauty. Suffragists often did the same, as demonstrated by the figure of Justice on the cover of *The Champion*, Canada's only magazine dedicated to suffrage (see page 85). | William Lyon Mackenzie King Papers, 1930 Election Posters, C-029363, Library and Archives Canada.

The 1928 Election: The Fall of a Liberal-Labour Lady

Mary Ellen always claimed a province- and nation-wide constituency. In 1928, this was tested when politics returned her to Vancouver Island, not to Nanaimo, but to Esquimalt, the home of another political clan. Charles Edward Pooley had served as a lawyer to the mine-owning and

This cartoon took for granted Mary Ellen's re-election. "Speaking of House-Cleaning," *Vancouver Sun*, July 13, 1928.

union-busting Dunsmuirs and as a Conservative MLA from 1882 to 1907. Mary Ellen faced his son, lawyer Robert Henry Pooley, a veteran of the legislature since 1912. She had already crossed swords with him in defending domestic science in the public schools, a cause without resonance for a man whose "most upper crust family" employed a Chinese chef and "uniformed maids."[9]

Many details of her move to hostile territory have disappeared, but press coverage reveals their outlines.[10] In February 1927, when the local Women's Liberal Club endorsed Mary Ellen "as a representative whose whole-hearted interest is for the women and children of British Columbia," she seemed fixed to stay in Vancouver.[11] Soon enough, however, arguably the city's two most prominent Liberal standard-bearers – Smith and Ian Mackenzie – became "lonely exiles" and "party deportees."[12] Like the transfer to North Vancouver of Mackenzie, another left Liberal victor in 1924, Mary Ellen's ejection from her stronghold appeared grounded in the internecine struggles bedevilling the Lower Mainland party. It may also have reflected a desire to bring younger blood into a seemingly safe seat. A Liberal nomination in Vancouver's multiple-member constituency (always better for women than single-member alternatives) went to Helen Douglas Smith, never known as a suffragist, whom party advertising reduced to "Mrs. Paul Smith."[13] Her social credentials as a granddaughter of former premier John Robson (1824–92) placed her in the upper echelons of both the Native Daughters of Canada and of British Columbia, as well as of the National Council of Women.[14] By choosing this descendant of privilege, the party could foreswear allegiance to an activist linked to the demands of feminists and workers for a fair deal.

According to the Liberal-minded *Vancouver Sun,* sending "one of the doughtiest campaigners" up against Pooley, the Conservative House leader and "hereditary member for Esquimalt," was an attempt by Premier John MacLean "to break into that solid phalanx of Tory representation."[15] In Ontario, the *Windsor Star* forecast that "the highlight to the coming provincial election" would be in "the nearest thing to a bomb-proof [Tory] stronghold in Western Canada." The paper also noted that Mary Ellen was no stranger to Esquimalt, as it had been part of Ralph's federal riding and she had been "his chief of staff when he entered the field against a leading scion of the eminent Dunsmuir family, then at the height of their power, politically, industrially and socially."[16] Mary Ellen attempted to fig leaf her ouster by referring to "her old friends in the constituency" who had spent "two years" encouraging her to return to Vancouver Island, "her old love."[17] In contrast, enemies reported that the Nanaimo Liberals had summarily rejected her.[18]

An observer for the Conservative *Vancouver Province* broke into verse in describing Smith's forced desertion of "the safe seat in Vancouver":

How Mary Ellen, overbold,
With queenly courage, high intent,

Packed up a carpet bag and went,
Determined, eloquent and coolly,
To strew the plain with Mister Pooley –
Whose only great outstanding fault
Was being sure of Esquimalt.

He clearly salivated at the prospects for "the failure of that splendid exhibition of courage."[19]

Esquimalt politics proved tumultuous even before Smith sparred with Pooley. She was parachuted in over Frank Carlow (1880–1940), former president of the local Liberal Association and the party's 1924 standard-bearer. However, Carlow had blotted his copybook by charging that government liquor sales were besmirched by corruption.[20] Eventually, by running as an Independent Liberal, he drained only a handful of votes from the mainstream Liberal Party. More significantly, he diminished enthusiasm for the Grit cause, which could only appear more immersed in partisan disagreements.[21] As that dissent within the local party organization foreshadowed, Mary Ellen would be readily tarred with government misdeeds. Being vilified was not a new experience, but the 1928 attack involved charges that her son Jack was in the pocket of the Liberal Party's "Vancouver liquor gang." Ian Mackenzie, dubbed by foes "the greatest political bluffer in the province," and Smith's sometime opponent within the party and former attorney general J.W. de Beque Farris, were imported to Esquimalt as her champions.[22] She herself passionately attacked the "cowardly" assault on her "wonderful son," who had "won his spurs on the battlefield and came home with the disabilities from which he is suffering to-day, and will suffer as long as he lives."[23] Nonetheless, some of the mud stuck.[24]

If press attention is any indication, however, Conservative efforts to deny Mary Ellen credit for progressive legislation and to claim it as their own were more damaging. Such appropriation was not unprecedented. Tory rival Edith Patterson and others had made such charges in the 1924 election. Pooley and his henchmen once again pilloried Mary Ellen because she had supported Oliver's efforts to "pass the buck to Ottawa" on labour legislation, health insurance, and maternity benefits.[25] They stressed her failure to support labour members' demands that British Columbia not wait for other provinces or the federal government to proceed with the progressive legislation inspired by the International Labor Organization.[26] Remaking history, they insisted that Conservatives had always sided with workers in favouring immediate reforms. Pooley

STARTLING EXPOSURE!

MacLean, His Cabinet, Mary Ellen Smith and Hon. Ian McKenzie Opposed and Obstructed Social and Labor Legislation

SESSION	Substance of Question Voted On.	MacLean's VOTE	MANSON	PATULLO	SUTHER-LAND	BARROW	Mary Ellen SMITH	Hon. Ian McKENZIE	A.D. Patterson (Lib. Whip.)
1920	BILL No. 8—Shall workers in sawmills, shingle mills, pulp mills and paper mills have an eight-hour day?	NO	NO	NO	NO	NO	Not in House	Not in House	Not in House
1921 (2nd)	BILL No. 9—Shall "Eight-hour Day Act" passed unanimously at 1st Session of 1921 come into force?	Not in House	Not in House	NO	YES	NO	NO	YES	NO
1921 (2nd)	BILL No. 7—Shall "Night Employment of Women Act" passed unanimously at 1st Session of 1921 come into effect ?	NO	Not in House	NO	NO	NO	NO	YES	NO
1921 (2nd)	BILL No. 5—Shall "Employment of Children Act" passed unanimously at 1st Session of 1921 come into force ?	NO	Not in House	NO	NO	NO	NO	YES	NO
1921 (2nd)	BILL No. 6—Shall "Night Employment of Young Persons Act" passed unanimously at 1st Session of 1921 come into force ?	NO	Not in House	NO	NO	NO	NO	YES	NO
1922	BILL No. 31—Shall "Eight-hour Day Act" passed unanimously at 1st Session of 1921 come into force?	NO	NO	NO	NO	Not in House	NO	NO	NO
1922	BILL No. 49—Shall "Night Employment of Young Persons Act" passed unanimously at 1st Session of 1921 come into force ?	NO	NO	NO	NO	NO	NO	Not in House	NO
1922	BILL No. 48—Shall "Night Employment of Women Act" passed unanimously at 1st Session of 1921 come into force ?	NO	NO	NO	NO	NO	NO	Not in House	NO
1922	BILL No. 52—Shall "Employment of Children Act" passed unanimously at 1st Session of 1921 come into force ?	NO	NO	NO	NO	NO	NO	Not in House	NO
1922	BILL No. 42—Shall coal miners be able to report dangerous places in mines in which they are working without being in danger of being discharged?	NO	NO	NO	NO	NO	NO	NO	NO
1922	MOTION—Should the government have been prepared to introduce legislation in the interests of the unemployed at this session ?	NO	NO	NO	NO	NO	NO	NO	Not in House
1922	MOTION—Will the House consider an adjournment to discuss the question of unemployment?	NO	NO	NO	NO	NO	NO	NO	Not in House
1922	MOTION—Will the House consider an adjournment to discuss the question of unemployment?	NO	NO	NO	NO	NO	NO	NO	NO
1922	MOTION—Will the House go into Committee to consider the question of State Health Insurance with a view to having a Bill brought in before the close of the Session?	NO	NO	NO	NO	NO	NO	NO	NO
1923	BILL No. 32—Shall "Eight-hour Day Act" come into effect on July 1st, 1924, instead of January 1st, 1925 ?	NO	NO	NO	NO	NO	NO	NO	NO
1923	MOTION—Will the House allow the introduction of a Bill to extend the benefits of the "Workmen's Compensation Act ?"	NO	NO	NO	NO	NO	NO	NO	NO
1923	MOTION—Will the House consider a motion to discuss labor conditions in Nanaimo?	NO	NO	NO	NO	NO	NO	NO	NO
1924	MOTION—Will Legislature disapprove of regulations made by Mothers' Pensions Commissioners, and that a woman must be deserted two years before she can receive assistance?	NO	NO	NO	NO	NO	NO	NO	Paired
1924	MOTION—Will House consider a motion to adjourn on a matter of urgency? Note—The matter of urgency was to meet a big delegation of unemployed which was waiting outside Parliament Buildings.	NO	NO	NO	NO	NO	NO	NO	NO
1925	BILL No. 74—Shall "Minimum Wage Act" apply to industries other than Lumbering and Coal Mining?	NO	NO	NO	YES	NO	NO	Not in House	NO
1925	BILL No. 75—Shall Sumas farmers retain their right to appeal for justice to the courts?	NO	NO	YES	NO	NO	NO	NO	NO
1928	MOTION—Will the House consider a resolution petitioning the Dominion Parliament that Old Age Pension age limit from 70 to 65 be lowered, and dependent pensioner's dwelling house from being subject to repayment of pension?	NO	NO	NO	NO	NO	NO	NO	NO

"Startling Exposure!" *Nanaimo Free Press*, July 17, 1928.

effectively used Mary Ellen's uncertain voting record to knock her claims that "she is the representative of the labor classes; who says she has fought to better workmen's conditions and to bring about social legislation to help the masses."[27] He went farther still, implying venality with regard to the expansion of social security, charging that "Mrs. Smith had been filling out pension applications, with her personal guarantee that the pensions would be guaranteed."[28] Conservative attacks, such as the *Nanaimo Free Press*'s "Startling Exposure," highlighted the apparent hollowness of Liberal claims to the progressive high ground. Of course, as long as the Tories remained in Opposition, their actual commitment to a better deal could not be tested.[29] After they took the reins in 1928, protective legislation found no friend in government.

Whatever truth they might hold, assaults on Mary Ellen were, as in the past, ridden with misogyny. References to her as "an alley cat" and an "old lady with a convenient memory" told a familiar story. Women's groups denounced such insults, promising to repay them in full at the voting booth. They also attempted to turn the tables, noting that

> with over forty seats at their disposal in this province, not one Conservative nomination has been offered or given to a woman. Why? Toryism resents the intrusion of women into politics, just as in England Toryism resented and fought extending the franchise beyond a few titled gentlemen controlling pocket boroughs ... Women ... [were] slowly fighting their way to freedom.[30]

In hearing of the slurs, Helen Douglas Smith issued a ladylike rebuttal from Vancouver, trusting "that the men of Esquimalt will show their innate chivalry and the women of Esquimalt unanimously will stand behind Mrs. M.E. Smith."[31] A Conservative enthusiast dismissed this "bleat about chivalry" and thundered that electoral loyalty should go to Pooley, not to a woman who had barged "incontinently into a distant riding."[32]

The Tories opened a second front by enlisting their own female shock troops, who demanded repudiation of the "stranger from Vancouver," other women's "cast-off."[33] Some three hundred women, welcomed to a garden party at the ornate mansion of Pooley's mother, heard charges that Mary Ellen "had ranged herself against social legislation." Also present was Mrs. Owen Rede Campbell (c. 1866–1953), a prominent Conservative activist and suffragist from Montreal with a sister in Victoria's well-to-do enclave of Uplands, who commended the "sane, honest, and progressive" choice of Pooley, announcing that "she was proud to hear Mr. Pooley state that he had cast his vote in the Legislature in favor of votes for women."[34] Another heavy-hitter, Mrs. George Black, wife of the sitting MP for the Yukon, justified the Tory failure to nominate female candidates: "women are home-makers and have no place in politics," a conclusion condemned by the *Vancouver Sun* as "out of tune with the spirit and the needs of the West."[35] In the Lower Mainland, a female Conservative declared herself honoured to recommend "such a wonderful set of businessmen" and insisted that the "foundation" for social legislation had been "laid by the previous Conservative government."[36] On Vancouver Island, Lottie Bowron (1879–1964), once the personal secretary to Premier McBride and soon to be appointed the BC rural teachers' welfare officer (women), likewise insisted that mothers' pensions were "stolen" from the Conservative platform.[37] Foes gleefully foresaw that the Liberal "machine" had sent Mary Ellen "to be politically buried."[38]

Local defenders nevertheless rallied. The Grit-inclined *Victoria Times* insisted that rumours that this "talented lady" could not "secure a nomination elsewhere" were "groundless," that "dissatisfaction" with Pooley was "widespread," and that his "citadel" was vulnerable.[39] A garden party of female Liberals protested Pooley's slanders and recalled "many scenes in the Legislature of which we as women are ashamed when indignities were heaped upon the lady member on many occasions."[40] In Victoria, the Liberal Women's Forum proudly hosted gatherings at which their candidate called for a "united womanhood" for "clean politics" and against men's "habit of throwing 'mud.'"[41]

Undeterred by slings and arrows, Mary Ellen ran a spirited campaign, working hard to recruit female voters, including those who were intimidated by formal political gatherings.[42] She resurrected old themes, suggesting that if voters "made her national housekeeper she would go into house cleaning, and go into the corners, and make this corner of Vancouver Island what it should be." At that rally, however, Mary Ellen made a rare misstep, suggesting that a king – Pooley – should be replaced by a queen.[43] This remark was hardly likely to win approval from the democratic voters whom she hoped to attract, and it played into the hands of her opponents.[44] She also promised that "if there is any rough stuff I will be right in the ring to put my opponents to shame."[45] Nevertheless, the *Victoria Times* reported that she kept to the high ground, delivering

> characteristic addresses – no personalities of any kind, but well-reasoned, convincing arguments in favour of the Government's return to power, based on its achievements in social legislation, the high credit it has secured

in the money markets of the world as the result of careful financing and its development of the Province in all lines of industrial, commercial and agricultural endeavour.

The good imperialist and churchgoer had only to mention Queens Elizabeth and Victoria and Old Testament prophet Deborah to allay fear about entrusting "the Esquimalt constituency in my hands."[46]

Right from the outset, alongside the premier and various cabinet ministers, Mary Ellen attempted to revive liberal-labourism with her endorsement of old age pensions, "a health insurance programme and a system of maternity benefits."[47] All of these had been "agitated for by women's organizations for more than twenty years," and unions had been similarly enthusiastic.[48] Mary Ellen reminded her sex of the importance of "greater organized effort." MLAs needed to be able to tell "the government [that] the women are behind it."[49] In a typical speech, she rejected the slur that she was a carpet-bagger, insisting that she was returning to her "first love" on the island; she also defended mothers' pensions because they kept women at home for their key duties, and she praised UBC for "teaching over 1,500 students to be good builders of the Empire." She explained her absence from the House during votes on improvements to social security as a non-issue: the votes had been unanimous and her presence would have done no more than confirm the result.[50] Since British Columbia had to await implementation of the ILO legislation by other jurisdictions in order to remain competitive, she could not be faulted. She demanded that Pooley apologize, stating that her "whole life" was a "sufficient answer" to his charges.[51] Frank Carlow muddied the waters, making Liberal disarray only too clear when, in criticizing Mary Ellen, he commended himself as the "father" of the BC Male Minimum Wage Act "as a solution to the Oriental problem."[52]

Despite the Liberal claim to progressive ground, the Tories triumphed and Mary Ellen fell in Esquimalt, where she received 1,077 votes, or 37.04 percent of ballots cast in the riding. Pooley was awarded 1,806 and 62.10 percent, whereas Carlow garnered only 25 and 2.86 percent. Province-wide, the Conservative Party took 53.3 percent of the vote, with thirty-five MLAs, and the Liberals won 40.04 percent, with twelve MLAs. The Independent Labour Party captured 4.95 percent and one seat. In Vancouver City, Helen Smith stood eighth in the six-person contest, with 12,514 votes and 6.94 percent. Two other women ran in the election, neither of them victorious: in Columbia, Gladys E. Cross, Independent, took 26 votes and 1.98 percent, whereas Alice E. McGregor, Independent Conservative, won 349 votes and .61 percent in Victoria City.[53]

Ultimately, the refugee from Vancouver had little to offer but past glories of her association with suffrage, minimum wage, and mothers' pension, as well as her invocation of Ralph. The feisty Alice McGregor, who defied her party's Victoria nomination of a man with questionable party credentials, later observed that she had known Smith for many years and "enjoyed a goodly number of heart-to-heart talks of mutual difficulties in our respective parties in the recognition of women."[54] The Liberal McClung, who had been defeated by a small margin in Alberta in 1926, shared still worse conclusions with Irene Parlby, the United Farmers of Alberta MLA: "the hostility to women in public life is not lessening, but rather growing."[55] Later, two prominent male Grit and Tory veterans of the 1928 campaign were casually recalled as unrepentant opponents of "women in public life."[56] The same commentator had previously noted that Mary Ellen's portrait had been "thrown out" of the legislature.[57] Its "club-like" environment remained a man's preserve. Even Mary Ellen had not attended state dinners, which kept men centre stage. A similar situation existed in Britain, but its Parliament boasted more female MPs, whose shared experience of exclusion fostered cross-party bonds in and out of Parliament. In British Columbia, Mary Ellen stood alone.[58]

SLIDING INTO OBSCURITY

After defeat on the island, Mary Ellen returned to Vancouver, where her family remained important to her, perhaps especially Jack, who, as an injured veteran, would eventually find permanent employment with the provincial government. Her son Robert's two daughters and a son, as well as the offspring of her brother, William Spear, and some of Ralph's kin, anchored her in a familiar Kitsilano apartment.[59] Civil service jobs, probably available because of political patronage, appear to have been significant for a family with limited resources. Robert's widow, Katherine (Kitty), was an assistant moving picture censor for British Columbia, employment that would have interested Mary Ellen and that helped send her granddaughters to private schools and a grandson to UBC.[60] Mary Ellen's stepdaughter, Mary Elizabeth Carr, was now a widow. Employed by the post office, she stayed in Victoria with her own daughter. Mary Ellen's other surviving son, Ralph, a salesman, lived in Seattle with his wife and son. Richard's family appears to have remained in Prince George. Although no relative worked in mining, Nanaimo connections bolstered personal life. Mary Ellen attended domestic celebrations and presided over reunions of that

The veteran, 1918. This photo of Mary Ellen Smith is formally dated 1918 but may well have been taken later in the 1920s. | Photo by Leonard Frank, accession no. 35220, Vancouver Public Library.

city's "Old Timers," many of whom shared roots in Northumberland and Durham.[61] Contact with other ex-pats, like visits to the United Kingdom, affirmed her long-held Britannic nationalism.

After Mary Ellen returned to Kitsilano, British Columbia lacked a female MLA until 1933. That loss was acknowledged even by the conservative *Victoria Colonist*:

> It is to be regretted that Mrs. Mary Ellen Smith has been eliminated from public life for the time being. She waged a good fight in a traditional Conservative stronghold.

> It is fitting at this time to remember the services Mrs. Smith has rendered to the Province ... The value of her influence in the Legislature cannot be over-estimated ... [It is] to be hoped that the public life of Mrs. Smith is by no means closed.[62]

In fact, far more than most defeated MLAs, the suffragist veteran refused to stand aside. The provincial and federal Liberal Parties had cause to thank her for shoring up their pretensions to represent women and she to thank them for their limited additions to her modest finances. Although her energy and ability to attract press ink were diminishing, Mary Ellen persevered with public talks, interviews, and writing that addressed times darkened by economic collapse, fascism's rise, and resilient misogyny.

Holding the presidency of the provincial Liberal Party allowed her to make discreet waves. The *Vancouver Province* was clearly fascinated as it observed – although, as a Tory newspaper, from a distance – Liberal machinations around replacing the defeated leader, MacLean, who slunk back east for federal gravy. It suggested that Mary Ellen was at odds with the obvious prince-in-waiting, Duff Pattullo, Prince Rupert's MLA since 1916.[63] Despite his readiness to reform capitalism in hopes of short-circuiting socialism, he treasured his blinkers when it came to women: "How fortunate to be a woman," he once wrote to a female friend, "and have nothing to do but play golf." Pattullo discouraged Mary Ellen from running in future provincial elections.[64] His slights to her and to other female activists, including Helen Douglas Smith, handicapped party progressives, setting the stage for a Liberal-Conservative coalition in the 1940s.[65]

For all their arrogance, BC Grits relied on female activists for organization and funding. The Liberal history of internecine discord required an especially adroit handling of egos. As president of the party until her death, Smith firmly mothered the boys into better behaviour and presented herself as a loyalist in endorsing Pattullo's calls for federal rescue during the Great Depression.[66] She also maintained at least the ghost of her old spirit. At the 1932 Liberal convention, she demanded that the party "seriously consider the needs of the people." Liberals possessed a proud history and they must "clean up our own act" in order "to give the people something to look forward to."[67] She spoke in favour of Pattullo's "new policy direction," which included a platform that declared "'nobody must be allowed to want for food, clothing and shelter' because of inability to obtain employment" and "'state health insurance, increased state aid to education, national employment insurance, a Provincial

Highways Board, progressive tax revisions and a Public Utilities Commission.'"[68] The *Vancouver Sun* highlighted female activists' support for her speech, which ultimately pictured "Liberalism as a war-machine against encroaching distress."[69] Despite her energy and charisma, however, Mary Ellen was now on the brink of her seventies, well past the age when the vast majority of women (or men for that matter) normally claim public authority. Despite generally good press, she faced a challenge to her presidency, termed "the most dramatic event of the convention."[70] Saved by the female delegates, she left the convention flush with the singing of "For She's a Jolly Good Fellow" and "She's a Daisy."[71]

Mary Ellen's party service extended to Ottawa. She remained president of the National Federation of Liberal Women until 1932. Her distance from the action in Ottawa, the federation's limited budget, the indifference of the national party to which it reported, and the Conservative victory of 1930 limited accomplishment. Most provinces remained without the associations for women and youth that had been anticipated.[72] Her term as president nevertheless kept Smith on call for partisan functions across Canada, where she often tried to align liberalism with a broadened nationality. In the spirit of optimism, or naïveté, she was heard to declare, "Canada has once and forever abandoned the word foreigner from her vocabulary." At least in the east, anti-Asian prejudice no longer seemed to be a stock-in-trade.[73] In 1932, Smith was quietly succeeded as federation president by Ontario's Glenora Bolton Kennedy (d. 1935), widow of William Costello Kennedy, William Lyon Mackenzie King's minister of railways and canals from 1921 to 1923.[74]

The remuneration for party services was limited, and Liberals had the unhappy experience of seeing their iconic MLA increasingly threadbare. During the fall of 1930, Mary Ellen joined a Chautauqua tour, giving paid lectures in the Ottawa Valley and northern Ontario as she struggled for the income to present herself as a respectable representative of Canadian womanhood.[75] For a time, there was talk of a pension from Victoria, linked firmly to one equal or larger for Lady McBride (Christine Margaret McGillivray, 1870–1937), widow of the early Tory premier. For all their many differences of service, both women were reduced to the dependants of once powerful men. After McBride's party agreed to rescue the relict of the "Province's Dick," however, Premier Tolmie nixed the suggestion of public assistance for the widow of Ralph Smith. Liberal leader Pattullo could not or would not find a bailout for the BC party president.[76]

Personal financial difficulty, as well as ambition and a call to public service, formed an incalculable backdrop to Smith's enthusiasm for elected or appointed posts. She remained publicly discreet about her income, but a 1929 visit from a sheriff as she hosted women Liberals at her Kitsilano flat offered an embarrassing reminder. Since she was about to leave for International Labour Association meetings in Geneva, he threatened to arrest her unless she paid $250 "owing the Reliance Financial Corporation Ltd." She told the press that the debt came from "a promissory note" that she had signed for a political supporter. She held her ground and her head high until she had served tea to her guests and then went to the sheriff's office with "a cheque for $320 which included interest and costs."[77] Her predicament, like the meagre funds she possessed at death, revealed real insecurity. All her family members had modest jobs, and none could offer much by way of financial help. She was not eligible for Canada's new means-tested old age pension until she reached the age of seventy, and applying for it would have entailed humiliation.

Given the bleak prospects of retirement, Smith remained receptive to offers of paid public service. In 1930, "a large delegation of men and women," the second in a row apparently, appealed to "the heroine of a number of contests in which her strategy and political ability have been of inestimable aid to her party" to run in Vancouver Centre against Conservative H.H. Stevens.[78] Given the slim hope of unseating the well-settled incumbent, such pleas counted for less than the possibility of appointed or patronage positions. In March 1929, her selection as Canadian representative to the League of Nations' ILO offered both travel to Britain and Switzerland and a stipend for duties to which Mary Ellen had long been committed.[79]

The ILO posting clearly reflected both Mary Ellen's advocacy of women's minimum and equal wages and her older history as the spouse of a well-known Ottawa Lib-Lab. When she arrived in London en route to her assignment, the English newspapers welcomed her warmly, albeit incorrectly, as a "woman labour minister."[80] Her feminist credentials were acknowledged by the hospitality of London's Minerva Club (founded in 1920 by the Women's Freedom League), where she told sympathizers that she had learned to "be a suffragist at her grandmother's knee, which was a very great heritage."[81] Her reception saw her hailed as having "probably achieved more for the working classes than any other woman alive today." Smith's political success was attributed to the quick wit and humour that she demonstrated in one laid-back retort to a heckler: "Don't be shy of me, sonny. I'm everybody's pal."[82]

During the 1929 London sojourn, Mary Ellen visited with Margaret Bondfield. As labour minister in Ramsay MacDonald's minority Labour government, Bondfield was the United Kingdom's first female cabinet member. In June, the *Nanaimo Free Press* clearly approved of the meeting between "our Mary Ellen" and "our Maggie," both touted as champions of women and children.[83] The *Victoria Colonist* preferred to jibe, observing that "Bondfield is as progressive in her ideas and as aggressive in her politics as Mrs. Mary Ellen Smith and Miss Agnes MacPhail." Since Macphail had urged the reform of Canadian penitentiaries, anyone could see that she was "as mad as a March hare."[84] The *Vancouver Province* was similarly biting in chiding the more progressive *Toronto Star* for its coverage of the visit: "It fairly bubbles with bonhomie and the get-together spirit so characteristic of Mrs. Smith's political outlook, and one would not be a bit astonished to learn that she either wrote or inspired it herself."[85]

Criticism came elsewhere in Canada as well. In the House of Commons, Tories objected to Smith "making partisan speeches when her expenses were being paid by the people of Canada." They pointed to Macphail as the appropriate representative of Canadian women abroad. The minister of labour responded that Macphail had refused the post. The latter explained that she had declined it because such appointments were always partisan. Though she too disapproved of giving speeches on behalf of a party in the course of official duties, Macphail defended Smith by noting her support from the National Council of Women.[86]

Mary Ellen soon found herself in even hotter water. When reflecting on the ILO meetings on her return, she told Toronto audiences that "Canada held an enviable place among the nations of the world in the matter of labor legislation." Her weeks in Geneva had taught her that Canada should help "less-favoured" nations reach the same high standards, an effort that offered the additional benefit of thwarting competitors with worse wages and conditions. She also applauded the fourteen women MPs, and Bondfield in particular, who had won their seats in the 1929 British election, adding, "I think it is a good thing for Merrie England that at this juncture the Labor Government has been returned. I have every faith in Ramsay MacDonald and the clever men he has chosen for his cabinet." She dismissed Ottawa's Conservative critics: "Mr. Bennett says I must not talk politics, but thank Heaven I am in a free country and under the Union Jack, and I am going to say what I think."[87] In St. Catharines, Ontario, the Women's Liberal Association heard her not only laud the British Labour Party but warn men "that the women of Canada intend to press on, and assert their rights and position as citizens of Canada, fighting for the principles they believe in." She finished by eulogizing King's administration, which soon faced an election.[88] In covering her post-Geneva speeches, the *Montreal Gazette* reported her declaration that

> Canada does not have to enact legislation to comply with the findings of the International Labor Council ... We have laws that cover them all. Our business now is to be big enough to forget the past and make the future secure for the world.
>
> Whenever the four woman delegates [from various countries] spoke at Geneva, they spoke wisely and well and always left an impression ... I do not think Canada suffered at my hands.[89]

All in all, the traveller, back home with the further reward of honorary memberships in the Royal Colonial Institute (soon the Royal Empire Society) and the Overseas League, seemed well satisfied with what would be her last visit to the Old Country.

Her compliments to British female MPs and the British Labour Party did not raise a public storm (though one wonders about the eyebrows of the Liberal brass), but her salute to the dominion's labour legislation did. Back in 1923, unions had condemned her recruitment of British immigrants, and now her claims regarding Canada's progressive leadership were disputed by two prominent figures, Charlotte Whitton (1896–1975) and Tom Moore (1878–1943). Whitton was director of the Canadian Council on Child Welfare and assessor to the Child Welfare Committee of the League of Nations, whereas Moore chaired the league's Child-In-Employment Section and was a long-serving president of Canada's Trades and Labor Congress. They denied that Canada led in child protection: it needed to do far more to meet ILO standards.[90] Just as she had some six years earlier, Mary Ellen retorted that her critics were misinformed.[91] She explained that she had been speaking generally of Canadian achievements. Canada was a young country, but

> in spite of her youth, through the farsightedness of her forefathers and foremothers, many of the old world mistakes had been avoided; that for the short period women had been enfranchised a great deal had been accomplished, and she had become the admiration of the world ... No one sympathizes more than I in the struggle for laws for the nations of the world that will make for peace. I am sorry that Miss Whitton and Mr. Moore did not find out from myself just what was meant as it would have avoided the cheap advertising we three have received.[92]

The contretemps, with its suggestion that Mary Ellen was out of step with knowledgeable opinion in Canada, like her failure to contain her admiration for Britain's Labour Party, could only damage her chances for further appointments in the gift of Mackenzie King.

In 1929, the Judicial Committee of the Privy Council finally pronounced that women were indeed "persons" under the British North America Act.[93] After that, the major recognition that any prime minister could offer Canadian women was elevation to the Senate (the post of the governor general was far in the future). That appointment had been discussed publicly since most women won federal enfranchisement in 1918. Mary Ellen had been regularly ballyhooed as a worthy candidate, as had Emily Ferguson Murphy, an Edmonton Juvenile Court judge and leader of Alberta's Famous Five who wrote under the pen name of Janey Canuck. In 1928, Mary Ellen had assailed the preceding negative judgment of the Supreme Court of Canada, asking what right had a man to "decree that his mother was not a person." She blamed women's lack of unity for allowing such injustice to continue.[94] In 1929, the *Vancouver Sun* editorialist welcomed "a place for Mary Ellen" in the Senate. This "woman of action" would change for the better a "more or less moribund body [that] has reached a stage of stagnation today where it is practically a brake on the progress of the county."[95] Such was not to be. In February 1930, King allocated the reward to Canadian-born Liberal activist, millionaire, and mother Cairine Reay Wilson.[96] She had never been known as a suffragist, and her lack of apparent threat to the status quo was readily celebrated. *Maclean's* reassured its readers that she was "first, last and always a woman – a wife and mother of eight children."[97] A surprise was waiting. In the 1930s, as an advocate for Jewish refugees from the Nazi Holocaust, Wilson proved a thorn in Mackenzie King's side.

Service to the Liberal Party, the ILO appointment, and the Senate were only the most talked about aspects of Mary Ellen's public life after 1928. In Vancouver, she embraced global and domestic causes, from peace advocacy and the condemnation of anti-Semitism to the defence of provincial mothers' pensions. The 1929 trip to Geneva, with its opportunities to talk to global feminists, and perhaps her release from legislative restraints, may have reinvigorated her activism: she found it "a revelation to see the positions that are occupied by women in Europe ... The question is not asked – is it a man or a woman who is needed for this position but always – who can fill this to the best advantage?"[98] The racism of the 1924 Janet Smith bill became less apparent. Recalling the "beauty and perfection of the English spoken by the delegation from India, Japan and the majority of those from China," the newly internationalized Smith urged Canadians to familiarize "themselves with the various languages of the world."[99] Women should act as global peacemakers, "using all influence to avoid future wars."[100] Speaking to the Vancouver League of Nations Society, the Kiwanis, and diverse women's clubs, she suggested that American membership in the League of Nations would remedy its weakness. As an advanced "English-speaking" country, the United States should lead the world "socially, spiritually, and politically."[101] The local Council of Jewish Women welcomed her enthusiasm for global security and her denunciation of fascism.[102] When its national council met at the Hotel Vancouver, she applauded the League of Nations' role in "functioning without barriers of race, religion or nationality" and women's critical role as interpreters.[103] Two years later, short weeks before her death, Mary Ellen stood with an ecumenical crowd of some 1,500 people in Vancouver to condemn Germany's oppression of "Jewish residents and citizens."[104]

As the Depression deepened, Smith maintained old activist networks with veterans such as Helen Gregory MacGill, Nellie McClung, and Emily Murphy, all of whom were worried about losing gains for women and children.[105] In 1929, MacGill had been sacked from her position as judge of the Vancouver Juvenile Court, which demonstrated the Tory mood for retribution.[106] In the midst of tumbling revenues, the Tolmie government, which increasingly conflated business and government interests, was determined to shed as many costs as possible. The 1932 Kidd Report, commissioned by Victoria, proposed the tough love of a wholesale assault on the nascent welfare state. Recommendations for the sterilization of the unfit, the repeal of minimum wage legislation, the curtailment of free education, the closure of employment service offices, major cuts to UBC, increased monitoring of mothers' and old age pensions, and a heightened role for the lieutenant governor set the stage for class war, just what Mary Ellen, and Ralph before her, had worked against. When social work leader Charlotte Whitton condemned the lax administration of mothers' pensions and assistance to women with only one child, Tolmie used her assessment to legitimize weakening the program.[107] In 1932, half of its costs were transferred to near-bankrupt municipalities, which were already culling desperate mothers from local relief.

In March 1932, under the auspices of the New Era League, Mary Ellen and other suffragist veterans rallied women's organizations to protest cutbacks.[108] At a mass meeting, Susie Lane Clark described the long fight for mothers' pensions,[109] and Mary Ellen declared war: "What we have we propose to hold." Mothers should not be forced to live on charity. She denied that the administration costs were excessive and urged a delegation to confront Victoria.[110] An all-male legislature should not sacrifice the BC initiative, the "best of its kind in the world."[111] In July, the New Era League heard her reassert "the necessity for women entering into affairs of the province and the expediency of forming a woman's party to safeguard the welfare of their sex."[112] Notably, however, the defence of wages did not rouse the same levels of public protest, whether because of the era's growing hostility to female earners or because loophole-ridden protective legislation was virtually toothless.[113] In any case, after the 1928 election, the old campaigner lost her visibility as one of British Columbia's foremost champion of fair or equal wages.

Mary Ellen's sympathies for vulnerable mothers sometimes had a counterpart in her concern about the male unemployed, many of whom were ex-soldiers, long a constituency she had claimed as a "mother politician." During the Great Depression, as during the general strikes of 1918–19, veterans inspired sympathy but sometimes raised the spectre of revolution.[114] As potentially dangerous men, they were not easily ignored. In March 1932, after the police cleared Vancouver's "hobo jungles," Smith stood against the Conservative government, arguing that hunger could justify theft. Accompanying her was Scottish-born Andrew Roddan (1882–1948), the outspoken minister of Vancouver's First United Church and author of the best-selling *God in the Jungles* (1931).[115] She was blunt: "When we remember the large number who have embezzled thousands, and that a man can be jailed for stealing a loaf of bread, I can only come to the conclusion that it is time the law was equalized and a fairer sense of justice meted to everyone."[116] Such a public stance took pluck, given that a May Day rally of that year sparked "rumors of Communist dynamite and violence that resulted in the greatest police precautions in the city's history." A "war vessel, H.M.C.S. Vancouver, with a squad of military machine gunners aboard from Victoria," greeted some "7000 persons, including spectators, [who] had collected to hear talk of revolution." Notably, however, no "hand was raised in violence" during the rally.[117] In October 1932, the provincial government set up relief camps for the male unemployed. It would not have been hard for Mary Ellen to remember how miners had suffered at the hands of state administrations effectively allied to the pit-owning Dunsmuirs.

Ultimately, however, her response to the Depression swerved to the right. She accepted that social hygiene legislation, including sterilization, would reduce welfare costs and produce a healthier population.[118] In the same spirit, she approved the *Vancouver Sun*'s call for an anti-crime "cleanup," including the "police search of all men suspected of carrying weapons." She declared that "the time has come in our national life when the protection of life and limb and peace and security should be our first consideration."[119] In July 1932, she set forth her evolving ideas. Maintaining her insistence on the importance of "planned prosperity," she described a world in which "our granaries are bursting with wheat and grain and yet industry is paralyzed. Every one deplores the fact that hundreds of thousands are hungry, and cannot get work of any kind. No one has any solution or gets at the root of the matter and yet the world is staggered by the grim monster of unemployment." In her view, joblessness owed much to the introduction of machinery and the failure "to harness the brains, intelligence and physical strength of the youth of the world." Pretty much unprecedented for her, at least in public pronouncements, was an apparent loss of confidence in democracy. Like most "business men, economists, financiers or men versed in industrial needs," governments had no answers for terrible times.[120] Much like British Columbia's first Social Credit group (associated with two *Vancouver Sun* reporters), she saw "poverty in the midst of plenty."[121] She urged the appointment of a "group of public-spirited citizens in every country, people with vision, courage and conviction, who will undertake to harness the brains of countries, bring the groups together whereby this bugaboo may as far as possible be expelled from our midst." Their term should last as long they got results. Such an expert-run state would serve "the mutual advantage of everyone concerned." More familiar was her recommendation for the cooperation of "industry and capital" to offer solutions, such as fewer hours of work, a public hospitalization plan, a revival of apprenticeships, and a "revised monetary system," by which she meant abandoning the gold standard. In short, the Depression required "a complete reconstruction of our social, industrial and economic system." Conspicuously absent from her proposal was explicit reference to women or unions.[122] Only businessmen and experts got the clear nod.

Seeming sympathies with Social Credit, again without direct mention by name, were visible a few months later, once more in the *Vancouver Sun*. This time, under the headline "Issue New Money," Smith urged "an improved monetary system for Canada." This too was to be managed by "practical and competent men" who would be appointed for an indefinite term with "full power to issue Dominion currency" to pay for federal, provincial, and municipal projects. An increase in the "volume of money" would "provide work for thousands and bring hope and relief to the overburdened taxpayer." Without such leadership, joblessness would increase, and "no one can tell what the outcome may be in the next 12 months." She cited the case of the United States to insist that more money should be circulated to ensure "a normal and natural demand for all goods and services." If the American president were to raise wages, consumption would increase and prosperity would return to his nation and its "intimate" associate, Canada.[123] Unfortunately, the two *Vancouver Sun* articles are the only sources yet discovered on Smith's possible flirtation with Social Credit doctrines. And it may have been no more than a fling. As the 1930s demonstrated, banking reform and trust in experts were broadly popular remedies for the failures of capitalism. In 1933, the new Liberal premier, Dufferin Pattullo, demanded a national bank, and a year later, millionaire Conservative prime minister R.B. Bennett created the Bank of Canada to manage currency and interest rates.[124]

Noteworthy in Death

The veteran suffragist did not have much time for reflection. She had always suffered from chest ailments, but in December 1932 her health provoked new concern when she badly injured an ankle on wintery pavements and retreated to the care of Jack and Mabel, her nearby son and his wife.[125] Now nearly seventy years old, she slowly resumed her engagements. In April, she collapsed with a stroke and was rushed to Vancouver General Hospital. Newspapers issued daily reports on her condition.

Mary Ellen died on May 3, 1933, never having regained consciousness. Her body lay in state in Vancouver's St. Andrew's Wesley United Church as women and men streamed by to pay their last respects, and the flag flew at half-mast in front of the legislature in Victoria. Dr. A.M. Sanford, former minister of Nanaimo's Wallace Street Methodist Church, eulogized her as "always at heart one of the common people and ever ready to lend aid to the victims of inequality and injustice."[126] Representatives from Vancouver's suffrage societies, the IODE, the LCW, League of Women Voters, New Era League, the Business and Professional Women's Club, the Lady Laurier Club, the Canadian Daughters' League, and the Native Daughters of British Columbia assembled as the casket was carried to Mountain View Cemetery in a send-off that matched that of her husband in 1917. Her honorary pallbearers included Pattullo and MLA John Hart for the Liberals; Conservative MLA Royal Maitland for the federal and provincial governments; Chief Justice Aulay Morrison; long-time friend, doctor, and UBC chancellor Robert McKechnie; and Vancouver mayor Louis D. Taylor.[127] Union leaders were conspicuously absent.

Mary Ellen's passing drew many press tributes. In London, England, the *International Suffrage News* remembered her as "a very active worker on behalf of women and children," and the same city's *The Vote* saluted her as a Northumbrian emigrant who had done her birthplace proud.[128] Her past was similarly centre front in the *Manchester Guardian*'s commendation of "Mrs. Mary Smith" as a "British" woman, whose merits included acting as the "chief helper" to her husband.[129] The *New York Times* reduced her to "Mrs. Ralph Smith" in an obituary that named her father, husband, and four sons while omitting her mother and stepdaughter and diminishing her contributions to her sex to four words – "sponsored laws for women."[130] The *Toronto Globe* paid her slightly greater respect, but its obituary, "Mary Ellen Smith Dies in Vancouver," was brief and did not mention her many commitments, from suffrage, wage equality, mother's pensions, and liberalism to Asian exclusion and mental hygiene.[131] In contrast, the "Page for Women" of *The Age*, published in Melbourne, Australia, lamented the loss of "an untiring fighter for woman's suffrage."[132]

At home in British Columbia, acknowledgments reflected closer and often partisan observation. The frequently unfriendly *Vancouver Province* faulted Smith for "associating herself too closely with party movements" but admitted, contradicting the slander that it had spread during the 1928 election, that she was a woman "of capacity and attainments" who was responsible for "much of the legislation on the statute book in the interests of women and children."[133] Her regular ally, the *Vancouver Sun*, hailed her life as one of "splendid usefulness." Women in particular would remember "her as a devoted public figure who contributed tremendously to the social welfare of her sex" and as someone "who proved in a practical way that the claims of the suffragettes were founded upon good sense rather than emotions alone." An "agent of civilization," she "added materially to the happiness and security of women in this province."[134] Notably, however, the *Labor Statesman*, successor to the *BC Federationist* as the official organ of the Vancouver Trades and Labor Council, which had previously followed her with considerable interest, was silent. Smith no longer interested such union activists.

As in life, Mary Ellen, much like UK suffragette Emmeline Pankhurst and Conservative MP Nancy Astor, remained a woman whose physical attractions and personality were credited as central to her success in a male-dominated world. The commemoration of the *Nanaimo Free Press* was especially fulsome in awarding her full marks: "There was no zenith to her career, no relegation to the ranks of departed glory, for until the end her vivacious but practical person ruled the ranks of the political party through which she chose to work."[135] In a "tribute to my old friend," an often curmudgeonly BC journalist mused similarly,

> it was my habit during her political career to poke a lot of fun in this place at some of her political doings. But did she get nasty and snooty about it? She did not ... When she was young she must have been beautiful. Her later years were marked by a fine and genial sense of humor – never completely clouded by the political fallacies she followed. We lose a good companion.[136]

More prosaic but equally expressive of Mary Ellen's public life was the size of her estate, only $630, which consisted largely of life insurance. After her funeral expenses were paid, $100 each remained for son Jack and stepdaughter Mary Elizabeth, with the same amount divided among Robert's three children.[137] As the *Toronto Globe* observed, "Mrs. Smith was among those who are impoverished rather than enriched by public life." The barb, for other politicians, lay in the next line: "There are both kinds."[138]

As the crisis of the Great Depression deepened, the memory of Mary Ellen slipped away. Her successor in Vancouver, Liberal Helen Douglas Smith was soon overshadowed by the province's third and fourth female MLAs, the outspoken CCFers Dorothy Gretchen Bierstaker Steeves (1891–1978) and Laura Jamieson. In 1938, at the inaugural meeting of the short-lived Mary Ellen Smith Club, which was created "with the purpose of maintaining charitable and social service work," Helen Douglas Smith attempted to claim a progressive legacy for herself. Her emphasis on "the need for constant vigilance in the fight for extension of social services" was timely and no doubt sincere,[139] but by then the Liberal Party in British Columbia and Canada showed little interest in justice for women. Mary Ellen had had high hopes for liberalism, but her legacy for the Liberal Party seemed infinitesimal.

Not to be ignored, however, was her initiation of a broader feminist genealogy in elections in downtown Vancouver. Her early victory set the stage for many voters in that neighbourhood to turn later to CCFers Jamieson and Grace Woodsworth MacInnis (1905–91). Although influence cannot be readily measured, it reflected the city's long-standing history of feminist activism of which Mary Ellen Smith was so important a part. Ultimately, the pioneer MLA and cabinet minister had significance well beyond one party.

Conclusion: British Columbia's Famous Pioneer Politician: Making History

How should the achievement of Mary Ellen Spear Smith be measured? For most women and men, families supply one test of accomplishment. The Smiths' hopes for their offspring had been a major cause of their departure from northern Britain. All their children and grandchildren escaped work in the mines. Some died early, some lived long, but none shared the extended public spotlight that focused on their emigrant forebears. To be sure, their only Canadian-born son, Jack, won France's Croix de Guerre for his services during the First World War, and his older brother, Robert, graduated from the University of Toronto and Osgoode Hall to set up a promising law and political career before his premature death. One of Robert's daughters, Jocelyn (Betty) Bosanquet Smith, a graduate of Vancouver's exclusive Crofton House School for girls, was hailed as "a patrician bride of great beauty" when she married at an Anglican church in select Shaughnessy in 1941.[1] Her brother, Robert Campbell Smith, a UBC alumnus, won honours during the Second World War and went on to a distinguished career in the federal Department of Trade and Commerce.[2] Such achievements help explain why many ambitious workers have preserved their hopes for capitalism and their faith in traditional parties.

Kin trajectories are, however, only one test of significance. For decades after her death, Mary Ellen Smith remained little more than a footnote in the history of Canada and the British world: as British Columbia's first female legislator and the Empire and Commonwealth's first female cabinet minister, she could be deemed demonstrable proof of British liberal enlightenment. That reductive snapshot does her no justice. Mary Ellen's devotion to settler aspirations and prejudices, liberal-labour politics, British imperialism, New Liberalism, and White first-wave feminism opened doors for the talent and industry of some women and men, even as it denied opportunity to others. That challenging legacy stands at the heart of the Anglocentric world that was and sometimes remains British Columbia and Canada.

As a determined Methodist coal miner's daughter and wife, Mary Ellen embraced unprecedented prospects for her sex and class. On the edge of empire, just as Ralph claimed the moniker "esquire," in effect announcing that character and behaviour, not birth, made the gentleman, she used hard work and moral responsibility, accessorized by tasteful dress and good manners, to assert respectable leadership and the status of a lady. Families like theirs, who had taken themselves from dark pits to legislative halls, deserved overseas realms. In claiming a better life and dignity for industrious and moral British women and men, this Liberal-Labour lady shared in the casual dispossession of Canada's Indigenous Peoples, who rarely caught her gaze. Far more self-conscious was her blunt rejection of Asian claimants to heightened prospects. Smith's endorsement of eugenics revealed as well her discrimination between the supposedly fit and unfit of the British "race," a distinction that corresponded to labourism's deep investment in rewards for talent and honest work. After the First World War, the rise of fascism and her sympathy for the League of Nations moderated some prejudices, but Mary Ellen always promoted a code that distinguished firmly between the worthy and the unworthy. In short, her life represented what has been termed "settlerism," which "converted emigration within the Anglo-world from an act of despair that lowered your standing to an act of hope that enhanced it."[3] Unfortunately, that enhancement could come at a brutal cost to others.

Working-class pride and settler privilege underlay Smith's faith in advanced liberalism. In her youth, she absorbed the politics of evangelism, self-help, and cooperation that wedded the ambitions of many British mining families to historic liberalism's commitment to class partnership in the furthering of democracy. For many working-class women and men, liberal-labourism stood for a politics of aspiration. They could partner with benevolent or otherwise interested elites. Earning their place in government, they could regulate the relations of capital and labour and promote gradual reform to forestall class warfare. Liberal legislation that extended democracy and social security would harness capitalism to human welfare, at least for White citizens. Central to this philosophy was an end to unearned class and sex privilege. This faith, aided, to what degree we cannot know, by hopes for personal advancement, explained the tenacity of both Smiths' allegiance to Liberal parties.

Too often, however, Canadian liberalism succumbed to reactionary influences that buttressed colonialism and capitalism. Largely satisfied that a small group of privileged White men were legitimate leaders, Canada's often ruling party became confident that workers and women would not vote as a block to force it significantly to the left. Champions of liberal-labourism and liberal-feminism frequently remained little better than interlopers, with unrequited dreams for full partnership. Ultimately, the left "liberalism of the British imperial world that sought to consolidate its project of rule by 'going beyond its immediate corporate interests to take into account the interests of other groups and classes'" failed in the years before the Second World War.[4] Little wonder that braver or less patient labour activists and suffragists forswore that creed in favour of the rival ideologies offered by the Canadian labour and socialist parties in the 1920s and the CCF or even the Communist Party in the 1930s. None proved entirely satisfactory, but they at least recognized that justice required far more radical politics than Canadian Liberal parties ever sustained.[5] As in Britain, liberalism's failure to respect and succour either working-class or female voters, displayed so well in Mary Ellen's life, reflected its common suspicion of democracy and ensured its electoral limitations.

Equally central to Smith's significance for British Columbia and Canada was her faith in women as deserving contributors to families and communities. She espoused a view of the past, the present, and the future in which her sex was in no way subordinate or inferior. Women's morality, talent, and industry matched those of the men who sought to dominate them. Like their fathers, brothers, husbands, and sons, women too were heirs of the world's races. In particular, industrious British women merited the opportunities and rights associated with Western capitalism and parliamentary democracy. Their potential as mothers, workers, and leaders need only be freed from patriarchal tyranny. Disdaining the fragility, self-absorption, and dependence associated with the decorative lady, Mary Ellen, like many suffragists, claimed strength, courage, and independence as her inheritance. Alongside natural gentlemen, ambitious working-class women would metamorphose into righteous ladies. A match and more for those who hoped to be their betters, they could demand a hearing from men, especially men on the imperial frontier who wished to count themselves civilized. Once conscious of their own merits and dedicated to human betterment, women could ensure the reward to British settlers that guaranteed the imperial project and liberal democracy's ability to ward off class war.

Many feminists, including Mary Ellen, like many subsequent scholars, repeatedly saw women everywhere as significantly responsible for post-enfranchisement disappointments. Enmeshed in class and race privilege, the commonplace story went, the female electorate, and indeed many feminist activists, largely failed the test of sisterhood. In her rise from British mining villages to prominence in British Columbia, Canada, and the British Empire, this Liberal-Labour lady should not, however, be reduced to her undeniable prejudices. Most contemporaries never matched even her flawed vision. The tribute of a woman who found her spellbinding highlighted the extraordinary, dubbed here almost supernatural, quality of her appeal:

> I attended a political meeting she hosted in Powell River in the late Twenties, when I was a child. Such charisma! Perfectly groomed, with a marvelous complexion, tastefully dressed, she was like a being from another world. Her message I have never forgotten ... "Inform yourself on the issues, listen, read, talk to the politicians. Then think over what you have learned, make your own decision as to who to choose, and Vote. Never forget to Vote."[6]

In defying the gender and class status quo of her day and demanding the enlargement of democracy, if far from complete, Mary Ellen Smith attempted to make history and perfect the future. The remarkable ambition of Canada's Liberal-Labour Lady merits close attention as we wrestle with its legacy in the twenty-first century.

Notes

Abbreviations

BCF	*BC Federationist*
BCS	*BC Studies*
CH	*Cranbrook Herald*
CHR	*Canadian Historical Review*
CUP	Cambridge University Press
DCB	*Dictionary of Canadian Biography*
EWW	*Everywoman's World*
GVC	*Greater Vancouver Chinook*
HS/SH	*Histoire sociale/Social History*
JCS	*Journal of Canadian Studies*
L/LT	*Labour/Le Travail*
MG	*Montreal Gazette*
MM	*Maclean's Magazine*
MQUP	McGill-Queen's University Press
MUP	Manchester University Press
NFP	*Nanaimo Free Press*
OC	*Ottawa Citizen*
OJ	*Ottawa Journal*
OUP	Oxford University Press
RBSCUBC	Rare Books and Special Collections, UBC
TC	*The Champion*
TG	*Toronto Globe*
UBCP	UBC Press
UTP	University of Toronto Press
VC	*Victoria Colonist*
VP	*Vancouver Province*
VS	*Vancouver Sun*

VT	*Victoria Times*
VW	*Vancouver World*
WCL	*Western Clarion*
WCLL	*Western Call* (Vancouver)
WT	*Winnipeg Tribune*
WWW	*Western Women's Weekly*

Introduction

1 See my *Liberal Hearts and Coronets: The Lives and Times of Ishbel Marjoribanks Gordon and John Campbell Gordon, the Aberdeens* (Toronto: UTP, 2015) for another example of the spousal partnerships that have often characterized politics. That study faced a different challenge in rescuing John Gordon from the reform shadows, and the title reflects its doubled gaze.

2 Lord Grey to Wilfrid Laurier, October 4, 1906, quoted in Mary Hallett, "A Governor-General's Views on Oriental Immigration to British Columbia, 1904–1911," *BCS* 14 (Summer 1972): 54. Albert Henry Grey, the fourth Earl Grey, was a fellow Northumbrian.

3 Craig Heron, *Working Lives: Essays in Canadian Working-Class History* (Toronto: UTP, 2018), 289. The espousal of a "fair deal" by both labour and suffragist movements goes unmentioned by Heron, but see the repeated reference in the classic Canadian suffrage argument by Nellie L. McClung, *In Times Like These* (Toronto: McLeod and Allen, 1915).

4 Adrian Bingham, *Gender, Modernity, and the Popular Press in Inter-War Britain* (Oxford: OUP, 2003), 11, 12. On the value and interpretation of historical press sources, see also Patricia Holland, "'The Politics of the Smile,'" in *News, Gender and Power*, ed. C. Carter, G. Branston, and S. Allen (London: Routledge, 1998), 17–32; Michelle E. Tusan, *Women Making News: Gender and Journalism in Modern Britain* (Champagne: University of Illinois Press, 2005); and Sarah Pederson, "Suffragettes and the Scottish Press during the First World War," *Women's History Review* 27, 4 (2018): 534–50. Reminders of the continuing significance of the press in Canada, and elsewhere, were also instructive. See François-Pierre Gingras, "Daily Male Delivery: Women and Politics in the Daily Newspaper," in *Gender and Politics in Contemporary Canada*, ed. François-Pierre Gingras (Toronto: OUP, 1995), 191–207; Elisabeth Gidengil and Joanna Everitt, "Tough Talk: How Television News Covers Male and Female Leaders of Canadian Political Parties," in *Women and Electoral Politics in Canada*, ed. Manon Tremblay and Linda Trimble (Toronto: OUP, 2003), 194–210; and Miki Caul Kittilson and Kim Fridkin, "Gender, Candidate Portrayals and Election Campaigns: A Comparative Perspective," *Politics and Gender* 4, 3 (September 2008): 371–92. Also invaluable in interpreting the press are the reflections of political theorist Nancy Fraser, notably her *Unruly Practices: Power, Discourse and Gender in Contemporary Social Theory* (Minneapolis: University of Minnesota Press, 1989).

5 Significant Canadian scholarship includes Marjory Lang, *Women Who Made the News: Female Journalists in Canada, 1880–1945* (Montreal and Kingston: MQUP, 1999); Barbara Freeman, *The Satellite Sex: The Media and Women's Issues in English Canada, 1966–1971* (Waterloo: Wilfrid Laurier University Press, 2001); Barbara Freeman, *Beyond Bylines: Media Workers and Women's Rights in Canada* (Waterloo: Wilfrid Laurier University Press, 2011); Janice Fiamengo, *The Woman's Page: Journalism and Rhetoric in Early Canada* (Toronto: UTP, 2008); and Carole Gerson, *Canadian Women in Print* (Waterloo: Wilfrid Laurier University Press, 2010). See also Veronica Strong-Boag, *The New Day Recalled: Lives of Girls and Women in English Canada* (Toronto: Copp Clark Pitman, 1988).

6 See Laura E. Nym Mayhall, "'It's Your Face That Is Carrying You Through!': Class, Gender, and Celebrity in Nancy Astor's 1919 Campaign for Parliament," *Feminist Media Histories* 2, 4 (2016): 64–83; and Laura Beers, "A Model MP? Ellen Wilkinson, Gender, Politics and Celebrity Culture in Interwar Britain," *Cultural and Social History* 10, 2 (2013): 231–50.

7 All critical readings appear in the notes to the chapters, and I am grateful to all authors. The work of Robert A.J. McDonald and Jean Barman has been especially influential. Both are deservedly celebrated for generosity in sharing their insights into the history of British Columbia and Canada. Bob's death in 2019 continues to be a great loss, but his inspiration lives on, most notably in his posthumous *A Long Way to Paradise: A New History of British Columbia Politics* (Vancouver: UBCP, 2021), an early version of which he shared with me. Jean Barman's *The West beyond the West: A History of British Columbia*, 3rd ed. (2007; repr., Toronto: UTP, 1991) and many other publications likewise stand as testaments to the significance and vitality of social and political movements in the province we have chosen as our home.

8 On workers, the key influences on this volume include Angela V. John, ed., *Unequal Opportunities: Women's Employment in England, 1800–1918* (Oxford: Blackwell, 1986); Alan Metcalfe, *Leisure and Recreation in a Victorian Mining Community* (London: Routledge, 2006); John Benson, *The Working Class in Britain, 1850–1939* (London: Longman, 1989); Dan Jackson, *The Northumbrians: North-East England and Its People: A New History* (London: Hurst, 2019); Valerie Gordon Hall, "The Anatomy of a Changing Consciousness: The Miners of Northumberland, 1898–1914," *Labour History Review* 66, 2 (Summer 2002): 165–86; Jonathan Rose, *The Intellectual Life of the British Working Classes* (New Haven: Yale University Press, 2001); John Belshaw, *Colonization and Community: The Vancouver Island Coalfield and the Making of the British Columbian Working Class* (Montreal and Kingston: MQUP, 2002); Robert G. McIntosh, *Boys in the Pits: Child Labour in Coal Mining* (Montreal and Kingston: MQUP, 2000); Greg Kealey, "Labour and Working-Class History in Canada: Prospects in the 1980s," *L/LT* 7, 1 (Spring 1981): 67–94; Allen Seager and Adele Perry, "Mining the Connections: Class, Ethnicity, and Gender in Nanaimo, BC, 1891," *HS/SH* 30, 59 (May 1997): 55–76; Linda Kealey, *Enlisting Women for the Cause: Women, Labour, and the Left in Canada, 1890–1920* (Toronto: UTP, 1998); Joan Sangster, *Dreams of Equality: Women on the Canadian Left, 1920–60* (Don Mills: McClelland and Stewart, 1989); Gordon Hak, *The Left in British Columbia: A History of Struggle* (Vancouver: Ronsdale Press, 2013); Mark Leier, *Red Flags and Red Tape: The Making of a Labour Bureaucracy* (Toronto: UTP, 1995); Heron, *Working Lives*; and Fred Burrill, "The Settler Order Framework: Rethinking Canadian Working-Class History," *L/LT* 83, 1 (Spring 2019): 173–97.

9 On British settlement and imperialism, see especially James Belich, *Replenishing the Earth: The Settler Revolution and the Rise of the Anglo-World, 1783–1939* (New York: OUP, 2009); Marjory Harper, "Rhetoric and Reality: British Migration to Canada, 1867–1967," Sarah Carter, "Aboriginal People of Canada and the British Empire," and Adele Perry, "Women, Gender, and Empire," all in *Canada and the British Empire*, ed. Philip Buckner (Oxford: OUP, 2008), 160–80, 200–10, 220–39; John Darwin, *The Empire Project: The Rise and Fall of the British World System, 1830–1970* (Cambridge: CUP, 2009); Patricia Roy, *Consolidating a White Man's Province, 1914–1941* (Vancouver: UBCP, 2003); Renisa Mawani, *Colonial Proximities: Crossracial Encounters and Judicial Truths in British Columbia* (Vancouver: UBCP, 2009); John Sutton Lutz, *Makúk: A New History of Aboriginal-White*

Relations (Vancouver: UBCP, 2008); and Jean Barman, *On the Cusp of Contact: Gender, Space and Race in the Colonization of British Columbia* (Madeira Park, BC: Harbour, 2020). Important studies illuminate the gendering of the imperial world. See, in particular, Antoinette Burton, *Burdens of History: British Feminists, Indian Women, and Imperial Culture, 1865–1915* (Chapel Hill: University of North Carolina Press, 1994); Robert Young, *Colonial Desire: Hybridity in Theory, Culture and Race* (London: Routledge, 1995); Julia Bush, *Edwardian Ladies and Imperial Power* (London: Leicester University Press, 2000); Catherine Hall and Sonya O. Rose, eds., *At Home with the Empire: Metropolitan Culture and the Imperial World* (Cambridge: CUP, 2006); Adele Perry, *On the Edge of Empire: Gender, Race, and the Making of British Columbia, 1849–1971* (Toronto: UTP, 2001); Christopher A. Bayly, "Moral Judgment: Empire, Nation and History," *European Review* 14, 3 (2006): 385–91; and Strong-Boag, *Liberal Hearts and Coronets*.

10 On liberalism and the state, see Ian McKay, "The Liberal Order Framework: A Prospectus for a Reconnaissance of Canadian History," *CHR* 81, 4 (2000): 617–45; Ian McKay, *Rebels, Reds, Radicals: Rethinking Canada's Left History* (Toronto: Between the Lines, 2005); Robert McDonald, "'Variants of Liberalism' and the Liberal Order Framework in British Columbia," and Ruth Sandwell, "Missing Canadians: Reclaiming the A-Liberal Past," both in *Liberalism and Hegemony: Debating the Canadian Liberal Revolution*, ed. Jean-François Constant and Michel Ducharme (Toronto: UTP, 2009), 322–46 and 246–73; Ruth Sandwell, "The Limits of Liberalism: The Liberal Reconnaissance and the History of the Family in Canada," *CHR* 84, 3 (September 2003): 423–50; Barry Ferguson, *Remaking Liberalism: The Intellectual Legacy of Adam Shortt, O.D. Skelton, W.C. Clark and W.A. Mackintosh, 1890–1925* (Montreal and Kingston: MQUP, 1993); Nancy Christie, *Engendering the State: Family Work and Welfare in Canada* (Toronto: UTP, 2000); Chris Clarkson, *Domestic Reforms: Political Visions and Family Regulation in British Columbia, 1862–1940* (Vancouver: UBCP, 2007); and Lisa Pasolli, *Working Mothers and the Child Care Dilemma: A History of British Columbia's Social Policy* (Vancouver: UBCP, 2015).

11 See the pioneering assessment by Ann Summers, *Damned Whores and God's Police: The Colonisation of Women in Australia* (Ringwood, AU: Penguin Books, 1975). Since its appearance, scholars and activists have exposed suffragists' role in both advancing and curtailing democracy in the British Empire and Commonwealth. The evolution in thinking is explored in the seven-volume series from UBC Press, beginning with Joan Sangster, *One Hundred Years of Struggle: The History of Women and the Vote in Canada* (2018), and including Lara Campbell, *A Great Revolutionary Wave: Women and the Vote in British Columbia* (2020). Sangster's "Exporting Suffrage: British Influences on the Canadian Suffrage Movement," *Women's History Review* 28, 4 (2019), 566–86, is also invaluable. Still important are earlier studies that concentrated on suffragists' shortcomings, such as Carol Lee Bacchi, *Liberation Deferred? The Ideas of the English-Canadian Suffragists, 1877–1918* (Toronto: UTP, 1998); and Mariana Valverde, *The Age of Light, Soap, and Water: Moral Reform in English Canada, 1885–1925* (Toronto: McClelland and Stewart, 1991). For an invaluable account of Canada's sometimes feminist imperialist members of a group patronized by Smith, see Katie Pickles, *Female Imperialism and National Identity: Imperial Order Daughters of the Empire* (Manchester: MUP, 2002), and of suffragist activists and politicians, see Veronica Strong-Boag, *The Last Suffragist Standing: The Life and Times of Laura Marshall Jamieson* (Vancouver: UBCP, 2018). Studies of minimum wage and mothers' pensions legislation are also important here, especially Gillian Creese, "Sexual Equality and the Minimum Wage in British Columbia," *JCS* 26, 4 (Winter 1991–92): 120–40;

Margaret Hillyard Little, "Claiming a Unique Place: The Introduction of Mothers' Pensions in B.C.," *BCS* 105–6 (Spring-Summer 1995): 80–102; and Megan Davies, "'Services Rendered, Rearing Children for the State': Mother's Pensions in British Columbia," in *Not Just Pin Money: Selected Essays on the History of Women's Work in British Columbia*, ed. B. Latham and R. Pazdro (Victoria: Camosun College Press, 1984), 249–63.

12 The key treatment of Ralph Smith remains Mark Leier, "Smith, Ralph," in *DCB*, vol. 14, University of Toronto/Université Laval, 2003, http://www.biographi.ca/en/bio/smith_ralph_14E.html.

13 On the complications of female identities for working-class women, see Beverly Skeggs, *Formations of Class and Gender: Becoming Respectable* (Thousand Oaks, CA: Sage, 2002), 13. On the dangers, see Steph Lawler, "'Getting Out and Getting Away': Women's Narratives of Class Mobility," *Feminist Review* 68 (Autumn 1999): 3–24.

14 On the pervasiveness of "adverse judgements on their femininity (transgressing gender codes)" for female politicians, see Marian Sawer, Manon Tremblay, and Linda Trimble, "Introduction," in *Representing Women in Parliament: A Comparative Study*, ed. Marian Sawer, Manon Tremblay, and Linda Trimble (London: Routledge, 2006), 5.

CHAPTER 1: SETTING THE STAGE IN BRITISH MINING VILLAGES, TO 1892

1 See Belich, *Replenishing the Earth*.
2 Ian Richards, "What Do They Know of Cornwall, Who Only Cornwall Know?" http://www.cornwall-online.co.uk/history/cmi/article2.htm.
3 On mining in Cornwall and Devon, see Gill Burke, "The Decline of the Independent Bal Maiden," in John, *Unequal Opportunities*, 179–204; and Lynne Mayers, *A Dangerous Place to Work! Women and Children of the Devon and Cornwall Mining Industries, 1300 to 1970* (Cinderford: Blaize Bailey Books, 2008).
4 John Benson, *British Coalminers in the Nineteenth Century: A Social History* (New York: Holmes and Meier, 1980).
5 Jackson, *The Northumbrians*, 137.
6 Benson, *British Coalminers*, 43.
7 See Hannah Elizabeth Martin, "'Tragedy, Death and Memory': The Commemoration of British Coal Mining Disasters in the Nineteenth and Early Twentieth Century" (bachelor's diss., Northumbria University, 2015), https://www.northumbria.ac.uk/about-us/academic-departments/humanities/research/history-research/history-dissertation-repository/-/media/corporate-website/documents/pdfs/departments/humanities/history/history-research/ug-dissertations/hannah-martin-tragedy-death-and-memory.ashx.
8 J. Kenyon Blackwell, Esq., quoted in Benson, *British Coalminers*, 45.
9 John Benson, "The Thrift of English Coal-Miners, 1860–95," *Economic History Review* 31, 3 (August 1978): 410.
10 On this reputation generally, see Jackson, *The Northumbrians*, which is distinguished by its inclusion of many notable women.
11 See D. Russell, "'We Carved Our Way to Glory': The British Soldier in Music Hall Song and Sketch, c. 1880–1914," in *Popular Imperialism and the Military: 1850–1950*, ed. John M. MacKenzie (Manchester: MUP, 1992), 50–79.
12 Metcalfe, *Leisure and Recreation*, 16.
13 Ibid., 18.
14 See Jackson, *The Northumbrians*, 141.

15 See I.H. Buchanan, "Infant Feeding, Sanitation and Diarrhea in Colliery Communities, 1880–1911," in *Diet and Health in Modern Britain*, ed. Derek J. Oddy and Derek S. Miller (Beckenham: Croom Helm, 1985), 148, 158–62; and Jane Long, "Conversations in Cold Rooms: Women, Work and Poverty in Nineteenth-Century Northumberland, c. 1834–1905" (PhD diss., University of Western Australia, 1995).
16 Jackson, *The Northumbrians*, 137.
17 Ibid., 118.
18 Valerie Gordon Hall, "Contrasting Female Identities: Women in Coal Mining Communities in Northumberland, England," *Journal of Women's History* 13, 2 (Summer 2001): 113.
19 See "Old English County Proud of Mrs. Smith's Cabinet Rank," *VW*, March 15, 1921; and Brian Hicks, "Mary Ellen Smith, Canadian Politician with Roots in the South-West of England," July 31, 2011, http://stoneposts-59.blogspot.ca/.
20 Jackson, *The Northumbrians*, 118.
21 See "Trade Unionism in Cornwall," Todpuddle Martyrs Museum, Todpuddle, Dorset, https://www.tolpuddlemartyrs.org.uk/story/tuc-150/new-unionism/trade-unionism-cornwall; and Richards, "What Do They Know of Cornwall?"
22 "One Who Knew Them," *Newcastle Weekly Chronicle*, February 1921, quoted in "Old English County Proud of Mrs. Smith's Cabinet Rank," *VW*, March 15, 1921.
23 Unattributed source, quoted in "Cornish Emigration to the North-East: How the Cornishmen Came to Cramlington," Pomeroy Family Association, https://pomeroyfamilyhistory.files.wordpress.com/2008/11/cornish-emigration-to-the-ne.pdf.
24 "Old English County Proud of Mrs. Smith's Cabinet Rank," *VW*, March 15, 1921.
25 "Holywell, Northumberland, 1873," GENUKI UK and Ireland Genealogy, https://www.genuki.org.uk/big/eng/NBL/Earsdon/Holywell1873.
26 "East Dereham Local Government District," *Norfolk News*, October 30, 1880, 5.
27 Note that Mary Ellen was born in October 1863 according to her birth certificate, but her marriage certificate gives her age as twenty-one in February 1883, when she would still have been nineteen.
28 *Newcastle Weekly Chronicle*, November 22, 1873, quoted in "Holywell, Northumberland, 1873."
29 Metcalfe, *Leisure and Recreation*, 15.
30 David M. Turner and Daniel Blackie, *Disability in the Industrial Revolution: Physical Impairment in British Coalmining, 1780–1890* (Manchester: MUP, 2018).
31 "Coast Pioneer Dies at Daughter's House," *VW*, December 13, 1913, 17. On this diaspora, see Shirley Ewart and Harold T. George, *Highly Respectable Families: The Cornish of Grass Valley, California, 1854–1954* (Grass Valley, CA: Comstock Bonanza Press, 1998); and Frederick Wolf, Bruce Finnie, and Linda Gibson, "Cornish Miners in California," *Journal of Management History* 14, 2 (2008): 144–60.
32 See Angus McLaren, *Birth Control in Nineteenth Century England* (New York: Holmes and Meier, 1978), 97–98.
33 Ibid., 221.
34 For a rare treatment of women in this debate, see Ellen Ross, "'Not the Sort That Would Sit on the Doorstep': Respectability in Pre-World War I London Neighborhoods," *International Labor and Working-Class History* 27 (Spring 1985): 39–59.
35 Benson, *The Working Class in Britain*, 103.
36 Hall, "Contrasting Female Identities," 122.
37 Ibid., 110.

38 Ibid., 113.
39 "Holywell, Northumberland, 1873."
40 Robert Moore, *Pitmen, Preachers, and Politics: The Effects of Methodism in a Durham Mining Community* (Cambridge: CUP, 1979), 146.
41 Eric Hobsbawm, "Methodism and the Threat of Revolution in Britain," in Eric Hobsbawm, *Labouring Men* (New York: Basic Books, 1964), 26.
42 "United Methodist Free Church, Seaton Sluice," *Morpeth Herald*, August 1, 1891.
43 "Services at Seaton Sluice," *Morpeth Herald*, October 12, 1889.
44 J.A. West, "Seaton Delaval Circuit, Northumberland," *Christian Messenger*, 1910, 315; My Primitive Methodists, https://www.myprimitivemethodists.org.uk/content/place-2/northumberland-2/seaton_delaval_circuit_northumberland.
45 Hall, "The Anatomy of a Changing Consciousness," 168.
46 See Brendan Duff, "The Progress of Education in the Northern Coalfield before 1870," *Northern History* 55, 3 (2018): 178–205.
47 Benson, *British Coalminers*, 136–37. For a portrayal of miners as conservative on schooling, see Brendan Duffy, "Late Nineteenth Century Popular Conservatism: The Work of Coalminers on School Boards of the North-East," *History of Education* 27, 1 (March 1998): 29–38.
48 The diversity of objectives has produced debate as to whether parents were more motivated by hopes for schooling or by prospects for early employment. See Robert Colls, "'Oh Happy English Children!': Coal, Class and Education in the North-East," *Past and Present* 73 (November 1976): 75–99; and A.J. Hessom and Brendan Duffy, "Coal, Class and Education in the North-East," *Past and Present* 90 (February 1981): 136–51. See also Robert Colls, "Coal, Class and Education in the North-East: A Rejoinder," *Past and Present* 90 (February 1981): 152–65.
49 See Rose, *The Intellectual Life*.
50 On its impact, see Anthony S. Wohl, "The Bitter Cry of Outcast London," *International Review of Social History* 13, 2 (August 1968): 189–245.
51 See "Hon. Ralph Smith's Death Causes Very Widespread Regret," *VP*, February 13, 1917.
52 "Notes from Nanaimo," *Ladysmith Daily Ledger*, August 22, 1906.
53 See Alon Kadish, "University Extension and the Working Classes: The Case of the Northumberland Miners," *Historical Research* 60, 142 (June 1987): 189; and Robert Davies Roberts, *Eighteen Years of University Extension* (Cambridge: CUP, 1891), especially 21–22.
54 Kadish, "University Extension," 199.
55 See Metcalfe, *Leisure and Recreation*, 39; Clifton Stockdale, "Mechanics' Institutes in Northumberland and Durham, 1824–1902" (PhD diss., University of Durham, 1993), http://etheses.dur.ac.uk/5614/1/5614_3030.PDF?UkUDh:CyT.
56 Kadish, "University Extension," 188–207.
57 "Concerning the Island Member," *NFP*, April 19, 1904.
58 Metcalfe, *Leisure and Recreation*, 44.
59 A labour aristocracy, based in pride in skill and respectability, has been much debated but does fit both Smiths. This social location has been offered as an explanation for the failure of most of the working class to champion socialist and communist politics. The literature on the labour aristocracy is extensive, but for an introduction, see E.J. Hobsbawm, "Debating the Labour Aristocracy," and E.J. Hobsbawm, "The Aristocracy of Labour Reconsidered," both in E.J. Hobsbawm, *World of Labour: Further Studies in the World of Labour* (London: Weidenfeld and Nicholson, 1984), 214–26, 227–51; Henry

Pelling, "The Concept of the Labour Aristocracy," in Henry Pelling, *Popular Politics and Society in Late Victorian Britain*, 2nd ed. (London: Macmillan, 1979), 37–61; and Brian H. Harrison, "Traditions of Respectability in British Labour History," in Brian H. Harrison, *Peaceable Kingdom: Stability and Change in Modern Britain* (Oxford: Clarendon Press, 1982), 157–84. On the Canadian phenomenon, see Mark Leier, "Ethnicity, Urbanism and the Labour Aristocracy: Rethinking Vancouver Trade Unionism, 1889–1909," *CHR* 74, 4 (December 1993): 510–34; and Heron, *Working Lives,* especially Chapter 7, "Labourism and the Canadian Working Class."

60 See Johnston Birchall, *Co-op: The People's Business* (Manchester: MUP, 1994).
61 Joan Allen, "A Question of Neutrality? The Politics of Co-operation in North-East England, 1881–1926," in *Labour and Working-Class Lives: Essays to Celebrate the Life and Work of Chris Wrigley,* ed. Keith Laybourn and John Shepherd (Manchester: MUP, 2017), 53.
62 Benson, *The Working Class in Britain,* 188.
63 Ibid., 193.
64 Barbara J. Blaszak, *The Matriarchs of England's Cooperative Movement: A Study in Gendered Politics and Female Leadership, 1883–1921* (Westport, CT: Praeger, 2000), 6.
65 Ibid., 11.
66 E.V. Neale, ed., *Handbook of the Co-operative Congress, Glasgow, 26–27–28 May 1890* (Manchester, 1890), CWS1/23/2/144, Glasgow City Archives.
67 See "The Canadian M.P. at Seaton Delaval," *Morpeth Herald and Reporter,* August 9, 1902.
68 Neale, *Handbook of the Co-operative Congress,* 8. See also J. Davis, "Primrose, Archibald Philip, Fifth Earl of Rosebery and First Earl of Midlothian (1847–1929)," *Oxford Dictionary of National Biography,* 2004.
69 Neale, *Handbook of the Co-operative Congress.*
70 See Carman Miller, "Grey, Albert Henry George, 4th Earl Grey," in *DCB*, vol. 14, University of Toronto/Université Laval, 2003, http://www.biographi.ca/en/bio/grey_albert_henry_george_14E.html; and Chester New, *Lord Durham* (Oxford: OUP, 1923). On the Earls of Durham (the Lambton family) and the importance of the coalfields to their income, see David Spring, "Earls of Durham and the Great Northern Coal Field, 1830–1880," *CHR* 33, 3 (September 1952): 237–53. The second Earl Grey was the architect of the first Great Reform Bill of 1832. The Lambtons and Greys were also kin.
71 Thomas Burt, *Thomas Burt M.P., D.C.L., Pitman & Privy Councilor: An Autobiography* (London: Garland, 1924), 214.
72 Ibid.
73 See Frank Prochaska, *Royal Bounty: The Making of a Welfare Monarchy* (New Haven: Yale University Press, 1995). Relations between seemingly altruistic elites and supposed beneficiaries could blunt radicalism and encourage sycophancy, charges to which liberal labourites were vulnerable. See Nicholas Owen, "MacDonald's Parties; The Labour Party and the 'Aristocratic Embrace,' 1922–31," *20th Century British History* 18, 1 (2007): 1–53. Elite allies had their own critics. See, for example, Martin Pugh, "'Class Traitors': Conservative Recruits to Labour, 1900–30," *English Historical Review* 113, 450 (February 1998): 38–64.
74 John Benson, "Miners, Coalowners and Collaboration: The Miners Permanent Relief Fund Movement in England, 1860–1895," *Labour History Review* 68, 2 (August 2003): 187.
75 "Mr. Ralph Smith Appointed Yukon Commissioner," *Morpeth Herald,* January 19, 1907.
76 Allen, "A Question of Neutrality?" See also the argument that "co-operation too, which is but an application of the principle of unionism, has had its influence on the social improvement of the miners of these two counties." Richard Fines, *The Miners of*

Northumberland and Durham: A History of Their Social and Political Struggles, from the Earliest Period Down to the Present Day (Blyth: John Robinson, Junior, 1873), 283.
77 Fines, *The Miners of Northumberland and Durham*, 274, 283.
78 William H. Maehl, Jr., "The Northeastern Miners' Struggle for the Franchise, 1872–74," *International Review of Social History* 20, 2 (April 1975): 199. On Canadian labourism, see Heron, *Working Lives*, especially Chapter 7.
79 On his role, see L.J. Satre, "Thomas Burt and the Crisis of Late-Victorian Liberalism in the North-East," *Northern History* 23, 1 (1987): 174–93.
80 Nicholas Thompson, quoted in "Hon. Ralph Smith's Death," *VP*, February 13, 1917.
81 "Imperial Parliament," *Shields Daily Gazette*, June 24, 1881.
82 "Proportional Voting," *Shields Daily Gazette*, December 31, 1884.
83 *Newcastle Weekly Current*, December 18, 1885.
84 Hall, "The Anatomy of a Changing Consciousness," 167.
85 David Powell, "The New Liberalism and the Rise of Labour, 1886–1906," *Historical Journal* 29, 2 (1986): 372. See too John Allett, *New Liberalism: The Political Economy of J.A. Hobson* (Toronto: UTP, 1981).
86 Hall, "The Anatomy of a Changing Consciousness," 166.
87 Christopher Radcliffe, "Mutual Improvement Societies and the Forging of Working-Class Political Consciousness in Nineteenth-Century England," *International Journal of Lifelong Education* 16, 2 (1997): 150.
88 "Concerning the Island Member," *NFP*, April 19, 1904.
89 Quoted in David Powell, "The Liberal Ministries and Labour, 1892–1895," *History* 68, 224 (1983): 414.
90 See Hall, "The Anatomy of a Changing Consciousness," 171; and John Benson, "Burt, Thomas (1837–1922)," *Oxford Dictionary of National Biography*, 2004.
91 "Northern Counties Women's Liberal Associations," *Northern Echo* (Durham), November 14, 1890.
92 Martin Pugh, "The Limits of Liberalism: Liberals and Women's Suffrage," in *Citizenship and Community: Liberals, Radicals and Collective Identities in the British Isles, 1865–1931*, ed. Eugenio F. Biagini (Cambridge: CUP, 1996), 52.
93 Metcalfe, *Leisure and Recreation*, 40–41.
94 John Shepherd, "Labour and Parliament: The Lib.-Labs. as the First Working-Class MPs, 1885–1906," in *Currents of Radicalism: Popular Radicalism, Organised Labour and Party Politics in Britain, 1850–1914*, ed. Eugenio Biagini and Alastair Reid (Cambridge: CUP, 1991), 188–89.
95 Carolyn Baylies, *The History of the Yorkshire Miners* (London: Routledge, 1993), 95.
96 "Success of a Northumbrian in Vancouver Island," *Newcastle Evening Chronicle*, September 21, 1895.
97 "Presentation at Holywell," *Morpeth Herald*, September 17, 1892.

CHAPTER 2: REPLENISHING THE EMPIRE, 1892–1900

1 Belich, *Replenishing the Earth*. See also Darwin, *The Empire Project*, which is especially good in its treatment of the White dominions as part of a "British World System." More particularly, see Harper, "Rhetoric and Reality," 160–80; and Carter, "Aboriginal People of Canada," 200–19.
2 Darwin, *The Empire Project*, 152.

3 British immigrants, working class and otherwise, were never homogeneous. The case of Edith Angell Hancox, born illegitimate in Wiltshire in 1874, who arrived in Winnipeg in 1904 and went on to support the Labor Church, the Winnipeg General Strike, and the Communist Party, serves as a reminder of alternatives to Mary Ellen's liberal-labour feminism. See David Thompson, "More Sugar, Less Salt: Edith Hancox and the Passionate Mobilization of the Dispossessed, 1919–1928," *L/LT* 85 (Spring 2020): 127–63.
4 On the onset of this process in British Columbia, see Perry, *On the Edge of Empire*. See also her "Women, Gender, and Empire," 220–39.
5 See especially her "Race, Greed, and Something More," in Barman, *On the Cusp of Contact*, 3–25.
6 Burrill, "The Settler Order Framework," 177.
7 See Tony Lane, *Liverpool: Gateway of Empire* (Liverpool: Liverpool University Press, 1987).
8 Belshaw, *Colonization and Community*, 54, 57. See the myth making regarding the Smiths' choice of destination, and by extension their status, in a much flawed entry, "Smith, Mary Ellen (1862–1933)," in *A Standard Dictionary of Canadian Biography*, ed. Charles G.D. Roberts and Arthur L. Tunnell (Toronto: Trans-Canada Press, 1938), 421. The piece claims that "southern Italy" was the alternative to British Columbia, which was ultimately chosen because Mary Ellen "had always dreamed of living there."
9 "Norway – Heritage," http://www.norwayheritage.com/p_ship.asp?sh=vanco.
10 *Papers in Reference to Atlantic Steamship Line between Great Britain and Canada* (Ottawa: S.E. Dawson, 1896), 26–27.
11 "Passenger Lists, 1865–1922," Library and Archives Canada, https://www.bac-lac.gc.ca/eng/discover/immigration/immigration-records/passenger-lists/passenger-lists-1865-1922/Pages/image.aspx?Image=e003551146&URLjpg=http%3a%2f%2fcentral.bac-lac.gc.ca%2f.item%2f%3fid%3de003551146%26op%3dimg%26app%3dpassengerlist&Ecopy=e003551146.
12 Both ambitious cities claimed the numbers were under-reported. See Patrick Dunae, "Making the 1891 Census in British Columbia," *HS/SH* 31 (November 1998): 234–35.
13 *Williams' Illustrated Official British Columbia Directory for Nanaimo* (Victoria: R.T. Williams, 1892).
14 Helen Brown, "Binaries, Boundaries, and Hierarchies: Spatial Relations of City Schooling in Nanaimo, British Columbia, 1891–1901" (PhD diss., University of British Columbia, 1998), 51.
15 *Williams' Illustrated Official British Columbia Directory*.
16 Lutz, *Makúk*, 172–74.
17 John D. Belshaw, "Cradle to Grave: An Examination of Demographic Behavior on Two British Columbia Frontiers," *Journal of the Canadian Historical Association* 5 (1994): 44. The city proper was considerably smaller, numbering some 4,595 in 1891. See Seager and Perry, "Mining the Connections," 67.
18 Seager and Perry, "Mining the Connections," 73.
19 Patrick Dunae, "Making the 1891 Census in British Columbia," *HS/SH* 31 (November 1998): 233.
20 *NFP*, May 7, 1891, quoted in Brown, "Binaries, Boundaries, and Hierarchies," 60.
21 Belshaw, *Colonization and Community*, 140.
22 "Durham Miner's Success," *Newcastle Evening Chronicle*, September 28, 1903.
23 William's business seems not to have been profitable. The *Nanaimo Free Press* mentions all stock being sold at a reduction of 30 to 60 percent. *NFP*, November 21, 1894.

24 McIntosh, *Boys in the Pits*, 130.
25 "Local Gossip," *VW,* November 26, 1896.
26 "Burns' Anniversary Concert!" *NFP,* January 23, 1900; "Scotch Concert Program," *NFP,* November 20, 1900.
27 Jan Peterson, *Hub City Nanaimo, 1886–1920* (Vancouver: Heritage House, 2003), 54.
28 See Janet Mary Nicol, "'My Brother Gave Me a Peddler's Kit': The Sabas in Early British Columbia," *British Columbia History* 42, 4 (2009): 19–21.
29 Higher wages help explain the presence of Nova Scotians in Nanaimo mines. See McIntosh, *Boys in the Pits,* 230n23.
30 *Statutes of British Columbia* (Victoria: Queen's Printer, 1898), 364.
31 See Peter Baskerville, "Women and Investment in Late-Nineteenth-Century Urban Canada: Victoria and Hamilton, 1880–1901," *CHR* 80, 2 (June 1999): 191–218. On the limitations of the Married Women's Property Law in British Columbia, which had no dower law, see Clarkson, *Domestic Reforms,* especially Chapter 4 and page 171.
32 Campbell, *A Great Revolutionary Wave,* 52, notes that "in Victoria and Nanaimo, married women who met the racial, property, and residency qualifications could vote. But in Vancouver and New Westminster, only unmarried or widowed women were initially allowed to vote municipally." But most women lacked sufficient property. See also Walter J. Meyer Zu Urpen, "Towards an Understanding of the Municipal Archives of Nineteenth Century British Columbia: A Case Study of the Archives of the Corporation of the City of Nanaimo, 1875–1904" (master's thesis, University of British Columbia, 1985), 58.
33 See Ian MacPherson, *Each for All: A History of the Co-operative Movement in English Canada, 1900–1945* (Montreal and Kingston: MQUP, 1979).
34 "Mr. R. Smith at Seaton Terrace," *Morpeth Herald and Reporter,* July 19, 1902.
35 For a discussion of this in the context of the 1890s' relatively stable wages, see John Belshaw, "The Standard of Living of British Miners on Vancouver Island, 1848–1900," *BCS* 84 (1989–90): 37–64.
36 "First Annual Exhibition," *NFP,* September 20, 1894.
37 Quoted in Peterson, *Hub City Nanaimo,* 95.
38 See Ralph's nomination as a candidate in the 1894 provincial election, "Elections Regulation Act," *NFP,* September 6, 1894; and the reference to William Spear in "Notice of Assignment," *NFP,* October 15, 1894; and *NFP,* May 3, 1895.
39 "Queen's Birthday," *NFP,* May 25, 1897.
40 On the significance of working-class women's use of dress as a source of power, see Nan Enstad, *Ladies of Labor, Girls of Adventure: Working Women, Popular Culture, and Labor Politics at the Turn of the Twentieth Century* (New York: Columbia University Press, 1999).
41 Darwin, *The Empire Project,* 152.
42 "Our Visitors," *NFP,* November 9, 1894.
43 Ibid.
44 "The Johnson-Smily Entertainment," *NFP,* September 27, 1894. On Johnson's role in legitimating but also questioning empire, see Veronica Strong-Boag and Carole Gerson, *Paddling Her Own Canoe: The Times and Texts of E. Pauline Johnson, Tekahionwake* (Toronto: UTP, 2000).
45 Burrill, "The Settler Order Framework," 194. Burrill draws on the assessment of Bryan Palmer, "Nineteenth-Century Canada and Australia: The Paradoxes of Class Formation," in "Australia and Canada Compared," special joint issue, *L/LT* 38 and *Labour History* 71 (Fall 1996): 35.

46 "Municipal Council," *NFP,* December 10, 1895.
47 *VW,* January 12, 1893.
48 *BC Report of the Minister of Mines* (Victoria: Queen's Printer, 1896), 593.
49 "Nanaimo Hospital: A Model Institution," *NFP,* February 9, 1892.
50 See, for example, "Hospital Notice," *NFP,* April 20, 1893.
51 "Death of Mrs. Spear," *NFP,* December 26, 1895.
52 Peterson, *Hub City Nanaimo,* 145.
53 "Vice-Regal Visit," *NFP,* August 30, 1900. In a further expression of the significance of public health initiatives for women, Mary Caroline Grey, the wife of Gilbert John Murray Elliot, Earl of Minto, later inspired the Lady Minto Nursing Association that sent nurses to India.
54 John R. Hinde, "Stout Ladies and Amazons: Women in the BC Coal-Mining Community of Ladysmith, 1912–14," *BCS* 114 (Summer 1997): 44–45. On women's support for miners, see also McIntosh, *Boys in the Pits,* 138–40.
55 For accounts of this controversial family that strive for balance, see Daniel T. Gallacher, "Dunsmuir, Robert," in *DCB,* vol. 11, University of Toronto/Université Laval, 2003, http://www.biographi.ca/en/bio/dunsmuir_robert_11E.html; and Clarence Karr, "Dunsmuir, James," in *DCB,* vol. 14, University of Toronto/Université Laval, 2003, http://www.biographi.ca/en/bio/dunsmuir_james_14E.html.
56 Undated letter from Cheerful, quoted in C.F.J. Galloway, *The Call of the West: Letters from British Columbia* (London: T. Fisher Unwin, 1916), 89–90, quoted in Seager and Perry, "Mining the Connections," 66. On the problem of drink, see also McIntosh, *Boys in the Pits,* 142.
57 "Drunken Brawl," *NFP,* March 28, 1892.
58 "A Drunken Row!" *NFP,* October 22, 1892.
59 "Man, Whiskey and Immorality," *NFP,* October 28, 1895.
60 "City Police Court," *NFP,* August 16, 1898.
61 See Melanie Ihmels, "The Mischiefmakers: Woman's Movement Development in Victoria, British Columbia, 1850–1910" (master's thesis, University of Victoria, 2008), 93; and Constance Backhouse, "The Shining Sixpence: Women's Worth in Canadian Law at the End of the Victorian Era," *Manitoba Law Journal* 23, 1–2 (1996): 570.
62 Peterson, *Hub City Nanaimo,* 84.
63 "Corporation of the City of Nanaimo, B.C.," *NFP,* January 25, 1896. The attempt to check such offences would have been familiar to the Smiths. Similar campaigns distinguished northern England. See Robert Storch, "The Policeman as Domestic Missionary: Urban Discipline and Popular Culture in Northern England, 1850–1880," *Journal of Social History* 9, 4 (Summer 1976): 481–509.
64 "Church Notes," *NFP,* August 31, 1894.
65 Heron, *Working Lives,* 292.
66 See Nancy Christie, "Young Men and the Creation of Civic Christianity in Urban Methodist Churches, 1880–1914," *Journal of the Canadian Historical Association* 17, 1 (2006): 79. The league was first established in Canada in Ontario in 1889.
67 "Lecture on 'Culture,'" *NFP,* October 28, 1896; "Brief Mention," *NFP,* October 7, 1896.
68 "Christian Duty," *NFP,* October 8, 1896.
69 "Service of Song," *NFP,* April 7, 1898.
70 "Epworth League," *NFP,* April 9, 1898. Barrett Browning has been recognized as someone for whom "spirituality and theological reflection held central place." See Alexandra M.B.

Worn, "'Poetry Is Where God Is': The Importance of Christian Faith and Theology in Elizabeth Barrett Browning's Life and Work," in *Victorian Religious Discourse*, ed. J.V. Nixon (New York: Palgrave Macmillan, 2004), 235.
71 "Christianity and the Toiler," *NFP*, March 26, 1895.
72 Freethought, letter, "Christianity and the Toiler," *NFP*, April 5, 1895. The significance of such secularism and anti-clericalism in BC history is well set out by Lynne Marks, *Infidels and the Damn Churches: Irreligion and Religion in Settler British Columbia* (Vancouver: UBCP, 2017).
73 Ralph Smith, "Reply to Freethought," *NFP*, April 13, 1895.
74 "Y.M.C.A. Concert," *NFP*, April 1, 1893; "Epworth League Meeting," *NFP*, June 23, 1893.
75 On the Odd Fellows and the soundness of the Nanaimo and other smaller lodges, see George Emery and J.C. Herbert Emery, *A Young Man's Benefit: The Independent Order of Odd Fellows and Sickness Insurance in the United States and Canada, 1860–1929* (Montreal and Kingston: MQUP, 1999).
76 "Loyal Orange Banquet," *NFP*, November 7, 1898.
77 "An Unqualified Success," *NFP*, November 10, 1899. See also her appearance in "For the Orphans Home," *NFP*, November 7, 1899; and "Protestant Orphanage Benefit," *NFP*, October 16, 1900.
78 "Fraternal Notes," *NFP*, July 15, 1898.
79 Campbell, *A Great Revolutionary Wave*, 28. The BC WCTU was not formally segregated by race. At times it had Black, Indigenous, and Jewish members. Unfortunately, Nanaimo features only marginally in Lyn Gough, *As Wise as Serpents, 1883–1939* (Victoria: Swan Lake, 1988), the otherwise useful history of the BC WCTU. Much of the information here is drawn from that volume, especially 57–61.
80 "W.C.T.U.," *NFP*, April 18, 1894.
81 See "Sunday Services at the Y.M.C.A.," *NFP*, March 24, 1894; "Lecture at Courtenay," *Nanaimo Weekly News*, September 18, 1894; and "The Temperance Cause," *NFP*, July 6, 1894.
82 "WCTU," *NFP*, July 26, 1895. On the shifting position of the labour leadership with regard to temperance, see Heron, *Working Lives*, Chapter 5, "Labour and Liquor."
83 "City and District," *Nanaimo Semi-Weekly Mail*, October 16, 1896; *NFP*, April 28, 1898.
84 J.D.P. Knox, "For God and Humanity," *NFP*, March 18, 1898.
85 "Brief Mention," *NFP*, December 19, 1900.
86 Helen Brown, "Gender and Space: Constructing the Public School Teaching Staff in Nanaimo, 1891–1914," *BCS* 105–6 (Spring-Summer 1995): 98.
87 Quoted in ibid.
88 McIntosh, *Boys in the Pits*, 8.
89 Ibid., 43. For boys' wages in Nanaimo, 1875–1900, see ibid., Table 3-3, page 58.
90 "The Kuper Island School," *NFP*, November 19, 1895. In 2021, the discovery of unmarked graves at residential schools across the country, including Kuper Island, further highlighted the nightmare of residential schooling.
91 "Discriminatory Legislation in British Columbia, 1872–1948," https://www2.gov.bc.ca/assets/gov/british-columbians-our-governments/our-history/historic-places/documents/heritage/chinese-legacy/discriminatory_legislation_in_bc_1872_1948.pdf.
92 Brown, "Binaries, Boundaries, and Hierarchies," 236.
93 Ibid., 177.
94 Ibid., 189.
95 Valerie Green, *If Walls Could Talk: Vancouver Island's Houses from the Past* (Victoria: Heritage House, 2004), 85.

96 T.W. Paterson, "'The Godfather' Was a Horticultural Hero," *Harbour City Star* (Nanaimo), March 1, 2006.
97 *Williams' Illustrated Official British Columbia Directory* (Victoria: R.T. Williams, 1892).
98 Brown, "Binaries, Boundaries, and Hierarchies," 57.
99 On the contrast between the two companies, see Barman, *The West beyond the West*, 127–29.
100 "Petition re Chinese and Japanese in Coal Mines," *BC Sessional Papers* (Victoria: Government Printer, 1892), 465.
101 Nanaimo Culture and Heritage, "A Walk through Time," https://www.nanaimo.ca/docs/social-culture-environment/heritage/heritage-walk-southend.pdf.
102 John D. Belshaw, "The British Collier in British Columbia: Another Archetype Reconsidered," *L/LT* 34, 3 (Fall 1994): 32.
103 Allen Seager, "Socialists and Workers: The Western Canadian Coal Miners, 1900–21," *L/LT* 16, 3 (Fall 1985): 32. The so-called Molly Maguires were an Irish secret society known for aiding immigrant coal miners in Pennsylvania.
104 Jeremy Mouat, "The Politics of Coal: A Study of the Wellington Miners' Strike of 1890–91," *BCS* 77 (Spring 1988): 29.
105 Heron, *Working Lives*, 278.
106 Seager and Perry, "Mining the Connections," 59. For an exploration of this link in general, see Campbell, *A Great Revolutionary Wave*.
107 Unnamed miner's wife and mother of ten children, quoted in Hinde, "Stout Ladies and Amazons," 54.
108 James Young, "Tully Boyce as a Unionist," *NFP*, October 23, 1900, 3. This writer offers a rare identification of Ralph's particular job. Wikipedia states that a "head timberman is a foreman who supervises workers installing timbers in a mine to support the roof and walls of haulage ways, passageways, and the shaft. Also called timber boss; timber foreman." See "Timberman," in "Appendix: Dictionary of Mining, Mineral, and Related Terms/T/3," https://en.wiktionary.org/wiki/Appendix:Dictionary_of_Mining,_Mineral,_and_Related_Terms/T/3.
109 James Young, "Tully Boyce as a Unionist," *NFP*, October 23, 1900.
110 "Trade Unionism," *NFP*, November 11, 1895.
111 For their identification of Ralph as a class traitor, see "For Sale Cheap," *WCL*, April 13, 1912. See also "Parm's Paragraphs," *WCL*, April 22, 1911.
112 Belshaw, "The British Collier," 14.
113 See Kenton Storey, *Settler Anxiety at the Outposts of Empire: Colonial Relations, Human Discourses, and the Imperial Press* (Vancouver: UBCP, 2016), 9.
114 As cited in "Ralph Smith Praised," *VW*, October 1, 1896.
115 *OJ*, September 24, 1898.
116 See *NFP*, September 29, 1898.
117 "Annexation Condemned," *Nanaimo Daily Telegram*, November 9, 1893.
118 "Importance of the Ballot," *NFP*, February 7, 1894; "The Northfield Meeting," *NFP*, March 13, 1894.
119 "Reform at Wellington," *NFP*, April 9, 1894.
120 Heron, *Working Lives*, 284.
121 "A Grand Rally," *NFP*, July 12, 1894; "Music and Dance," *NFP*, May 2, 1894.
122 "Meeting at Northfield," *NFP*, June 13, 1894.
123 Quoted in "The Temperance Cause," *NFP*, July 6, 1894.

124 This was Premier Theodore Davie, a former Nanaimo lawyer. See David Ricardo Williams, "Davie, Theodore," in *DCB*, vol. 12, University of Toronto/Université Laval, 2003, http://www.biographi.ca/en/bio/davie_theodore_12E.html. See also Elections British Columbia, *Electoral History of British Columbia, 1871–1986* (Victoria: Elections BC, 1988), 63, https://elections.bc.ca/docs/rpt/1871-1986_ElectoralHistoryofBC.pdf.
125 "Telegraphic News," *NFP,* October 22, 1895; "Manitoba School Question," *NFP,* October 23, 1895; "Terminal City Notes," *NFP,* July 7, 1896.
126 "Editorial Notes," *Chilliwack Progress,* July 20, 1898.
127 Jeremy Mouat, "Semlin, Charles Augustus," in *DCB*, vol. 15, University of Toronto/Université Laval, 2003, http://www.biographi.ca/en/bio/semlin_charles_augustus_15E.html.
128 Robert A.J. McDonald and H. Keith Ralston, "Carter-Cotton, Francis Lovett," in *DCB*, vol. 14, University of Toronto/Université Laval, 2003, http://www.biographi.ca/en/bio/carter_cotton_francis_lovett_14E.html.
129 "Legislative Assembly," *NFP,* February 11, 1899.
130 "Woman Suffrage," *NFP,* February 25, 1899.
131 Leier, "Smith, Ralph," in *DCB*.
132 "Telegraphic News by Wire," *Nelson Tribune,* February 4, 1899.
133 "Provincial Legislature," *NFP,* July 26, 1900. See also Peter G. Silverman, "Military Aid to Civil Power in British Columbia: The Labor Strikes at Wellington and Steveston, 1890, 1900," *Pacific Northwest Quarterly* 61, 3 (July 1970): 156–61. On the significance of Dunsmuir and anti-labour legislation, see Belshaw, *Colonization and Community,* especially 146–47.
134 *Nelson Daily Miner,* September 20, 1899.
135 On Smith's role, see J. Webber, "Compelling Compromise: Canada Chooses Conciliation over Arbitration," *L/LT* 28, 3 (Fall 1991): 23.
136 "Interesting Sermon," *NFP,* December 26, 1899.
137 "Provincial Legislature," *NFP,* January 5, 1900, 4. On Rosebery, see Peter D. Jacobson, "Rosebery and Liberal Imperialism, 1899–1903," *Journal of British Studies* 13, 1 (November 1973): 83–107. On Burt, see Jon Lawrence, *Speaking for the People: Party, Language and Popular Politics in England, 1867–1914* (Cambridge: CUP, 1998), 221; and John W. Auld, "The Liberal Pro-Boers," *Journal of British Studies* 14, 2 (May 1975): 78–101.
138 "The Men in Khaki's [sic]," *NFP,* December 18, 1899.
139 "Tommy's Night," *NFP,* December 15, 1899.
140 "Ralph Smith's Address," *NFP,* May 18, 1900.
141 "Unionists in Politics," *OJ,* September 19, 1900.
142 J.W. Patterson, "The Labor Party and Its Leader," *OJ,* September 22, 1900.
143 "Ralph Smith's Trouble," *OJ,* October 19, 1900; "Another Reputation Gone," *Nelson Miner,* September 29, 1900.
144 Robert H. Babcock, *Gompers in Canada: A Study in American Continentalism before the First World War* (Toronto: UTP, 1974), 70.
145 Heron, *Working Lives,* 282.
146 "Anniversary Celebration," *NFP,* November 13, 1900.

CHAPTER 3: FROM NANAIMO TO OTTAWA AND BACK AGAIN, 1900–11

1 Norman Gidney, "From Coal to Forest Products: The Changing Resource Base of Nanaimo, B.C.," *Urban History Review/Revue d'histoire urbaine* 1, 2 (June 1978): 20.

2 "Nanaimo: Carr-Smith," *Ladysmith Daily Ledger*, November 2, 1905. Miss Brenton may have been Sadie, the daughter (or perhaps sister) of Charles J. Brenton, who in 1911 was the manager of Vancouver's Standard Milk Company. He was born in Calstock, Cornwall, and his mother was Ellen Eliza Jackson, presumably a cousin or sister of Mary Ann Jackson Spear. In the 1890s, he was working in Nanaimo as a miner and a piano-tuner, the latter occupation a further confirmation of the family's musicality. See "Brenton Charles Jewell (1871–1948)," WestEndVancouver, https://westendvancouver.wordpress.com/biographies-a-m/biographies-b/brenton-charles-jewell-1871-1948/.
3 "Shepherd's Meeting Saturday Night," *NFP*, January 28, 1907; "Strongly Endorse Ralph Smith, M.P.," *VT*, December 3, 1907.
4 *NFP*, May 21, 1906.
5 "Services Appreciated," *VT*, September 28, 1911.
6 *VP*, August 14, 1907.
7 "Personal," *NFP*, August 23, 1902.
8 "They Want Settlement," *VP*, December 21, 1905. See also "McCarter v. York County Loan Company," *Ontario Law Review* 14 (1907): 420.
9 "Number of Vancouver Investors," *VW*, December 21, 1905.
10 "Local and Other Items," *Chilliwack Progress*, June 26, 1901.
11 "What Is Success?" *NFP*, July 3, 1901.
12 *OJ*, May 7, 1908.
13 A "Spinster," letter, "Communication," *NFP*, November 29, 1911; and see Ralph's speech, "Mr. Ralph Smith Promises Support," *NFP*, May 22, 1908.
14 *NFP*, May 7, 1907.
15 *NFP*, November 25, 1911.
16 "The Concert Programme," *Ladysmith Daily Ledger*, November 22, 1905.
17 "Annual Banquet of the Wallace Street Church," *NFP*, February 22, 1906.
18 *CH*, June 20, 1907.
19 See "The Anniversary," *NFP*, November 16, 1903; *NFP*, February 27, 1904; "Excellent Concert Given Last Night," *NFP*, September 26, 1908; "Benefit Concert," *NFP*, January 11, 1902; *NFP*, January 15, 1904; "Sacred Cantata!" *NFP*, December 4, 1902; and "To Take Donations for Fernie Relief," *NFP*, August 6, 1908. Although dominated by the British, membership in the Native Sons was not restricted to them, particularly for "skilled labourers, white-collar employees, small businessmen, and minor professionals." Not until 1925 were British Columbians of Asian descent formally excluded, and a few early members were of Indigenous and African descent. See Forrest D. Pass, "'The Wondrous Story and Traditions of the Country': The Native Sons of British Columbia and the Role of Myth in the Formation of an Urban Middle Class," *BCS* 151 (Autumn 2006): 5, 16. See in contrast the emphasis on racism in Ian G. Baird, "An Anti-Racism Methodology: The Native Sons and Daughters and Racism against Asians in Nanaimo, British Columbia," *Canadian Geographer/Le Géographe Canadien* 62, 3 (2018): 300–13. Baird's great-grandparents, members of a mining family, emigrated from northeastern England in 1908. Ibid., 303. Whereas the Native Sons was founded in 1899, the Native Daughters did not appear until 1919.
20 "Annual Banquet of the Wallace Street Church," *NFP*, February 22, 1906.
21 "The Women's Auxiliary," *NFP*, March 20, 1903.
22 "New Ward Dedicated," *NFP*, January 2, 1904.
23 "Interesting Ceremony at the Hospital," *NFP*, January 2, 1904.

24 "Nanaimo Receives Earl Grey," *NFP,* September 27, 1906.
25 See *NFP,* November 10, 1904.
26 *NFP,* December 2, 1904.
27 "Honored Mrs. Smith," *OC,* December 26, 1907.
28 See John H. Taylor, *Ottawa: An Illustrated History* (Ottawa: Canadian Museum of Civilization, 1986).
29 *OJ,* April 24, 1902; "Ministerial Association," *OC,* April 7, 1902.
30 "Mr. Smith on 'the Hope of Canada,'" *VW,* February 3, 1906.
31 See "Local Briefs," *OC,* August 1, 1903; and "Social Affairs," *OC,* February 13, 1911. See also Sheila Lloyd, "Ottawa Typhoid Epidemics of 1911 and 1912," *Urban History Review/Revue d'histoire urbaine* 8 (June 1979): 66–89.
32 See Sharon Anne Cook, "Webster, Ella Hobday (Bronson)," in *DCB,* vol. 15, University of Toronto/Université Laval, 2003, http://www.biographi.ca/en/bio/webster_ella_hobday_15E.html.
33 Tarah Brookfield, *Our Voices Must Be Heard: Women and the Vote in Ontario* (Vancouver: UBCP, 2018).
34 Ibid., 107.
35 Sandra Gwyn, *The Private Capital: Ambition and Love in the Age of Macdonald and Laurier* (Toronto: McClelland and Stewart, 1984), 397.
36 Domino [Augustus Bridel], *The Masques of Ottawa* (Toronto: Macmillan of Canada, 1921), 9.
37 Sandra Gwyn, "Scott, Agnes Mary (Davis)," in *DCB,* vol. 15, University of Toronto/Université Laval, 2003, http://www.biographi.ca/en/bio/scott_agnes_mary_15E.html.
38 Gwyn, *The Private Capital,* 223.
39 Ibid., 398.
40 "Lady Laurier Interviewed," *Brandon Daily Sun,* March 7, 1910.
41 Domino, *The Masques of Ottawa,* 39–44.
42 Gwyn, *Private Capital,* 245–46.
43 "Proud to Notice the Important Part of the Women: Keep Up Standard of Canadian Life," *TG,* August, 11, 1910.
44 "A Canadian Labour Leader in the North," *Morpeth Herald and Reporter,* July 5, 1902.
45 See the astringent comments in "Labor," *VW,* August 25, 1902.
46 See Paul Craven, *'An Impartial Umpire': Industrial Relations and the Canadian State, 1900–1911* (Toronto: UTP, 1980); see also Webber, "Compelling Compromise," 15–57.
47 "Labour Matters Were Discussed in House," *OJ,* May 7, 1903.
48 See "How Labor Gets 'Something Now' by Way of the Ralph Smith Route," *WCL,* August 27, 1904. See also "Ralph Smith, of Nanaimo," *WCL,* May 27, 1905.
49 See "The Week Ahead at Ottawa," *VC,* February 12, 1905; Leier, "Smith, Ralph," in *DCB;* and Powell, "The New Liberalism," 384.
50 "Old Age Bill," *WT,* July 6, 1908; "Parliament Got Down to Work," *OC,* December 6, 1910.
51 "For the Suffrage," *OC,* March 6, 1909.
52 *OJ,* January 20, 1909.
53 "Equal Suffragists," *OC,* February 1, 1911. See also Sue Jones, "Labour and the Suffragettes: An Uneasy Relationship," *North East History* 44 (2013): 86–103.
54 *Ladysmith Chronicle,* February 3, 1909.
55 "The Chinese Question," *TG,* February 11, 1903.

56 "Sessional Notes," *OC,* May 14, 1904.
57 See, for example, "Smith as Leader," *NFP,* March 18, 1903.
58 Jeremy Mouat, "The Genesis of Western Exceptionalism: British Columbia's Hard-Rock Miners, 1895–1903," *CHR* 71, 3 (September 1990): 335. On the United Kingdom, see Duncan Tanner, *Political Change and the Labour Party, 1900–1918* (Cambridge: CUP, 1990); Martin Petter, "The Progressive Alliance," *History* 58, 192 (1973): 45–59; and Andrew Chadwick, "Aristocracy or the People? Radical Constitutionalism and the Progressive Alliance in Edwardian Britain," *Journal of Political Ideologies* 4, 3 (1999): 365–90. See also Hak, *The Left in British Columbia,* 44.
59 "Ralph Smith, M.P., Liberal Organizer," *Prince Rupert Optimist,* October 17, 1910.
60 See King's self-satisfaction that his brand of liberalism and British New Liberalism were "the same" in "holding true to the principles of moderate reform." "The Diaries of William Lyon Mackenzie King," September 11, 1921, Library and Archives Canada, https://www.bac-lac.gc.ca/eng/discover/politics-government/prime-ministers/william-lyon-mackenzie-king/Pages/item.aspx?IdNumber=7840&.
61 Ibid., January 30, 1901, September 30, 1901.
62 Ibid., October 1, 1901. Harper died tragically in December 1901 while attempting to rescue a drowning woman. See H. Blair Neatby, "Harper, Henry Albert," in *DCB,* vol. 13, University of Toronto/Université Laval, 2003, http://www.biographi.ca/en/bio/harper_henry_albert_13E.html.
63 "The Diaries of William Lyon Mackenzie King," March 15, 1906.
64 "The Grand Trunk," *NFP,* October 13, 1904.
65 Allen Seager, "Hawthornthwaite, James Hurst," in *DCB,* vol. 15, University of Toronto/Université Laval, 2003, http://www.biographi.ca/en/bio/hawthornthwaite_james_hurst_15E.html.
66 On the closeness of this contest, see Seager, "Socialists and Workers," 23–59.
67 Quoted in James T. Stott, "Letters to the Editor," *VC,* October 22, 1908. See too A.R. McCormack, "Arthur Puttee and the Liberal Party: 1899–1904," *CHR* 51, 2 (June 1970): 141–63.
68 Heron, *Working Lives,* 283.
69 "Not Expecting Much of Change," *OC,* January 18, 1911. There is an extensive literature on the 1911 election, now often dated, but for a summary of the issues, see Richard Johnston and Michael Percy, "Reciprocity, Imperial Sentiment, and Party Politics in the 1911 Election," *Canadian Journal of Political Science* 13, 4 (December 1980): 711–29.
70 Darwin, *The Empire Project,* 301.
71 *VW,* April 15, 1911.
72 "Some Details about Cabinet Ministers," *VW,* November 29, 1916.
73 "State Ball at Government House," *OC,* April 3, 1902.
74 *OJ,* December 2, 1907; "At the Vice Regal Drawing Room," *OC,* November 15, 1909; "Dresses Worn at Parliament Opening," *OC,* January 22, 1909; *OJ,* March 19, 1909. On the importance of dress in the assertion of self-respect and competence for working-class women, see Enstad, *Ladies of Labor, Girls of Adventure;* and Diana Crane, *Class, Gender and Identity in Clothing* (Chicago: University of Chicago Press, 2000).
75 See "The Social Round," *OJ,* May 1, 1902; and Brian P. Clarke, "Scott, Sir Richard William," in *DCB,* vol. 14, University of Toronto/Université Laval, 2003, http://www.biographi.ca/en/bio/scott_richard_william_14E.html.
76 See *OJ,* April 2, 1908; and *OJ,* April 3, 1908.

77 *OJ*, March 19, 1909.
78 *OJ*, April 8, 1911. See also Elizabeth Smith, *A Woman with a Purpose: The Diaries of Elizabeth Smith, 1872–1884*, ed. Veronica Strong-Boag (Toronto: UTP, 1980).
79 See "Margaret Graham (1870–1924)," Canadian Writing Research Collaboratory/Le Collaboratoire scientifique des écrits du Canada, https://cwrc.ca/islandora/object/ceww%3A26b63943-91f9-4829-a319-43d9b7c56fb6.
80 Margaret Graham, "Of Interest to Women," *VW*, June 25, 1904.
81 "Hon. Ralph Smith," *OJ*, February 21, 1917. For similar sentiments, see *CH*, June 20, 1907.
82 *OJ*, April 10, 1907.
83 "Sir Wilfrid at the Exhibition," *VP*, August 17, 1910.
84 See Margot Blanchard, "Féministes canadiennes face à la traite des blanches: Le cas du National Council of Women of Canada (1904–1914)" (master's thesis, Université du Québec à Montréal, 2017). See especially Chapter 3 for Gordon's identification of "White" slavery as involving female victims of all races and classes. Blanchard compares Gordon to Josephine Butler, the British campaigner against the Contagious Diseases Acts. Ibid., 53.
85 Ibid., 54.
86 "To Hold Evangelical Services in Nanaimo," *NFP*, January 25, 1908.
87 See "Franchise Drill in the Y.W.C.A.," *OJ*, April 16, 1907; and "Woman's Suffrage," *OC*, April 16, 1907. The women were not more fully identified but must have been Isabel Flemming Laurence (1844–1938) and Mary Bartlet Sutherland, wives of Nova Scotian Liberal Frederick Andrew Laurence and Ontario Liberal Robert Franklin Sutherland. Unfortunately, we know nothing more about their suffragism.
88 See "Suffragettes Not Endorsed," *OC*, May 20, 1908; and "Suffragettes Will Organize," *OC*, May 22, 1908.
89 "Suffragettes in Ottawa," *OC*, May 19, 1908.
90 "Women's Right to Franchise," *OC*, February 10, 1909. See also the favourable coverage in "Votes for Women," *MG*, February 10, 1909.
91 It had regular columns, titled "Suffragette Sermons," which were written by Vancouver's Florence Huzzey Hall (1864–1917), who insisted on spiritual equality between women and men. See Campbell, *A Great Revolutionary Wave*, 23.
92 Mary Ellen Smith, "Franchise for Women," *Western Methodist Recorder*, January 1909, 1–2. My thanks to Blair Galston, BC archivist for the United Church of Canada in Vancouver, for his generosity in the midst of the COVID-19 pandemic in scanning this article for me.
93 Patrice Dutil and David MacKenzie, *Canada 1911: The Decisive Election That Shaped the Country* (Toronto: Dundurn Press, 2011), 17.
94 "British Columbia Went Solidly Conservative," *NFP*, September 22, 1911.
95 "Mr. Ralph Smith Coming," *VP*, December 11, 1911.
96 "Ralph Smith Feted by Citizens," *NFP*, December 8, 1911.
97 Ibid.

Chapter 4: Boom, Bust, War, and Death, 1912–17

1 "Ralph Smith Engages in Active Business," *VW*, June 7, 1912. See also "Interest in Real Estate Is Reviving," *VW*, June 22, 1912, which notes that Ralph Smith had sold a house at 2800 Marine Drive for $12,000 and bought a house on the corner of First Avenue and Balsam through the Federal Investment Company.

2 *Canadian Engineer*, August 7, 1914, and *Henderson's Greater Vancouver City Directory* (1914), part 2.
3 "New Industry Here," *VP*, July 11, 1914.
4 James Conley, "'Open Shop' Means Closed to Union Men: Carpenters and the 1911 Vancouver Building Trades General Strike," *BCS* 91–92 (Autumn-Winter 1991–92): 129.
5 "Feminine Splendor Marks the Vice-Regal Reception," *VS*, September 20, 1912. Prince Arthur, Duke of Connaught and Strathearn, and the Duchess Louise Margaret of Prussia were Canada's viceregal couple from 1911 to 1916.
6 On these key figures, see Irene Howard, *The Struggle for Social Justice in British Columbia: Helena Gutteridge, the Unknown Reformer* (Vancouver: UBCP, 1992); and Strong-Boag, *The Last Suffragist Standing*.
7 On the shift toward greater inclusiveness in the IODE during the First World War, see Steve Marti, "Daughter in My Mother's House, but Mistress in My Own: Questioning Canada's Imperial Relationship through Patriotic Work, 1914–18," in *Fighting with the Empire: Canada, Britain, and Global Conflict, 1867–1947*, ed. Steve Marti and William J. Pratt (Vancouver: UBCP, 2019), 38. See also the identification of the continuing evolution of the IODE as a nationalist group in Pickles, *Female Imperialism and National Identity*. On Tupper, see R.A.J. McDonald, "Charles Hibbert Tupper and the Political Culture of British Columbia, 1903–1924," *BCS* 149 (Spring 2006): 63–86.
8 On the significance of "at homes" in Vancouver, see R.A.J. McDonald, *Making Vancouver: Class, Status and Social Boundaries, 1863–1913* (Vancouver: UBCP, 1996), 165.
9 "At Home," *VW*, April 18, 1913; "Society," *VW*, April 15, 1913.
10 "Smith-Johnson," *'DE LUXXE' Magazine* (Victoria), August 1913.
11 See "Liberals Met at Bursill Institute," *GVC*, July 10, 1915; and "Will MacDonald or McCrossan Be Our Liberal Nominee?" *GVC*, July 17, 1915.
12 *VS*, October 6, 1916.
13 *VP*, December 13, 1913.
14 *VW*, May 26, 1916.
15 McDonald, *Making Vancouver*, 120.
16 Ibid., 93.
17 See Jean Barman, *Stanley Park's Secret: The Forgotten Families of Whoi Whoi, Kanaka Ranch, and Brockton Point* (Vancouver: Harbour, 2006); "Race, Greed, and Something More" and "Erasing Indigenous Indigeneity in Vancouver," in Barman, *On the Cusp of Contact*, 3–25, 26–59; Renisa Mawani, "Imperial Legacies (Post) Colonial Identities: Law, Space and the Making of Stanley Park, 1859–2001," *Law, Text, Culture* 7 (2003): 98–141; and Douglas C. Harris, "Property and Sovereignty: An Indian Reserve in a Canadian City," *UBC Law Review* 50, 2 (2017): 321–92. On the province-wide theft of Indigenous lands in these years, see McDonald, *A Long Way to Paradise*, Chapters 3 and 4.
18 The details of corporate land dealings are unlikely to be retrieved, but see "Being Paid Three Times Over for Coming Here," *VP*, March 6, 1913, for Ralph's interest in False Creek.
19 On this story, see Strong-Boag and Gerson, *Paddling Her Own Canoe*.
20 See "Canada's Poetess Is Laid to Rest," *VP*, March 10, 1913.
21 Banfield is a major figure in Vancouver women's clubs. She was vice-president of the Woman's Employment League, whose board and representatives included many suffragists during the war years, such as Smith, Gutteridge, Jamieson, Mrs. W.H. Griffin, and Mrs. J.O. Perry. See "Will Start Exchange Help for the Women," *VS*, October 1, 1914, 5.

For a rare identification of Banfield as a suffragist, see "Suffrage Pioneers Meet to Discuss Activities," *VW,* March 18, 1921. Her husband, insurance broker John Joseph Banfield, was a Conservative, which may have limited her official involvement.
22 See Jennifer S.H. Brown, "Nickawa, Frances," in *DCB,* vol. 15, University of Toronto/ Université Laval, 2003, http://www.biographi.ca/en/bio/nickawa_frances_15E.html.
23 See Gerald Thomson, "'A Baby Show Means Work in the Hardest Sense': The Better Baby Contests of the Vancouver and New Westminster Local Councils of Women, 1913–1929," *BCS* 128 (Winter 2000–01): 5–36.
24 Katharyne Mitchell, "Conflicting Geographies of Democracy and the Public Sphere in Vancouver BC," *Transactions of the Institute of British Geographers* n.s. 22, 2 (1997): 166.
25 McDonald, *Making Vancouver,* 162.
26 On the Tuppers, see ibid., 151, 174. Obituaries for Janet Tupper stressed her commitment to the IODE and otherwise suggested modest accomplishments. Certainly, they are difficult to find. On the Bell-Irvings, see R.A.J. McDonald, "'He Thought He Was the Boss of Everything': Masculinity and Power in a Vancouver Family," *BCS* 132 (Winter 2001–02): 5–30. Marie Isabella retreated into illness as she dealt with repeated pregnancies and an overbearing and philandering husband. Contributions to the community are hard to find in her obituaries.
27 See Sylvie McClean, *A Woman of Influence: Evlyn Fenwick Farris* (Victoria: Sono Nis Press, 1997), 107–8.
28 See the many references in McClung, *In Times Like These.*
29 See the implied criticism of the UWC in "What Women Are Doing," *VS,* March 10, 1913.
30 See Elsie Gregory MacGill, *My Mother the Judge: A Biography of Judge Helen Gregory MacGill* (Toronto: Ryerson Press, 1955); and Strong-Boag, *The Last Suffragist Standing.*
31 This phrase is the title of Chapter 7 in McDonald, *Making Vancouver.*
32 See Linda Hale, "The British Columbia Woman Suffrage Movement, 1890–1917" (master's thesis, University of British Columbia, 1977), Appendix I, "Biographies of the British Columbia Woman Suffrage Leaders, 1890–1917." Evlyn Farris is notably absent from this list, and no top member of the BC social elite is included in it.
33 *TC,* August 1912.
34 *BCF,* June 11, 1915, quoted in C. Cleverdon, *The Woman Suffrage Movement in Canada* (1950; repr., Toronto: UTP, 1974), 84n2.
35 By 1913, the Women's Forum "represented approximately 1,700 female municipal franchise holders in the city." Campbell, *A Great Revolutionary Wave,* 55.
36 In ibid., 77, Campbell notes that 71 percent of MLAs voted against a suffrage resolution in 1913 and that 80 percent followed suit in 1916.
37 "Fort George Women Send to Vancouver for Help in Straits," *VS,* July 19, 1913.
38 "Editor's Notes," *TC,* July 1913.
39 "Editor's Notes: The Outlook," *TC,* January 1914.
40 See "Women Accomplish Great Work to Help Men on the Firing Line," *VS,* February 7, 1916. Mary Ellen chaired Vancouver's Ward Six Branch.
41 Lisa Pasolli, "'A Proper Independent Spirit': Working Mothers and the Vancouver City Creche, 1909–20," *BCS* 173 (Spring 2012): 69–95.
42 Marjory Lang and Linda Hale, "*Women of the World* and Other Dailies: The Lives and Times of Vancouver Newspaperwomen in the First Quarter of the Twentieth Century," *BCS* 8 (Spring 1990): 14, 21.

43 Robin Anderson, "Domestic Service: The YWCA and Women's Employment Agencies in Vancouver, 1898–1914," *HS/SH* 25, 50 (November 1992): 311.
44 See Star Rosenthal, "Union Maids: Organized Women Workers in Vancouver, 1900–1915," *BCS* 41 (Spring 1979): 36–55.
45 Hinde, "Stout Ladies and Amazons," 33–57.
46 G. Colmre, "Shame!" *TC,* July 1913.
47 Indiana Matters, "Public Welfare Vancouver Style, 1910–1920," *JCS* 14, 1 (Spring 1979): 8, 14.
48 Lang and Hale, "*Women of the World* and Other Dailies."
49 McDonald, *Making Vancouver,* 176.
50 "Woman and Her Part in the World War," *VW,* August 27, 1915.
51 "The Cause of Women (Contributed by Women's Suffrage Societies)," *VW,* February 26, 1916.
52 See the decision of the Provincial Political Equality League to oppose the referendum in principle but to work for the "yes" vote. "Will Trust to Men to Give Just Vote," *VW,* May 17, 1916.
53 *BCF,* April 14, 1916.
54 Campbell, *A Great Revolutionary Wave,* 198.
55 See the condemnation in "Parker Williams Wins," *BCF,* September 15, 1916.
56 "Serious Rioting at Vancouver," *VT,* January 29, 1912.
57 For the prohibition referendum, see Robert Campbell, *Demon Rum or Easy Money: Government Control of Liquor in British Columbia from Prohibition to Privatization* (Ottawa: Carleton University Press, 1991).
58 "Voters' Educational League Hear Inaugural Address of President," *VS,* November 4, 1916. See also *VS,* November 2, 1916.
59 "Items of Social and Personal News," *VP,* January 23, 1917. On league branches in Victoria, New Westminster, and North Vancouver, see *VT,* November 9, 1916; "Mrs. Wiggins Is First President," *VW,* December 1, 1916; and *VP,* February 16, 1917.
60 See A.W. Purduc, "The Liberal and Labour Parties in North-East Politics 1900–14: The Struggle for Supremacy," *International Review of Social History* 26, 1 (April 1981): 1–24.
61 See Leier, "Smith, Ralph," in *DCB.*
62 "Liberals to Contest the Elections," *VP,* March 1, 1912, 5. See also "Holds to Free Trade Ideals," *VP,* March 16, 1912.
63 "Parliamentarian Tells of Value of Individual Effort," *VS,* March 11, 1912. See also Ralph Smith, "Man's Strength and Destiny Lies with Himself," *VS,* March 11, 1912.
64 "The Liberal Convention," *VW,* March 12, 1912; "Candidates Are Severely Just in Arraignment," *VW,* March 14, 1912.
65 "Liberal Candidates Throw Down the Gage of Battle," *VW,* March 13, 1912.
66 "Ralph Smith Is Heard in a Fine Effort," *VW,* March 15, 1912; "Young Liberals Hear Candidates," *VW,* March 16, 1912; "Government of Humbug and Tyranny," *VW,* March 23, 1912.
67 "Mr. Ralph Smith and His Political History," *WCLL,* March 22, 1912.
68 See *BCF,* June 29, 1912; and *BCF,* November 9, 1912.
69 "For Sale Cheap," *WCL,* April 13, 1912.
70 See "Ralph Smith Will Take Stump Again," *VW,* June 12, 1912; and "Says Federation Would Not Help Bonds of Empire," *VS,* August 15, 1912, 5.
71 *VS,* June 2, 1913.

72 "Democratic Principles Are Upheld," *VS*, June 6, 1913.
73 "Tory Machine of Golden under Parson's Thumb," *VW*, October 10, 1913.
74 "Asks All to Unite to Defeat Government," *VW*, November 12, 1913.
75 "Ralph Smith and the Liberal Party," *Revelstoke Mail Herald*, November 22, 1913. See also "Ralph Smith on Liberal Party," *Revelstoke Mail Herald*, October 18, 1913; and "Wants Coalition to Defeat McBride," *Delta Times*, October 18, 1913.
76 "Patriotic Address by Mr. Ralph Smith, Ex-M.P., Setting Forth Principles of Liberalism, Stirs People of South Hill," *GVC*, February 21, 1914.
77 "Bar Hindus from Canada Says Meeting," *VP*, June 24, 1914; H.F. West, "That Phantom Komagata Maru," *Canadian Courier*, July 11, 1914. See also Sarah I. Wallace, *Not Fit to Stay: Public Health Panics and South Asian Exclusion* (Vancouver: UBCP, 2017), 144.
78 "Provincial Progressive," *VS*, June 2, 1914, 2. Contradictions were also evident in 1915 when this group hosted a federal Liberal speaker who condemned the provincial government for giving funds to the Indians, which he compared to "giving loaded weapons to children." "Provincial Progressives," *VS*, July 6, 1915.
79 Quoted in "Says True Patriotism Is Not Flag-Flapping," *VS*, June 30, 1914.
80 See his letter, "Comparison of Methods," *VS*, August 10, 1914.
81 "Solidarity of the Empire Increased by War," *VW*, October 7, 1914.
82 "Patronage System Secures Adherents," *VS*, October 9, 1914.
83 "Greater Prosperity Enjoyed in Canada under the Liberals," *VS*, December 14, 1914.
84 "Liberals Select Candidates and Draft Platform," *VW*, March 31, 1915.
85 "Confusion Worse Confounded," *Prince Rupert Journal*, April 1, 1915; J.E. Rea and Patricia E. Roy, "Martin, Joseph," in *DCB*, vol. 15, University of Toronto/Université Laval, 2003, http://www.biographi.ca/en/bio/martin_joseph_15E.html.
86 "Why Act with Caution When Interning Aliens Who Menace Community?" *VS*, June 19, 1915.
87 "Liberalism Eternal Enemy of Privilege," *VT*, July 19, 1915.
88 "Who's to Be the Victim?" *WCLL*, December 24, 1915.
89 *BCF*, March 10, 1916.
90 "Brewster Is the Unanimous Choice of Liberal Party," *VT*, February 17, 1916.
91 "Witness Testified That He Saw Macdonald Hand Money to Gosden," *Prince Rupert Journal*, May 17, 1916; "No Rubber Stamp about Mr. Smith," *VW*, June 19, 1916. See also "Brewster Writ Finds Support," *VW*, July 19, 1916.
92 "A Trio of Speakers Champion the Cause of Woman Suffrage," *VS*, June 6, 1916.
93 *VS*, August 28, 1916; *Lillooet Prospector*, July 21, 1916.
94 *Vancouver Standard*, August 26, 1916.
95 "Says Alien Enemies Given White Men's Jobs in Coal Mines," *VS*, September 11, 1916.
96 "Some Details about Cabinet Ministers," *VW*, November 29, 1916.
97 See "Ralph Smith's Place," *Prince Rupert Journal*, December 3, 1916.
98 See "No Candidate Nominated by Conservatives," *VW*, December 16, 1916; and "McTaggart Replies to Opponents' Charges," *VW*, December 19, 1916.
99 "Development of Business Depends on Co-operation," *VW*, December 6, 1916.
100 See R.A.J. McDonald, "The Quest for 'Modern Administration': British Columbia's Civil Service 1870s to 1940s," *BCS* 161 (Spring 2009): 22. On the significance of Shortt and others for Canadian New Liberalism, see Ferguson, *Remaking Liberalism*.
101 "Stocktaking of B.C. Affairs Inaugurated by Hon. Ralph Smith," *VS*, December 12, 1916.
102 "Wish to Know about Capital," *VW*, January 4, 1917.

103 "Must Respond to Duty's Call," *VS*, January 19, 1917.
104 "Civil Servants Should Enlist," *VW*, January 19, 1917.
105 Roger Stonebanks, "Goodwin, Albert," in *DCB*, vol. 14, University of Toronto/Université Laval, 2003, http://www.biographi.ca/en/bio/goodwin_albert_14E.html.
106 *NFP*, November 25, 1911.
107 See Marks, *Infidels and the Damn Churches*.
108 "Report of W.C.T.U. Convention," *Lillooet Prospector*, October 3, 1914.
109 "What Women Are Doing," *VS*, October 25, 1912. See also "Society: In Club Circles," *VW*, October 25, 1912.
110 *WCLL*, November 22, 1912.
111 "Women Bound to Get Franchise: Are Essential in Political Life," *VS*, October 28, 1912.
112 See "Suffrage Movement Is 'a Divine Unrest,'" *VS*, November 12, 1913; "On Dit," *VS*, April 9, 1913, 8; "Women's Suffrage Makes Headway," *VS*, May 17, 1913; "Society," *VW*, April 8, 1913; "Says Women Must Have the Ballot: Two Votes Needed from Homes," *VS*, June 6, 1913; "Society: In Club Circles," *VW*, July 30, 1913; and "Society: In Club Circles," *VW*, August 29, 1913.
113 "Suffrage Lecture Tonight," *VS*, July 28, 1913; "Great Epworth League Meeting," *WCLL*, August 1, 1913.
114 "Injustice of the Laws to Our Women," *VS*, September 17, 1913.
115 "Awakening of South Vancouver Liberals," *GVC*, July 12, 1913.
116 "Better Land Policy Wanted," *New Westminster News*, July 28, 1913.
117 "Liberals Enjoy Great Rally at Annual Picnic," *VW*, July 28, 1913.
118 "Awakening of South Vancouver Liberals," *GVC*, July 12, 1913.
119 "South Vancouver and Ward Eight Liberals Hold Big Social Gathering at Ash's Hall," *GVC*, July 26, 1913. See also on these themes, "Society: In Club Circles," *VW*, July 23, 1913.
120 "If Women Get Vote No Babies Will Toil," *VS*, July 23, 1913.
121 *TC*, September 1913, 16. See also "No Fear of Militancy in Province," *VS*, October 29, 1913.
122 "If Women Get Vote No Babies Will Toil," *VS*, July 23, 1913. Evlyn Farris, who also understood the benefits of attractiveness, self-consciously deployed the "feminine devices of new clothes and a bewitching smile." Farris to the new Liberal premier, Brewster, quoted in McClean, *A Woman of Influence*, 118.
123 "Will Go On Forever," *VP*, November 12, 1913.
124 "Liberal Speakers Pointedly Condemn Brazen Government," *VS*, July 28, 1913.
125 "Crowds Turned Away at Suffrage Meeting," *VS*, November 18, 1913.
126 "The Suffrage Movement News and Views," *VW*, November 24, 1913.
127 Quoted in Howard, *The Struggle for Social Justice*, 76.
128 See "Social Events," *VS*, March 20, 1914, 5; "Cedar Cottage Jottings," *GVC*, April 4, 1914; and "Mrs. Ralph Smith Addresses Meeting in Mountain View Church," *GVC*, May 2, 1914.
129 "The Woman's Place in Modern Life," *TC*, February 1914.
130 "Social Events," *VS*, May 28, 1914. The fair seemed most (if little) attentive to protecting White women and affirming a racial hierarchy. See Abigail M. Markwyn, "Queen of the Joy Zone Meets Hercules: Gendering Imperial California at the Panama-Pacific International Exposition," *Western Historical Quarterly* 47, 1 (Spring 2016): 51–72.
131 "Women's Propagandist Campaign," *VS*, June 22, 1914, 6. See the inclusion of de Lavelaye in Theodore Ruyssen, "The Final Efforts of the European Pacifists to Prevent the War," *Advocate of Peace* 76, 10 (November 1914): 236–38.

132 Mrs. J.A. Clarke, "Votes for Women," *BCF,* July 24, 1914.
133 *BCF,* August 21, 1914. On Smith's August campaigns, see "Personal Mention," *VS,* August 19, 1914.
134 See "Will Start Exchange Help for the Women," *VS,* October 1, 1914. "Social Events," *VS,* October 2, 1914; "Society: In Club Circles," *VW,* October 3, 1914.
135 "Society: In Club Circles," *VW,* November 24, 1914.
136 Lorna R. McLean, "'The Necessity of Going': Julia Grace Wales's Transnational Life as a Peace Activist and a Scholar," in *Feminist History in Canada: New Essays on Women, Gender, Work, and Nation,* ed. Catherine Carstairs and Nancy Janovicek (Vancouver: UBCP, 2013), 77–95. See also David S. Patterson, *The Search for Negotiated Peace: Women's Activism and Citizen Diplomacy in World War One* (New York: Routledge, 2008).
137 "Women's Council Review Work of Very Busy Year," *VW,* February 3, 1915; "Local Council Has Annual Assembly: Many Important Matters Discussed," *VS,* February 2, 1915.
138 "Cedar Cottage Notes," *GVC,* April 24, 1915.
139 "Must Protect Women: To Take Active Steps," *VS,* February 17, 1915; "Frances Willard Day: Vancouver's Tribute," *VS,* February 18, 1915.
140 "Want Full Franchise on Terms with Men," *VS,* February 27, 1915.
141 "War and Suffrage," *NFP,* March 18, 1915.
142 "Women of B.C. Must Have Vote: Look to Liberal Party to Give It," *VS,* March 5, 1915.
143 "Governmental Stand Influences Women," *VT,* March 4, 1916.
144 Dorothy E. Arnold, letter, "Women's Liberal Association," *VS,* June 17, 1915.
145 "Liberal Women Have Confidence in Party," *VW,* June 1, 1916. See also "Women Are Aroused over Misgovernment of British Columbia," *VS,* June 1, 1915; and "'What Can Be Women's Part in the Struggle': Topic of Mrs. McClung's Address," *VS,* August 27, 1915.
146 "Liberal Principles Aim of Organization Formed among Women," *VS,* June 10, 1915.
147 "Census of Liberals Is Made by Ladies through Vancouver," *VS,* July 9, 1915.
148 "Women Will Hold Big Gathering: Liberal Association Sounds Call," *VS,* September 18, 1915.
149 Almroth Wright, *The Unexpurgated Case against Woman Suffrage* (New York: Paul B. Hoeber, 1913). For the full text, see https://en.wikisource.org/wiki/The_Unexpurgated_Case _Against_Woman_Suffrage.
150 "Women Win Argument on Woman Suffrage," *VW,* November 30, 1915; "Snapshots of the City: Debate on Woman's Suffrage," *VW,* November 27, 1915.
151 "Declares That Women Must Ford Prejudice River before Ballot," *VS,* December 6, 1915. See also "Mrs. Ralph Smith on Women's Work in War," *NFP,* December 7, 1915; and "Women's Night at the People's Forum," *BCF,* December 10, 1915.
152 "Housewives Support B.C. Consumers' League," *WCLL,* April 2, 1915; "New Local Magazine," *VW,* December 21, 1915. Mary Ellen also wrote for the league's magazine.
153 J. Herbert Welch, "Aims of the B.C. Consumers' League," *VW,* July 5, 1915. See also "Organize to Support B.C. Brand of Goods," *VS,* December 2, 1914; and "Consumers' League," *WCLL,* February 12, 1915.
154 "Social Events," *VS,* June 29, 1915.
155 "New Westminster Campaign Is Formally Open," *VW,* August 4, 1916.
156 "Recruiting League Will Start Vigorous Campaign," *WCLL,* May 26, 1916.
157 "Vancouver Women's Work for Soldiers," *OJ,* May 26, 1916.
158 "Irene Moody (1879–1958)," Canadian Writing Research Collaboratory, https://cwrc.ca/ islandora/object/ceww%3A6e9c8d5c-d00e-4103-8961-da6eab243eee.

159 "Women Are Gratified at Election Results," *VW,* January 14, 1916; "Criticisms Are Hurled by Speaker," *VS,* January 12, 1916.
160 "Women Going to Celebrate Victory: Manitoba Suffragists Signal Success," *VS,* February 7, 1916. See also "In Club Circles," *VW,* February 3, 1916.
161 "Suffrage Delegation Received by Premier," *VW,* February 26, 1916.
162 "Mr. Brewster in Kerrisdale," *VW,* July 13, 1916; "New Westminster Campaign Is Formally Open," *VW,* August 4, 1916.
163 "Will Support Woman's Side," *VW,* June 15, 1916.
164 See *OC,* May 23, 1916, 6; *OC,* May 27, 1916, 4; and "Personal and Social," *VS,* May 30, 1916.
165 "Tells of Conditions in Eastern Canada: Mrs. Smith Returns," *VS,* June 6, 1916.
166 "Mrs. Pankhurst Tells Local Suffragists of Women's Work in War," *VS,* June 10, 1916.
167 "Suffragist Leader Tells of Kitchener's Orders to Soldiers," *VS,* June 10, 1916.
168 "Mission City Meeting," *Pacific Canadian,* July 21, 1916.
169 "Dastardly Tory Plot Is Bared," *VS,* July 5, 1916.
170 "Women's Suffrage," *NFP,* September 1, 1916.
171 "Women Celebrate Enfranchisement through Return of Liberal Party," *VS,* September 22, 1916.
172 "How Women of B.C. Cleaned Up Province," *TG,* October 31, 1916.
173 "Liberals Hold a Pleasant Social," *VT,* December 6, 1916, 7. Farris reinforced her message by asking Brewster for four Liberal organizers to tour the province to recruit women. E. Farris to Brewster, December 14, 1916, cited in McClean, *A Woman of Influence,* 122.
174 Leier, "Smith, Ralph," in *DCB.*
175 See "Hon. Ralph Smith's Death," *VP,* February 13, 1917; "Hon. Ralph Smith Taken by Death," *VT,* February 24, 1917; "Eloquent Tribute to Dead Minister," *VW,* February 13, 1917; "Immense Concourse Pays Last Tribute of Respect," *VW,* February 16, 1917; "Hon. Ralph Smith, Minister of Finance in G.C. Cabinet Dies Suddenly in Victoria," *VS,* February 13, 1917; "The Passing of Ralph Smith," *TG,* February 14, 1917.
176 "A Good Man Gone," *Vancouver Standard,* February 17, 1917.
177 J.M. "Hon. Ralph Smith," *OJ,* February 21, 1917; "Hon. Ralph Smith, Minister of Finance in G.C. Cabinet Dies Suddenly in Victoria," *VS,* February 13, 1917.
178 "Hon. Ralph Smith Dies in Victoria," *VW,* February 13, 1917.
179 Leier, "Smith, Ralph," in *DCB.*
180 Heron, *Working Lives,* 302.
181 Tanner, *Political Change and the Labour Party,* 338.
182 "A Good Man Gone," *Vancouver Standard,* February 17, 1917.
183 "Hon. Ralph Smith's Death," *VP,* February 13, 1917.
184 "Hon. Ralph Smith Taken by Death," *VT,* February 24, 1917.
185 "Hon. Ralph Smith Dies in Victoria," *VW,* February 13, 1917.

CHAPTER 5: INDEPENDENT LIBERAL LADY? 1917–20

1 See Eleanor A. Bartlett, "Real Wages and the Standard of Living in Vancouver, 1901–1929" (master's thesis, University of British Columbia, 1980).
2 "Exploring the First Century of Canada's Consumer Price Index," Statistics Canada, https://www150.statcan.gc.ca/n1/pub/62-604-x/62-604-x2015001-eng.htm#n9.

3 Bettina Liverant, "The Promise of a More Abundant Life: Consumer Society and the Rise of the Managerial State," *Journal of the Canadian Historical Association* 19, 1 (2008): 229–51.
4 Julie Guard, *Radical Housewives: Price Wars and Food Politics in Mid-Twentieth-Century Canada* (Toronto: UTP, 2019), 12.
5 The 1917–19 Victory Loans were part of a Canadian "war finance plan [that] consisted entirely of borrowing." Shirley Tillotson, *Give and Take: The Citizen-Taxpayer and the Rise of Canadian Democracy* (Vancouver: UBCP, 2017), 22. Tillotson stresses women's support. Ibid., 367. See also Karen A. Reyburn, "Blurring the Boundaries: Images of Women in Canadian Propaganda of World War I" (master's thesis, University of Guelph, 1998), 147.
6 Some of these workers were organized by Vancouver's female activists. Complaints of their low wages and poor working conditions divided suffragists. See "Mrs. Kemp Holds Fort against Critics," *VP*, September 13, 1917. On the similar problems in Ontario, see Joan Sangster, "Mobilizing Women," in *Canada and the First World War: Essays in Honour of Robert Craig Brown*, ed. David McKenzie (Toronto: UTP, 2018), 174–75.
7 Reyburn, "Blurring the Boundaries," 92.
8 See Ryan Van den Berg, "'Thank Goodness We Have a He-Man's School': Constructing Masculinity at the Vancouver Technical School in the 1920s," *Historical Studies in Education* 28, 1 (Spring 1916): 96–124.
9 Mrs. Ralph Smith, "Statistics Necessary in Canada," *VS*, February 9, 1919.
10 For a good survey of unrest, see Hak, *The Left in British Columbia*, 49–60.
11 Stonebanks, "Goodwin, Albert," in *DCB*; Mark Leier, "Plots, Shots, and Liberal Thoughts: Conspiracy Theory and the Death of Ginger Goodwin," *L/LT* 39, 1 (Spring 1997): 215–24.
12 Tillotson, *Give and Take*, 33.
13 See Sarah Buchanan, "Spanish Influenza in the City of Vancouver, British Columbia, 1918–1919" (master's thesis, University of Victoria, 2012); and M. Andrews, "Epidemic and Public Health: Influenza in Vancouver, 1918–1919," *BCS* 34 (Summer 1977): 22–44.
14 "Tendency to Forget the Women and Give Glory to Man, Declares Mrs. Smith," *VS*, February 6, 1919.
15 For a broad view, see Greg Kealey, "The Canadian Labour Revolt," *L/LT* 13, 1 (Spring 1984): 11–44.
16 "Union Jack Is Worn by Many," *VW*, June 12, 1919.
17 Plain Working Woman, "Why I Approve of the Strike," *VW*, June 13, 1919. For the support in Winnipeg of another working-class British woman, see Thompson, "More Sugar, Less Salt," 127–63.
18 Esther Crosfield, letter, "A Strike or a Revolution?" *VW*, June 16, 1919.
19 "Strike Methods Tabooed by Local Council of Women," *VW*, June 3, 1919; "Mrs. Pankhurst Brands Bolshevism as General Effort to Ruin World," *VS*, November 29, 1919; "Strikes Must Cease, Says Mrs. Pankhurst," *VP*, November 28, 1919.
20 "Need Individual Reconstruction Says Mrs. R. Smith, M.L.A.," *VS*, May 26, 1919.
21 "Remold the Here and Now Is the Call to Social Reform," *VW*, June 4, 1919. See also her earlier claim that female influence in capital-labour disputes "would result in much good" in "Place of Woman in New World," *VS*, December 30, 1918.
22 Mrs. Ralph Smith, "Industrial Conferences Sidelights," *VS*, September 25, 1918.
23 "'The World Aflame' Wonderful Picture," *OC*, September 19, 1919. One Vancouver reviewer described the film filling seats at a local theatre as showing "the earnest desire of a businessman

of influence to get his fellow men, no matter what their condition, to live better and to be better." "Deals with Capital and Labor and Social Struggles," *VW*, September 9, 1919.
24 On their divisions, see Elizabeth Lees, "Problems of Pacification: Veterans' Groups in Vancouver, 1918–1922" (master's thesis, Simon Fraser University, 1985).
25 Margaret Ormsby, *British Columbia: A History* (Toronto: Macmillan, 1958), 406–7.
26 Ingrid Sharp and Matthew Stibbe, "Introduction: Women's Movements and Female Activists in the Aftermath of War: International Perspectives, 1918–1923," in *Aftermaths of War: Women's Movements and Female Activists, 1918–1923*, ed. Ingrid Sharp and Matthew Stibbe (Leiden, Netherlands: Brill, 2011), 8.
27 See "Will Women Have Vote, They Ask," *VW*, June 18, 1919; "The Federal Franchise Act," *VP*, March 12, 1920; "Election Talk," *VP*, December 15, 1919; "Elections Act Amendment Is Explained," *VP*, July 5, 1919; "Women of Capital Are Also on War Path over Election Act," *VP*, July 3, 1919; and "Franchise Act Is Postponed," *VW*, June 25, 1919.
28 For criticism of partyism and candidate selection, see "Items of Social and Personal News," *VP*, January 23, 1917. See also the enthusiasm described in "Women's Views on Publicity Policy," *VS*, May 8, 1919; and "Will Vancouver Have P.R. in Provincial Election?" *VW*, April 9, 1920. On Mary Ellen's support for parliamentary reform, see *VW*, January 18, 1919; and "Premier's Views on Proportional Representation," *NFP*, January 24, 1919.
29 Anne Anderson Perry, "Future of Women's Clubs in Canada," *VS*, April 13, 1919.
30 "Signs of the Times: Some Notes on the Progress of Women in Public Life," *EWW*, September 1917. See also suffragist Mrs. W.J. ["Annie" or Hannah] Gale, "Canada's First Woman Alderman," *MM*, September 1919. Gale ran unsuccessfully in the 1921 provincial election as a Labour candidate, but in Calgary's 1917 municipal election she stressed non-partisanship. See also Christopher Armstrong, "The Great Fight for Clean Government," *Urban History Review/Revue d'histoire urbaine* 5, 2 (October 1976): 50–66, which criticizes the tendency to see urban reform as "elitist" and "anti-democratic."
31 May L. Armitage, "Canada's First Woman Member," *MM*, August 1917.
32 M.M. [Mary Murphy], "We Nominate as Leading Woman of Alberta – Nellie McClung," *EWW*, October 1917.
33 Mary Hilson, "Women Voters and the Rhetoric of Patriotism in the British General Election of 1918," *Women's History Review* 10, 2 (2001): 325.
34 On Pankhurst's group, see June Purvis, "The Women's Party of Great Britain (1917–19): A Forgotten Episode in British Women's Political History," *Women's History Review* 25, 4 (2016): 638–51. Purvis emphasized that despite its anti-pacifist and pro-imperialist war policies, the Women's Party had not surrendered feminism and pointed to its advocacy of equal pay for equal work and equality in marriage and divorce, as well as co-operative housekeeping. In the 1918 British election, Christabel Pankhurst stood for the Women's Party, with the support of Lloyd George's coalition.
35 "Opinions, Local Women on British Elections," *VS*, January 1, 1919. See also Smith's hopes for positive results in later British elections. Mrs. Ralph Smith, "Matters of Public Interest: The British Elections," *WWW*, February 8, 1919.
36 See Sangster, *One Hundred Years of Struggle*, Chapter 7.
37 "Personal," *OJ*, April 5, 1917.
38 "Appeal for Unity," *VW*, August 6, 1917.
39 "Compulsion Is Favored by I.O.D.E." *VS*, June 1, 1917. "Selective" conscription meant various things, including the exclusion of farmers' sons, certain age groups, and married

men, but was rarely spelled out by speakers, as it was expected to evolve with shifts in wartime demands. Silence on details had the additional advantage of keeping dissension in check.
40 See "Protests to Be Vigorous," *VW,* August 11, 1917; "Strong Support for Conscription," *VW,* August 14, 1917, 5; and "Society," *VS,* September 3, 1917.
41 "Five Thousand People Urge Union Government," *VW,* August 22, 1917.
42 "Vancouver Women Demand National Government – Now," *VW,* August 20, 1917.
43 "Five Thousand People Urge Union Government," *VW,* August 22, 1917.
44 J. Kavanagh, "A Patriotic Crowd at Horse Show Building," *BCF,* June 22, 1917.
45 "Society," *VS,* September 3, 1917. Thompson would run in Vancouver in the 1928 election. See "Vote the Straight Liberal Ticket," *VS,* June 30, 1928.
46 "Premier Brewster Will Give His Support to New Union Government," *VW,* November 1, 1917. See also Patricia E. Roy, "Brewster, Harlan Carey," in *DCB,* vol. 14, University of Toronto/Université Laval, 2003, http://www.biographi.ca/en/bio/brewster_harlan_carey_14E.html.
47 See Tanner, *Political Change and the Labour Party,* Conclusion.
48 "Local Liberals Range Up under Laurier's Banner," *VW,* August 2, 1917.
49 "Pupils from 22 Nationalities," *VW,* June 30, 1917. See also her endorsement of Canadianization for the IODE. "Order Discusses Educating Aliens," *VC,* May 31, 1917; "Makes Strong Plea to Canadianize Foreigner," *VW,* June 28, 1917.
50 On its significance in the west, see Lyndsay Campbell, "The War-Time Elections Act and Women Voters in 1917," November 1, 2019, Active History, https://activehistory.ca/2019/11/the-war-time-elections-act-and-women-voters-in-1917/. See also Nanaimo's Lady Orange Lodge's criticism of her defence of foreigners. "Is Heavily Scored," *VC,* October 24, 1917.
51 See the condemnation of BC Conservative MP H.H. Stevens by the BC United Suffrage Societies in "Admits Switching on Suffrage Bill," *VW,* September 29, 1917.
52 "Mrs. Ralph Smith Has Busy Journey," *VS,* October 12, 1917.
53 "Votes for Foreigners," *VW,* October 4, 1917; "Economic War after This War," *TG,* October 4, 1917. See also "Sergt. Walter Drinnan Fusionist Candidate to Oppose Mrs. Ralph Smith," *VW,* January 12, 1918.
54 "Economic War after This War," *TG,* October 4, 1917.
55 "Mrs. Ralph Smith Pleads for True Liberalism," *TG,* October 5, 1917. See also Evlyn Farris's anger at the Wartime Elections Act's denial of her right to vote as one reason for remaining Liberal. "Cooper Friend of Property Interests," *VS,* December 13, 1917.
56 See "Whirlwinds of Oratory Loose," *VW,* December 13, 1917; and J. Castell Hopkins, *The Canadian Annual Review War Series: 1917* (Toronto: Canadian Annual Review, 1918), 632. Typical of its preoccupation with English Canada, the *Review* missed Montreal. See Tarah Brookfield, "The Montreal Council of Women and the 1917 Election," *CHR* 89, 4 (December 2008): 473–501.
57 Jean Blewett, "A Word with the Mother," *EWW,* December 1917; "Canadian Women Opposed to Conscription," *EWW,* May 1917.
58 See the assertion by long-time Liberal and LCW president, Mrs. W.H. Griffin, "Deliberate Attempt TO MISLEAD Women of Vancouver," *VS,* December 17, 1917 (capitalization in original).
59 "Exit the Political Machine," *VW,* December 22, 1917.

60 See Lees, "Problems of Pacification"; Gregory S. Kealey, "State Repression of Labour and the Left in Canada, 1914–20: The Impact of the First World War," *CHR* 73, 3 (1992): 281–314; and Allen Seager, "Nineteen Nineteen: Year of Revolt," *Journal of the West* 23, 4 (1984): 4–7.
61 "Are Anxious to See Women in the Legislature," *VP,* February 15, 1917.
62 "Farris Might Not Be Opposed," *VW,* May 12, 1917.
63 "Mrs. Ralph Smith Is Now in Field," *VC,* December 30, 1917.
64 See "To Accept Important Portfolio," *VS,* May 23, 1917. See also the later, unsubstantiated, and far from credible claim by John Sedgwick Cowper (1876–1947), a progressive Liberal MLA from 1916 to 1920, that he had engineered Smith's nomination. J.S.C., "'Mary Ellen' Paved Way for Nancy," *VP,* February 16, 1943. See also his quick positive response to her presence in the legislature. J.S. Cowper, "The Woman in 'the House,'" *WWW,* July 6, 1918.
65 "Mrs. DeB. Farris Speaks," *VT,* March 30, 1917, 6. Many long-time suffragists dismissed Farris as very much a latecomer to the cause. See Campbell, *A Great Revolutionary Wave,* 205.
66 "Liberal Association Held Good Meeting," *VS,* May 26, 1917.
67 "Conscription of Wealth Favored," *VW,* June 30, 1917; "Important Resolutions Are Endorsed by the Women's Liberal Association," *VS,* June 30, 1917.
68 "Mrs. Ralph Smith Pleads for True Liberalism," *TG,* October 5, 1917; "Marriage Laws Defective in B.C.," *TG,* October 3, 1917.
69 "Puts Principle before Party," *VW,* October 9, 1917.
70 Elizabeth Kalmakoff, "Naturally Divided: Women in Saskatchewan Politics, 1916–1919," *Saskatchewan History* 46, 2 (1994): 3–18.
71 "Mrs. R. Smith's Candidature," *VS,* December 30, 1917.
72 "Mr. Farris' Comment on Candidature," *VS,* December 31, 1917. See too Alastair Gleg, "Margaret Bayne and the Vancouver Girls' Industrial School," *Historical Studies in Education* 18, 2 (Fall 2006): 201–23.
73 "Chilliwack Is Fine Says Acting Premier," *VT,* May 6, 1918.
74 *VS,* March 29, 1917, quoted in McClean, *A Woman of Influence,* 125.
75 McClean, *A Woman of Influence,* 160.
76 "Mrs. Smith Makes Platform Public," *VS,* January 3, 1918.
77 Ibid. In sharp contrast to Smith, when Edith McTavish Rogers (1876–1974) ran in the 1920 Manitoba election, she did not single out women or issues such as mothers' pensions and equal wages. Focusing far more narrowly and much less controversially on veterans, she became the second female Liberal elected to a provincial legislature.
78 "Can Mrs. R. Smith Do Any Good for Labor?" *BCF,* January 4, 1918.
79 Editorial, *WWW,* January 3, 1918.
80 Editorial, *WWW,* January 10, 1918. See also the half-page ad "Vote for Mrs. Ralph Smith," *WWW,* January 10, 1918.
81 Quarter-page ad "Electors, Attention!" *VS,* January 6, 1918; "Protest against Oriental Influx," *VS,* January 15, 1918.
82 "Liberals Face Stiff Problem," *VW,* January 12, 1918. See also "'Hobson's Choice,'" *VP,* December 31, 1917. As Smith would have known, liberalism was also deeply divided in the United Kingdom, where Herbert Asquith and David Lloyd George headed rival camps. The disarray helped contribute to the dissolution of the Progressive Alliance with the Labour Party and the latter's emergence as the chief opposition to the Conservative Party.

See E. David, "The Liberal Party Divided, 1916–1918," *Historical Journal* 13, 3 (1970): 509–33; and P. Clarke, *Liberals and Social Democrats* (Cambridge: CUP, 1978).
83 See "The O'Brien Hall," *VP,* January 22, 1918; and "Conley Talk of 'Inside Stuff,'" *VP,* January 23, 1918. For more on James Conley's opposition to Mary Ellen, see "Convention Is Urged by P.P.L.A. [Provincial Progressive Liberal Association]," *VP,* January 8, 1918. See the Liberal Party's internal critics, Conley and Joseph Martin, apparently speaking for the "Progressive Club," in "Liberals Should Run a Candidate," *VS,* January 8, 1918. See also Conley's threat to run against Smith in "Three to Run in Vancouver By-Election," *VW,* January 17, 1918.
84 "Liberals Will Not Put Up Candidate in By-Election," *VW,* January 16, 1918; "Mr. Farris' Comment on Candidature," *VS,* December 31, 1917.
85 "Support Mrs. Ralph Smith," *VW,* January 21, 1918.
86 "Organization Now Permanent," *VW,* January 3, 1918. See also "No Acclamation for Mrs. Smith, Say Opponents," *VW,* January 4, 1918.
87 See "Not Officially in Fight," *VS,* January 4, 1918.
88 "No Acclamation for Mrs. Smith, Say Opponents," *VW,* January 4, 1918.
89 "Mrs. Smith Is Out for Legislature," *VS,* December 30, 1917; "Speculation about Vancouver Contest," *VT,* December 26, 1917; "The Chameleon Has Nothing on Mrs. Smith," *VP,* January 23, 1918; and Irene Moodie's speech in favour of Walter Drinnan, the wished-for soldier candidate, in "Urges the Need of Soldiers in the Legislature," *VP,* January 23, 1918.
90 For splits among Conservative, see "Opposition Likely for Mrs. Smith," *VS,* January 2, 1918.
91 See "Organization Now Permanent," *VW,* January 3, 1918; and "Sergt. Walter Drinnan Fusionist Candidate to Oppose Mrs. Ralph Smith," *VW,* January 12, 1918.
92 "Opposition for Mrs. Ralph Smith," *VW,* January 7, 1918. See also "To the Electors of Vancouver," *VW,* January 11, 1918; and "Robinson Is in Field for By-Election," *VS,* January 7, 1918. A veteran of the 1877 Zulu War and the "first Boer war" in 1881, Robinson was employed as a registrar under the Military Services Act. See also the *Vancouver World*'s earlier enthusiasm for a medical veteran, Dr. Archibald Procter, who never joined the fray. "The Officer and the Lady," *VW,* December 31, 1917.
93 "R.H. Young," *VS,* January 14, 1918; "Drinnan Nominated; Three Are Already Chosen Candidates," *VS,* January 12, 1918.
94 See "Three to Run in Vancouver By-Election," *VW,* January 17, 1917. For a sympathetic view of Pritchard that ignores the by-election, see Peter Campbell, "'Making Socialists': Bill Pritchard, the Socialist Party of Canada, and the Third International," *L/LT* 30, 3 (Fall 1992): 45–63.
95 See "Convention Call Is Issued by Fusionists," *VW,* January 10, 1918.
96 "Sergt. Walter Drinnan Fusionist Candidate to Oppose Mrs. Ralph Smith," *VW,* January 12, 1918.
97 "Sergt. Walter Drinnan Fusionist Candidate to Oppose Mrs. Ralph Smith," *VW,* January 12, 1918. See also "Drinnan Nominated; Three Are Already Chosen Candidates," *VS,* January 12, 1918. The veterans' association was itself divided, with the president of the New Westminster branch, Private Barnard, defending Smith. See "G.W.V.A. Head Is for Mrs. Smith in Today's Vote," *VS,* January 24, 1918. FitzGibbon was the niece of Agnes Bernard Macdonald, the wife of Conservative John A. Macdonald, Canada's first prime minister. Little has been discovered about the so-called Good Government Association. It seems to have been a short-term instrument to allow Conservatives to appear to join in the clamour for political reform.

98 "Sergt. Walter Drinnan Fusionist Candidate to Oppose Mrs. Ralph Smith," *VW,* January 12, 1918.
99 "Urges the Need of Soldiers in the Legislature," *VP,* January 23, 1918; "Opening Guns Signal Start," *VW,* January 16, 1918.
100 "Correspondence: Mrs. Moody's Remarks," *VS,* January 24, 1918.
101 "Mrs. Smith's Platform," *BCF,* January 18, 1918.
102 "Believe Ministers Favor Mrs. Smith," *VS,* January 20, 1918.
103 "Need Viewpoint of Women at Victoria," *VS,* January 22, 1918.
104 Beatrice, "Society," *VS,* April 11, 1920.
105 "Need Viewpoint of Women at Victoria," *VS,* January 22, 1918. On her repudiation of being easy on aliens and Asians, see also "Sharp Replies by Mrs. R. Smith," *VW,* January 19, 1918.
106 "Bowser Is Flayed by Cooke," *VS,* January 23, 1918.
107 "High Time Tongue Scandal Checked," *VS,* January 24, 1918.
108 "An Appeal to the Women of Vancouver by the United Suffrage Societies of Vancouver," *VS,* January 24, 1918.
109 "The Chameleon Has Nothing on Mrs. Smith," *VP,* January 23, 1918.
110 "Three Candidates Confident on Eve," *VS,* January 24, 1918.
111 "Official Count of By-Election Ballot," *VS,* January 30, 1918.
112 "The Provincial Elections," *VW,* January 25, 1918. At the time, four by-elections were under way in British Columbia. This *Vancouver World* editorial emphasized that none of them produced a government victory.
113 "Three Women and Politics," *TG,* February 14, 1918.
114 "Society," *VS,* January 30, 1918.
115 *Grand Forks Sun and Kettle Valley Orchardist,* January 25, 1918.
116 Mrs. Walter Smith, quoted in "Presentation to Mrs. Ralph Smith," *VS,* February 1, 1918.
117 "New Members Both Favor Minimum Wage," *VS,* February 2, 1918.
118 *VS,* March 2, 1918.
119 "Presentation to Mrs. Ralph Smith," *VS,* February 1, 1918.
120 Whenever suffrage bills were debated in the legislature, long-time Victoria leader Maria Grant had carried "a model of the ship of state when she headed up delegations." Campbell, *A Great Revolutionary Wave,* 96.
121 "Women's Ship of State Is Launched," *VS,* February 8, 1918.
122 "Mrs. Smith Takes Member to Task," *VS,* March 24, 1918.
123 By One of the Gods, "Mrs. Ralph Smith Makes Maiden Speech, as Heard from the Gallery," *CH,* March 21, 1918. See also "Making History in Legislature Today," *VT,* March 1, 1918.
124 "Mrs. Ralph Smith Perfectly at Home," *VT,* March 22, 1918.
125 By One of the Gods, "Mrs. Ralph Smith Makes Maiden Speech, as Heard from the Gallery," *CH,* March 21, 1918.
126 "Notes and Comments," *TG,* May 8, 1918.
127 "Ten Dollars a Pair," *VS,* April 23, 1918.
128 J.S. Cowper, "The Woman in 'the House,'" *WWW,* July 6, 1918. See also the mayor of Vancouver's similar emphasis on Mary Ellen's domestic and womanly qualities, including a flair for cooking flapjacks. Mayor Gale, "Who's Who in British Columbia," *WWW,* September 28, 1918.
129 "Off to London to Plead for Provincial Rights," *VW,* May 21, 1919.

130 By One of the Gods, "The Legislative Story," *CH,* February 20, 1919.
131 "A Woman's Party," *WWW,* March 28, 1918.
132 The Editor, "Call to Arms! Women of Canada," *EWW,* March 1918. See also "Citizenship or Politics? – What Next?" and Nellie McClung, "Mobilization of Canadian Women," both in *EWW,* March 1918.
133 "The 'Mothers of Consolidation,'" *EWW,* April 1918.
134 Sangster, "Mobilizing Women," 176.
135 Quoted in ibid., 177.
136 McDonald, *A Long Way to Paradise,* 101. Patricia Roy's description of Brewster as an honest and largely progressive Liberal seems on the mark, although perhaps generous. See Roy, "Brewster, Harlan," in *DCB.*
137 Unfortunately, Oliver's views of women remain unexplored, but for his lack of sympathy for workers, see Andrew Yarmie, "The State and Employers' Associations in British Columbia: 1900–1932," *L/LT* 45 (Spring 2000): 53–101. See also David Mitchell, "Oliver, John," in *DCB,* vol. 15, University of Toronto/Université Laval, 2003, http://www.biographi.ca/en/bio/oliver_john_15E.html.
138 McDonald, *A Long Way to Paradise,* 101.
139 "Kiwanians Hear Lady Legislator," *VS,* April 4, 1919.
140 "Women's Interests," *VS,* September 19, 1918.
141 Mrs. Ralph Smith, "The Woman's Movement," *VS,* September 19, 1918.
142 See Mrs. Ralph Smith, "Cultivate Spirit of Optimism," *VS,* July 24, 1919.
143 Mrs. Ralph Smith, "Looking Forward," *VS,* January 27, 1919.
144 Mrs. Ralph Smith, "Women's Place after the War," *VS,* November 17, 1918. See also her "Must Women Be Driven Back?" *VS,* August 3, 1919.
145 Mrs. Ralph Smith, "Women in Industry," *VS,* January 20, 1919.
146 Mrs. Ralph Smith, "Policing Our City," *VS,* January 9, 1919.
147 Mrs. Ralph Smith, "Educators Have to Live," *VS,* November 4, 1919.
148 Mrs. Ralph Smith, "The Question of Nursing," *VS,* January 23, 1919.
149 Mrs. Ralph Smith, "Statistics Necessary in Canada," *VS,* February 9, 1919.
150 Mrs. Ralph Smith, "Room at the Top," *VS,* March 9, 1919.
151 Mrs. Ralph Smith, "Contented Discontent," *VS,* November 3, 1918.
152 Mrs. Ralph Smith, "Peace, Liberty and Democracy," *VS,* November 10, 1918.
153 Mrs. Ralph Smith, "Enfranchisement of Canadian Women," *VS,* June 10, 1919.
154 Mrs. Ralph Smith, "Our Illiterate Population," *VS,* August 16, 1919.
155 Mrs. Ralph Smith, "Madame Breshkovsky – Her Work," *VS,* February 23, 1919.
156 Mrs. Ralph Smith, "New Japan and Modern Africa," *VS,* January 5, 1920.
157 Mrs. Ralph Smith, "Lady Legislator Urges All Women to Learn Power of Franchise," *VS,* November 16, 1919. On this extraordinary person, see Goolam Vahed, "Race, Empire, and Citizenship: Sarojini Naidu's 1924 Visit to South Africa," *South African Historical Journal* 64, 2 (June 2012): 319–42.
158 Mrs. Ralph Smith, "Showing Respect for Our Flag," *VS,* April 19, 1919.
159 Mrs. Ralph Smith, "Immigration Prospects Now Demanding New Regulations," *VS,* October 12, 1919; "Mrs. Ralph Smith in Ottawa Working for the Welcome to British Women to the Dominion," *VS,* January 16, 1920.
160 Mrs. Ralph Smith, "Child Welfare," *VS,* December 8, 1918.
161 Mrs. Ralph Smith, "The Child and the War," *VS,* January 17, 1919.
162 Mrs. Ralph Smith, "Canada's Greatest Asset," *VS,* October 28, 1918.

163 Mrs. Ralph Smith, "Making Provision for Mothers," *VS*, May 25, 1919.
164 Mrs. Ralph Smith, "Industry and the Family," *VS*, January 13, 1920.
165 Mrs. Ralph Smith, "Commissions and Commissioners," *VS*, December 30, 1919.
166 Mrs. Ralph Smith, "Loyalty to Our Province," *VS*, May 9, 1919.
167 Mrs. Ralph Smith, "A Step Forward," *VS*, January 13, 1919. She hailed England's Lever Brothers as a model for Canadian capitalists. See David J. Jeremy, "The Enlightened Paternalist in Action: William Hesketh Lever at Port Sunlight before 1914," *Business History* 33, 1 (1991): 58–81.
168 See Greg Patmore, *Worker Voice: Employee Representation in the Workplace in Australia, Canada, Germany, the UK and the US, 1914–1939* (Liverpool: Liverpool University Press, 2016).
169 Mrs. Ralph Smith, "Industry and the Family," *VS*, January 13, 1920.
170 Consumers' campaigns could be both conservative and progressive. See Donica Belisle, "Conservative Consumer Advocacy in Woman's Century Magazine during and after World War One," *HS/SH* 48, 93 (May 2014): 111–38; and Guard, *Radical Housewives*. See the delegation on high prices from Vancouver women's organizations, including Smith, to Victoria. "Are Irate at Present High Prices of Food," *VP*, May 9, 1919.
171 Mrs. Ralph Smith, "Meat Again," *VS*, March 3, 1919. See also her condemnation of war profiteering in "Conscript Every Man and Plant Is Mrs. Smith's Plea," *Seattle Star*, March 30, 1918; and "Claims Fifteen Men in Canada Control Prices," *Edmonton Journal*, March 20, 1919. Her target was probably Toronto millionaire meat merchant Joseph Flavelle. See Michael Bliss, "Flavelle, Sir Joseph Wesley," in *DCB*, vol. 16, University of Toronto/Université Laval, 2003, http://www.biographi.ca/en/bio/flavelle_joseph_wesley_16E.html. In 1920, as Canadians worried about sugar prices and shortages, Mary Ellen was appointed to British Columbia's legislative committee on the problem. Despite her substantial experience with consumer issues, she was denied the chair, which went to M.B. Jackson, KC, who had no obvious credentials. On the committee and public concern, see *Canadian Annual Review of Public Affairs* (Toronto: Canadian Annual Review, 1921), 199.
172 Mrs. Ralph Smith, "The High Cost of Living," *VS*, May 2, 1919.
173 See Elaine Bernard, "Last Back: Folklore and the Telephone Operators in the 1919 Vancouver General Strike," in *Not Just Pine Money: Selected Essays on the History of Women's Work in British Columbia*, ed. Barbara Latham and Roberta J. Pazdo (Victoria: Camosun College, 1984), 279–86, and Greg Kealey, "*The Canadian Labour Revolt,*" *L/LT*, 13 (Spring 1984): 11–44.
174 Mrs. Ralph Smith, "Proletariats and Plutocrats," *VS*, June 3, 1919. See also her talk along similar lines at the Kitsilano Methodist Church. "Announcements," *VS*, June 4, 1919.
175 "Society: Ottawa Audience Applauds Address of Mrs. R. Smith," *VS*, September 28, 1919. See also "Industrial Reconstruction Could Be Helped by Women," *VS*, November 9, 1919.
176 Mrs. Ralph Smith, "Industrial Reconstruction Could Be Helped by Women," *VS*, November 9, 1919.
177 See Mrs. Ralph Smith, "Purchasing in Home Market," *VS*, January 31, 1919; and her "B.C.'s Climate," *VS*, February 3, 1919.
178 Mrs. Ralph Smith, "Alberta Institute Conference," *VS*, March 16, 1919.
179 Mrs. Ralph Smith, "Women on the Land," *VS*, July 17, 1919.
180 Mrs. Ralph Smith, "Looking Forward," *VS*, January 27, 1919.
181 See, for example, N. DeBertrand Lugrin in collaboration with Mrs. Ralph Smith, "Problems in B.C.," *Canadian Courier*, May 25, 1918.

182 See "Dope Evil Is on Increase Here," *VS*, January 28, 1919, 4. See also Emily Murphy, *The Black Candle* (Toronto: Thomas Allen, 1922); and Catherine Carstairs, *Jailed for Possession: Illegal Drug Use, Regulation, and Power in Canada* (Toronto: UTP, 2006).
183 Lugrin with Smith, "Problems in B.C."
184 See her enthusiasm for resource development when she presided over both a Revelstoke mining convention, where admirers saluted her as the cabinet's "best man," and the NCWC's Committee on Natural Resources. *CH*, July 18, 1918.
185 BC Legislative Assembly, *Journals* (April 3, 1918), 119, http://archives.leg.bc.ca/civix/document/id/leg_archives/legarchives/62409636.
186 "Women Must Wage War on 'Snobocracy,' Says Mrs. Ralph Smith, M.L.A.," *VS*, April 7, 1919.
187 "On Behalf of the Jews in Poland," *VP*, May 22, 1919.
188 The best treatment of the legislative machinations is Clarkson, *Domestic Reforms*, especially Chapter 6. On Smith's support for dower, see "Approves Principle of Dower Rights," *VC*, March 25, 1919. On the gendering of the welfare state, see Christie, *Engendering the State*.
189 See, for example, Creese, "Sexual Equality and the Minimum Wage," 120–40; Bob Russell, "A Fair or a Minimum Wage? Women Workers, the State and the Origins of Wage Regulation in Western Canada," *L/LT* 28, 3 (Fall 1991): 59–88; and Little, "Claiming a Unique Place," 80–102.
190 Russell, "A Fair or a Minimum Wage?" 60.
191 "Lady Legislator Tells of Session," *VS*, April 6, 1919.
192 Paul Martin, "Canada and the International Labour Organization," *Public Affairs* (Dalhousie University) 7, 4 (1944): 196.
193 See Adelle Blackett, *"This Is Hallowed Ground": Canada and International Labour Law*, Canada in International Law at 150 and Beyond 22 (Waterloo: Centre for International Governance Innovation, 2018).
194 See the criticism of its failure in "Eight-Hour Bill Is Defeated at Victoria," *BCF*, April 2, 1920. In 1921, the Vancouver TLC would sponsor the *British Columbia Labor News*, the masthead of which read, "Devoted to the Interest of the International Labor Movement," a description that highlighted keen attention to global developments, including the work of the ILO.
195 Her failure to support ILO bills confirmed her as a target for their sponsor, Richard Burde, the Independent Soldier MLA for Port Alberni (sometimes identified as an Independent Liberal or Labour). He charged her with hypocrisy. See "Boodle Was Used Says Maj. Burde," *VS*, October 27, 1921. On Burde, see Gordon Hak, "The Socialist and Labourist Impulse in Small-Town British Columbia: Port Alberni and Prince George, 1911–33," *CHR* 70, 4 (December 1989): especially 532–33.
196 "Successful Trip State Delegates," *VS*, March 22, 1918.
197 "New Members Both Favor Minimum Wage," *VS*, February 2, 1918.
198 "Will Sit on Capital Steps Till They Are Heard," *BCF*, February 15, 1918; "Speaks of Minimum Wage for Women," *VC*, March 7, 1918. See too the credit to Smith in "Minimum Wage Bill at Last on Its Way," *BCF*, March 29, 1918.
199 "Women Are Their Sisters' Keepers," *VW*, October 3, 1919.
200 Mary Ellen Smith, quoted in Pasolli, *Working Mothers and the Child Care Dilemma*, 57.
201 "Legislation Is Lop-Sided, Says Mrs. R. Smith," *VS*, May 10, 1920.
202 "To Stand Together for Each Other," *OJ*, June 26, 1920. See also "Mrs. Ralph Smith Strongly Supports Mothers' Pension Bill, Read for Second Time," *VS*, April 10, 1920.

203 Many Prairie and BC women remained suspicious that the NCWC catered to eastern interests, and the platform was never fully endorsed. See "Calgary L.C.W. Opposes Forming Women's Platform," *VS*, April 27, 1919; and "Urges Council against Party," *VS*, July 27, 1919. On these persisting strains, see Veronica Strong-Boag, *The Parliament of Women: The National Council of Women of Canada* (Ottawa: National Museum, 1976), Chapter 6.

204 Mrs. Ralph Smith, "Women Who Bring Something to Progress," *WWW*, July 5, 1919; "National Leader Brings Message," *VS*, April 15, 1919. See also "Mrs. Ralph Smith M.L.A., Very Popular in the East," *VS*, July 11, 1920.

205 "Society: Lady Legislator Tells of Her Visit to Eastern Cities," *VS*, October 7, 1919.

206 "Women Candidates Warmly Endorsed," *OJ*, September 19, 1919. On women's poor prospects for election in Ontario, see Frederick B. Scollier, "The Woman Candidate for the Ontario Legislative Assembly, 1919–1929," *Ontario History* 104, 2 (Fall 2012): 1–27.

207 This was the conclusion of the majority interviewed by Catherine Cleverdon in her classic study, *The Woman Suffrage Movement in Canada*.

208 Mrs. Ralph Smith, "Legislation and the Lady," *WWW*, March 29, 1919. See also "Remold the Here and Now Is the Call to Social Reform," *VW*, June 4, 1919.

209 Mrs. Ralph Smith, "Legislation and the Lady," *WWW*, March 29, 1919.

210 On her emphasis on her welcome in Victoria, see "Mrs. Ralph Smith Speaks of Session," *VS*, April 30, 1918; and "Women Must Wage War on 'Snobocracy,' Says Mrs. Ralph Smith, M.L.A.," *VS*, April 7, 1919.

211 "Woman Legislator Holds High Place," *VS*, April 21, 1918.

212 "Premier Oliver Heard," *Enderby Okanagan Commoner*, December 4, 1919.

213 "Mrs. Ralph Smith in New Role of Scenario Writer," *VS*, March 18, 1920.

214 "Mrs. Ralph Smith Speaks of Session," *VS*, April 30, 1918.

215 "Abuses Home Government," *VS*, March 13, 1919.

Chapter 6: From Hope to Disillusion, 1920–28

1 See "Seeks Equality in Divorce Laws," *VS*, November 13, 1920; and "Mrs. Smith Is Mentioned as New Senator," *VS*, June 22, 1921.

2 See Jean Barman, "Neighbourhood and Community in Interwar Vancouver: Residential Differentiation and Civic Voting Behaviour," in *Vancouver Past: Essays in Social History*, ed. R.A.J. McDonald (Vancouver: UBCP, 1986), 127, who notes that by the 1930s, female candidates for school board "consistently received the highest level of support."

3 See Agnes C. Laut, "Our Election Enigma – Woman!" *MM*, November 15, 1921.

4 See McClung, *In Times Like These*, Chapter 5.

5 Robin Fisher and David J. Mitchell, "Patterns of Provincial Politics since 1916," in *The Pacific Province: A History of British Columbia*, ed. Hugh Johnston (Vancouver: Douglas and McIntyre, 1996), 257.

6 Heron, *Working Lives*, 298.

7 Ormsby, *British Columbia*, 413.

8 "Opinions, Local Women on British Elections," *VS*, January 1, 1919, 4. For the same conclusion, see Beatrice, "Reflections," *VP*, December 4, 1920.

9 Henrik J. von Winthus, "The Influence of Political Leaders on the Provincial Performance of the Liberal Party in British Columbia" (master's thesis, Wilfrid Laurier University, 1977), 8.

10 See H. Blair Neatby, "King, William Lyon Mackenzie," in *DCB*, vol. 17, University of Toronto/Université Laval, 2003, http://www.biographi.ca/en/bio/king_william_lyon_

mackenzie_17E.html. Margaret Ormsby's classic "'Honest John' and the Liberals," Chapter 14 in her *British Columbia,* remains a useful guide to BC Liberal debates, albeit without sensitivity to Mary Ellen's predicament. See also Lloyd George's move to the right in the United Kingdom, which left liberalism vulnerable to the rise of the Labour Party. Gavin Freeman, "The Liberal Party and the Impact of the 1918 Reform Act," *Parliamentary History* 37, 1 (2018): 47–73. Pat Thane argues that Britain's Liberal women, unlike those affiliated with the Labour Party, were "unafraid" to name themselves feminists. See her "Women, Liberalism and Citizenship, 1918–1930," in Biagini, *Citizenship and Community,* 66–92.

11 "Capt. Jack Smith Is in Hospital," *VS,* January 10, 1923. See Mabel Quesnel in "Patroness of Patriotic Dance," *VS,* March 23, 1919.
12 "Miss M. Quesnell Becomes Bride of Capt. Jack Smith," *VS,* August 9, 1923. Quesnel's name is variously spelled.
13 "R.W. Smith, Ill, Returns to City," *VS,* June 13, 1925.
14 "Robert Smith, Lawyer, Passes," *VP,* July 6, 1927.
15 "Prohibition," *CH,* February 12, 1920. See too "Doings at Victoria from Our Correspondent," *Abbotsford Post,* February 13, 1920.
16 "Women Interested in Social Work of the Government," *VT,* June 13, 1924.
17 *BCF,* May 7, 1920.
18 "Recognition of Ability," *MG,* February 8, 1921.
19 See "Political Education League Nominates Two Women Legislature Candidates," *WT,* April 1, 1920; and "Mrs. Smith to Enter Eastern Politics," *TG,* April 18, 1921.
20 See "Will Vancouver Have P.R. in Provincial Election?" *VS,* April 9, 1920. Those broad networks had been essential to the city's suffrage campaigns. See Campbell, *A Great Revolutionary Wave.*
21 Beatrice, "Reflections," *VP,* December 4, 1920.
22 Hak, *The Left in British Columbia,* 70.
23 "Mrs. Smith Has New Programme," *VS,* November 11, 1920.
24 "Liberals Select Candidates for Vancouver City," *VS,* November 2, 1920.
25 See the discussion of Edith Patterson in Joan Brockman, "Exclusionary Tactics: The History of Women and Visible Minorities in the Legal Profession in British Columbia," in *Essays in the History of Canadian Law 6,* ed. Hamar Foster and John McLaren (Toronto: Osgoode Society for Canadian Legal History, 1995), 508–62. In 1929, Patterson would be appointed by the new Conservative provincial government to replace MacGill, who was effectively fired as a Juvenile Court judge. In 1950, as Mrs. Hamilton Read, she would be elected the first female president of Vancouver's conservative civic party, the Non-Partisan Association. Crosfield, the other 1920 candidate, argued that mothers' pensions and other reforms resulted from popular agitation, not the Liberals. See "New Legislation Forced by People," *VP,* November 24, 1920; and "Urge the Election of Independents," *VP,* November 16, 1920.
26 "Claim Charges Were Unproved," *VS,* November 18, 1920.
27 "Bonds Issued on Same Basis in Bowser's Day," *VS,* November 17, 1920. See also Mary McConkey, letter, "Regrets Attitude of Miss Patterson," *VS,* November 15, 1920; Susie Lane Clark, letter, "Lady Suffragist Tells of Fight," *VS,* November 29, 1920; and "M.A. Macdonald Scores Bowser's Peanut Politics," *VS,* November 26, 1920, 3.
28 "Campaign Jottings," *VS,* November 20, 1920.
29 "Fears Cupid Will Catch Miss Edith," *VS,* November 27, 1920.

30 Editorial, "The Women Candidates," *WWW,* November 27, 1920.
31 "Rally for Women," *WWW,* November 27, 1920.
32 Mary McConkey, letter, "Regrets Attitude of Miss Patterson," *VS,* November 15, 1920. For the same criticism of Conservative Party claims to support woman suffrage, see Susie Lane Clark, letter, "Lady Suffragist Tells of Fight," *VS,* November 29, 1920.
33 "Why They Will Vote the Straight Liberal Ticket," *VW,* November 30, 1920.
34 "Labor Nominees Open Campaign," *VW,* November 13, 1920. On Corse, see "Alberta Woman Has Gained Distinction," *VW,* January 20, 1920; and "Former Calgary Lady to Contest Vancouver Seat," *Calgary Herald,* September 14, 1921. See also David Bright, "'We Are All Kin': Reconsidering Labour and Class in Calgary, 1919," *L/LT* 29 (Spring 1972), 64.
35 See the typical election ad, "Women's Rights – without Restriction," *VS,* November 19, 1920.
36 "Mrs. M.E. Smith Speaker of B.C. Legislature," *MG,* February 8, 1921.
37 "Charge Bowser Failed to Pay Minimum Wage," *VS,* November 18, 1920. See also "Bowser Discusses Women Opponents," *VS,* November 26, 1920.
38 "Scots Foregather on Night o' Nights," *VS,* December 1, 1920.
39 "Lady Legislator Is Waging Hot Campaign," *VS,* November 15, 1920; "Mrs. Smith Speaks to Huge Audiences," *VS,* November 24, 1920.
40 See "Farris Will Not Return to Cabinet," *VS,* January 6, 1922.
41 "Women's Rights – without Restriction," *VW,* November 6, 1920.
42 "Women's Rights – without Restriction," *VS,* November 19, 1920.
43 *Electoral History of British Columbia 1871–1986* (Victoria: Elections British Columbia, 1988), 139.
44 "Members Thank Their Electors," *VS,* December 2, 1920.
45 Heron, *Working Lives,* 289.
46 Editorial, "The Election Returns," *WWW,* December 4, 1920.
47 "Victorious Liberals Hold Big Celebration at Hotel Vancouver," *VS,* December 4, 1920. See also "Osculatory Precedents," *VC,* December 16, 1920; "A Fresh Dignity," *Montreal Star,* published in *WT,* February 18, 1921; and "A Scandal Creditable to All," *Independent* (Dearborn, MI), January 8, 1921.
48 "Kissing as a Vote-Getter," *OJ,* December 22, 1920, reprinted from the *London Free Press.*
49 "Kissing Bee for Lady Member at Vancouver," *OJ,* December 13, 1920.
50 "When John Kissed Mary Ellen," *BCF,* December 10, 1920.
51 "Kissing as a Vote-Getter," *OJ,* December 22, 1920, reprinted from the *London Free Press.*
52 "Vancouver Women in Political Fight," *VS,* September 9, 1921.
53 See, for example, Kiwanis, letter, "What Is Your Opinion?" *VS,* October 31, 1921; and Chaugeur, letter, "What Is Your Opinion? Mothers' Pension Act," *VS,* November 4, 1921.
54 "Get-Together-Luncheon Given by Women's Forum," *VS,* October 21, 1922.
55 "Many Speakers Heard at New Era League Luncheon," *VW,* March 22, 1923.
56 "Lady Legislator Asked to Extend Franchise," *VW,* February 3, 1922.
57 By a Woman, "Milady in Politics," *VS,* November 28, 1921. See also "Trades Council Discusses B.C. Electric," *BCF,* June 9, 1922.
58 "Pensions Are to Be Investigated," *VS,* November 16, 1922.
59 Mary Ellen Smith to A. Manson, undated but July-August 1923, Alexander Manson Fonds 1350, box 62, folder 062-18, RBSCUBC. My thanks to Pat Roy for this and following references.

60 A.W. Manson to E.S.H. Winn, Esq. KC, Chairman, Workmen's Compensation Bd., August 20, 1923, marked "Personal and Confidential," Alexander Manson Fonds 1350, box 62, folder 062-18, RBSCUBC.
61 Smith to Manson, March 11, 1924, Alexander Manson Fonds 1350, box 82, folder 082-02, RBSCUBC.
62 See "Policewoman to Be Transferred," *VS*, April 11, 1922; "New Era League Afternoon Affair Is Huge Success," *VW*, June 21, 1922; and "Women Excited over Dismissal of Policewoman," *VW*, June 23, 1922.
63 On this inclusion, see Creese, "Sexuality, Equality and the Minimum Wage," 127. This law was in fact directed at the lumber industry, but its wage orders later extended to restaurants. In any case, it had little effect.
64 "Labor Deputation Alleges Factories Violate Agreement," *VS*, June 21, 1921; "As a Result of the Meeting Between ...," *VP*, June 21, 1921.
65 D.L. Matters, "A Report on Health Insurance," *BCS* 21 (Spring 1974): 28–32; Margaret W. Andrews, "The Course of Medical Opinion on State Health Insurance in British Columbia, 1919–1939," *HS/SH* 16, 31 (May 1983): 129–41; Martin, "Canada and the International Labour Organization," 195–99; Blackett, *"This Is Hallowed Ground."* For criticism from the Vancouver TLC, see "Oliver and Bowser Combine against 8-Hour Bill," *British Columbia Labor News*, November 25, 1921.
66 See "Lady Member Speaks in City," *Chilliwack Progress*, June 1, 1922. See also Margaret Hobbs, "Equality and Difference: Feminism and the Defence of Women Workers during the Great Depression," *L/LT* 32, 3 (Fall 1993): 201–23.
67 "Much Business Brought before New Era League," *VS*, October 13, 1922. See also Eleanor Weld Mathewson, "Old Age Pensions in British Columbia: A Review of Trends in Eligibility" (master's thesis, University of British Columbia, 1949).
68 Clarkson, *Domestic Reforms*, 174.
69 Unfortunately, this proved almost impossible to enforce. See Patricia Reed, "Maintenance Collections from Putative Fathers" (master's thesis, University of British Columbia, 1950), 2–3.
70 See her speech delivered to the YMCA, "How to Establish a Single Standard of Morality," *VW*, February 18, 1922; and "Seeks Equality in Divorce Laws," *VS*, November 13, 1920.
71 "Mrs. Ralph Smith May Be First Lady Speaker," *VT*, January 6, 1921. The legislature discussion of venereal disease was effectively ignored by the press, but on the issue, see Dorothy E. Chunn, "A Little Sex Can Be a Dangerous Thing: Regulating Sexuality, Venereal Disease and Reproduction in British Columbia," in *Challenging the Public/Private Divide: Feminism, Law, and Public Policy*, ed. Susan Boyd (Toronto: UTP, 1997), 62–86; and Renisa Mawani, "Regulating the 'Respectable' Classes: Venereal Disease, Gender, and Public Health Initiatives in Canada, 1914–35," in *Regulating Lives: Historical Essays on the State, Society, the Individual, and the Law*, ed. John McLaren, Robert Menzies, and Dorothy E. Chunn (Vancouver: UBCP, 2002), 170–95.
72 "'M.A.' Is Chosen as Liberal Party Leader," *VW*, September 30, 1922.
73 "Women to Sit on B.C. Juries," *VP*, December 15, 1922.
74 "Delegation Goes Over to Victoria," *British Columbia Labor News*, May 5, 1922, 1. See also Veronica Strong-Boag and Kathryn McPherson, "The Confinement of Women: Childbirth and Hospitalization in Vancouver, 1919–1939," *BCS* 69–70 (Spring-Summer 1986): 159; and Harry Cassidy, *Public Health and Welfare Reorganization: The Postwar Problem in Canadian Provinces* (Toronto: Ryerson Press, 1945).

75 *British Columbia Labor News,* May 5, 1922.
76 Quoted in Russell R. Walker, "British Columbia Leads All Canada in Social Legislation," *VP,* March 26, 1923.
77 "Greater Devotion to Home Is Urged," *VS,* January 10, 1921.
78 See Mawani, "'The Most Disreputable Characters': Mixed–Bloods, Internal Enemies, and Imperial Futures," in Mawani, *Colonial Proximities,* 166–99.
79 "Women of City United in Crusade against Drugs," *VS,* February 3, 1922. On this, see Catherine Carstairs, "Deporting 'Ah Sin' to Save the White Race: Moral Panic, Racialization, and the Extension of Canadian Drug Laws in the 1920s," *Canadian Bulletin of Medical History* 16, 1 (Spring 1999): 65–88.
80 "Christmas Meeting of Wesley W.M.S. Held on Tuesday," *VS,* December 15, 1920. Some critics understandably interpreted this appointment to recruit immigrants as no more than party patronage, a response that signalled growing press disenchantment with Smith. See R.B.D., "Note and Comment," *VC,* July 11, 1923.
81 "Mary Ellen Smith Defends Policy of Immigration," *VS,* January 15, 1924.
82 See "Preponderance of Women," *Hartlepool Northern Daily Mail,* December 5, 1923.
83 See "Hon. Mrs. R. Smith Honored Guest at Liberal Luncheon," *VS,* May 14, 1921; "Mrs. Ralph Smith Home from East," *VS,* April 6, 1922; "British Girls Eager to Come to Canada, Declares Mrs. Smith," *VW,* October 18, 1923; "Girls to Flock Here in Hundreds," *VS,* October 18, 1923; and "Maturing Generation in Britain Looking to Canada as Chief Hope," *VS,* October 19, 1923.
84 "Mrs. Smith and Immigration," *BCF,* July 13, 1923.
85 "Mary Ellen Is Heckled, but Scores Again," *VW,* November 24, 1923.
86 "Capital as Well as Immigrants Coming Says Mary Ellen," *VS,* October 25, 1923.
87 See "Hungry Blame Mary Ellen for Unemployment," *VW,* November 20, 1923; and "Mrs. Smith Denies Charge of Local Unemployed," *NFP,* November 23, 1923.
88 See Thompson, "More Sugar, Less Salt," especially 156–59.
89 See "Mrs. Smith Is Favorite of Liberals," *VS,* September 2, 1921. Conservative women also preached against her. See "Conservative Lady Speaker Addresses Kimberley Meeting," *CH,* September 9, 1921.
90 "Hon. Mrs. Smith Takes 'Stump,'" *VS,* July 14, 1921.
91 See "Disabled Vets Join Together," *VS,* May 12, 1921.
92 See "Evolve New Relief System," *VS,* February 4, 1922.
93 "Urges an Effort for Immigration," *VS,* November 25, 1922. See also John Rodenhizer, "The Student Campaign of 1922 to 'Build the University' of British Columbia," *BCS* 4 (Spring 1970): especially 33–35.
94 "COAL INVESTIGATION IS DEMANDED," *VS,* January 12, 1921 (capitalization in original); "Coal Inquiry Is the Citizen's Demand," *VS,* January 20, 1920.
95 "Gossip of Lobbies in Legislature," *VW,* October 27, 1921. See also A.B. Clark, *An Outline of Provincial and Municipal Taxation in British Columbia, Alberta and Saskatchewan* (Winnipeg: University of Manitoba, 1919), 12, which noted that only British Columbia and Prince Edward Island levied income tax, "now the largest individual item in the Provincial Revenue."
96 See "Ten Million Dollar Iron and Steel Plant for B.C. Assured," *VS,* August 5, 1922; "Bear Again Holds House for Session: Workingmen Silent," *VT,* March 18, 1921; "Case of Coast Range Steel Placed before Premier and Minister," *VP,* June 6, 1923; and "Reviews Visit to Motherland," *VP,* October 31, 1923.

97 See "Break Precedent in Legislature," *VS*, February 18, 1921; "Moderation No Party Question," *VP*, February 18, 1921; and "Co-operation Urged in Shopping Week," *Toronto Star*, April 26, 1928.
98 "Eight-Hour Bill Is Beaten 22–18 as Trade Burden," *VT*, December 8, 1922. See "Eight-Hour Day Bill Defeated in Legislature by 9," *VS*, November 25, 1921; Yarmie, "The State and Employers' Associations," 53–101.
99 See "Mrs. M.E. Smith Congratulated," *VS*, September 7, 1921; "Mass Meeting to Be Held Tomorrow at Stanley Park," *VW*, July 29, 1922; "Stanley Park Meeting Passes Resolution against Further War," *VP*, July 31, 1922; "International Board Would Ensure Peace," *VW*, September 13, 1922; "Many Attractive Teas on Friday's Calendar," *VW*, September 23, 1922; and "Clubs," *VW*, January 22, 1924.
100 Tanner, *Political Change and the Labour Party*, 341.
101 "Women Agree on 'Mary Ellen' for Seat in Cabinet," *VS*, December 19, 1920.
102 "Liberals Insisting on Cabinet Rank for Mrs. Smith," *CH*, February 21, 1921. See also James Conley in "Cabinet Seat for Mary Ellen, He Says," *VP*, January 19, 1922.
103 See "What Style of Hat Shall Be Worn by First Lady Speaker?," *VS*, January 11, 1921; "WORLD'S FIRST WOMAN SPEAKER," *VS*, January 6, 1921 (capitalization in original). See also "What to Do with Mary Ellen," *CH*, January 27, 1921.
104 "What to Do with Mary Ellen," *CH*, January 27, 1921.
105 "Mary Ellen Not Attending Caucus of Liberal Party," *CH*, February 17, 1921; "Woman Minister Is Absentee from Caucus," *VS*, October 22, 1921.
106 "Cabinet Split over Popular Mrs. R. Smith," *VS*, February 8, 1921. For more on Liberal divisions, see "Breach between Factions Grows over Mrs. Smith," *VW*, February 10, 1921.
107 Editorial, "Too Much Mary Ellen," *VS*, February 9, 1921.
108 "Premier Oliver Has Played a Little Shell Game on Mrs. Ralph Smith," *Cumberland Islander*, April 9, 1921, reprinted from the *Kamloops Standard-Sentinel*. See also "'I Am President to the Council,' States Hon. Mrs. Ralph Smith," *VS*, March 30, 1921; and speculation that she was to become minister of education, "Woman Cabinet Minister," *Manchester Guardian*, January 31, 1921.
109 "Honoring Woman but with Caution," *Abbotsford Post*, April 1, 1921. See too W.L.M. King's mean-spirited response in his diary entry for April 6, 1921: "I felt she was much carried away with her position ... To be frank I do not care for women in public life." "The Diaries of William Lyon Mackenzie King," April 6, 1921.
110 Quoted in Catherine Anne Cavanaugh, "In Search of a Useful Life: Irene Marryat Parlby, 1868–1965" (PhD diss., University of Alberta, 1994), 98.
111 "Cabinet Split over Popular Mrs. R. Smith," *VS*, February 8, 1921.
112 "Hon. Mary E. Smith Speaks of Honor Women Received," *OC*, April 4, 1921. See also "Says Women Have Power to Control All the Country," *OC*, April 7, 1921.
113 Editorial, "A Canadian Woman Senator," *VS*, August 26, 1921.
114 "Vancouver Women in Political Fight," *VS*, September 9, 1921.
115 "Not a Compliment – a Necessity," *VS*, September 25, 1921. On the continuing interest in Smith as a senator, see "Will Mary Ellen Get Senatorship from J. Canuck?" *VS*, April 5, 1922.
116 "Women Fire the First Shot in Election Fight," *VS*, September 5, 1921. See also "Hon. Mary Ellen Smith Will Not Enter Federal Field at the Present," *NFP*, September 24, 1921; "Coast Liberals Fear Move for Federal Honors," *WT*, September 24, 1921; and "Mrs. M.E. Smith Congratulated," *VS*, September 7, 1921. For the claim that Vancouver's Liberal

chief, John Wallace Farris, strongly opposed Smith's entry federal politics lest her departure weaken the provincial party, see "Liquor Takes Its Old Role in Politics," *VS*, September 20, 1921.
117 *BCF*, September 9, 1921, 2. See also Editorial, *BCF*, September 23, 1921.
118 "Farris Holds Out Bait for Mary Ellen," *VS*, September 11, 1921. See also "Mrs. Smith Expects Portfolio Soon," *VP*, October 21, 1921.
119 A.E. Garvey to King, December 28, 1921, William Lyon Mackenzie King Papers, vol. 60, microfilm reel C-1946, pages 52197–98, MG26-J, Library and Archives Canada. My thanks to Patricia Roy for this reference and to Sarah Bellefleur Bondu, reference archivist at Library and Archives Canada, for finding the up-to-date citation in the midst of the COVID-19 pandemic. The *Vancouver Province* had identified this "definite understanding" between the Oliver administration and Mary Ellen. "Mrs. Smith Expects Portfolio Soon," *VP*, October 21, 1921.
120 "R.H. Gale Is Liberal Choice as Candidate," *VW*, October 1, 1921.
121 "Wallflower No Longer, Says Mrs. Smith," *VP*, November 21, 1921.
122 "Mrs. Ralph Smith Has No Regrets," *VS*, November 21, 1921. For the letter of sympathy sent by the Vancouver Mothers' Pension Association when Smith became ill shortly after the height of the conflict, see "Pension Society to Aid Sons of Widowed Mothers," *VS*, December 1, 1921.
123 "MRS. R. SMITH RESIGNS: MUST UPHOLD TRUST PLACED IN HER BY WOMEN OF B.C.," *VS*, November 20, 1921 (capitalization in original). By that time, the *Vancouver Sun* was a leading critic of suspected government corruption. See "Is This Right or Wrong?" *VS*, November 21, 1921.
124 By a Woman, "Milady in Politics," *VS*, November 28, 1921.
125 "Women in Politics," *VS*, December 2, 1921.
126 Quoted in Winthus, "The Influence of Political Leaders," 68. See also Ormsby, *British Columbia*, 414; "Leaders Gather against Premier," *VS*, January 17, 1922; "H.G. Perry Now Man of the Hour," *VS*, October 4, 1921; and "Mrs. Ralph Smith Has No Regrets," *VS*, November 21, 1921. The final article in this list described a pervasive revolt against Oliver.
127 See "King Mission to Stimulate Party in B.C.," *VS*, January 10, 1922; "Leaders Gather against Premier," *VS*, January 17, 1922; and "Whitewash for Oliver; Convention by March 29," *VS*, January 21, 1922.
128 "Thinks Activity Presages Election," *CH*, June 22, 1922.
129 "Major Burde of Alberni in the Legislature," *NFP*, February 16, 1921. See also "Women Demand Apology Be Given to Mrs. Smith," *VT*, February 17, 1921.
130 "Wallflower No Longer, Says Mrs. Smith," *VP*, November 21, 1921.
131 M.E. Smith to A.M. Manson, no date but clearly July-August 1923, and A.M. Manson to M.E. Smith, August 20, 1923, both in Alexander Manson Fonds at RBSCUBC. Thanks to R.A.J. McDonald and Patricia Roy for these references.
132 "Warm Liberal Debate Won by Women," *VP*, April 12, 1922. See also "Liberal Women Discuss Union," *VS*, March 4, 1922; "Subordinate Associations Keep Identity," *VW*, April 12, 1922; "Despite Opposition the Woman's Liberal Association Is Intact," *VS*, April 12, 1922; "Committee to Investigate," *VS*, April 26, 1922; and "Why City Detective Appeared at Meeting," *VW*, April 4, 1922. The Vancouver City and District Liberal Association attempted mediation between female activists and the party leadership. See "Arbitration Board to Promote Harmony," *VW*, April 26, 1922.
133 "Visiting Ministers Set Precedent at Reception," *VW*, July 21, 1922.

134 "Liberal Women Score Methods of Medical Board," *VS*, March 2, 1923. See also "Liberal Women Elect President," *VW*, September 22, 1923; and "Women Still Are Fighting," *VS*, September 22, 1923.
135 "Legislature Faces Two Vexed Problems at Opening, Oct. 30," *VS*, September 11, 1922.
136 Attorney General Manson, quoted in "Want University Built Promptly," *VS*, September 30, 1922.
137 "Woman's Platform Necessary Is Opinion of Mrs. R. Smith," *VS*, March 22, 1923.
138 "Hon. Mr. Manson Defines Woman's Part in Politics," *VS*, June 14, 1923.
139 "Mrs. M.E. Smith Says Woman Must Defend Her Laws," *VS*, June 20, 1923.
140 "Women Liberals Form Federation for All Canada," *TG*, June 4, 1923 (emphasis added). On the limited effect of the national federation, see Patricia A. Myers, "'A Noble Effort': The National Federation of Liberal Women of Canada, 1928–1973," in *Beyond the Vote: Canadian Women and Politics*, ed. Linda Kealey and Joan Sangster (Toronto: UTP, 1989), 39–62. See also the unprepossessing story of unrequited loyalty in *Report: First Assembly of the National Federation of Liberal Women of Canada* (Ottawa: n.p., 1928), https://ia801006.us.archive.org/19/items/reportofthefirstoonati/reportofthefirstoonati.pdf. On the American-born Ramsland, also a widow who took her husband's seat, see Melissa K. Bennett, "Sarah Ramsland: Pioneer in Politics and Library Service," *Canadian Parliamentary Review* 43, 1 (Spring 2020), http://www.revparlcan.ca/en/sketches-of-parliaments-and-parliamentarians-of-the-past/. Although Edith McTavish Rogers was the first Métis woman elected to a Canadian legislature, she was married to a successful White businessman and moved in Winnipeg's elite circles, where she made her reputation as an advocate for First World War veterans and disadvantaged children. She is difficult to locate as a suffragist. Her appeal to electors in the 1920 election was a bland, non-specific endorsement of the reform sympathies of the sitting Liberal government. She makes no mention of women or suffrage. See "To the Electors of Winnipeg," *WT*, June 28, 1920.
141 See Andrews, "The Course of Medical Opinion," 129–41.
142 "Mrs. J. Robinson Declines Honor of Nomination," *VS*, May 21, 1924. For the support of Liberal activists, see also "Liberal Women Are Pledged to Support Mrs. M.E. Smith," *VS*, May 17, 1924.
143 Campaign ad, "Vote for the Oliver Six – and Prosperity," *VS*, June 16, 1924.
144 Patricia E. Roy and Peter Neary, "Mackenzie (McKenzie), Ian Alistair," in *DCB*, vol. 17, University of Toronto/Université Laval, 2003, http://www.biographi.ca/en/bio/mackenzie_ian_alistair_17E.html. Like Smith, the Scottish immigrant Mackenzie was committed to both the advancement of social security and anti-Asian policies.
145 On the UK shift, see Tanner, *Political Change and the Labour Party*, 434.
146 *Some Plain Facts about the Oliver Government* (Vancouver: Provincial Liberal Association, 1924), 24.
147 Smith, cited in [Pattullo?] to M.A. Macdonald, March 4, 1924, Dufferin Pattullo Papers, AddMss003, A01798, vol. 18, file 19, Royal British Columbia Archives. My thanks to Patricia Roy for this reference and the next.
148 M.A. Macdonald to John Oliver, March 6, 1924, Dufferin Pattullo Papers, AddMss003, A01798, vol. 18, file 19, Royal British Columbia Archives.
149 "Women to Take Prominent Part in Elections," *VS*, May 30, 1924.
150 "Public Money Well Spent in Many Branches," *VS*, June 11, 1924.
151 "Big Audience Heard Hon. Wm Sloan and J.S. Cowper Pour Hot Shot into Opponents," *NFP*, June 19, 1924. Unfortunately, the cartoons haven't been located.

152 For their election statements, see "Why I Want to Be Elected," *VP,* June 9, 1924.
153 Hall tried to emphasize female support. See "Many Women Signers of Mrs. J.Z. Hall's Nomination," *VP,* May 30, 1924. See also "Third Party Opens Barrage on Opponents," *VP,* May 31, 1924, in which Hall, "a native daughter," identified as a former Liberal who would desert the Provincial Party if it did not remain true to "good principles." Later, she said she needed no women's committee, as "third party women were throwing in their lot with the men." "'Tea a Day' Their Motto," *VS,* June 3, 1920, 16. By the 1926 federal election, Hall was speaking for the Liberals. See "Mass Meeting," *VP,* September 12, 1926. By the 1928 provincial contest, she was rumoured as a replacement for Mary Ellen in Vancouver. See "City Nominees Being Sifted by Two Parties," *VS,* April 28, 1928; and her refusal to endorse any party, "Four Certain of Place on Grit Slate," *VP,* June 21, 1928.
154 Benjamin Isitt, "Elusive Unity: The Canadian Labor Party in British Columbia, 1924–28," *BCS* 163 (Autumn 2009): 31. The Canadian Labor Party also endorsed Asian enfranchisement in the 1924 and 1928 provincial elections. See also Hak, *The Left in British Columbia,* 67. Confusion over the names (not to mention the platforms) of the political parties seeking to represent the Canadian working class has often confounded contemporaries, as well as historians. As one sympathetic observer in the *Dalhousie Review* noted in 1923:

> There are not fewer than eight Labour parties in the Dominion. There is the Canadian Labour party, – a political offshoot of the Trades and Labour Congress of Canada, – the parliament of international unionism in the Dominion. Besides this we have the Dominion Labour party, the Independent Labour party, the Labour party, the Socialist Representation League, the Federal Labour party, the Socialist party of Canada, and the workers' party of Canada. Some of these are confined to one province, others are found in several provinces.

Francis A. Carman, "Labour Party in Parliament," *Dalhousie Review* 2, 4 (1923), 456. Confusion is only compounded since spelling often varies between "labour" and "labor" when referring to the same organization.
155 "'Tea a Day' Motto of Lady Workers," *VS,* June 3, 1924; "Women to Take Prominent Part in Elections," *VS,* May 30, 1924.
156 Graves had run unsuccessfully for Victoria City Council in January 1919, with a platform holding that "women and children of Victoria require more intimate representation" and stressing soldiers' re-establishment. "Mary Gertrude Graves," *VT,* January 11, 1919. She also served a term on the city's Library Commission, 1920–22.
157 See "Annie Garland Foster (1875–1974)," Canadian Writing Research Collaboratory, https://cwrc.ca/islandora/object/ceww%3A7cceb359-4ea5-4607-a199-154901892e30. Foster was better known as the writer Mrs. Garland Foster.
158 Ormsby, *British Columbia,* 423.
159 Elections British Columbia, *Electoral History of British Columbia.*
160 See "Mrs. Smith Replaces McRae for Seat in Next Legislature," *NFP,* July 18, 1924.
161 "Our Lady Representative," *BCF,* July 25, 1924.
162 "Vancouver Woman Again in Legislature," *TG,* August 4, 1924.
163 Gertrude E.S. Pringle, "Outstanding Canadian Women," *Edmonton Journal,* August 30, 1924.
164 Fisher and Mitchell, "Patterns of Provincial Politics since 1916," 258.
165 See Ormsby, *British Columbia,* 433; and Winthus, "The Influence of Political Leaders," 77. See also Anne Wood, *Idealism Transformed: The Making of a Progressive Educator* (Montreal and Kingston: MQUP, 1985), Chapter 8, "Putnam-Weir Survey."

166 Martin Robin, quoted in McDonald, *A Long Way to Paradise*, 124.
167 McDonald, *A Long Way to Paradise*, 126.
168 See "Ask Mrs. Smith to Run in Burrard," *VS*, September 1, 1925. See also the very different treatments of the powerful Stevens in John Nelson, "Harry Stevens Never Lost a Fight," *MM*, May 1, 1926; and Jagmeet Mann, "History Catches Up with Komagata Maru Villain – and It's Good Riddance," *Toronto Star*, August 9, 2019.
169 See the discussion in "Liberal Leaders in Vancouver for Big Rally," *NFP*, July 26, 1926. See also "Senate Seat for Mrs. Smith Urged," *VS*, October 22, 1924.
170 "Vancouver Sets Pace for Canada in Returning Tide of Prosperity," *VS*, October 22, 1924.
171 "Mrs. Smith Gives Interesting Talk on Recent Legislation," *Chilliwack Progress*, March 3, 1926. See also "Mass Meeting of N. Burnaby Women Hear Mrs. Smith," *VS*, October 13, 1925; and "Women Present Lieut.-Governor with Gilded Trowel Following Corner-Stone Laying Today," *VS*, May 1, 1926.
172 J. Butterfield, "The House in Session," *VP*, November 29, 1925.
173 See Rose Henderson, "Woman and Marriage," *Canadian Labor Advocate*, July 31, 1925; and, on Jamieson, see the coverage of her talk "Woman and Peace," *Canadian Labor Advocate*, October 2, 1925. On Henderson, see Peter Campbell, *Rose Henderson: A Woman for the People* (Montreal and Kingston: MQUP, 2010). Henderson ran unsuccessfully as a Labor candidate in New Westminster in the 1925 federal election, and Jamieson would successfully run for the Co-operative Commonwealth Federation in a 1939 provincial by-election.
174 P.C.R., "The Greatest Show on Earth," *VP*, January 23, 1927.
175 "Nearly $400 Taken by Army Taggers," *VS*, November 29, 1926.
176 See "Government Ready but Tories Seek Delay in Business," *VT*, January 19, 1927; J. Butterfield, "The Common Round," *VP*, January 20, 1927; and "New Era Is Surprised by Letter," *VP*, February 11, 1927. The relationship between BC women and taxation deserves attention. See its importance elsewhere in Shirley Tillotson, "Relations of Extraction: Taxation and Women's Citizenship in the Maritimes, 1914–1955," *Acadiensis* 39, 1 (Winter-Spring 2010): 27–57.
177 "Legal Hints," *VS*, April 4, 1927.
178 "Extend P.G.E. to G.T.P. Line Now, Mrs. Smith Urges," *VT*, January 21, 1927. See also her earlier suggestion that municipalities absorb half the costs of mothers' pensions as a deterrent to transferring mothers to that program. "Mothers' Pensions Act Is Defended," *VC*, November 15, 1924.
179 "Rock Pile Place for Husbands Who Desert Families," *VT*, February 16, 1927.
180 "Extend P.G.E. to G.T.P. Line Now, Mrs. Smith Urges," *VT*, January 21, 1927.
181 "Protest Court Decision on Picketing," *VS*, July 7, 1926.
182 "Mary Ellen Smith Advocates Diploma for House Workers," *Saskatoon Star-Phoenix*, June 29, 1926. See also "Urges Domestic Service Placed among Professions," *VS*, June 25, 1926; and Lee Stewart, *It's Up to You: Women at UBC in the Early Years* (Vancouver: UBCP, 1990), Chapter 4, "The Proper and Logical Study for Womankind: Home Economics at UBC."
183 Magdalena Dorothy Kean, "'The Bob-Shingle Regime that Rules the Feminine World': Consumerism, Women and Work in 1920s British Columbia" (master's thesis, University of British Columbia, 2004), 28, https://open.library.ubc.ca/cIRcle/collections/ubctheses/831/items/1.0099775.
184 Ibid., 39.
185 "Woman Politician in Critical Vein," *MG*, January 26, 1925.

186 See Scott Kerwin, "The Janet Smith Bill of 1924 and the Language of Race and Nation in British Columbia," *BCS* 121 (Spring 1999): 83–114. On the fears associated with interracial contacts, see Roy, *Consolidating a White Man's Province;* and Mawani, *Colonial Proximities.*
187 *BCF,* December 12, 1924. On divisions among organized White workers regarding Asians, see Gillian Creese, "Exclusion or Solidarity? Vancouver Workers Confront the 'Oriental Problem,'" *BCS* 80 (Winter 1988–89): 24–51.
188 "Playing Politics," *VP,* November 29, 1924.
189 "Kumtuks Discuss Janet Smith Bill," *VT,* December 2, 1924.
190 Kerwin, "The Janet Smith Bill," 97, 100.
191 See "Ask House to Urge Repeal of Treaties Restricting Canada's Oriental Control," *VT,* December 9, 1924.
192 See "Sterilization Is Advocated" and "Sterilization Again Urged," *VS,* December 2, 1925.
193 "Commission Urges Strong Measures to Cope with Insanity Problem Here," *VT,* March 13, 1928. See also BC Royal Commission on Mental Hygiene, *Report of the Royal Commission on Mental Hygiene* (Victoria: Government Printer, 1927), https://open.library.ubc.ca/collections/bcsessional/items/1.0228017.
194 "Plebiscite to Test People's Views on Economy Suggested," *VT,* December 2, 1925. For her discussion of schooling and institutionalization of the feeble-minded, see "Local Council of Women to Have Speakers' Bureau," *VS,* April 3, 1928.
195 Heron, *Working Lives,* 288. Craig Heron does not make this link, but it seems very significant for Mary Ellen Smith.
196 "Interesting Sidelights on the Week at Victoria," *BCF,* November 28, 1924. See also "Lash Is Advocated for Women Drug Peddlers," *WT,* November 19, 1924.
197 "Extend P.G.E. to G.T.P. Line Now, Mrs. Smith Urges," *VT,* January 21, 1927.
198 "Two Bills Pass; No Opposition," *VS,* December 18, 1925.
199 "Mrs. Mary Ellen Smith, M.L.A.," *VP,* December 27, 1924.
200 "Honored Guest Liberal Women," *OJ,* January 24, 1925.
201 "Woman Politician in Critical Vein," *MG,* January 26, 1925.
202 On Quebec feminists' struggles with Taschereau, see Denyse Baillargeon, *To Be Equals in Our Own Country: Women and the Vote in Quebec* (Vancouver: UBCP, 2020), especially Chapter 4.
203 "Cabinet Members to Attend Event for Premier," *VS,* November 30, 1927.
204 "Nelson Honors Party Leaders," *VS,* October 15, 1927. See also "Mrs. Mary Ellen Smith's New Role as Accompanist," *VT,* October 15, 1927.
205 J. Butterfield, "The Common Round," *VP,* October 16, 1927.
206 Edith K. Hall, letter, "What Is Your Opinion? Declares Women Will Support Liberal Policy of Development for the West," *VS,* October 26, 1925.
207 Genevieve Lipsett-Skinner, "Mirrors of Ottawa," *VS,* April 12, 1926.
208 "Mrs. Mary Ellen Smith May Represent City in Cabinet as Provincial Secretary," *VP,* February 17, 1927.
209 "Mme. Speaker Swings Gavel in Legislature," *VP,* February 23, 1928.
210 Anne Anderson Perry, "Is Women's Suffrage a Fizzle? Has the Woman Voter Sacrificed the Interests of Her Sex to Mere Party Allegiance?" *MM,* February 1, 1928. See also Kay, "What Women Are Doing," *VP,* April 19, 1928.
211 "Women's Laurier Club Is Formed," *VT,* November 15, 1927.
212 For a thoughtful description of these divisions, see "Hon. M.E. Smith First President of Liberal Women," *MG,* April 19, 1928. For a positive and superficial assessment, see "A

Tribute to Mrs. Smith," *NFP,* April 27, 1928. In the United States, under the influence of Eleanor Roosevelt, another political wife, but one better placed than Smith to shape policy, the Democratic Party seemed more promising than Canadian Liberals. See John T. McGuire, "Beginning an 'Extraordinary Opportunity': Eleanor Roosevelt, Molly Dewson, and the Expansion of Women's Boundaries in the Democratic Party, 1924–1934," *Women's History Review* 23, 6 (2014): 922–37.

213 "Hon. M.E. Smith First President of Liberal Women," *MG,* April 19, 1928. See also "Women Urged," *OJ,* April 18, 1928.
214 Anne Anderson Perry, "Women Begin to Speak Their Minds," *Chatelaine,* June 1928. See also her "Stag Politics," *Chatelaine,* May 1930.

Chapter 7: On the Margins, 1928–33

1 Isitt, "Elusive Unity," 64.
2 For an assessment of Conservative difficulties that ignores all issues of gender, see Ian Parker, "Simon Fraser Tolmie: The Last Conservative Premier of British Columbia," *BCS* 11 (Fall 1971): 21–36.
3 "The Confessions of a She-Politician," *MM,* June 1, 1922.
4 M. Ada Dickey, quoted in "In the Editor's Confidence," *MM,* July 1, 1922.
5 Nellie L. McClung, quoted in "In the Editor's Confidence," *MM,* Nov. 15, 1922.
6 Ibid. My discussion of the *Maclean's* article is a slightly revised version of Veronica Strong-Boag, "Fake News Canada 1922: Designed to Diminish and Deceive," Active History, March 29, 2018, http://activehistory.ca/2018/03/fake-news-canada-1922-designed-to-diminish-and-deceive/.
7 H.F. Gadsby, "Letters of a Woman M.P.," *MM,* February 15, 1929, and March 1, 1929. A third installment was promised but failed to appear.
8 Dora M. Sanders, "Women Won't Be Free," *MM,* August 15, 1933.
9 James K. Nesbitt, *VS,* January 28, 1971.
10 For one Conservative columnist's reflections on the "mystery" of the removal of both Smith and Ian Mackenzie, who was relocated to North Vancouver, see J. Butterfield, "The Common Round," *VP,* July 7, 1928.
11 "Voice Confidence in Woman M.L.A.," *VS,* February 26, 1927.
12 Editorial, "Exiles and Deportees," *VP,* July 13, 1928.
13 On the limitations of single-member organization, see Sawer, Tremblay, and Trimble, "Introduction," in Sawer, Tremblay, and Trimble, *Representing Women in Parliament,* 1–24.
14 Smith would win Burrard in the 1933 election. Although her talents surpassed those of many men appointed to cabinet, the party never promoted her. See also Cassidy Rose Ellis, "Preserving the 'Glory of the Past': The Native Daughters of British Columbia and the Construction of Pioneer History in the Hastings Mill Museum" (master's thesis, University of British Columbia, 2002). Although Helen Smith is hard to find as a suffragist, John Robson, BC premier from 1889 to 1892, was an ally. The cause "was rooted in his Christian faith and commitment to both temperance and representative government." He did, however, oppose the enfranchisement of First Nations and Chinese residents. Campbell, *A Great Revolutionary Wave,* 50, 52.
15 "Mrs. Smith Likely to Oppose Pooley," *VS,* April 12, 1928.
16 "Stronghold of Tories in B.C. Invaded," *Windsor Star,* April 27, 1928.

17 "Eastern Women Look to West for Leadership," *VS,* May 2, 1928.
18 See E.E. Billinghurst, letter, "Esquimalt Politics," *VC,* June 23, 1928; and E.E. Billinghurst, letter, "Mrs. M.E. Smith and Unemployment," *VC,* July 17, 1928.
19 J. Butterfield, "The Common Round," *VP,* April 18, 1928.
20 See Campbell, *Demon Rum or Easy Money,* 66–67. See also "Carlow May Run in Esquimalt Riding," *VP,* April 30, 1928.
21 For Carlow's denial that he was Pooley's "pawn," see Frank Carlow, letter, "Political Machine Tactics," *VC,* July 1, 1928.
22 "Ian Mackenzie Nails Pooley's 'Fabrications,'" *VT,* June 30, 1928; "Farris Proves Mrs. Smith's Social Legislation Claims," *VT,* July 17, 1928.
23 "Ian Mackenzie Nails Pooley's 'Fabrications,'" *VT,* June 30, 1928.
24 Trevor Keene, letter, "Cobble Hill Meeting," *VC,* July 5, 1928.
25 "Who First Sought Health Insurance?" *VP,* March 15, 1928.
26 Rather ironically, the federal Conservatives under R.B. Bennett introduced legislation "to enable Canada to fulfil her treaty obligations under the 1922 [League of Nations] Conventions." These included a Minimum Wages Act and an Hours of Work Act, which were declared ultra vires, or beyond the jurisdiction of the dominion government, in 1937. See J.R.H. Wilbur, "R.B. Bennett as a Reformer," *Historical Papers of Canadian Historical Association* 4, 1 (1969): 108–9.
27 "Scrutiny of Votes Invited," *VC,* July 15, 1928.
28 "Pooley Flings Many Charges at Royal Oak," *VT,* July 6, 1928. For his rejection of criticism of his family, see also "Mr. Pooley Is Indignant at Charges," *VC,* July 18, 1928.
29 "Social-Labor Legislation of B.C. Analyzed," *VC,* May 31, 1928; "Startling Exposure," *NFP,* July 17, 1928.
30 "Thain Says Remark Was 'Angry Cat,'" *VS,* July 12, 1928; Editorial, "'That Old Woman,'" *VS,* July 10, 1928. Conservative women sympathizers are mentioned in "Resentment on Attacks Shown by Club Women," *VS,* July 17, 1928.
31 "What Is Your Opinion? Letter from 'Voger,'" "Resents W.C. Shelly's Remarks about Mary Ellen Smith Going to Esquimalt," *VS,* July 17, 1928.
32 J. Butterfield, "The Common Round," *VP,* July 18, 1928.
33 "Women Decide Pending Poll," *VC,* July 5, 1928.
34 "Urges Women to Exercise Vote," *VT,* July 5, 1928. See also "East and West Should Unite," *VC,* June 28, 1928. Active in the Montreal Women's Club and the Women's Auxiliary of the Presbyterian Church, Campbell was the president of the Montreal Women's Conservative Club. See also her later address to the WCTU, "Feminism Was Topic," *MG,* February 27, 1930, and the obituary "Prominent Church Worker, Mrs. O.R. Campbell, 87, Dies," *MG,* October 2, 1953.
35 Editorial, "Is This What Women Think?" *VS,* July 14, 1928. See also the extended report on similar remarks made by Black, always referred to with her married name, in support of Conservative leader Simon Fraser Tolmie in Vancouver. "Tolmie Is Given Ovation in Vancouver," *VP,* July 12, 1928.
36 Mrs. Howard Lloyd, quoted in "Assails Election Printing," *VS,* July 13, 1928.
37 "Women Assure Mr. Davie Aid," *VC,* July 18, 1928. See also J.D. Wilson, "'I Am Here to Help If You Need Me': British Columbia's Rural Teachers' Welfare Officer, 1928–1934," *JCS* 5, 2 (Summer 1990): 94–118. Bowron, who was not a teacher but a clubwoman, was to offer "pastoral care," not to question the salaries or working conditions of teachers. Ibid., 96.
38 "Shelley Here to Aid Fight," *VT,* July 10, 1928.

Notes to pages 183–86

39 Observer, letter, "Mrs. M.E. Smith," *VT,* May 1, 1928.
40 Mrs. Stewart Henderson, quoted in "Women Protest Epithets Applied to Mrs. Smith," *VT,* July 11, 1928.
41 "Premier's Wife One of Speakers," *VC,* July 17, 1928.
42 "Public Conference for Women (Auspices Liberal Women's Forum)," *VC,* July 15, 1928.
43 "Mrs. Smith Begins Fight in Esquimalt," *VC,* May 15, 1928.
44 See Pooley's retort that "there was never any bowing of the knee on the part of the residents of this district." "Sharp Reply Is Made by Mr. Pooley," *VC,* May 23, 1928.
45 "Candidate Welcomed," *VC,* May 16, 1928.
46 "Voters of Metchosin Condemn Tactics of Opposition Campaign," *VT,* July 14, 1928.
47 Ormsby, *British Columbia,* 43. In contrast, Henrik J. von Withus dismissed Liberal policies presented during the election as little more than retreading. See his "The Influence of Political Leaders," 82.
48 "Fighting Speech by Mrs. M.E. Smith Delights Saanich," *VT,* March 21, 1928. See also "Fighting for Mothers' Care," *VT,* June 23, 1928.
49 "Local Council of Women to Have Speakers' Bureau," *VS,* April 3, 1928.
50 "Mrs. M.E. Smith at East Sooke," *VT,* May 30, 1928.
51 "Need of Change Fully Realized," *VC,* July 18, 1928.
52 "Meeting Holds Carlow Honest," *VT,* July 4, 1928.
53 Cross, of Golden, British Columbia, was particularly distinguished as perhaps the only candidate to use an airplane during the campaign. See "Woman to Carry on Campaign by Plane and Radio," *WT,* July 6, 1928. Cross may be the Dr. Cross who wrote *Through the Land of Living Gods: My Pilgrimage at the Wish of the Master* (1930). A medical doctor who worked in China, the author was the wife of Major Wallace H. Cross. McGregor, a widow (and not yet further identified), had argued that there should be "no discrimination between men and women." She was the nominee of the Conservative Women's Current Events Club. "Conservatives Barred Women," *VT,* July 12, 1928. See also "Equal Rights for Women," *VT,* July 11, 1928.
54 Alice McGregor, letter, "A Tribute to Mrs. Smith," *VT,* May 6, 1933.
55 Quoted in Cavanaugh, "In Search of a Useful Life," 147.
56 James K. Nesbitt, "Victoria Report," *Interior News* (Smithers), August 27, 1975. The two offenders were Liberal John Hart and Conservative Royal Maitland.
57 James K. Nesbitt, *VS,* December 6, 1972. Pictures of Tilly Jean Rolston, Canada's first female cabinet minister with a portfolio, and of Thomas Uphill, Fernie's long-time Labour MLA, suffered the same fate.
58 See Brian Harrison, "Women in a Men's House: The Women M.P.s, 1919–1945," *Historical Journal* 29, 3 (1986): 623–54.
59 One nephew, Joseph Smith (d. 1957), lived in Vancouver with his wife, Catherine, son Ralph, and a daughter. Another nephew, Matthew, who had boarded with her in Nanaimo, remained there as an employee of the post office. See "Matt Smith Is Remembered by His Comrades," *NFP,* March 31, 1932; and "Many Happy Returns," *NFP,* April 6, 1939. He seems to have died in 1945.
60 "W.D. Carter Is Superannuated," *VT,* April 1, 1936.
61 See "Vancouver Nanaimoites to Hold Big Banquet," *NFP,* February 26, 1932; and "Old Timers of Nanaimo in Vancouver," *NFP,* March 19, 1932. See also "Diamond Wedding Is Celebrated by Aged City Couple," *VP,* August 31, 1928; and "Nanaimo Pioneers Mark Golden Wedding Anniversary," *VP,* February 28, 1932.

62 "Mrs. Smith," *VC*, July 19, 1928.
63 "Can Liberal Ship Be Hauled Off the Rocks?," *VP*, January 20, 1929.
64 Quoted in Robin Fisher, *Duff Pattullo of British Columbia* (Toronto: UTP, 1991), 199.
65 See Robin Fisher, "The Decline of Reform: British Columbia Politics in the 1930s," *JCS* 25, 3 (Fall 1990): 74-89.
66 See the Liberal convention's call for a royal commission "to ascertain the extent to which British Columbia has failed to secure the quality of benefit and the quantity of advantage that the other provinces have enjoyed." "Red Letter Day for Liberalism Says Mary Ellen Smith," *NFP*, October 4, 1932.
67 "Liberal Convention Votes Confidence in Pattullo," *VT*, October 3, 1932, 2.
68 McDonald, *A Long Way to Paradise*, 136-37.
69 Pat Terry, "Fighting Liberals United in Idealism," *VS*, October 4, 1932. See also Editorial, "The Job of Liberalism," *VS*, October 4, 1932, 6; and J. Edward Norcross, "MADAME President's BIG JOB," *VS*, October 4, 1932 (capitalization in original).
70 "Mary Ellen Succumbs to Illness," *VS*, May 4, 1933.
71 "Liberals Favor Unemployment Insurance Plan," *VP*, October 5, 1932.
72 See Myers, "'A Noble Effort,'" 39-62.
73 "Voice Optimism for Outlook in Every Province," *OC*, May 17, 1929.
74 Glenora Kennedy actively toured the country in the interest of liberalism before her sudden death. See "Liberal Women Lose President of Federation," *OC*, March 15, 1935. Her qualifications, other than her marriage, are unclear.
75 See "Mary Ellen Smith Returns to Coast," *VS*, November 17, 1930.
76 On this complicated story, which may have included an initial payment, see "Widows of Legislators Pensioned," *VP*, April 25, 1931; "Mrs. Smith and Lady McBride Got Cheque," *VP*, June 25, 1931; "Lady M'Bride and Mrs. Smith Given Pensions," *NFP*, April 25, 1931; J. Butterfield, "The Common Round," *VP*, June 24, 1931; "Government Decides Not to Pension Lady McBride and Mrs. Smith, After All," *VP*, June 23, 1931; "Political Pensions," *WT*, June 25, 1931; "Payments Made to Lady McBride and Mrs. Mary E. Smith," *VS*, June 25, 1931; "Tories to Provide for Lady M'Bride," *VP*, July 2, 1931.
77 "Writ Served on Mrs. M.E. Smith," *VS*, May 4, 1929.
78 "Mr. Pattullo for Cabinet," *VP*, May 17, 1930. See also "Mary Ellen May Run for Federal House," *VP*, February 20, 1929.
79 The first woman to be appointed as the ILO representative for Canada, in 1923, was the British anti-suffragist but "feminist" Violet Markham Carothers (1872-1959). Her main qualification seemed to be that she had befriended (and financed) W.L.M. King. See Helen Jones, "Markham, Violet Rosa," *Oxford Dictionary of National Biography*, 2004.
80 "Woman Labour Minister," *Liverpool Echo*, May 27, 1929.
81 "First Woman Cabinet Minister," *London Vote* (Women's Labor League), May 12, 1933.
82 "A Liberal Woman Minister," *Birmingham Daily Gazette*, May 28, 1929.
83 "'Mary Ellen' Pays a Visit to 'Our Maggie,'" *NFP*, July 10, 1929.
84 R.B.D., "Note and Comment," *VC*, June 20, 1929. The correct spelling is Macphail.
85 J. Butterfield, "The Common Round," *VP*, July 19, 1929.
86 "Appointment of Mrs. Ralph Smith Objected To," *NFP*, June 13, 1929. See also "Refusal Revealed as House Debates Geneva Delegates," *TG*, June 13, 1929.
87 "Proud of Canadians, States Mrs. Smith after Visit Abroad," *TC*, July 30, 1929. Her admiration for Ramsay MacDonald might well have owed something to his intention that the Labour Party "should evolve as a party that united the social classes," an aspiration that

matched the Smiths' hopes for liberalism. See Pugh, "'Class Traitors,'" 40. The post-war Labour government's "devotion to free trade, Home Rule, social welfare and Gladstonian foreign policy" also offered a "comforting sense of continuity" with left liberalism. Pugh, "'Class Traitors,'" 43.
88 "Women in Politics Still Wield Broom," *TG,* August 3, 1929.
89 "Labor Laws Here Model to World," *MG,* July 31, 1929.
90 "Say Statement Not Accurate," *VC,* August 4, 1929. See also "Answer Is Given to Hon. Mrs. Smith," *TG,* August 5, 1929.
91 "Hon. Mary E. Smith Makes Statement on Regent Speech: Makes No Apologies," *TG,* August 6, 1929.
92 "Views on Labor Are Explained by Mary Ellen Smith," *VP,* August 13, 1929.
93 See Robert J. Sharpe and Patricia McMahon, *The Persons Case: The Origins and Legacy of the Fight for Legal Personhood* (Toronto: Osgoode Society for Legal History and UTP, 2007).
94 "Mrs. Smith Hits Senate Verdict," *VP,* April 25, 1928. See also "Women Use Vote Sanely," *Windsor Star,* May 9, 1928.
95 Editorial, "A Place for Mary Ellen," *VS,* October 21, 1929.
96 See Valerie Knowles, *First Person: A Biography of Cairine Wilson, Canada's First Woman Senator* (Toronto: Dundurn Press, 1988).
97 John Leslie Scott, "Our New Woman Senator," *MM,* April 1, 1930.
98 "Views on Labor Are Explained by Mary Ellen Smith," *VP,* August 13, 1929.
99 "Mrs. E. Smith Returns Home from Geneva," *NFP,* August 12, 1929.
100 See "American Club Holds Luncheon," *VS,* October 15, 1929; and "Women Urged to Take Interest in Affairs of World," *VP,* September 15, 1931.
101 See "U.S. Should Join League," *VP,* September 13, 1929.
102 "Many Organizations Comprised in Jewish Council," *VS,* December 12, 1930.
103 "Introspective Report Interests Jewish Conference Meeting," *VS,* June 9, 1931.
104 "Hitler Tyranny Protest," *VS,* April 7, 1933.
105 For her welcome of these women to her home, see "Mrs. Mary E. Smith Entertaining for Noted Visitors," *VS,* July 21, 1931.
106 For a fond daughter's defence of her mother's judicial independence, see MacGill, *My Mother the Judge,* Section X.
107 See Pasolli, *Working Mothers and the Child Care Dilemma,* 61–66; and Barman, *The West beyond the West,* 269.
108 "Women's Mass Meeting Will Protest Pensions," *VP,* March 17, 1932; and "Mothers' Pension Protest Meeting," *VP,* March 22, 1932.
109 Clark, the president of the New Era League, contributed to the *BC Federationist* and ran for school board for the ILP. Later, she joined the CCF and was elected to the Vancouver Park Board in 1937. See Campbell, *A Great Revolutionary Wave,* 41.
110 "Protest Use of Act as Football," *VT,* March 24, 1932.
111 "Urges Pensions Basis Remain," *VP,* March 24, 1932.
112 "New Era League," *VS,* July 11, 1932.
113 Hobbs, "Equality and Difference," especially 207–13.
114 Mary Ellen was to address Burnaby's Ex-Service Men's Unemployment Association. See "Notice," *VS,* November 22, 1932.
115 See Todd McCallum, "The Reverend and the Tramp, Vancouver, 1931: Andrew Roddan's *God in the Jungles,*" *BCS* 147 (Autumn 2005): 51–88.

116 "Broke and Hungry Should One Steal?" *VS*, January 23, 1932. This article cited interviews published in the *New Outlook*, the magazine of the United Church of Canada. See also approval of her statement in John Ahern, letter, "Damn the Consequences," *VS*, January 30, 1932.
117 "4500 'Reds' Demonstrate: No Disorder," *VS*, May 2, 1932.
118 "Social Hygiene Council," *OJ*, May 11, 1929.
119 "Citizens Rallying against Gunmen," *VS*, March 5, 1932.
120 Mrs. Mary Ellen Smith, "Planned Prosperity a Modern Necessity," *VS*, July 16, 1932.
121 Leonard Kuffert, "'Reckoning with the Machine': The British Columbia Social Credit Movement and Social Criticism, 1932–52," *BCS* 124 (Winter 1999–2000): 13.
122 Mrs. Mary Ellen Smith, "Planned Prosperity a Modern Necessity," *VS*, July 16, 1932.
123 "'Issue New Money and Go to Work,'" *VS*, September 26, 1932.
124 On the relationship between Canada's central bank and Social Credit, see Robert L. Ascah, *Politics and Public Debt: The Dominion, the Banks and Alberta's Social Credit* (Edmonton: University of Alberta Press, 1999).
125 See "Ex-M.L.A. Injured," *VS*, December 17, 1932; and "In and Out of Town," *VS*, December 20, 1932.
126 "Thousands Pay Warm Tribute to 'Mary Ellen,'" *VP*, May 7, 1933. During Sanford's service to BC mining communities, he had been "a leading liberal social gospel advocate," but by the Great Depression he captained United Church conservatives. Unlike so-called Reds within the church, Sanford favoured individual salvation and effort. See Marilyn J. Harrison, "The Social Influence of the United Church of Canada" (master's thesis, University of British Columbia, 1975), 74–75.
127 "Body Lies in State," *VS*, May 5, 1933.
128 "Obituary," *International Suffrage News*, June 1933; "First Woman Cabinet Minister," *The Vote*, May 12, 1933.
129 "Obituary: First British Woman Cabinet Minister: Mrs. Mary Smith," *Manchester Guardian*, May 5, 1933.
130 "Mrs. Ralph Smith, Legislator, Dead," *New York Times*, May 5, 1933.
131 "Mary Ellen Smith Dies in Vancouver," *TG*, May 5, 1933, 3.
132 "Current Events," *The Age*, August 1, 1933.
133 "Mrs. Mary Ellen Smith," *VP*, May 4, 1933.
134 Editorial, "Mary Ellen Smith," *VS*, May 4, 1933.
135 "Women Legislator Dies in Vancouver," *NFP*, May 4, 1933.
136 J. Butterfield, "The Common Ground," *VP*, May 5, 1933.
137 "Mary Ellen Smith's Estate $630," *VS*, June 22, 1933. The small sum prompted a letter that concluded "Had there been a score or more of her character and sex in the legislature throughout her political career British Columbia would today be the banner province of the Confederation." S.D., letter, *VS*, June 27, 1933.
138 "Notes and Comments," *TG*, June 24, 1933.
139 "Inaugural Meeting of Mary Ellen Smith Club," *VS*, March 3, 1938.

Conclusion

1 "Granddaughter of Political Pioneers Wed," *VS*, March 29, 1941.
2 See "City Man Weds Belgian Girl," *VP*, December 11, 1944; and "City Man Given Post in London," *VP*, December 28, 1951.

3 Belich, *Replenishing the Earth*, 164.
4 McKay, "The Liberal Order Framework," 630, quoted in Burrill, "The Settler Order Framework," 186.
5 See Strong-Boag, *The Last Suffragist Standing*. On the failure of the "true" liberalism, see the condemnation in E.J. Urwick, "Liberalism True and False," *University of Toronto Quarterly* 7, 3 (April 1938): 289–97. Urwick was a progressive political economist at the University of Toronto and a former associate of London's Toynbee Hall. In this 1938 article, he suggested that a "political liberalism" had emerged, "which has seized upon the least attractive dogmas of the liberal creed – economic *laissez-faire* and freedom for commercial enterprise – and converted these into instruments for the protecting of existing privileges and power." Ibid., 289. Had Mary Ellen been able to read his comment, she might have agreed.
6 Kelsey McLeod, "Mary Ellen Smith," *B.C. Historical News* 30, 2 (Spring 1997): 17.

Index

Note: MES refers to Mary Ellen Smith and RS refers to Ralph Smith. Page numbers with (f) refer to illustrations.

Aberdeen, Lord John and Lady Ishbel, 25–26, 39, 153, 204*n*1
Aboriginal Peoples. *See* Indigenous Peoples
Addams, Jane, 99
agriculture. *See* farming
Alberta: E. Murphy, 132, 155, 192, 193; farmers' parties, 141; I. Parlby, 155, 176, 185; non-partisanship, 110, 230*n*30; Persons Case (1929), 155, 174, 192; Senate candidates, 155; women cabinet members, 155; women MLAs, 7–8, 123, 153, 155; women's enfranchisement, 110. *See also* McClung, Nellie L.
alcohol. *See* temperance movement
anti-Asian racism. *See* Asian people
anti-feminism. *See* feminist movement; suffrage movement; women's movement
Asian people: anti-Asian racism, 34, 39, 47–48, 50, 52, 92, 121, 152, 161, 167, 188; demographics, 33, 34; enfranchisement politics, 46, 173, 246*n*154, 249*n*14; immigration, 47, 53, 66–67, 167; job bans, 37, 46, 47–48, 50, 167;

"maleness," 34; MES's views, 3, 5, 50, 73, 121, 132, 167; miners, 14–15, 46, 47–48, 50, 52–53, 130; in Nanaimo, 34, 37, 46–48, 50, 52–53, 59, 121, 130; in Ottawa, 61; royal commission (1902), 47, 53; RS's views, 50, 52–53, 54, 66–67; segregated space, 82, 121; social exclusion, 32, 34, 50, 59, 76, 130, 133, 218*n*19; stereotypes, 132, 152, 167–68
Astor, Nancy Langhorne, 6, 119, 157, 197
Australia, suffrage, 6, 74, 97, 197

baby contests, 82, 99, 107
Baird, Ian G., 218*n*19
Banfield, Harriet Oille and John, 82, 222*n*21
Barman, Jean, 31–32, 205*n*7
BC Federationist (newspaper): anti-suffragism, 89; *Labor Statesman* (as successor), 5–6, 165, 197; TLC newspaper, 88, 91–92, 117, 134; views on MES, 112, 117, 143, 147, 152, 156, 163, 167; views on RS, 91–92, 94; women writers, 99, 253*n*109. *See also* labour movement

257

BCFL (British Columbia Federation of Labor), 84–85, 95, 101, 104
Bell-Irving, Henry and Marie Isabella, 83, 223n26
Belshaw, John, 49
Bennett, R.B., 174, 190, 196, 250n26
Besant, Annie, 26
Black, Martha Munger, 174, 183, 250n35
Black people, 4, 39, 89–90, 215n79
Bondfield, Margaret, 8, 189–90
Booth, Herbert, 38–39
Borden, Laura Bond, 70
Borden, Robert: election (1917), 109–13; mock election (1915), 88–89; naval policies, 92; Union government, 106, 109–10, 111–12, 113, 119–20; views on women, 110, 128; Wartime Elections Act, 109–10, 111–12, 113, 129, 231n55
Bowron, Lottie, 183, 250n37
Bowser, William John: anti-suffragist, 102–3; elections (1915, 1916), 89, 94, 102, 103; elections (1920, 1924), 144–45, 163; MES's by-election (1918), 117; opposition leader, 112–13, 120; patronage, 95; referenda (1916), 89, 94
Boyce, Tully, 48
Bradlaugh, Charles, 26–27
Brenton, Charles J., 56, 218n2
Brewster, Harlan Carey: death (1918), 128; Liberal divisiveness, 114; New Liberalism, 94; personal qualities, 161, 235n136; RS as finance minister, 95; suffrage legislation, 100, 103, 228n173
Britain. See United Kingdom
British Columbia: demographics, 33–34. See also Nanaimo; Nanaimo, mining industry; Vancouver; Victoria
British Columbia, political parties. See Conservative Party of BC; Liberal Party of BC; political parties
British Columbia, premiers. See Conservative Party of BC; Liberal Party of BC, premiers
Bronson, Ella Webster, 62
Brookfield, Tarah, 62
Browning, Elizabeth Barrett, 43, 214n70
Bryden, John, 51

Burde, Richard, 237n195
Burns, John, 65, 91, 104
Burrill, Fred, 39
Burt, Thomas, 21, 25, 26–28, 53, 65
Butler, Josephine, 221n84

Campbell, Mrs. Owen Rede, 182–83, 250n34
Canadian Collieries, 47–49, 51
Canadian Labor Party, 162–63, 173, 246n154
Canadian Women's Press Club, 71, 82, 87
capitalism: liberal-labourism approach, 194–96, 200–1; MES's views, 3, 5, 57, 131, 152–53, 194–96, 236n167; models, 57, 131, 236n167; war profiteering, 108, 236n171. See also economy; labour movement; women and work; work
Carlow, Frank, 180, 184
Carothers, Violet Markham, 252n79
Carr, John, 17, 56
Carr, Mary Elizabeth Smith (RS's daughter and MES's step-daughter), 16–17, 18, 36, 46, 56, 81, 185, 198
cartoons, 87(f), 90(f), 124(f), 149(f), 158(f), 175(f), 178(f)
CCF (Co-operative Commonwealth Federation), 140–42, 173–74, 198, 201, 253n109
The Champion (suffragist magazine), 5–6, 84, 85(f), 98, 177
children and youth: child custody, 86, 97, 128, 133; child labour, 13, 97, 134; child support, 151, 166; child welfare, 130–31; ILO recommendations, 134; juvenile courts, 83, 116–17; MES's views, 118(f), 121, 151, 168; New Liberalism, 133; underage marriage, 128; unwed mothers, 3, 136, 152. See also education; marriage and divorce; mothers' pensions
Chinese people, Nanaimo, 34, 37, 39, 46–48, 50. See also Asian people
Christianity: Christian socialism, 25; conflict with racism, 50; Lord's Day Alliance, 58; Presbyterians, 36, 58, 61; social gospel, 43–44, 74; United

Church, 194, 254*n*126. *See also* Methodists; Methodists (UK)
city elections. *See* municipal elections
Clark, Susie Lane: about, 83, 253*n*109; MES's political ally, 83–84, 125; mothers' pensions, 135(f), 193–94; socialist, 168; suffragist, 83–84, 98, 99
class. *See* social class
coal mines. *See* mining industry; Nanaimo, mining industry; United Kingdom, mining towns
Communist Party, 153, 173–74, 201, 212*n*3
Comrades of the Great War, 120, 123
"The Confessions of a She-Politician" (*Maclean's*), 175–76, 175(f)
Conley, James, 119
Conservative Party of BC: by-election, Vancouver (1918), 120–21, 123; elections (1920, 1924), 145, 163–64; election (1928), 173, 177–85; women candidates, 182–83. *See also* Bowser, William John; McBride, Richard; Tolmie, Simon Fraser
Conservative Party of Canada: election (1911), 76; election (1917), 113; election (1930, 1935), 174; women in, 170. *See also* Bennett, R.B.; Borden, Robert; Meighen, Arthur; Tupper, Charles
consumer issues: consumers' campaigns, 154, 236*n*170; Consumers' League, 96, 101, 236*n*170; MES's views, 131, 153; war profiteering, 108, 236*n*171. *See also* cooperative movement
Co-operative Commonwealth Federation (CCF), 79, 140–41, 142, 173, 174, 198, 201, 253*n*109
cooperative movement: MES and RS's support for, 24–26, 37, 66; UK movement, 23–26, 210*n*76; women in, 19, 24
Cornwall, England, 10–11
Corse, Mary Insley, 144–45
Cowper, John Sedgwick, 127, 232*n*64
Crawford, William, 27
Creery, Andrew, 163
Crosfield, Esther Margaret Biddle, 144, 145, 239*n*25
Cross, Gladys E., 184, 251*n*53

Davie, Theodore, 52, 217*n*124
de Lavelaye, Baroness, 99
democracy: liberal-labourism, 200–1; MES's views, 118(f), 129–30, 133, 194–96; proportional voting, 91, 118(f); RS's views, 51. *See also* enfranchisement; suffrage movement
Deserted Wives' Maintenance Act (1919), 128, 133, 165. *See also* marriage and divorce
Devon, England, 10–11
Dickey, M. Ada, 175–76
diseases. *See* healthcare and public health
divorce. *See* marriage and divorce
Drake, Montague Tyrwhitt, 42
Drinnan, Walter, 120–21, 123, 233*n*89
Dunsmuir, James, 41, 47–49, 51, 53, 59–60, 178, 179
Dunsmuir, Laura Surles, 59–60
Dunsmuir mines, Nanaimo, 41, 47–49, 172, 178, 194. *See also* Nanaimo, mining industry
Durham. *See* United Kingdom, mining towns
Durham, Lord, 26

economy: Depression, 140–41, 193–96; First World War impacts, 78, 107, 108; free trade, 68–69; market crash (1929), 173; MES's views, 132, 194–96; in Nanaimo, 37–38, 56, 60; recession (1913), 78. *See also* capitalism; labour movement; resource development
education: domestic science, 62, 178; MES's education in UK, 9, 15, 21–23; Nanaimo, 45–46, 56–57; school boards, 46, 86, 102, 140, 238*n*2; voter education, 90, 110. *See also* University of British Columbia (UBC)
Edwards, R.P., 36
Elections Act Amendment Act (1915), 100
Emerson, Ralph Waldo, 91
enfranchisement: Australia, 6, 74, 97, 197; international networks, 6, 66, 84, 99; international standards, 111; New Zealand, 38, 74, 97; United Kingdom, 27–28, 110–11; United States, 111. *See also* suffrage movement

enfranchisement, British Columbia: about, 112, 114; bills and resolutions (1883, 1913, 1916), 44, 223*n*36; demographics, 114; foreign-born male enfranchisement, 101; legislation (1917), 89–90, 90(f), 112; MES's legacy, 199–202; municipal elections, 37, 140, 213*n*32; property qualifications, 37, 213*n*32; school boards, 46, 86, 102, 140, 238*n*2. *See also* suffrage movement

enfranchisement, Canada: election (1917), 109–16; enemy aliens, 110, 113, 121; Military Voters Act, 109–10; Wartime Elections Act, 109–10, 111–12, 113, 129, 231*n*55. *See also* suffrage movement

England. *See* United Kingdom

Epworth League, Nanaimo, 43, 57–58, 74–75, 96, 97, 214*n*70

Equal Franchise Association, Ottawa, 62, 74

Equal Franchise League, 97, 103

equal pay for equal work, 3, 8, 101, 118(f), 134, 136, 151, 160. *See also* women and work

Esquimalt, 5, 68, 69, 177–80

eugenics: better baby contests, 82, 99, 107; MES's views, 3, 131, 132, 152, 167–68, 200; physical ideals, 82, 107, 152; sterilization of mentally unfit, 3, 167–68, 193, 194, 200

Everywoman's World (periodical), 110, 113, 127–28

Fallis, Iva Campbell, 174

farming: farmers' parties (1919, 1921), 141; minimum wage, 150; veterans' programs, 118(f), 132

Farris, Evlyn Fenwick: about, 83; Liberal Party, 231*n*55; views on MES, 83, 116, 119; views on suffrage, 83, 100, 103, 223*n*32, 228*n*173, 231*n*55, 232*n*65; WLA (Women's Liberal Association), 100, 114

Farris, John Wallace de Beque: about, 83; candidate opposition MES (1920), 144, 145; elections (1924, 1928), 156, 163, 180; MLA, 89, 119, 145, 161, 163, 243*n*116; views on MES, 116, 155, 156

Fearn, Mrs. H., 150. *See also* Gutteridge, Helena

Federated Labour Party, 144–45, 154, 160

Federationist. *See* BC Federationist (newspaper)

females. *See* gender/sexuality; women

feminist movement: about, 4, 8–9; anti-feminism, 8–9, 64, 66; election (1917), 111–12; First World War's impacts, 107–8; historical sources, 5–6; liberal-feminism, 104; maternal feminism, 8, 19, 24; MES's friendships, 96; MES's legacy, 199–202. *See also* suffrage movement; women and work; women's movement

First Nations. *See* Indigenous Peoples

First World War: about, 106–11; casualties, 106; conscription, 108, 110, 112–13, 114, 230*n*39; election (1917), 109–13; enemy aliens, 94, 110, 113, 121; "Ginger" Goodwin (war resister), 95, 108; MES's views, 99–100, 102–3, 112, 114; peace movement, 99; profiteering, 108, 236*n*171; recruitment, 101; Red Cross and relief, 86, 99–100, 107; RS's views, 92–94, 95; suffragists, 99–100; Union government, 106, 111–12, 113, 119–20; women's war conference (1918), 128; women's work, 87, 107. *See also* veterans

FitzGibbon, Clare (Lally Bernard), 120–23, 233*n*97

Flavelle, Joseph, 236*n*171

foreign relations. *See* international affairs

Foresters, Independent Order of, 44

Foster, Annie H., 162

Free Press. *See* Nanaimo Free Press (newspaper)

French, Mabel Penery, 89

Gale, "Annie" or Hannah, Mrs. W.J., 230*n*30

Gale, H.O., 156

gender/sexuality: Asian "maleness," 34; barbers and hairdressers, 166; birth control, 18–19, 139, 152; charm offensives, 143, 155; demographics, 60; double entendres, 176; double standard, 41, 139, 147, 151; gender relations (UK),

Index

11, 13–15, 17–20, 28–29; gradualism in collaboration, 49; historical sources, 5–6; interwar years, 140–41; misogyny, 169, 170, 172, 173, 176, 182, 187; patriarchy, 3, 5, 48, 73, 133, 140, 175, 201; prostitution, 35, 41–43, 88, 98–99, 214n63; White slavery, 73, 221n87; women politicians and code transgressions, 207n13; women's auxiliaries to men's civic groups, 44. *See also* suffrage movement; women and work; women's movement
Gilbertson, Belfrage, 62–63
Gilman, Charlotte Perkins, 84
Gladstone, William Ewart, 18, 27, 29, 52, 64
Good Government League, 120, 122–23
Goodwin, Albert "Ginger," 95, 108
Gordon, Amelia Roe, 73–74, 221n84
Gordon, Ishbel and John. *See* Aberdeen, Lord John and Lady Ishbel
Graham, Margaret, 71–73
Grant, Helen Maria, 84, 126, 234
Graves, Mary Gertrude, 162, 246n156
Great War. *See* First World War
Great War Veterans' Association (GWVA), 117, 120–21, 161
Grey, Albert Henry, Lord, 4, 23, 26–28, 59–60, 62, 204n2, 210n70
Grey, Alice Holford, 59–60
Grey, Mary Caroline, 214n53
Griffin, Margaret, 100
Gutteridge, Helena: about, 83–84; collectivist liberalism, 128; first female alderman, 140; MES's political ally, 125; minimum wage, 134–35, 150; suffrage referendum (1916), 89, 94; suffragist, 79–80, 83–84, 86, 98, 101; women's clubs, 99
GWVA (Great War Veterans' Association), 117, 120–21, 161
Gwyn, Sandra, 63

Hall, Florence Huzzey, 221n91
Hall, Jessie, 162–63, 246n153
Hancox, Edith Angell, 153, 212n3
Hardie, Keir, 65

Harper, Henry Albert, 68, 220n62
Hawthornthwaite, James, 58, 68, 125–26
healthcare and public health: diseases, 39–40, 128; hospital auxiliaries, 40–41, 59; hospitals, 82, 151, 168; mining towns, 12, 17–18, 40; Nanaimo, 39–41, 58–59; Oliver government, 161; pandemic (1918–19), 106, 108; RS and MES's support for, 40–41, 58–59; venereal disease, 128, 151, 241n71
Henderson, Rose, 165, 247n173
Heron, Craig, 48, 51, 104, 204n3, 248n195
Heron, Mary Ann, 70
Hobson, John A., 28
Holywell, England, 16–18, 20–21. *See also* United Kingdom, mining towns
How the Vote Was Won (play), 100

illnesses. *See* healthcare and public health
ILO (International Labor Organization), 134, 151, 154, 180–81, 184, 189–91, 192–93, 237nn194–95, 252n79
immigrants: Asian immigration, 47, 53, 66–67, 167; British in Nanaimo, 34–38; employment, 130; immigrant and "bride" ships, 33, 35; MES's support, 152–53, 166–67, 191; MES's tour of UK (1923), 152–53, 242n80; preferred countries, 152, 167; royal commission (1902), 47, 53; RS as MP, 67–68; statistics, 33; White supremacy, 166–69, 200. *See also* Asian people
Imperial Order Daughters of the Empire (IODE), 79–80, 82, 96, 102, 110, 112, 196, 206n11, 222n7, 223n26
In Times Like These (McClung), 7, 140, 204n3, 223n28
Independent Labour Party, 184, 246n154, 253n109
Indigenous Peoples: ban on land sales to, 34; cartoons, 90(f); Coast Salish people, 81; Douglas Treaty (1854), 31; E. Pauline Johnson, 39, 81–82; Edith Rogers as first Métis woman MLA, 245n140; education of children, 46; exclusion from hospitals, 59; First World War military service, 81; MES's

views, 3, 73, 200; Nanaimo area, 31–32, 34, 39, 59; RS's views, 52, 62; Snuneymuxw people, 31–32, 34; social exclusion, 34, 59, 62, 73, 76, 81–82, 130, 133; Tolmie as Métis premier, 173
international affairs: League of Nations, 132, 154, 189, 250*n*26; MES's views, 132, 154; Russian Revolution (1917), 129, 132–33. *See also* First World War
International Labor Organization (ILO), 134, 151, 154, 180–81, 184, 189–91, 192–93, 237*nn*194–95, 252*n*79
international suffrage networks, 6, 66, 84, 99, 132, 149. *See also* suffrage movement
interwar years: decline in labour and socialist vote, 149; post-war reconstruction, 127–28, 139–40, 143–44. *See also* Smith, Mary Ellen, political life as MLA (1918–28); Smith, Mary Ellen, political life as MLA (1918–28), political issues; Smith, Mary Ellen, later life (1928–33); veterans
IODE (Imperial Order Daughters of the Empire), 79–80, 82, 96, 102, 110, 112, 196, 206*n*11, 222*n*7, 223*n*26

Jackson, Ellen Eliza, 218*n*2
Jamieson, Laura Marshall: about, 83–84; CCF member, 142, 165, 168, 198, 247*n*173; Federated Labour Party, 160; MLA, 198; suffragist, 83–84, 99, 103; women's clubs, 79–80, 98, 99, 128
Janet Smith Bill, 167, 192
Japanese people, 37, 47, 53, 73, 132. *See also* Asian people
Jewish people, 133, 192, 193
Johnson, E. Pauline, 39, 81–82
Johnson, Katherine (Kitty), 80
judges, juvenile court, 83, 116–17, 133, 165, 193, 239*n*25
juveniles. *See* children and youth

Keith, Thomas, 48
Kemp, Janet, 84, 120, 157
Kennedy, Glenora Bolton and William, 188, 252*n*74
King, William Lyon Mackenzie: election (1926), 141, 164; on "group government," 160; New Liberalism, 220*n*60; old age pensions, 141–42; patronage, 169–70; on RS and MES, 67–68, 164; on women, 29, 141, 169–70, 243*n*109
King's Daughters, 144
Kipling, Rudyard, 53
Kitsilano, 78–79, 130(f). *See also* Smith, Mary Ellen, life in Vancouver (1911–33); Smith, Ralph, life in Vancouver (1911–17); Vancouver
Knights of Pythias, 44
Komagata Maru incident, 92
Kuper Island Industrial School, 46, 215*n*90

Labor Party, Canadian, 162–63, 173, 246*n*154
Labor Statesman (newspaper), 5–6, 165, 197
labour movement: arbitration, 65; BCFL (BC Federation of Labor), 84, 95, 101, 104; coal miners, 48–49, 53, 87–88; Depression, 140–41, 193–96; "fair deal" and justice, 4, 8, 204*n*3; foreign workers, 152–53; general strikes, 108, 131, 194; gradualism, 49; historical sources, 5–6; international movement, 134, 237*n*194; jurisdictional conflicts, 134; labour aristocracy, 35, 49–53, 209*n*59; Liberals as allies, 64–66; MES's legacy, 199–202; MES's views and allies, 96, 108–9, 121, 131; post-war unrest, 108–9, 113, 140–41; RS as ally and MP, 35, 49, 60, 62, 65–68; socialism and social democracy, 65, 174; suffragists and allies, 48, 84–86, 98; TLC (Trades and Labor Council), 65, 84, 88, 120, 150, 151, 166, 237*n*194; UK activism, 14, 26, 28, 65; women's union auxiliaries, 87–88. *See also BC Federationist* (newspaper); ILO (International Labor Organization); liberal-labourism; minimum wage; mothers' pensions; political parties; women and work
Ladner, Leon, 89
Ladysmith (near Nanaimo), 40, 47, 48–49, 87–88
Laurence, Isabel Flemming, 74, 221*n*87

Laurier, Wilfrid: election (1911), 60, 76; MES's friendship, 102, 113; mock election (1915), 88–89; personal qualities, 64; as prime minister, 64–69, 76; RS and, 52, 54, 60, 66; views on suffrage, 64, 66, 110, 170
Laurier, Zoe Lafontaine, 63–64, 70, 102, 113
Laurier Club, 170, 196
LCW (Local Council of Women): better baby contests, 82, 99, 107; vs general strikes, 108; MES and, 96, 99, 125–26, 144; post-war progressivism, 174; vs red-light districts, 86; vs Union government, 113; Vancouver, 84, 86, 88, 108, 113, 125–26; Victoria, 126; women and work, 88; women's suffrage, 74
League of Nations, 132, 154, 189, 193, 250*n*26
Leier, Mark, 104
"Letters of a Woman M.P." (*Maclean's*), 176
Liberal Party of BC: attacks on affiliated groups, 159; divisiveness, 114, 116, 119–20, 141, 173, 179; elections (1920, 1924), 145, 163–64; election (1928), 172, 177–85, 178(f), 181(f); election (1933), 173–74; labour movement, 67; MES as officer, 159, 168–69, 187; MES's legacy, 199–202; MES's support, 60, 97, 124. *See also* Smith, Mary Ellen, political life as Ralph's wife (1898–1917); Smith, Mary Ellen, political life as MLA (1918–28); Smith, Ralph, politician (1898–1911, 1916–17); WLA (Women's Liberal Association)
Liberal Party of BC, premiers. *See* Brewster, Harlan Carey; MacLean, John Duncan; Oliver, John; Pattullo, Dufferin
Liberal Party of Canada: election (1917), 109–16; elections (1930, 1935), 174, 176, 177(f); national women's federation, 160, 170–71, 188; post-war divisiveness, 141, 170; RS as MP (1900–11), 54–55, 57–69, 61(f), 76–78; women candidates, 174. *See also* King, William Lyon Mackenzie; Laurier, Wilfrid; Smith, Ralph, politician (1898–1911, 1916–17)
liberal-labourism: about, 29–30, 104, 128; collectivist liberalism, 128; conflict with racism, 50; cross-class alignment, 116; MES's legacy, 199–202; RS's views, 55, 57–59, 60, 64–69, 116
liquor. *See* temperance movement
Lloyd George, David, 28, 91, 92, 101, 110–11, 230*n*34, 232*n*82
Local Council of Women. *See* LCW (Local Council of Women)
local elections. *See* municipal elections
Loyal Legion of Young People (WCTU), 45

MacAdams, Roberta, 123
Macaulay, Thomas Babington, 22
Macdonald, Malcolm Archibald, 95, 162
Macdonald, Ramsay, 161, 189–90, 252*n*87
MacGill, Helen Gregory: *Daughters, Wives and Mothers in BC*, 86; jury service, 151; juvenile court judge, 83, 116–17, 133, 165, 193, 239*n*25; MES's ally, 114, 116–17, 141, 165, 193; on political parties, 111; suffragist, 83–84, 86; voter education, 90
MacInnis, Grace Woodsworth, 198
Macken, Jean K., 135(f)
Mackenzie, Ian, 161, 163, 179–80, 181(f), 245*n*144, 249*n*10
MacLean, John Duncan, 141, 164, 169, 179, 181(f), 187
Maclean's (magazine), 175–76, 175(f), 192
Macphail, Agnes Campbell, 8, 142, 174, 176, 190, 252*n*84
MacRae, Christopher, 161, 163
magazines. *See* press coverage
Maidu, Mrs. Sarajin (Sarojini), 129
males. *See* gender/sexuality
Manitoba: E. Rogers, 160, 170, 232*n*77; enfranchisement (1916), 102
Manning, Henry Edward, 26
Manson, Alexander Malcolm, 150, 158–60
marriage and divorce: about, 139–40; birth control, 18–19, 139, 152; deserted wives' support, 128, 133, 165; dower rights, 133, 140, 151; family property, 133, 151; federal jurisdiction over divorce, 156; married women's property law

(1873), 37; unwed mothers, 3, 136, 152.
    See also children and youth
Martin, Joseph, 94, 119
maternal feminism, 8, 19, 24. *See also*
    feminist movement
Maternity Protection Act (1921), 150–51
McBride, Christine Margaret
    McGillivray, 188
McBride, Richard: anti-suffragist, 86,
    87(f), 100, 168; auditing of, 95;
    elections (1912, 1915), 89, 91–92, 94;
    RS and, 57
McClung, Nellie L.: on "dope" (flattery),
    140, 160, 176; on "gentle ladies," 83;
    MES's friendship, 89, 153, 193; MLA in
    Alberta (1921–26), 7–8, 153, 160, 176,
    185; mock election (1915), 88–89;
    political parties, 100, 110, 114, 116;
    suffragist, 82, 84, 88–89; *In Times Like
    These*, 7, 140, 204*n*3, 223*n*28; on women
    in politics, 176
McDonald, Robert A.J., 128, 164,
    205*n*7, 238*n*2
McGregor, Alice E., 184–85, 251*n*53
McKechnie, Robert E., 39, 46–47, 52,
    104, 197
McKinney, Louise, 110, 123, 176
Mechanics' Institutes, 22
medical care. *See* healthcare and public
    health
Meighen, Arthur, 141–42, 164, 169, 170
men. *See* gender/sexuality
mentally unfit, sterilization. *See* eugenics
Menzies, Bertha Grace Kidd, 157
Methodists: about, 42–43; for democracy,
    129; Epworth League, 43, 57–58, 74–75,
    96, 97, 214*n*70; MES's support for, 96,
    121–22, 129; Nanaimo, 42–43, 57–58;
    Ottawa, 62; RS's support for, 42–43,
    57–58; social gospel, 43–44, 74;
    Vancouver, 96; *Western Methodist
    Recorder*, 74–75, 221*nn*91–92. *See also*
    Christianity
Methodists (UK): about, 20–21; Epworth
    League, 43, 214*n*70; female preachers,
    19–21; MES's support for, 15, 20, 30;
    mining towns, 11–12, 15, 19; Primitive
    Methodists, 11, 15, 16–17, 20, 23, 27; RS
    as lay preacher, 16, 20–21; social
    activism, 20, 23
Métis people: Edith Rogers as first Métis
    woman MLA, 245*n*140; Tolmie as Métis
    premier, 173. *See also* Indigenous Peoples
migrants. *See* immigrants
Military Voters Act, 109
Mill, John Stuart, 19, 91
minimum wage: administration, 150, 154;
    collectivist liberalism, 128; ILO
    recommendations, 134, 250*n*26; MES's
    views, 117, 118(f), 121, 132–33; Minimum
    Wage League, 117, 125; New Liberalism,
    133; Tolmie government, 193; for
    women, 4, 128, 133–36, 150, 166
mining industry: Alberta, 79; Asian
    miners, 46, 47–48, 50, 130; Canadian
    Collieries, 47–49, 51; child labour, 46;
    Kootenay mines, 53; Ladysmith, 40, 47,
    87–88; Nova Scotia, 46, 213*n*29; strikes,
    48–49, 87–88; women miners, 34–35.
    See also Nanaimo, mining industry;
    United Kingdom, mining towns
Minto, Governor General, 70, 79, 214*n*53
Minto, Lady, 40, 214*n*53
misogyny, 169, 170, 172, 173, 176, 182, 187.
    See also gender/sexuality
Montreal: MES's press coverage, 71, 143,
    145, 191; MES's speeches, 113, 169;
    strikes, 65
Montreal Gazette, 143, 145, 191
Moody, Irene Hawkins, 102, 120
Moore, Tom, 191
Morrison, Aulay, 196–97
mothers' pensions: about, 4, 133–36,
    135(f), 165–66; administration, 150, 154,
    157, 165–66, 193–94, 247*n*178;
    collectivist liberalism, 128; MES's views,
    118(f), 121, 133–34, 135(f), 150, 165, 184,
    247*n*178; New Liberalism, 133; Oliver
    government, 150; racial exclusions, 133;
    Tolmie government cutbacks, 193–94
municipal elections: first female alderman,
    140; library boards, 140; property and
    age qualifications, 37, 213*n*32; school
    boards, 46, 86, 102, 120, 140, 238*n*2

Index

Murphy, Emily, 132, 155, 192, 193
MWMLPA (Mine Workers and Mine Laborers Protective Association), 45–49

Nanaimo: about, 4, 34–46, 42(f), 55–56; agriculture, 37–38; Asian people, 34, 37, 46, 47–48, 50, 53, 121, 130; British immigrants, 34–38; churches, 42–43; civic life, 36–41, 44, 58; demographics, 34, 60, 212*n*17; early history, 31–32, 34; economy, 37–38, 56, 60; education, 45–46, 56–57; healthcare, 39–40, 59; homeownership, 35–36, 37, 56–57; Methodists, 42–43, 51, 57–58, 196; public morality laws, 42, 214*n*63; publications, 38; Snuneynuxw people, 31–32, 34; suffrage movement, 44–45, 58–59, 62; WCTU, 44–45, 58–59; women's auxiliaries, 40–41, 59–60; women's work, 35, 37. See also *Nanaimo Free Press* (newspaper); Smith, Mary Ellen, life in Nanaimo (1892–1911); Smith, Ralph, life in Nanaimo (1892–1911)
Nanaimo, mining industry: about, 33, 36–37, 46–50; Canadian Collieries, 47–49, 51; disaster (1887), 47; Dunsmuir mines, 41, 47–49, 172, 178, 194; labour aristocracy, 35, 49–53, 209*n*59; Ladysmith mines, 40, 47, 87–88; MWMLPA (union), 45–49; non-British miners, 34, 35–36, 46, 47–48, 50, 53, 130; NVCMLC mines, 34, 35, 46–47, 57; strike (1890–91), 47, 48
Nanaimo Free Press (newspaper): on the Aberdeens, 39; on MES and RS, 58, 68, 96, 100, 190, 197–98; progressive views, 38, 41, 43–44, 59, 182; suffrage news, 38, 100
Nation, Carrie, 41
National Women's Liberal Federation, 160, 170–71, 188
Native Daughters of BC, 162, 179, 196, 218*n*19
Native Sons of BC, 58, 218*n*19
NCWC (National Council of Women of Canada), 39, 73, 107, 110, 136, 171, 190, 238*n*203

New Era League: anti-Asian racism, 152; leadership, 125, 135(f), 253*n*109; MES's political allies, 144, 156, 159, 196; mothers' pensions, 135(f), 193–94; peace activism, 154; political issues, 111; Tolmie government cutbacks, 193–94
New Liberalism: about, 91, 133, 153–54; in Britain, 4, 28; "key pillar of post-war politics," 153–54; King's views, 220*n*60; Liberal Party, 91, 94, 144, 153–54; MES's legacy, 199–202; MES's views, 133, 153–54; vs patriarchy, 133; peace activism, 154, 192–93; post-war reconstruction, 153–54; progressive policies, 66, 91, 144
New Woman ideal, 7
New Zealand, franchise, 38, 74, 97
newspapers. See press coverage
Nickawa, Frances, 82
non-British settlers: assimilation, 101, 113, 130, 152, 167. See also immigrants
Northumberland. See Smith, Mary Ellen, life in England (1863–92); Smith, Ralph, life in England (1858–92); United Kingdom, mining towns
Northumberland Miners' Association (NMA), 15, 23, 27–28
NVCMLC (New Vancouver Coal Mining and Land Company), 34, 35, 46–47, 57. See also Nanaimo, mining industry

O'Boyle, William Patrick, 98
Odd Fellows, Nanaimo, 36, 42(f), 44, 58
Odlum, Victor, 161, 163
old age pensions. *See* pensions
Oliver, Harriet Dunlop, 70
Oliver, John: about, 128, 137; death (1927), 141; elections (1920, 1924), 141, 143, 145–46, 161–64; MES's cabinet post, 154–58; MES's views, 127; personal qualities, 157, 161; poem on, 147; social programs, 134, 150–51; views on labour, 128, 134, 180; views on MES, 137; views on women, 128, 155, 235*n*137
Ontario: farmers' parties (1919, 1921), 141; MES's endorsements, 136, 153; MES's speeches, 188, 190–91. *See also*

Macphail, Agnes Campbell; Ottawa
Ormsby, Margaret, 163
Ottawa: demographics, 60–61; MES as MP's wife, 60–64, 69–76; public health, 62; religious affiliations, 61; RS as MP (1900–11), 60–69, 61(f); social life, 63–64, 69–71; suffrage movement, 62–64, 66, 70, 72–74; women's work, 60, 62
Owen, Robert, 24

Pankhurst, Christabel, 230*n*34
Pankhurst, Emmeline Goulden, 66, 84, 102–3, 108, 197
Parlby, Irene Marryat, 155, 176, 185
patriarchy, 3, 5, 48, 73, 133, 140, 201. *See also* gender/sexuality
Patterson, Edith Louise, 144–45, 180, 239*n*25
Pattullo, Dufferin, 161–62, 173–74, 187–88, 196
peace movement, 154, 192–93
pensions: BC's enabling legislation (1927), 168; federal old age pensions, 66, 91, 141–42, 189; MES's views, 184, 189; old age pensions for women, 151, 160, 189; Oliver government, 150–51; Tolmie government cutbacks, 193–94
periodicals. *See* press coverage
Perry, Harry G., 157
Persons Case (1929), 155, 174, 192
Political Equality Leagues, 45, 84, 92, 99, 101, 224*n*52. *See also* PPEL (Pioneer Political Equality League)
political parties: about, 110–11, 246*n*154; Canadian Labor Party, 162–63, 246*n*154; Communist Party, 153, 173–74, 201, 212*n*3; farmers' parties, 141; Federated Labour Party, 144–45, 154, 160; MES's non-partisanship, 99, 103, 110, 112, 114–16, 115(f), 143; MES's views, 126; non-partisanship, 95, 101, 103, 114–16, 115(f), 116; Progressive Party, 67, 141–42, 174; reforms, 110–11, 143–44; Social Credit, 195–96; women's party, 103, 114, 116, 157, 194, 230*n*34; working class parties, 246*n*154. *See also* socialism and social democracy

political parties, mainstream. *See* Conservative Party of BC; Conservative Party of Canada; Liberal Party of BC; Liberal Party of Canada
Pooley, Charles Edward, 172, 177–78, 182–83
Pooley, Robert Henry, 172, 178–84, 178(f)
Poulet, Naomi, 48
PPEL (Pioneer Political Equality League), 79–80, 89–90, 97, 99–100, 102, 144, 160
Presbyterians, 36, 58, 61
press coverage, 5–6, 204*n*4
press coverage, periodicals. *See BC Federationist* (newspaper); *The Champion* (suffragist magazine); *Everywoman's World* (periodical); *Maclean's* (magazine); *Nanaimo Free Press* (newspaper); *Vancouver Sun*
Primitive Methodists, 11, 15, 16–17, 20, 23, 27. *See also* Methodists (UK)
Pritchard, W.A., 120
Progressive Party, 67, 141–42, 174
prohibition: plebiscite (1898), 45; referenda (1916, 1920), 89, 94, 142–43. *See also* temperance movement
proportional representation, 27–28
Protestants. *See* Christianity
Provincial Party, 160–63
Provincial Women's Suffrage Referendum Association, 89
public health. *See* healthcare and public health
Puttee, Arthur, 68

Quebec: anti-suffrage sentiment, 159; federal election (1917), 109–10, 112; MES's speeches, 112, 159, 169; Smiths and, 61. *See also* Montreal

racialized people: about, 4, 31–32, 50; assimilationism, 101, 113, 130, 152; *Komagata Maru* incident, 92; Ku Klux Klan, 164; liberalism vs racism, 50; MES's views, 3, 5, 73, 113, 130; miscegenation, 152; racial hierarchy, 50; social exclusion, 130, 218*n*19;

xenophobia and unemployment, 108.
  See also Asian people; Black people;
  Indigenous Peoples; White people
Ramsland, Sarah McEwen, 160, 245*n*140
Read, Mrs. Hamilton, 239*n*25
Recorder. See *Western Methodist Recorder*
Reform Club, 45, 49, 51, 169
religion: Jewish people, 133, 192, 193.
  See also Christianity; Methodists;
  Methodists (UK)
resource development: MES's views, 132,
  153. *See also* mining industry; Nanaimo,
  mining industry; United Kingdom,
  mining towns
Riddle, Sarah (RS's first wife; mother of
  Mary Elizabeth Carr), 16–17
Robin, Martin, 164
Robins, Samuel Matthew, 47
Robinson, James, 120–21, 233*n*92
Robson, John, 179, 249*n*14
Roddan, Andrew, 194
Rogers, Edith McTavish, 160, 170, 176,
  232*n*77, 245*n*140
Rolston, Tilly Jean, 251*n*57
Rosebery, Lord, 25, 49, 53
Royal Commission on Chinese and
  Japanese Immigration (1902), 47, 53
Royal Commission on Industrial
  Relations (1919, Mathers Commission),
  109, 131
Royal Commission on Mental
  Hygiene, 167
Russell, Bob, 133
Russian Revolution (1917), 129, 132–33

Sanders, Dora, 176
Sanford, A.M., 196, 254*n*126
school and library boards, 46, 86, 102,
  120, 140, 238*n*2, 253*n*109
schools. *See* education
Scott, Agnes Mary, 63
Scott, Frances Mary, 70
Scott, Richard, 70
Scott, Thomas and Jessie Read, 80
Seaton Delaval, England, 14
Semlin, Charles, 52
Senate: first woman senator, 174, 192;
  MES and RS as potential candidates,
  68, 155–56, 164, 192; Persons Case
  (1929), 155, 174, 192
sexuality. *See* gender/sexuality
Shaughnessy Heights, Vancouver, 82
Shortt, Adam, 95
Sifton, Elizabeth Burrows, 70
Smith, Helen Douglas, 174, 179, 182, 184,
  187, 198, 249*n*14
Smith, Inness Ogilvy (Ralph Gladstone
  Smith's wife), 81
Smith, Jocelyn (Betty) Bosanquet
  (Robert's daughter, granddaughter of
  MES and RS), 199
Smith, John (RS's brother), 16
Smith, John Wesley (Jack, youngest son of
  MES and RS), 18–19, 35, 36, 40, 56, 81,
  104, 106, 142, 180, 185, 196, 199
Smith, Joseph (RS and MES's nephew),
  57, 251*n*59
Smith, Katherine Winnifred Johnson
  (Robert's wife), 80, 142, 185
Smith, Mabel Catherine Quesnel (John
  Wesley Smith's wife), 142, 196
Smith, Mary (RS's mother), 16
Smith, Mary (RS's sister), 16
Smith, Mary Ellen Spear (1863–1933):
  about, 7, 122(f), 130(f), 186(f); birth
  (1863), 10, 208*n*27; children, 18, 35–36,
  40, 56–57, 68, 104, 185–86; education,
  9, 15, 21–23; finances, 57, 60, 63, 104,
  143, 188; historical sources, 5–6; homes
  in Nanaimo, 35–36, 56–57; homes in
  Vancouver, 76–79, 130(f), 148; marriage
  to Ralph (1883), 3–4, 17–18, 104–5,
  208*n*27; Methodist, 20, 30, 35, 42–43,
  58, 129. *See also* Smith, Ralph
  (1858–1917)
Smith, Mary Ellen, personal qualities:
  about, 8–9, 58, 127, 202;
  conversationalist, 8, 10, 58, 127, 143, 155,
  163; fashion and style, 16, 38, 69–70,
  79, 80, 124(f), 127; femininity, 8, 54,
  67–68, 122(f), 127, 143, 164–65, 169,
  202; health, 18–19, 148, 196; musician,
  7–8, 53–54, 58, 63–64, 169; photos and
  illustrations, 115(f), 122(f), 130(f),

146(f), 148(f), 149(f), 158(f), 186(f); physical attractiveness, 4, 67, 143, 163, 197–98, 202; political skills, 8, 58–59, 60, 67–68, 70–73, 145, 163, 169; sewing and knitting, 15–16, 38, 63, 127; speaker, 8, 58–59, 97–98, 124, 143

Smith, Mary Ellen, life in England (1863–92): about, 4, 7, 10; childhood and youth, 10–12, 15; Cornwall and Devon, 10–12; education, 9, 15; marriage to Ralph (1883), 3–4, 17–18, 208*n*27; Northumberland, 12–17, 20–24; return visit (1902, 1923), 65, 152–53; seamstress, 15–16, 35; stepmother to Mary Elizabeth, 17; travel to Canada (1892), 30, 32–34, 32(f). *See also* Smith, Ralph, life in England (1858–92); United Kingdom, mining towns

Smith, Mary Ellen, life in Nanaimo (1892–1911): about, 4; homes, 35–36, 56–57; Methodist, 35, 42–43, 58; musician, 7–8, 36, 38, 43, 44, 45, 51, 53–54; politician's wife, 58–59; seamstress, 35, 38; travel from UK (1892), 30, 32–34, 32(f); WCTU member, 35, 58–59; women's auxiliaries, 40–41, 44, 59. *See also* Nanaimo; Nanaimo, mining industry; Smith, Mary Ellen, political life as Ralph's wife (1898–1917)

Smith, Mary Ellen, life in Vancouver (1911–33): family life, 80–81; homes, 130(f); Methodist, 79; move from Nanaimo (1911), 76–79; social life, 79–80; women's clubs, 83–86, 96–103, 105, 112, 136. *See also* Smith, Mary Ellen, political life as Ralph's wife (1898–1917); Smith, Mary Ellen, political life as MLA (1918–28); Vancouver

Smith, Mary Ellen, political life as Ralph's wife (1898–1917): about, 7, 51–55, 58–59, 67–77, 96–105; family devotion, 96; femininity and style, 54, 67–68, 70, 76; King's views on, 67–68; Lauriers' friendship, 102; Nanaimo, 58–59; non-partisanship, 99, 101, 103, 110, 112, 114–16; political skills, 53–54, 70–73, 76; press coverage, 71–73, 95, 104–5; respectable feminism, 96; RS as MLA (1898–1900, 1916–17), 53, 95, 96–103; RS as MP (1900–11), 54–55, 67–77, 179; RS's death (1917), 104–5; social life, 63–64, 69–71, 79–80; speeches, 97–101; Vancouver, 96–103; women's clubs, 83–84, 96–103, 105. *See also* Smith, Ralph, politician (1898–1911, 1916–17)

Smith, Mary Ellen, political life as MLA (1918–28): about, 4, 135(f), 139–42, 146(f), 148–49, 148(f), 149(f), 186(f); anti-Asian politics, 121, 161, 167; by-election (1918), 4, 114–26, 115(f), 118(f), 122(f), 234*n*112; cabinet post, 148, 154–60, 244*n*119; cabinet resignation, 156–59, 162; election (1920), 4, 141, 142–47, 146(f); election (1924), 5, 160–66; election (1928), 5, 172, 177–85, 178(f), 181(f); endorsements by MES, 136, 153, 161–62; federal elections (1917, 1926), 111–13, 114–16, 164; first female cabinet minister in British Empire, 199–200; first female MLA in BC, 199–200; first female speaker, acting (1928), 170; gradualist approach, 134; Independent Liberal, 115(f), 117, 121; King's views on, 66–67; labour allies/foes, 148, 152–53, 154; Liberal MLA, 143–44, 153, 156–58; Liberal Party divisiveness, 119–20; Liberal Party service, 168–71; maiden speech as MLA, 126–27; male allies, 137–38, 144, 159; misogyny, 172, 182, 185; name change to "Mary Ellen Smith," 145; non-partisanship, 110, 112, 114–16, 115(f), 143; options for other seats, 143, 156, 160, 164; political allies, 122–23, 143–44, 148, 172; press coverage, 123–24, 124(f), 126–27, 143–46, 146(f), 151, 155, 158(f); relations with colleagues, 148, 157–60, 158(f); Senate candidacy, 155–56, 159, 164, 192; UK tour (1923), 152–53, 163

Smith, Mary Ellen, political life as MLA (1918–28), political issues: about, 126–38; anti-corruption, 122; consumer issues, 131; democracy, 118(f), 129–30, 133;

deserted wives' welfare, 128, 133, 165; dower rights, 133, 140, 151; equal pay for equal work, 118(f), 134, 136, 151; liberal-labour politics, 29, 134, 168–71, 237*n*195; minimum wage, 117, 118(f), 121, 132–33; New Liberalism, 133, 153–54; newspaper articles by MES (1918–20), 128–37; oversight of women's programs, 150; political legacy of MES, 199–202; postwar reconstruction, 139–40, 143–44; prohibition, 118(f), 142–43; reform agenda (1918–20), 126–38; tax policies, 153, 242*n*95, 247*n*176; veterans benefits, 118(f); women's workplace safety, 118(f). *See also* children and youth; eugenics; marriage and divorce; minimum wage; mothers' pensions; veterans

Smith, Mary Ellen, later life (1928–33): about, 5, 172–77, 186(f), 196–202; ageism and misogyny, 9, 172, 182, 185; civic life, 187–94; death and funeral (1933), 5, 196–97; discouragement, 172–77; election (1928), 172, 177–85, 178(f), 181(f); Esquimalt, 5, 177–80, 178(f); family life, 185–86; federal elections (1930, 1935), 174, 176, 177(f); finances, 188–89, 198, 254*n*137; Great Depression, 140–41, 187, 193–96; ILO representative, 189–90, 192–93; Liberal Party president, 187–88; liberal-labourism, 184, 187–88; Nanaimo visits, 185–86; political legacy, 196–202; press coverage, 178(f), 179, 183–84, 186–90; press tributes after death, 197–98; UK visits, 189–91

Smith, Mary Ellen, works: "Franchise for Women" (1909), 74–76; lost manuscript (1920), 137; newspaper articles (1918–20), 128–37; "The Woman's Place in Modern Life" (1914), 98

Smith, Mary Elizabeth. *See* Carr, Mary Elizabeth Smith (RS's daughter and MES's step-daughter)

Smith, Mathew (RS's brother), 16, 18, 36, 57

Smith, Matthew (RS and MES's nephew), 251*n*59

Smith, Priscilla Janet, 162–63

Smith, Ralph (1858–1917): about, 3–4, 7, 61(f), 93(f); children, 18, 35–36, 40, 56–57, 68, 104; death and funeral (1917), 4–5, 27, 46, 104–5; finances, 57, 60, 63, 68, 76, 79, 81, 104, 221*n*1; historical sources, 5–6; marriage to Mary Ellen (1883–1917), 3–4, 7, 17–18, 208*n*27; Methodist, 42–43, 57–58, 62. *See also* Smith, Mary Ellen Spear (1863–1933); Smith, Ralph, politician (1898–1911, 1916–17)

Smith, Ralph, personal qualities: health, 21, 40, 62, 76; masculinity, 54; musician, 41; photos and illustrations, 61(f), 93(f); speaking abilities, 52, 95

Smith, Ralph, life in England (1858–92): birth (1858), 16; cooperative movement, 16, 24–25; early life, 16–17, 27; marriage to Mary Ellen (1883–1917), 3–4, 7, 17–18, 208*n*27; marriage to Sarah (1880–82), 16–17; Methodist lay preacher, 16, 20; miner, 27; Northumberland, 4, 11–16, 20–24; public lectures, 24–25; return visit (1902), 65; social activism, 16; temperance movement, 23; travel to Canada (1892), 30, 32–34, 32(f). *See also* Smith, Mary Ellen, life in England (1863–92); United Kingdom, mining towns

Smith, Ralph, life in Nanaimo (1892–1911): about, 4; anti-Asian racism, 52; civic leadership, 44–45; family life, 56–57; labour aristocracy, 35, 49–53, 209*n*59; Liberal MP (1900–11), 54–55, 57–69, 61(f), 76–78; miner, 35–36, 49, 216*n*108; move to Vancouver (1911), 76–79; suffragist and temperance ally, 45, 52, 58, 66; TLCC leadership (1896–1902), 4, 50, 53, 54, 55, 162; travel from UK (1892), 30, 32–34, 32(f). *See also* Nanaimo; Nanaimo, mining industry; Smith, Mary Ellen, life in Nanaimo (1892–1911); Smith, Mary Ellen, political life as Ralph's wife (1898–1917); Smith, Ralph, politician (1898–1911, 1916–17)

Smith, Ralph, life in Vancouver (1911–17): business career, 79, 81; death and funeral (1917), 104–5; Liberal MLA (1912–17), 91–95; Methodist, 79; move from Nanaimo (1911), 76–79; suffrage ally, 92, 94. *See also* Smith, Mary Ellen, life in Vancouver (1911–33); Smith, Mary Ellen, political life as Ralph's wife (1898–1917); Smith, Ralph, politician (1898–1911, 1916–17); Vancouver

Smith, Ralph, politician (1898–1911, 1916–17): about, 4, 51–55, 93(f); civic events, 57–58, 61–62; elections, federal (1900–11), 55–56, 60, 68–69, 76–78; elections, provincial (1912), 88, 91; gradualist approach, 66; immigration commission, 53; labour ally, 65, 67–69; Liberal Party (BC), 67, 89–95, 93(f); Liberal Party (Canada), 67–69; as liberal-labour reformer, 51–55, 57–58, 60, 64–69, 104–5; Methodist, 62; minister of finance, 4, 95; as MLA (1898–1900, 1916–17), 51–55, 89–95; as MP (1900–11), 54–55, 57–69, 61(f), 76–78; New Liberalism platform, 91; press coverage, 50, 93(f), 94–95; suffragist ally, 52, 58, 66, 94; temperance, 94; travel to UK (1902), 65–66. *See also* Smith, Mary Ellen, political life as Ralph's wife (1898–1917)

Smith, Ralph, works: "Are We Owners or Stewards," 43; "Culture of the Human Being," 43; "Disestablishment and Disendowment," 29; "High and Low Dividends," 24–25; "Peace and Warfare as Introduced by the Lord Jesus," 53; "What Christianity Has and Is Doing for the Toiler," 43

Smith, Ralph Gladstone (son of MES and RS), 18, 36, 56–57, 81, 104, 185

Smith, Richard William (eldest son of MES and RS), 18, 36, 56–57, 62, 81, 104, 142, 185

Smith, Robert (RS's brother), 16

Smith, Robert (RS's father), 16

Smith, Robert (son of MES and RS), 18, 36, 56–57, 80–81, 104, 142, 185, 199

Smith, Robert Campbell (Robert's son, grandson of MES and RS), 199

Snuneymuxw First Nation, 31–32, 34
social class: about, 31–32; charm offensives, 143, 155; cross-class collaboration, 4, 23, 26–28, 29–30, 100, 116, 210*n*73; gradualism in relations, 49; immigration policies, 67; liberal-labourism, 116; MES's views, 9, 43, 108, 133; Nanaimo area, 31; post-war unrest, 108–9
Social Credit, 195–96
social gospel, 43–44, 74, 254*n*126
socialism and social democracy: Canadian Labor Party, 162–63, 173, 246*n*154; CCF party, 79, 140–41, 142, 173, 174, 198, 201, 253*n*109; Christian socialism, 25, 43–44; feminist allies, 88, 165; vs gradualism, 65–66; labour allies, 88, 165; MES's friendships, 96; MLAs, 68, 125; political candidates, 120, 125; political parties, 246*n*154; RS's views, 28, 37, 43–44, 55, 65, 91–92; Social Democratic Party, 86; Socialist Party, 79, 86, 88, 91–92, 125, 246*n*154; suffrage alliances, 84–86; *Western Clarion* (newspaper), 86, 92; Western Federation of Miners, 65
South African War, 53
Spear, Edgar (William's son, RS and MES's nephew), 81
Spear, Elizabeth Edwards (William's wife, MES's brother), 36
Spear, Mary Ann Jackson (Richard's wife, MES's mother), 10–11, 13–15, 18, 33, 35–36, 40, 218*n*2
Spear, Reginald Gordon (RS and MES's nephew), 106
Spear, Richard Sleep ("Dick," MES's father), 10–15, 18, 33, 35, 36, 40, 47, 56, 81
Spear, William John (MES's brother), 11, 18, 33, 35, 36, 38, 57, 81, 185, 212*n*23
Spencer, Herbert, 22
St. George Society, Ottawa, 61–62
Steeves, Dorothy, 198
sterilization of mentally unfit, 3, 167–68, 193, 194, 200. *See also* eugenics
Stevens, Henry Herbert, 92, 156, 164, 189
Storey, Kenton, 50

Studholme, Alan, 68
suffrage movement: anti-suffragism, 29, 75, 87(f), 98, 101; arguments for suffrage, 62, 74–75, 98, 100; *The Champion* (magazine), 5–6, 84, 85(f); duty of care, 96–97; "fair deal" and justice, 4, 8, 62, 204*n*3; First World War's impact on, 99–100; historical sources, 5–6; international networks, 6, 66, 84, 99, 132, 149; male allies, 58–59, 88; maternal virtues, 8; MES's allies, 122–23, 125–26; MES's "Franchise for Women" (1909), 74–76; MES's legacy, 199–202; MES's support for, 58–59, 62–64, 72–75, 89, 98–103, 105, 117; MES's views, 59, 72–73, 126, 129; Ottawa, 62–64, 66, 72–73; Pankhursts (British suffragettes), 66, 84, 102–3, 197, 230*n*34; post-suffrage politics, 169–70; press coverage, 5–6, 72–73; referendum (1916), 78, 89–90, 94, 102–3; RS as ally, 52, 58, 66, 92; taxation and fairness, 62, 74; Toronto, 66; Vancouver, 83–86; WCTU as ally, 45, 58–59. *See also* enfranchisement; enfranchisement, British Columbia; enfranchisement, Canada; women's movement
suffrage movement, leaders: about, 83–86. *See also* Clark, Susie Lane; Gutteridge, Helena; Jamieson, Laura Marshall; MacGill, Helen Gregory; McClung, Nellie L.
suffrage movement, organizations: about, 110; Political Equality Leagues, 45, 84, 92, 99, 101, 224*n*52; WLA (Women's Liberal Association), 100; Woman's Suffrage League, 83–84. *See also* PPEL (Pioneer Political Equality League)
Sutherland, Mary Bartlet, 70, 74, 221*n*87

Taschereau, Louis-Alexandre, 169
Taylor, Louis D., 88, 197
Taylor, Mrs. H.G., 135(f)
teachers, 150
temperance movement: British mining towns, 11, 23; maternal virtues, 8; MES's support for, 23; Methodists as allies, 23; prohibition plebiscite (1898), 45; prohibition referenda (1916, 1920), 89, 94, 142–43; public morality laws, 42, 214*n*63; RS as ally, 23, 52; self-help, 23; suffragist allies, 45. *See also* WCTU (Woman's Christian Temperance Union)
Thatcher, Margaret, 13
Thompson, Nicholas, 27, 79, 104, 112, 231*n*45
TLC (Trades and Labor Council), 65, 84, 88, 120, 150, 151, 166, 197, 237*n*194. *See also BC Federationist* (newspaper); labour movement
TLCC (Trades and Labor Congress of Canada), 4, 50, 53, 54, 55, 162, 191, 246*n*154
Tolmie, Simon Fraser, 173, 188, 193, 250*n*35
Toronto Suffrage Association, 66
Tupper, Charles, 82–83, 104
Tupper, Janet McDonald, 80, 82–83, 112, 223*n*26

UBC. *See* University of British Columbia (UBC)
unions. *See* labour movement
United Kingdom: birth control, 18–19; British settler entitlements, 166–68; Coalition government, 112; democratizing presses, 21; education, 9, 15, 21–23; female factory workers, 13; Labour Party, 161, 190–91, 252*n*87; liberal divisions, 232; Liberal Party, 4, 25, 28, 29–30, 161; MES's visits, 65, 152–53, 163, 186, 189–91; old age pensions, 66; press tributes on MES's death, 197; suffragettes, 66, 74, 83; women office-holders, 75, 185; women's enfranchisement, 110–11; women's party, 230*n*34. *See also* Methodists (UK); Smith, Mary Ellen, life in England (1863–92); Smith, Ralph, life in England (1858–92)
United Kingdom, mining towns: about, 4, 11–16; ban on women miners, 13, 34; child labour, 11, 46; cooperative movement, 23–24; Cornwall and Devon, 10–12, 14–15; education, 21–23; gender relations, 11, 13–15, 17–20, 28–29; labour movement, 4, 14–15; liberal-labourism, 4;

living conditions, 11–12, 17–18, 20; MES's family life, 10–11; miners' associations, 26–27; NMA (Northumberland Miners' Association), 15, 23, 27–28; Northumberland and Durham, 12–14, 16–17, 20–24, 26, 29, 186; social hierarchies, 13; temperance movement, 11, 23. *See also* Smith, Mary Ellen, life in England (1863–92); Smith, Ralph, life in England (1858–92)
United States: first female federal Representative (1916), 111; migration to/from BC, 33–34; women's enfranchisement (1920), 111
United Suffrage Societies, 122–23
University of British Columbia (UBC), 46, 151, 153, 166, 168, 184, 193
University Women's Club (UWC), 23, 83, 103, 154, 174
Uphill, Thomas, 251*n*57
Urwick, E.J., 255*n*5

Vancouver: about, 33–34, 81–88; demographics, 33–34, 81, 212*n*12; Indigenous Peoples, 81–82; labour movement, 86–88; men's clubs, 82; school boards, 86, 102, 120, 140; social hierarchy, 82–84; suffragists, 83–86; unemployment, 88; Women's Building, 84, 112. *See also* labour movement; Smith, Mary Ellen, life in Vancouver (1911–33); Smith, Ralph, life in Vancouver (1911–17); suffrage movement; women's movement
Vancouver Sun: cartoons, 87(f), 90(f), 178(f); MES's articles (1918–20), 128–37; MES's obituary, 197; MES's press coverage, 116, 123, 137, 155–56, 178(f), 179, 183, 188, 192, 194–96; mock election (1915), 88–89; on RS, 104
Vancouver Trades and Labor Council. *See* TLC (Trades and Labor Council)
veterans: about, 194; agricultural settlers, 118(f), 132; civil service preference, 118(f); Comrades of the Great War, 120; GWVA advocacy, 117, 120–21, 161; MES's allies, 137; MES's views, 109, 117,
118(f), 121, 132–33, 137, 153, 194; pensions, 133, 153, 161; political allies, 232*n*77, 245*n*140; political candidates, 120; post-war unrest, 113; women's resocialization of, 109
Victoria: about, 33–34; *The Champion* (magazine), 5–6, 84, 85(f); demographics, 33–34, 212*n*12; PEL chapter, 84; Protestant Orphanage, 44
Voters' Educational League, 90
voting rights. *See* enfranchisement; enfranchisement, British Columbia; enfranchisement, Canada; suffrage movement

Wales, Julia Grace, 99
War, First World. *See* First World War
Wartime Elections Act, 109–10, 111–12, 113, 129, 231*n*55. *See also* enfranchisement, Canada
WCC (Women's Canadian Club), 79–80, 82, 89, 96, 101–2, 110
WCTU (Woman's Christian Temperance Union): about, 44–45; Frances Willard's leadership, 44, 45, 96, 100; MES's support for, 35, 40, 45, 73, 96, 142; Nanaimo, 215*n*79; prohibition plebiscite (1898), 45; prohibition referenda (1916, 1920), 89, 94, 142–43; racialized members, 215*n*79; suffragist allies, 45, 58. *See also* temperance movement
Weatherburn, Mary, 28–29
Wellington (Nanaimo area), 47
Western Clarion (socialist newspaper), 86, 92
Western Federation of Miners, 56, 65
Western Methodist Recorder, 74–76, 221*nn*91–92
Western Women's Weekly, 117, 127
"When John Kissed Mary Ellen" (poem), 147
White people: about, 152; eugenics ideals, 82, 107, 152; racism in White working class, 39; stereotype of White beauty, 176, 177(f); White supremacy, 101, 152, 166–69, 200. *See also* racialized people

Whitton, Charlotte, 191, 193
Wilkinson, Ellen, 6
Willard, Frances, 44, 45, 96, 100
Williams, Parker, 89
Wilson, Cairine Reay Mackay, 174, 192
Wilson, Mrs. Hugh, 135(f)
Winch, Ernest, 79
WLA (Women's Liberal Association): England, 29; MES's allies, 143; MES's nomination for MLA, 114; Nanaimo, 114; national federation, 160, 170–71, 188; Vancouver, 100–1, 103, 112, 114, 159; as woman's group, 114
Woman's Century, 5–6
Woman's Christian Temperance Union. *See* WCTU (Woman's Christian Temperance Union)
Woman's Employment League, 99
Woman's Suffrage League, 83–84
women: demographics, 60; MES's legacy, 199–202; New Woman, 7–8; Persons Case (1929), 155, 174, 192; public respectability, 7. *See also* children and youth; enfranchisement, British Columbia; enfranchisement, Canada; feminist movement; gender/sexuality; marriage and divorce; suffrage movement; women and work; women's movement
women and work: about, 35, 37, 129, 140; auxiliaries for men's unions, 87–88; equal pay for equal work, 3, 8, 101, 118(f), 134, 136, 151, 160; First World War's impacts, 107–8, 129; ILO recommendations, 134, 151; male entitlement, 107–8; maternal ideal, 8, 35; maternity protection, 150–51; MES's legacy, 199–202; MES's platform (1918), 118(f); misogyny, 173; Nanaimo, 35, 37; Ottawa, 60, 62; sexual exploitation, 88; Vancouver, 86–88; women's movement, 73–74. *See also* ILO (International Labor Organization); labour movement; minimum wage
women and work, occupations: ban on miners, 13, 34–35; civil service, 60; domestic service, 37, 129, 130, 150, 152, 166, 173; dressmaking, 37; factory work, 166; hairdressers, 166; nurses, 129; police officers, 129; presswomen, 86–87; teachers, 37, 129
Women's and Girls' Protection Act, 167
Women's Canadian Club (WCC), 79–80, 82, 89, 96, 101–2, 110
Women's Forum, 84, 96, 98, 102, 148, 183, 223*n*35
Women's Institutes, 132
Women's International League for Peace and Freedom, 99, 154, 174
Women's Liberal Association. *See* WLA (Women's Liberal Association)
women's movement: about, 73–74; civic auxiliaries, 40–41, 44, 59; dower rights, 133, 140, 151; First World War's impact on, 99–100, 107; gradualism, 49, 66; historical sources, 5–6; international networks, 84, 99, 108, 149; labour allies, 48, 88; MES's support for, 59, 73–74, 83–84, 96–103; misogyny, 126; non-partisanship, 101, 103, 110, 114–16, 115(f); political candidates, 90; post-war reconstruction, 127–28, 139–40, 143–44; self-improvement, 83; socialist allies, 88; voter education, 90, 110; Women's Building, 84, 112. *See also* children and youth; feminist movement; marriage and divorce; suffrage movement; women and work
women's movement, clubs and organizations: about, 83–84, 110. *See also* IODE (Imperial Order Daughters of the Empire); LCW (Local Council of Women); University Women's Club (UWC); WCC (Women's Canadian Club); WLA (Women's Liberal Association); Women's Forum
Women's Voters' League, 137
Wong Foon Sing, 167
Wood Scott, Emma, 162–63
Woodsworth, James S., 97, 142, 144, 145, 174
Woodward, Charles, 161, 163
work: hours of work, 134, 237*nn*194–95, 250*n*26; ILO recommendations, 134,

250*n*26; workman's compensation, 91, 141, 150. *See also* ILO (International Labor Organization); labour movement; minimum wage; women and work; women and work, occupations
The World Aflame (photoplay), 109, 229*n*23
World War One. *See* First World War

Wright, Almroth, 100
Wright, Annie, 36
Wylie, Barbara, 84

YMCA, Nanaimo, 44
Youmans, Letitia, 44
Young, R.H., 120
youth. *See* children and youth